Cross-Platform Game Programming

Cross-Platform Game Programming

Steven Goodwin

CHARLES RIVER MEDIA, INC.
Hingham, Massachusetts

Publisher: Jenifer Niles
Cover Design: The Printed Image

CHARLES RIVER MEDIA, INC.
10 Downer Avenue
Hingham, Massachusetts 02043
781-740-0400
781-740-8816 (FAX)
info@charlesriver.com
www.charlesriver.com

This book is printed on acid-free paper.

Steven Goodwin. *Cross-Platform Game Programming.*
ISBN: 1-58450-379-3

Library of Congress Cataloging-in-Publication Data
Goodwin, Steven, 1973-
Cross platform game programming / Steven Goodwin.— 1st ed.
p. cm.
Includes bibliographical references and index.
ISBN 1-58450-379-3 (pbk. with cd-rom : alk. paper)
1. Computer games—Programming. 2. Cross-platform software development. I. Title.
QA76.76.C672G66 2005
794.8'1526—dc22
2004029828

Printed in the United States of America
05 7 6 5 4 3 2 First Edition

To my sister, Angela...

...the brainy one of the family.

Contents

Acknowledgments

The completion of this book is the result of many people and their inspiration, experience, ideas, and time. Writing the actual words appears insignificant by comparison.

I would like to thank my readers, editors, and other assorted developers who have provided invaluable feedback, comments, and suggestions, especially Michael Braithwaite, Ben Crossman, Dan Evans, Mal Lansell, David Manley, Jerome Muffat-Meridol, and Dave Wall.

To my friends and colleagues that have encouraged my writing: John Hearns, Anne Mullane, Colin Murphy, Steve Porter, John Southern, and Dean Wilson.

To those with whom I've worked, and whose great ideas have found some form within these words, I thank you: The development teams at Bits Studios, Computer Artworks (R.I.P.), Criterion and Edcom, and notably Mat Cook, Dominic Giles, Vlad Kapietsky, Nat Presson, Alan Troth, Mark Walker, and Darren Ward.

I would like to thank Jenifer Niles and all her team at Charles River Media for this book, and for making me appear competent!

Finally, I would like to thank my close network of family and friends who know all about me, but seem to like me anyway—especially David Eade, Ed and Margaret Grabowski (without whom...), Justine Griffith, Phillip Hart, William Siddons, Fiona Stewart, Maria Thomson, and all of TULS, Lonix, Gllug, 2600, and Slashdot-London.

And, of course, I want to thank Grandma, Granddad, Shirley and Ken, Juliette and Dean, Melanie, Mum, Dad, and my sister Angela.

Preface

With nearly every game on the market today being released simultaneously on all platforms, the need for a good cross-platform development strategy is crucially important. Every hour spent reinventing the wheel is an hour wasted. Or put another way, every hour spent writing cross-platform code constitutes three saved hours. This means being able to write code that behaves identically on all machines. Not similar—identical! This book covers myriad problems that exist within every cross-platform games, and gives you the understanding and ability needed to solve them.

This book is intended for developers working (or hoping to work) in the games industry who need a mentor to guide them through the jungle of abstractions, design patterns, and engine architectures that support a cross-platform game. You'll learn the particular rules and methods by which code must be written, why these rules exist, and how to harness them to create good cross-platform code.

The book is also for those looking to start crossing their project from one platform to another, and for those building a new engine with the intention of making it cross-platform from the ground up. This book will help senior and lead programmers determine where the platform-specific features should start and end, and the best way to achieve their cross-platform goals. Gameplay programmers will develop according to these same rules, preventing the common problems and thereby speeding their ascent to lead and senior level.

For those already working in the upper echelons of their company, this book provides a solid reference of development practices and a detailed breakdown of all the required cross-platform game components, with a comprehensive task list for the team. You also get detailed explanations of new technologies, such as multiprocessing and threaded environments, and how they will affect the next generation of consoles.

For those using middleware, the problem is not over because every programmer still needs to be able to handle memory, the filesystem, and gameplay code in a generic, cross-platform manner to make efficient use of the purchase. Who knew that in our world the standard libraries are not standard? This book covers the rarely discussed world of cross-platform game programming and gives you the understanding to develop your games effectively.

We begin by explaining the 10 basic tenets for development that must be adhered to throughout a project for it to work, whether it involves engine or gameplay coding. We then cover specific areas in detail, such as the abstraction of a filesystem, the graphics engine, the memory manager, and how to handle different hardware specifications without changing the code. Seemingly general topics (such as debugging and UI design) take on new meaning and raise different issues when the platform changes and the old tricks no longer work.

A plethora of new ideas and techniques need to be adopted across the spheres of memory allocation, file handling, graphics, audio, and networking. These are all areas of knowledge that were once deemed magic by the knowledgeable few, and unobtainable by the rest of the populous. They are now available to all, and I hope to teach you some new tricks in this book.

–Steven Goodwin

1 Introduction

In This Chapter

- Background of Cross-Platform Programming
- Overview of Cross-Platform Components
- The Development Process
- About the Book
- Non-Disclosure Agreements
- Notes to the Reader

BACKGROUND OF CROSS-PLATFORM PROGRAMMING

Cross-platform development is the art, skill, ability, and general know-how required to write software that works on multiple platforms. "Working on multiple platforms" means that the same code will compile, link, run, and behave identically on whichever platform is targeted. Granted, the compiler and tools will be specific to each machine, and the underlying Application Programming Interface (API) may vary, but the code itself will be identical as both the game and engine should be reusable across each platform; that is, developed once, and deployed often.

To be considered a cross-platform project (as opposed to a port), work must be carried out concurrently on at least two different target machines using a common code base that remains live throughout. This is a delicate skill because algorithms, libraries, compilers, and data structures cannot be changed in an arbitrary fashion as a benign modification to one system could cause catastrophic problems for one (or more) of the other platforms. This is especially true of the data structures containing game assets, where the effects can range from a nuisance to code breakdown, to fluctuations in the memory footprint and large-scale project delays.

Also, a cross-platform game must act identically on these different machines once compiled. This is the main difference between a project that can be compiled and run on different machines, and one that is truly cross-platform. Most of the available OpenGL® code, for example, will compile and run anywhere, but its runtime behavior often relies on the target platform and varies according to the operating system, memory, processor speed, filesystem, byte order, and graphics capabilities.

History

Before the current crop of games, cross-platform development only occurred rarely. Usually, a game was written first, and then ported to other platforms. The amount of work required varied according to the project, but was usually small. Often, when the same development team carried out the port, a set of libraries would be rewritten for each machine using common names and calling conventions. Various portions of the game code were then changed, amended, and generally hacked around to compile or assemble on the new platform. There would be moderate reuse of the game code, but very little reuse of the engine.

Throughout most of the 1980s, a different programmer (or team) would rewrite the entire game whenever the game was ported to a new platform. Because most games of this time were written in assembler, it was rare to find a programmer expert enough in more than a couple of machine code variations to write both versions. The newness of the industry also meant that very few conversion tools were available because these were highly specialized languages. The game engines consisted of highly optimized sprite renderers and animation code that would usually belong to the conversion programmer himself and tied into the new game with whatever customizations were needed for that project.

As games became more complex in the 1990s, bringing in a different developer (or team) for the new platform became a less viable option. Development cycles were no longer measured in weeks, but months. Publishers didn't want to wait another six months for the conversions to appear because this prevented any attempt at a short-term marketing and advertising blitz. This meant both versions of the game had to be developed in tandem, requiring more code reuse as was demonstrated within the game development cycles of the Commodore™ Amiga® and Atari® ST, which shared a common processor in the Motorola® 68000. Software houses created their own graphics library (now called engines) and developed both products concurrently in the first cases of true cross-platform development. In this situation, both game and engine code would get reused on each platform.

Even though technology was marching on, the industry was diverted from this early cross-platform view because it was not distributed evenly between projects. On one hand, the IBM® PC (and its myriad clones) encouraged highly complex strategy games, flight simulators, and war games using high-powered Intel® chips and hard drives for mass storage. Programmed in C and C++, these games used multimedia drivers for graphics, sound, and networking. The structure of these drivers varied between hardware, requiring an abstraction of their basic functionality—a technique still used today. On the other hand, the market for standalone consoles was growing by using smaller machines with customized chips for improved graphics and sound, and by focusing its market on children and teenagers playing platform and shooting games. These games were largely written in assembler with very little code sharing because every ounce of processing power needed to be squeezed out of the machine for each game. However, more engine code was being reused because each game was shipped for several platforms in the same time frame, as common libraries (with identical names, but written in different languages) again came to the forefront. Code reuse became more pronounced as the console market grew and became license-driven with very short lead times. Every other game, it seemed, was connected to a film release and so needed to be available on as many machines as possible (and as quickly as possible) to maximize the revenue streams. The jokes about "change the name, change the graphics, and reship" weren't funny, as it brought about a downturn in fortunes within the industry.

The first step back to the cross-platform path began with the Sony® PlayStation™, Nintendo® 64, and Sega® Saturn™ series of consoles, as gamers became more adult, and console programmers rediscovered the joy of the C language. During this time, speed was not as vital as it had been previously. It was important certainly, but whereas programmers would previously have spent days trying to claw back one or two processor cycles, attention now focused on other areas for many reasons. First, when working in a high-level language, such as C, you have less opportunity to optimize at the low level because the assembler code is now the compiler's responsibility. Second, the balance of processing moved away from the CPU and onto the graphics chip. This meant that an extra cycle saved on the CPU didn't make any difference to the speed if the game was still bound by slow graphics processing. Third, the increase of code size and team members required a more maintainable development environment. Maintenance-friendly programming rarely involves assembler.

This scenario is consistent with the present day, and the desire for a maintainable engine takes precedence over speed or memory issues because those gains can be made in areas other than code. In recent years, only one notable console engine has been written entirely in assembler: *Jak and Daxter*™ for the PS2™. It was not cross-platform, and still used a scripting language to implement gameplay. Almost all games are presently written in C++ (with some still chained to C code, where an old engine is still in use), and most of these are cross-platform.

The Importance of Cross-Platform Development

Cross-platform game development is important for many people, not just programmers. For the marketing department, it means they can sell four games at once with one budget, and don't need to remind the public about the game with each new platform release. One advertisement, with the line "Available on PC, PS2, Xbox™ and GameCube™" hits all the bases. It also means marketing can answer "Yes" to any question concerning its availability, giving a very positive message to the retail chains.

Cross-platform development helps publishers, too. They are still holding the game industry's purse strings, and so need some way of recouping their costs. Having the game available on every platform, especially at the start of a console's lifetime, means that publishers can hedge their bets concerning from where the big money will come. It has never been "obvious" that the Sony PlayStation and PS2 would be the big sellers they have become in the marketplace. Even with the success of the original PlayStation, publishers and developers would both mutter the words "lightning" and "twice" in sentences that also contained the phrase "PS2." This is true in any industry. When VCRs were first available to the public, the war between VHS and Betamax™ was the stuff of legends. Film companies released movies on both formats, siding with both camps, just in case they backed the wrong proverbial horse. Game publishers are doing the same now. Even when one platform has a strong dominance, it's still good to sell the same product to as many people as possible providing the costs involved aren't excessive. There's no reason why any particular platform should be excluded without good reason.

And finally, cross-platform development helps the developers—although it might never appear that way. With the exception of the very biggest developers (that is, the likes of Id®, Blizzard®, and Valve), no one gets to dictate their marketplace; Id could release *Quake™ 17*—requiring five 12.8 GHz graphic cards attached to monitors placed in a cube around the players head—and it would still sell enough copies to make back development costs and draw a tidy profit. Market forces—whatever the public is prepared to pay for—drive the rest of us.

The state of the industry is most apparent in the mass-market field of casual gamers, as they own nothing more than a single platform and a handful of games. If your first-person shooter isn't released on their platform, they'll buy someone else's, and all your hard work will be for naught. Unless you're working on the next *Zelda®*, heed this advice.

Technology

From a technical programmers perspective, cross-platform development encourages a modular approach to development. Because it's not possible to run Nintendo code on a Sony platform, for example, every individual component must be isolated: processing and presentation, platform-specific and common, game and engine. Each module must then provide a common interface to the rest of game, hiding the specific details beneath it. This conforms to the traditional view of good software design. A cross-platform project enforces this distinction that might otherwise become blurred in a single target environment. Whereas modular programming often encourages this method of abstraction and isolation, cross-platform development requires it.

Under this regime, it's no longer possible to rely on any internal side effects of the API. Nor is it possible to surreptitiously add an access function, or make a `private` member variable `public`, because the implementation details—or information upon which you rely—might not exist on every platform. Consequently, a very rigid demarcation must exist between the various components.

Cross-platform code is also more stable and more accurate. This is not a generalization on the people that write it, but as a consequence of it being written. After all, if your code compiles without warnings on three different compilers, and runs identically on three different machines, then it is more likely to have been written solidly. It can be an illuminating experience to compile code under the GNU™ C Compiler (gcc) when you're over-familiar with Microsoft™ Visual C++™. Not because gcc is better, *per se*, but because it's different. An unfamiliar set of warnings can inspire—as well as exasperate.

Teamwork

Most of the games currently available have been written to work cross-platform. They are usually available on PS2 and Xbox, at least, with many also appearing on PC and GameCube. Unfortunately for the majority of the industry, this is a new field, and developers are the only ones solving these problems when the market goes cross-platform. Marketing can easily add stickers to boxes claiming "PS2 version out now. Xbox due Q4." Publishers only need to snap their wallets shut and say, "Give us a GameCube version, too, or else" and they can consider their job over. For developers, however, it represents a significant amount of extra effort. Most of this extra effort is unknown (or ignored) by everyone else. Of the three main departments in a development team— the code, the art, and the design—cross-platform development directly affects all three.

Even when all the individuals within the team have understood (and solved) the problems involved, the managerial glue that holds them together has other problems. The producer must decide where to spend the money; for example, should it be spent on another artist to convert and re-interpret textures, on a new art tool to convert them automatically, or on hiring a programmer to write a custom tool. They also need to manage the time devoted to each platform, making sure the focus is suitable for the product in question: Has a competing product been released on GameCube that means our game is dated? Has the market changed? Do we need to consider supporting network play now? And even before the game is signed and the contracts exchanged, producers must consider how much extra money is needed to develop each platform, and how hard can they push to drop the PC version of the game in favor of giving more time over to Xbox, and so on.

Management

One particular management problem that is specific to new cross-platform games is snobbery. Every console manufacturer believes its machine is the best on the market. They demonstrate this by releasing their first-party games for their own consoles alone. So while Nintendo is still building machines, *Zelda*, *Mario*, and its other game licenses are only available for the latest Nintendo platform. This makes good business sense for Nintendo. The "Exclusively on..." flash on the game packaging nurtures a fan base wanting to play that particular Nintendo game on that particular Nintendo console. It implies that the game is better tailored to the hardware because there were no other considerations during development. Although this can limit the range of potential consumers, it can benefit the developers because it increases the selling power of a game if the console manufacturer helps with advertising features (which the manufacturer should do, because it helps sell the console too) and more technical support in times of trouble.

However, wanting a cross-platform release can create bad feelings on the part of the console manufacturers that weren't approached first. Because the manufacturers hold a monopoly on their console and development kits, they can withhold materials and support that would otherwise be forthcoming.

Finances

Because most development studios are cash strapped, cross-platform development can help massage the budget by eliminating the need for excessive hardware. Any game, including those destined for a single console, can benefit here. After all, if a game works identically on a PS2 and a PC, then the majority of developers can spend most of their time working with the PC version, while periodically testing their work on a shared development kit. Exclusive access to development kits is usually limited to the lead and senior programmers, the console-specific engine coders, and those in charge of the control system and technical requirements.[1] In many cases, however, the lead programmer handles these last two tasks. For the other developers that need access to hardware (such as testers), less expensive kits are often available from the console manufacturers that do not support the full range of debugging facilities, but provide adequate preview features so that the artists and level designers can view their work in position.

In some cases, sharing hardware presents a double saving because there's less software to buy in the form of compilers, profilers, and customized debuggers. These savings depend on whether your toolset supports a roaming license. If you haven't encountered these yet, this simply allows you to install the software anywhere you like, but you can only use it on a limited subset of these machines at any one time. Shared kit is not a recommended way to build games, but frugal developers should take note anyway.

Growth

From a human resource management point of view, cross-platform development can profit the company by helping grow the ability of the team much quicker than usual. Even junior programmers, often consigned to in-house scripting languages and menial tasks, will understand the ramifications of the various platforms because their code will be reused on each of them. So what might initially appear to them as a simple loop with a "pointer to function" callback, will soon be understood as a potential problem involving cache misses.

In the initial stages of development, instruction of this kind will come from the senior programmers (and this book), but afterwards, programmers will be able to use this knowledge themselves to write and fix more involved code. They will also be able to teach the new junior programmers. This continues to increase the average ability of the team and cultivate an awareness of the project as a whole. The junior programmers' knowledge will become very valuable to the team (and the company) over the forthcoming years as they graduate to lead, and senior, status.

OVERVIEW OF CROSS-PLATFORM COMPONENTS

The three main development components to a cross-platform project are

- The design of the generic, cross-platform, interfaces that handles the various modules within the game, such as graphics, audio, or input.
- The technical, platform-specific, implementation of the low-level driver that talks to the hardware to bring the interface to life.
- The gameplay code that effectively uses these components.

The balance between each section varies significantly according to the module in question. An input library, for example, has a simple design and implementation, but the gameplay mechanics that use it are much more complex. The gameplay mechanics will, for example, have to cope with controller configurations, in which the sidestep might be assigned to the joystick, a button, or a pressure-sensitive shoulder control.

Software interface design is a big topic, so we'll limit our discussions to the specific design patterns suitable for cross-platform game development. This includes many multi-layered solutions because even though a graphics renderer is considered the code that "draws stuff," it's wise to separate this into multiple components to deal with specific jobs. In this example, a renderer can be split into two distinct cases: one component that determines what objects to draw, and a second component to draw them. This moves a lot of common engine code away from the low-level driver, enabling more code to be reused.

The low-level implementation of the driver is the only part of the game that should interface with the platform-specific API. Even when this API is middleware, the interface layer should still exist to prevent the game from accessing any component directly as this limits the control the engine can exert on the platform. The more control the engine has, the greater its opportunity for creating faster games and the less chance the game has for slowing it down.

One additional distinction to make at this point is between platform-specific code and platform-dependent code. The former indicates code that is intended for a single platform, but can be compiled and run anywhere. Dependent code, on the other hand, requires the underlying API or hardware to be present for it to work. So if we revisit the example of the input library, code that makes a character side-step left when the PS2 circle button is pressed is platform-specific. However, the code that actually polled the controller would be platform-dependent.

Within a cross-platform game, often a complex relationship exists between these two categories because much of the platform-specific code becomes platform-dependent. This is through workflow problems more than technical ones; if a programmer needs to change a piece of platform-specific code, he is often likely to solve it with the idea that "It's only ever on PS2, so I can just call this PS2-specific function…." In many cases, this isn't a valid argument. For example, if you're converting data assets on the target machine using platform-dependent code, it becomes very difficult to move that conversion routine offline into the PC-oriented tool chain at a later date. Also, platform-specific code is only one step away from the targeted grail of cross-platform code. Dependent code is two steps. A simple abstraction can often generalize specific code, which means there's less code to write, debug, and maintain. This creates a greater amount of commonality between platforms, and should be the goal for any developer. Throughout the book, the terms platform-specific and platform-dependent are used in very specific cases. However, because this can depend on the precise implementation employed, we tend to err toward the use of platform-specific.

The Lead Platform

From the start of any cross-platform project, only one question is more important than "which platforms?" and that is "which platform?" Singular. The *lead* platform in any project always takes priority and everyone else must be flexible around this. Determining the platform is normally a difficult choice because they all have fairly equal technological plumage. But aside from flame wars, this is a question that never will be solved by developers arguing the various merits of each platform. Fortunately, the answer comes from outside the development team, usually from the publisher. The publisher often dictates a lead platform based on market forces, the genre of game, or political alliance—although not necessarily in that order. If the decision has not been made for you, then role-play the position of a publisher to determine the appropriate focus for your game.

Cross-Generation, Cross-Platform Game Programming

In some cases, a new generation of machines will arrive midway through development. This can happen for several reasons, and not necessarily due to bad planning or elongated schedules on the part of the developers. For instance, a platform might die unexpectedly early, console launch dates might change, or a new half-breed console might be released that is worth adopting. This means your development work might be extended across a wide dynamic range of platforms. Even when looking at the single-platform PC, there is a large gap between the high-end, mid-range, and low-end machines. To create a good project on all platforms, you must take a scalable approach, and adapt the gameplay and resources to match the machine on a case-by-case, and game-by-game, basis. Programmers for the current range of mobile phones will have an advantage here because the PDA market is moving at a very fast and, more importantly, *continuous* rate. Over the next year, phones will become as powerful as game consoles. There will be no opportunity to stop and rewrite your game using a completely different "PDA-only" engine. Each game will use an evolution of the existing technology, and despite some techniques being confined to new consoles, the base technology of the *game* will need to be cross-generation as well as cross-platform.

During this transition, don't worry about losing out financially. The PlayStation 2 sold many millions of units, but for the first few years of its existence, many games were still written, released, and (more importantly) sold for the original PlayStation. No one stopped buying PlayStations, or their games, because a better machine was available. It's highly unlikely this will change during the next generation shift, either.

With mid-generational platforms, such as the Sony PSP™, the same cross-platform approach is needed. Although its heritage is routed in the lore of PlayStation 2, the scalability argument should win out over the desire to create a PS2-specific engine that is then tweaked into a PSP engine. Such tweaking inevitably becomes a crowbar.

> *When converting code between two consoles, it's often easier to port the whole game to a PC first, and then back onto the new target.*

The Theoretical Process

The world of game development is very large and there is no "one size fits all" approach to any part of the process. Different engines run games of different genres using different tools with different design philosophies and different styles. Attempting to mention all such situations would be a foolhardy exercise. However, providing game solutions without an example framework is difficult at best, and a confusing jumble of theoretical retorts at worst. With that in mind, this book will adopt a theoretical game, tool chain, and environment for its examples.

The Game

The majority of examples within this book have a direct connection with the process of developing a first-person shooter (FPS). Not because they have any special cross-platform qualities, but because the scenarios involving non-player characters (NPCs), explosions, players, and bullets provide a familiar host of good examples from which we can draw, as most people will have a natural instinct for the design of at least one FPS without needing any groundwork to be explained.

Naturally, it makes no difference what sort of game you're writing because the problems involved in cross-platform game programming are the same within all genres. Where an FPS doesn't sensibly support a particular feature or technique, we'll indicate a suitable example and include a brief background instead of creating contrived examples within the example FPS.

The Tool Chain

Game development probably has the heaviest data use of any modern application. Each frame consists of several megabytes of data, stored as sounds, polygons, and textures. Getting this data from a raw asset into game memory is one of the continuing problems in game development.

The start of the process involves an application for creating assets, such as 3ds max®, Maya®, or Adobe™ Photoshop®. This data is then exported using custom code to a platform-independent version on disc. From here, the generic data is converted into custom versions that are optimized for each platform and then built into disc image files for the various platforms, if required. This is shown in Figure 1.1.

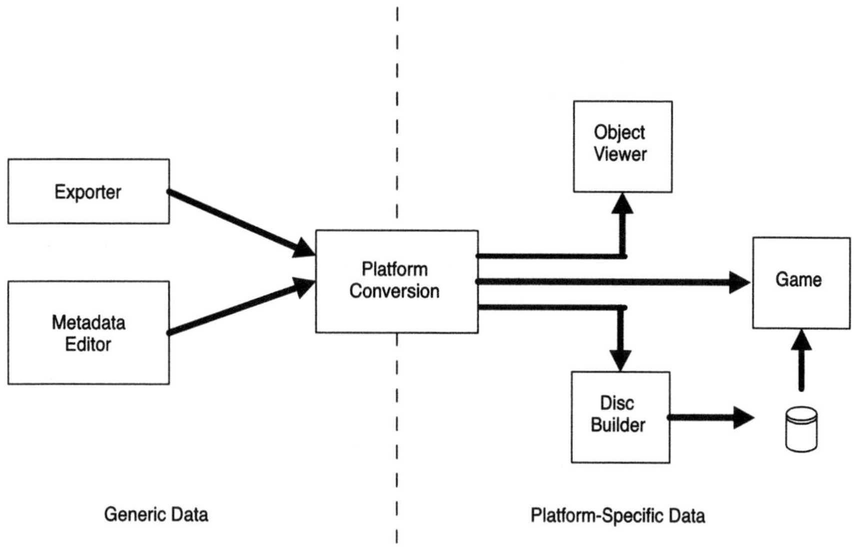

FIGURE 1.1 The cross-platform tool chain.

This is typical of most development houses, and is mirrored by most of the commercial middleware providers. It is a multi-layered solution that allows each section of the pipeline to be changed as required, and ensures the minimum modifications to our platform-specific data.

NOTE

Although not essential, we have introduced platform-specific image viewers into our tool chain that help improve the turn-around time because they are less bulky than a complete game engine.

This conversion process is consequently written as two halves; you have half of a converter that adapts an image file into generic raw data, and another half to build a platform-specific asset from the generic resource. Splitting the conversion routines into two makes it easier to cross onto new platforms, such as Xenon®, because you only need to add the missing half.

When building assets for a cross-platform pipeline, you need to make a few considerations over and above that of a single-platform game. We'll look at these considerations in Chapter 2.

The Engine

The engine running your game has the greatest scope for variation. Trying to predict every breed of engine is impossible. All we'll assume is that you have some form of code to process the game objects, each derived from a common base class, and a means for their inter-communication. Throughout the text, we'll refer to this as an event system, or message passing system, depending on context. These messages are assumed to arrive instantaneously.

Any API calls not described within these pages, and all classes referred to, are similarly theoretical and are assumed to fulfill any basic functionality ascribed to them. The implementation will conform to the rules of cross-platform development (as laid out in Chapter 2), but won't be described in detail unless a new idea or concept needs to be presented.

THE DEVELOPMENT PROCESS

The physical act of developing code has been discussed many times. When applied to cross-platform development, however, this role changes.

Code Is Code

Writing cross-platform code is somewhat different from writing standards-compliant code, although the two are not mutually exclusive. Indeed, to write anything that is cross-platform without adhering to standards would be the gentle equivalent of changing the preprocessor macro of `TRUE` to `0`, or `PI` to `3`. It would be more true to say that cross-platform code is like writing to standards on steroids. You have to make sure that the compiler cannot misinterpret any line of code, that it says exactly what you mean, and that you mean exactly what you say. Running the code through checkers such as Lint can be very useful here, as can adopting peer reviews, and compiling with stringent warning settings on alternate compilers.

More complications occur because of buggy compilers, in which certain language constructs cause incorrect code to be generated or fail to build entirely. Granted, this is not as common now as it has been in the past, but it still happens. There are also places where the C standard states that the behavior of certain code is "undefined." Although the compiler might be standards compliant, the three little words of "undefined," "undetermined," and "unknown" indicate that each compiler is at liberty to process your code in any way it sees fit. The classic interview question of "what result does `a = a++;` give" is a prime example, and should naturally be avoided. This is just one of many similar examples throughout the book. Chapter 2 highlights some of them, but during the course of development, you'll discover your own favorites.

Standards-compliant code, however, is only half the story. The typical scenario of a present day developer reveals the other half. Consider for a moment this set up:

> "The developer will be experienced with Microsoft Visual C++ or .NET™, running under Windows 2000™ using the Win32™ API on an Intel machine. The developer's PC will have a 128-channel sound card (as standard), a 256-MB graphics card, a large hard drive (containing an equally large swap file), 2 GB of RAM and a 19-inch monitor."

How much of this seems familiar? Most of it, no doubt. This is not an atypical environment, as the development tools required to build and play modern games require this amount of processing grunt. In cross-platform games development, everything presented in that scenario is so far wide of the goal posts, it's not even in the same stadium.

Most PC programmers can become spoiled by being able to write clever algorithms that use a lot of memory, are very compute-intensive, or both. They can also get used to the safety net of a swap file, and never check their memory allocation function returns safely. On a console, memory can (and sometimes does) run out, so you still need to keep the game running, even though some particular feature cannot be allocated. Not only that, with each console having a different amount of memory (and the game resources using a different memory footprint), you might run out of memory during different parts of the game on the various consoles. You need to cope with that, too. And, if you're developing without a console development kit, how do you determine the effect of your code on the real hardware?

A further consideration stems from the fact that Microsoft Developer Studio™ is not the only environment. It compiles code differently from other compilers (including .Net), with different resultant code and different warnings and error messages. Furthermore, the Win32 API is, obviously, not available on the PS2 or GameCube, and only partially implemented on the Xbox. So, anyone who's used to `OpenFile` should get used to something else.

Another important, but also less obvious problem in this scenario, is the fact that the byte order of the data on a GameCube is different from the PC. This is known as *endian-ness* and makes it more difficult to load binary data (such as graphical texture images) into memory. A number saved as 0x12345678 on the PC (which is *Little Endian*) appears as 0x78563412 when loaded into a GameCube (a *Big Endian* machine). Although the endian-ness of a number is of no concern while it remains within memory, as soon as it is transferred to or from disk, the data needs to be converted.

Finally, those working on the console-side of cross-platform development don't even have the luxury of a monitor to preview their work. Consoles have television sockets. That means low resolution (usually a 480 horizontal line maximum), color bleed, and brightness and contrast settings that can (and will) vary extensively between make, model, and age of the TV. Although the visuals are normally a problem assigned to artists, the inability to display more than a few lines of debugging text onscreen can be prohibitive for the programmer.

Console Limitations

When working on the PC platform (under Windows, Linux™, or BSD™), you have remarkably few limitations. If the game runs too slowly, buy a faster processor. If the graphics aren't good enough, add more polygons, increase the texture sizes, and upgrade the graphics card. If you can only play five gunshot noises at once, replace the sound card. In some cases, you can even just postpone the game for six months until the entry-level PC hits a suitable specification to show off your game at its best.

Unfortunately, console programmers have none of these benefits. The console machine you have now is the only version of the machine you need to consider because it cannot be upgraded[2] with more RAM, a different graphics card, or a faster processor. There's no swap file to fall back on if memory gets tight or easy upgrade path to cover hardware bugs. Although these problems are not unique to cross-platform development, their effect multiplies when you have to simultaneously consider these effects on different machines. For example:

- The memory footprint for the level data might be 12 MB, 20 MB, or 40 MB.
- The same code might compile to 4 MB, 6 MB, or 12 MB.
- The graphics engine might be bound by fill rate on one platform, and computation on another.
- The CPU might be fast enough to process all the Artificial Intelligence (AI) in one frame, or it might not.
- Any number of other equivalent problems can also occur.

Each console is a finely balanced machine. If it's lacking in one area, another area is usually super-charged to compensate. This ensures that each console, when considered on its own merits, is roughly as good as its competitors. When the same game needs to run across all platforms, you have to either look for ways to scale back certain features (perhaps the AI will only think every other frame), or build everything to run on the lowest common denominator and pad out the game with bonus code in each particular area where the console is under-used.

Several methods for tackling this problem are covered later in the book. No matter which method is used, programmers (along with artists and designers) need to take the initiative, consider the limitations, agree to the confines, and stick to them.

The Processor(s)

The processor(s) will always be fixed, but you need to take into account whether there is one large behemoth CPU that controls everything, or if the work needs to be split between a lot of smaller, slower chips.

Working with a single CPU means that every game feature will (more than likely) run in sequence. So if the AI takes a little longer to process, the graphics engine can compensate by using a lower level of detail when rendering the meshes. In contrast, having separate CPUs running in parallel means the game can only be as fast as the slowest process. If this is the AI (for example), how does it react if more enemy characters are being processed? To use the vernacular, does it scale?

Disk Access

Disk access has two main variables: speed and size. If the disk is very slow (in combined terms of latency and transfer rate), but the processor is fast, then it's a fairly simple process to store all the data on the disk in a compressed format, and decompress it while it's being read. Conversely, the opposite may be true. Additionally, the disk size might be small (having to reside on a 650-MB CD-ROM, instead of a 4.7-GB DVD), necessitating the need for compression, but the processor will then require a larger memory buffer to handle the decompression within a reasonable time frame. As we said before, this problem may exist on any of the consoles, but the method for handling it in each specific case will vary depending on the platform. This in turn will have an impact on the tool chain, and the way in which artists create their work.

Libraries

One beneficial facet of cross-platform development is the ability to use standard libraries. These might be Open Standards (with a capital "O") such as OpenGL or Simple Directmedia Layer (SDL), closed ones such as RenderWare® or Gamebryo®, or internal ones developed by the in-house technology team or senior developers. Each library allows multiple platforms to be serviced directly through a common API, abstracting the hardware—and operating system-specific—details away from the game code.

Employing such a library prevents you from having to reinvent a lot of wheels, and there are many examples on the Web of OpenGL code that's been written for Unix®, but works flawlessly on Windows, and vice versa. A few years ago, a company called Loki Entertainment ported Windows games to Linux by modifying existing DirectX® code to use the SDL API instead. In both of these cases, the common interface between platforms helped speed up development.

A common API is essential in a cross-platform engine; but it isn't the only requirement for a cross-platform *project*. After all, a computer game is more than just its engine, the engine is not just the graphics code, and the graphics code is not defined by its capability to push polygons. The following paragraph will tackle these issues in order.

The game engine needs to consider how to access the disk and allocate memory. These simple tasks take on a new complexity in our world. The sample code for an OpenGL application might read a text file using the `fopen` function, for example. This is part of the C standard library, and not guaranteed to exist on a games console. Even when it does exist on the consoles for which you're currently developing, the function must exist on all of them to be used effectively. Will your publisher come back after a year and say "It's going well, here's some cash, just do another port?" If so, every instance of `fopen` will have to be retroactively replaced. Furthermore, `fopen` is a blocking function, which means it doesn't exit until it has completed its task. In a single threaded environment, this means the whole machine cannot do anything until the file has been opened. If the disk cover is open or the CD-ROM has been removed, you won't be able to access the file, and because the program has been suspended, you won't be able to print a message onto the screen saying "Please put the disc back in" either. On its own, the standard library isn't powerful enough. It was never intended to be. So we either need to create an abstraction layer for the filesystem to hide our use of nonstandard library calls, or make sure we're always using threads. In reality, we'll use an abstracted filesystem anyway because it provides other benefits. We'll also often employ an abstracted thread library because the most common threading library, *pthreads*, is not available on consoles since they exist within a different set of standards. Not only that, but after you have abstracted the basic filesystem, you need to handle the different conventions for filenames. Windows uses names that appear as, `c:\projects\game\mymesh`, whereas Linux might use `/home/steev/game/mymesh`. Furthermore, filenames might be case sensitive or limited to a certain number of characters. All these possibilities need to be considered.

In the same vein, the graphics code is not just about drawing the polygons. The polygonal mesh data needs to come from somewhere, so most sample code or magazine articles include a list of vertices in an array, hard-coded into the source. In the real world, this cannot work because the amount of game data easily outstrips available memory. Instead, you need to write a data-driven component that loads arbitrary data from an external package and prepares it for the graphics code. This again uses the abstracted filesystem, but it also uses platform-specific code to set up the graphics chip correctly. In addition, we'll also need some extra cross-platform resourcing code that allows the game to reference these (platform-specific) polygons from our (common) code, because we must be able to say "draw this object in this position."

In theory, you only need a single rendering function to write a 3D graphics engine—`DrawOnePolygon`—but the overhead of sending each polygon individually to the hardware is prohibitively expensive. Instead, each hardware API will have its own method for storing and referencing groups of polygonal data that has no relevance to the outside world, or any other API. This platform-specific data then needs to be manipulated in a cross-platform manner for tasks such as collision, movement, and animation. This often requires a duplicate set of structures for each of render data and collision data. This apparent waste will pay for itself very quickly, however, with the increased ease by which all platforms can optimize their specific half of the equation without intruding on the other half.

ABOUT THE BOOK

In attempting to deliver as much information as possible, code explanations are kept to a minimum, all utilizing the same rules and guidelines as follows.

Coding Style

Throughout the text, code samples are given either in their entirety or in fragments. They have been taken from the author's own engine and chosen to illustrate the points within the text. The naming conventions used within the code are:

`sgxInitialCaps`: A global function, datatype, or enumeration ready for cross-platform work, meaning it could be used on any platform without problems. It may present an abstraction with platform-dependent code underneath, or a completely generic function.

`SGX_UPPERCASE`: A macro, ready for cross-platform work.

`OS_ANY_CASE`: A pseudo-function indicating OS-specific functionality. The name is not intended to reflect any existing function, merely present the role of an equivalent routine within the API.

`PS2_ANY_CASE`: A pseudo-function indicating PS2-specific functionality. Again, the name does not reflect any existing PS2 function. This is used to distinguish between a generic "any OS" code, and specifics.

`XBOX_ANY_CASE`: As above.

`GC_ANY_CASE`: You get the idea.

We've chosen this naming convention for two reasons. First, and most obviously, it highlights the cross-platform abstractions that exist within the function and reminds us of the task at hand. Second, by including uppercase letters in the name, it cannot conflict with any of the standard C types, functions, or other third-party library's features.

Several functions and classes are also prefixed with letters such as PS2, Xbox, or GC. Again, these are meant to illustrate examples, and no connection with the actual platform or its API should be inferred.

NON-DISCLOSURE AGREEMENTS

There have been many dissenting voices about the use of NDAs, with them being called "the scourge of our industry" and "monopolistic." Many find it strange that a scientific discipline such as computing should hide behind this cloak, allowing us to stand only on the shoulders of proverbial giants in our local vicinity. But there is nothing we can do about this. All consoles have an NDA, and we must abide by it. To that end, we cannot, and will not, reveal any secrets about the APIs for PlayStation 2, Xbox, or GameCube. Nor will there be any named functions, macros, or magic numbers. All the information presented in this book, including the machine specifications shown in the appendixes, has been gleaned from magazines, press packs, clean room engineering projects, and numerous Web sites around the world. These appendixes have been presented separately because a side-by-side comparison is both unfair and nonrepresentative. After all, the clock speed of the G5™ and Intel processors do not reflect their relative power. Where a direct comparison is not possible or the information is under NDA (or could not be ascertained from a public source), the entry is left blank.

Any time the workings of a platform need to be explained, imaginary stub functions will be invented to process the theoretical data, and return theoretical results. There is no connection, intentional or otherwise, between the name used here and that of the official version. Wherever possible, samples will use openly published APIs such as OpenGL and DirectX.

NOTES TO THE READER

All the examples given within the text are correct at the time of going to press. However, tools change, compilers are updated, libraries are patched, and new bugs are added. It is entirely possible that a particular example might fail to work in exactly the same manner as given here. That's life. This doesn't negate the point itself, but reiterates it. Along with the fundamental rules of test, test, and test again. The principle arguments are exactly the same.

ENDNOTES

1. All consoles have a list of requirements that the game must fulfill to be approved by the manufacturer before release. These lists vary between consoles, and are private. It dictates criteria such as maximum load time and the wording for various error messages.
2. Even when the console does support upgrades (such as with broadband adapters), you still need to work toward the lowest common denominator; that is, a machine without upgrades.

2 Top Ten Tips

In This Chapter

- Abstraction
- Commonality
- Limitations
- Modularization
- Resource Creation Path
- Granularity
- Separation and Isolation
- Debugging and Profiling
- Predictability
- Turn-Around

THE BASIC ISSUES

Cross-platform development is an issue that affects a game's entire code base. The graphics and audio programmers aren't the only ones that have a job to do. All programmers working on the game need to always remember that their code will be compiled, run, and very often debugged on platforms other than the one on which it was originally written and tested. This might seem obvious, but it's frequently overlooked. What difference does it make anyway? Why isn't it enough to use the C language?

To explain this, we offer a number of fundamental ideas that need to be adhered to across all code within the cross-platform environment. With so many differences between platforms, we need to know how to consider, cover up, or isolate those differences. Each idea is supplemented with code samples, demonstrating where the methods can be applied. The methods can be applied elsewhere as well; example-ridden references to the filesystem will contain ideas that are just as applicable to the audio code, input library, or network code.

ABSTRACTION

If this book were condensed into a single paragraph, line, or word, the word *Abstraction* would be on the short list of words to use. It is the cornerstone of everything we do. Abstraction means to generalize, ignoring details and specifics. For programmers, it's being able to write code without being concerned about the hardware, and knowing in advance that the behavior of every platform will be identical—not similar, but identical. Everything you do needs to be abstracted in some way and at some level. Even the code you write, although it's all C, is just an abstraction. It abstracts the low-level machine code away, allowing you to write a more general program. When you declare an integer variable, for instance, you're abstracting a datatype. When you read from a file, you're abstracting the filesystem, and so on. Some abstractions are simple, consisting of nothing more than a well placed `#define` or `typedef` in a header file. Sometimes they are more complex, where one function hides a wealth of code behind a simple nomenclature, such as `PlayThemeMusic`.

What matters is that when you abstract something, no side effects are introduced in the process. For example, the standard library function `qsort` hides the basic implementation details from you, but it *doesn't* behave identically on all platforms because each compiler will provide its own implementation of `qsort`. Because the language specification isn't strict enough to prevent side effects, `qsort` only has to perform a sort, not necessarily a *quicksort*. An example of this difference can be seen if the `qsort` function is required to sort a list containing two identical primary keys. In that case, the algorithm (not the `qsort` callback function) is responsible for the list's final order. The strict requirements placed on cross-platform development mean that functions with side effects are unacceptable.

So what needs to be abstracted?

Game: Should be programmed in a generic manner, using only the abstractions provided by the engine.

Engine: Although parts will be platform specific (for example, graphics driver), the majority of code (such as geometry calculations) should be common. The interface that the engine presents to the rest of world must therefore be common, too.

Everything Else: You should use nothing that is compiler-specific or platform-specific. This includes memory management routines and datatypes.

Also, do not be afraid to consider multilayered abstractions. They are both necessary and useful. The best example in this category is the filesystem.

At one level, C's standard library has provided a layer of abstraction for you with the `fopen`, `fread`, and `fclose` functions; however, they are, for most purposes, limited and only cover the basic file-handling capabilities. They are so basic, in fact, that some platforms do not consider it worthwhile to include them in the standard libraries. We'll most likely need a series of wrapper functions that use the platform-specific versions, such as `OpenFile`, to provide the much needed features. On top of these wrapped functions, we'll then produce another layer of abstraction that allows us to access different types of files, such as a memory card file or a single file within a *.ZIP* package, as if they were identical. The latter becomes important on the PlayStation 2 where a strict *ISO 9660* standard is applied, and we need to overcome the limit of 30 files in a directory as seen in Chapter 5, "Storage."

If you are using a third-party library or middleware solution, you should abstract large portions of it too. At the very least, abstract the input library, the debugging helper routines, and the memory allocation code. Even if you call the same function with the same parameters, wrapper it with your own code. This will make it easier to add debugging code around the API calls and quicker to determine whether the parameters for a specific function call are valid. This is especially useful when the third-party function is called from several places, and you have no library source on which to place a breakpoint. Additionally, wrapping these functions will even make life a little simpler if you change middleware products during development. Although if you do need to change middleware solution during development, this is probably the least of your problems.

Abstracting middleware also helps if your adopted solution doesn't support a platform that later becomes a requirement. This might be a new platform that becomes available due to an extended deadline, or an old platform that gains a resurgence of interest due to a change in the publisher's allegiance. Although abstracting middleware doesn't make the task of writing a new engine any easier, it does give you an idea of how many middleware functions need to be replaced, which lets you judge a more realistic timeline.

So much of cross-platform development involves abstractions that it should become second nature after a while. Much of this book gives full examples on how to abstract various components at the game, engine, and system level.

COMMONALITY

Commonality follows on directly from the discussion of abstraction. When abstracting part of the engine (for example, the renderer), consider carefully which components are truly platform-specific, and which can be made common across all platforms. The render component might be comprised of code to determine which areas of the level are visible (through a portal system or potentially visible set) and separate code to send this list of textured polygons to the graphics chip. The first step in this pipeline is cross-platform. The second is not. This commonality needs to be determined to build a mutual, stable, base.

These interfaces extend across every minutia in the project. At one end of the scale, you must ensure that the size of every datatype is common to all platforms, even if the structures they build are not. This (as we shall see in Chapter 3, "Memory") means that the standard types, such as `short`, `int`, and `long` must not be used and should be replaced with `tUINT16` and `tINT32`, for example.

At the other end of the scale, the graphics engine API should implement common functions, for example, `DrawWorld`, which is implemented once and available for all platforms, and the platform-specific `DrawWorldMesh` function that it calls. Followers of design patterns will recognize this as something similar to a *bridge*. Furthermore, if a function inside one driver needs to change a global state within the engine, the function should reset that state before it exits to remove any side effects and maintain commonality. This topic is explored further in the "Granularity" section later in this chapter.

LIMITATIONS

Every part of the game development process involves limitations that you must overcome. A cross-platform game has more limitations than most, and extends beyond the usual questions about polygon counts. You also need to consider the language, compiler, and its libraries.

Language Limitations

The first limitation to overcome is the language. If we succumb to these limitations, we can't even compile our game, let alone run it to the point of exhaustion. The language in question is probably C or C++, so we must focus our attention on the minutiae of C—namely, *standard C.*

A programming language is usually learned by example. We copy the code samples in our book of choice, change them, add to them, delete bits from them, and make them our own. As time goes by, we collect more examples. Rarely do we look behind the scenes of a language to find out what makes it tick and why the examples work the way they do. When a lot of our work is in a single environment (perhaps the PC—usually under Microsoft Windows, but more frequently under Linux), we adapt our coding style to the compiler and platform we are using (often subconsciously). This might include involuntary use of vendor-specific functions that appear in the so-called standard libraries (such as `_gvct`, or `stricmp`), compiler-specific extensions (such as the `<?` operator), or special datatypes (such as `qword`). In extreme cases, you might be tempted to write code for a specific compiler to gain extra speed. It's imperative that every line of code written for a cross-platform project is completely standard to ensure that the code cannot be misinterpreted in any way, by any compiler.

To illustrate this point, consider these questions concerning language.

Language Questions:

1. How many bytes constitute a `long` variable?
2. Is a `char` signed or unsigned, by default?
3. What is the value of `a` after this code?
   ```
   int a = 1;
   a = a++;
   ```
4. What is the value of `sizeof('a')`?
5. In which directory does the header file live, given the following code?
   ```
   #include "graphics.h"
   ```

Language Answers:

1. Depends on the platform. Usually 4 bytes on a 32-bit machine, but it's 8 on the PlayStation 2.
2. Depends on the compiler. You must explicitly state `signed` or `unsigned` when using `char`s. All font code, for example, should use an `unsigned char` to cope with accented characters. Games using Unicode will use their own (nonchar oriented) datatype.
3. Depends on the compiler. The expression is undefined because the value of `a` is changed twice before the sequence point (that is, the semicolon, in this example). It could be 1 or 2, or, in really perverse compilers, 934537.
4. Depends on the language. If it's compiling as C, it will be compiler-dependent, and its result will be identical to `sizeof(int)`. When compiled a as C++, it will report 1 byte.
5. Depends on the compiler. The double quotes usually mean current directory, but if used within a header file, the compiler might interpret this as the directory of the current header file, or the source file where the compiler started building. This makes it inadvisable to nest headers in different directories, although in practice this is difficult to avoid.

As you can see, building the code to see what the compiler does is not good enough because you'll ultimately be building the game with more than one compiler. Cross-platform programming requires a deeper understanding of the language. The only way you can acquire this knowledge is by reading. Your first stop should be *comp.lang.c* newsgroup's excellent FAQ at *http://www.faqs.org/faqs/C faq/faq/index.html.* This FAQ contains many good questions and answers concerning how to handle several tricky constructs. Should the phrase "not portably" appear in the answer, avoid using it, even if it appears to work on your current set of compilers.

For a more definitive, but slightly drier, coverage of the language, the best document to read is the ANSI® standard itself. The ANSI standard is a big, and occasionally unwieldy, document that describes every facet of the C language, and what each compiler must implement to be considered "ANSI-compliant." Any competent programmer can understand most (if not all) of this document. Experienced programmers with a good working grasp of the language can avoid this step.

The completed ANSI/ISO® standard is not free,[1] although the final draft can be downloaded from the Internet. Some choose to purchase the much less expensive book entitled *The Annotated ANSI C Standard* instead;[2] although its annotations are sometimes wrong or misguided. It is, however, an inexpensive way to get the majority of the standard, but keep in mind that not all of the standard is included.

This might appear like a lot to read, but it's easier to learn what is legal (and apply only that knowledge), than it is to learn every extension on every platform and explicitly avoid them. After all, the legal features constitute a finite set. However, it is possible to make an educated guess as to what is nonstandard. For instance, any function or macro featuring one or more underscores is probably an extension (`size_t` is one notable exception). Those that begin with an underscore are almost certainly extensions. Any function name in MixedCapitals is probably an extension, too. This is a sign of *Hungarian Notation*, which originated from Charles Simonyi at Microsoft.

In contrast, names that are comprised solely of lowercase alphabetic characters are likely to be standard, unless they're the typical gotchas, such as `stricmp`. If in doubt, look for the prototype in the header files. It's very likely such names will be sandwiched between `#ifndef __STRICT_ANSI` macros, or similar. The MSDN® has extensive (and very good) documentation on the standard library. Under .NET, pressing #F1 on any library function opens the appropriate help page for you and states whether the function is a Microsoft extension.

As always, prevention is better than cure. Most compilers provide a way to switch off these extensions, either through a dialog box or a macro that must be defined before including any standard header files. Depending on the compiler, this can be more trouble than it's worth because each platform likely *needs* these extensions to pack structures correctly, or to use specific datatypes that access and control the hardware. With careful modularization, you can limit these occurrences and compile the game under a strict ANSI compiler.

Although we have concentrated on C here, the same ideas apply to C++. There's just more scope in C++ for problems. For example, the construction order of globally instantiated classes is not fixed, so any interdependencies will not behave portably (we'll cover this in Chapter 11, "The Bits We Forget About"). Fortunately for the game programmer, after the basic architecture has been completed, any new functions only use a small, well-known subset of C++, such as references, templates, and the standard template library (STL).

NOTE

Some of the more complex templating techniques will not work under some compilers. One typical example is partial template specialization, which fails under Microsoft Visual C++ 6.0.

Library Limitations

For any C compiler to be ANSI-compliant, it must have a set of standard libraries. C++ also includes the standard template library (STL). All of these are standard, tested components that can be used without fear in a gaming environment. Unfortunately, a cross-platform gaming environment might raise problems because the implementation might differ slightly between compilers, as you've already seen with the `qsort` function.

STL implementations also differ between platforms. Even the versions on PC and Xbox (despite their heritage) are different from each other. If you are using STL out-of-the-box for basic single platform work, then the default implementation is usually good enough because it behaves well enough for end users to consider it identical to anything they've used before.

On the other hand, if you use your own memory management code, you might need to work around specific issues in STL. The amount of work will increase as effort is duplicated across each specific implementation and each platform. In these situations, you might decide to ignore your vendor's implementation, and use a set of third-party libraries, such as *STLPort* (*http://www.stlport.org*), or those provided by *Boost* (*http://www.boost.org*). This is a case when reinventing the wheel is a good thing. Only here, someone else has done the reinventing for you. You just need to test it.

Compiler Limitations

We rarely need to consider compiler limitations because the compiler's sole job is to implement the language standard, and we only practice our art according to that standard. However, you should consider four issues about compiler limitations.

Standard Interpretations

Standards are good, but there are so many to choose from. Although a compiler can adhere to the letter of the law, it doesn't necessarily behave according to the spirit. This might be due to bugs in the compiler, extensions that cannot be switched off, or undefined behavior that is permitted by the standard. However, before your project ships, you'll find at least one really annoying problem that exists between compilers: variable scope in C++, for example.

```
for (int i=0;i<10;i++)
{
    // ... do stuff ...
}
```

The loop counter `i` exists only between the braces because that is its scope. It increments from 0 to 9, and forces the loop to exit when it reaches 10. This is true of every compiler.

When the loop terminates at 10, `i` goes out of scope and it is destroyed. This is *not* true of every compiler. Some compilers do not destroy `i`, allowing it to be used in another loop later on in the function. This causes problems when another loop in the same function declares `i` again—perhaps in another `for` loop. This produces a "redeclaration of i" error on some compilers. If the declaration is removed, then every other compiler will complain that `i` hasn't been declared. The solution is simply to move the declaration outside the `for` loop.

NOTE

Under Visual C++, this error can be avoided by using the Disable Language Extensions option; however, this can cause more problems than it solves because some of the official header files are not compliant. .NET 2003 does not suffer this problem because a better option is available in the form of `/Zc:forScope`.

Creating these workarounds is a nuisance, but that's par for the course with cross-platform development. To stop other developers from falling into the same traps, you should create a small document of these differences, and keep it in your source control tool. If you work with code reviews, reference that document as part of your process.

Abstracting Compiler-Specific Features

Each compiler has three separate categories of macros and extensions. First, some are part of the C standard, such as `__FILE__` to indicate the current file, and `__LINE__` for the current line number in the source. Both of these will find a use when we look at memory allocation in Chapter 3, "Memory" and Chapter 6, "Debugging." These are language features, so we don't need to worry about them.

Next are the features that exist in all compilers, but in different forms. For example, to distinguish between a release and debug build of the game, the compiler often predefines a special symbol. A debug build might be indicated with any of the following:

- DEBUG
- NRELEASE
- _DEBUG
- __DEBUG
- DEBUG_BUILD

The vendor could also use any other macro it deems appropriate. These macros could be declared with either

```
#define DEBUG
```

or

```
#define DEBUG    1
```

Because each platform requires a different compiler, we can't rely on any particular standard and so must create a separate header file for each platform-compiler combination like this:

```
// For the CodeWarrior compiler, running on a Nintendo GameCube
#ifdef DEBUG
#define SGX_DEBUG_BUILD      1
#undef SGX_RELEASE_BUILD
#endif
```

The implementation then requires

```
#if SGX_DEBUG_BUILD
#endif
```

to be placed around cross-platform, debug-only code. This method is favored because it's possible to upgrade an `#if` to `#ifdef` (using the preprocessor function, `defined`), whereas you cannot change an `#ifdef` to an `#if`.

The third subcategory of compiler specifics are those that hide in `#pragma` statements, or are extensions, usually prefixed with one or two underscores. For games programmers, the most often used directives are `__inline` and `__force_inline`.

Again, these should be abstracted as cleanly as possible, usually in the same header file as `SGX_DEBUG_BUILD`, because these directives vary according to compiler.

```
#define SGX_FORCE_INLINE __forceinline
```

Compiler attributes that align structure elements to specific boundaries also fit in this category. They often require separate begin and end macros and surround the structure in question.

Pragmas are invariably never cross-platform, although many are common to at least two compilers. This includes

```
#pragma once
```

which should be banned in favor of traditional header guards such as

```
#ifndef SGX_DATATYPES_HPP
#define SGX_DATATYPES_HPP
    /* Rest of code here... */
#endif /* SGX_DATATYPES_HPP */
```

A Compiler's Result Is Not Cross-Platform

This is obvious if only from a literal standpoint: the result is assembly that is always specific to a particular platform. Because of this, the final code size may bear no relation to that of other platforms (PlayStation 2 executables, known as ELFs, are large regardless of compiler). Therefore, do not use one platform's executable size to prepare memory footprints for the other machines—even on a single module.

The reasons for the differences in size are numerous, but often revolve around specific criteria. A RISC (Reduced Instruction Set Computing) instruction set will cause a larger footprint, as will statically bound libraries. This is more common on consoles. PC executables usually use dynamic link libraries (DLLs) and very small link libraries. Also, extra debugging information may be present in the build, so be sure to strip the symbols out if you need to ascertain an accurate memory footprint.

Compilers Change

Finally, remember that any code workaround for version 1.2 of the compiler may not work in 1.3. This may even be true of perfectly valid code that suddenly breaks in later versions (even compiler writers produce bugs). Before changing the compiler, make sure you've run your games test suite over the whole code base, and don't migrate the rest of the team until you're completely happy. If you're producing an engine for several teams, make sure this occurs after a stable build has been produced; otherwise, you'll be forcing others to upgrade at a potentially controversial time. Treat it with the paranoia of a completely new compiler and platform, and you'll be fine.

CAUTION *If you work without the source to your engine, remember that the name mangling present in C++ can prevent libraries from one version of the compiler from working with another. Upgrade with care.*

Remember, too, that most new tools start as very immature pieces of code, and suffer many changes during their initial roll-out phase, which provides yet another reason not to write compiler-specific code.

Platform Limitations

One common, and perhaps overused, mantra in games development is the idea of targeting the worst platform, the lowest common denominator. Every generation of consoles has a pecking order. In 1989, Commodore Amiga and Atari ST waged titanic battles. Super NES® and the Sega Megadrive® (a.k.a. Genesis®) battled in 1993. Currently, PlayStation 2, Xbox, and Nintendo GameCube are involved in a three-pronged attack. The PC doesn't directly compete in this race because it's infinitely more upgradeable than a console, and consequently doesn't suffer limitations in the same way. Consoles have hard limits.

Some believe that if you write a game (or design a level, or build a character) for the lowest spec platform at the time, you can guarantee a similar experience on all existing machines. This might be done by limiting the number of polygons in each part of the level, the number of characters onscreen at once, or the number of texture maps (or materials) allowed.

This is a common fallacy, however, because each machine has its own unique strengths in particular areas; for instance, the Nintendo GameCube has a very powerful general-purpose processor, allowing for complex AI path-finding algorithms. Conversely, the PlayStation 2 has customized chips (VU0 and VU1) to perform compute-intensive matrix transformations, making these chips better suited to mathematics than AI.

To truly focus on the lowest common denominator, you would need to consider the slowest CPU combined with the worst graphics chip, the lowest polyphonic sound chip, and the smallest memory—in other words, the worst of all worlds, which, at the time of writing, would be little improvement on the old Amiga 1200.

Instead, the limitations must be set on a dynamic basis that can be varied between platforms. Outdoor scenes in most 3D games have fogging to obscure distant detail. Racing games especially are known for culling large portions of their world, and fading them in gently as the camera approaches. This is a very suitable example because the fogging distance is completely arbitrary. As long as it's not too close to hinder gameplay, the player doesn't generally worry if the scene clips at 100 meters or 110—or if the PlayStation 2 version clips at 100 meters, and the Xbox version clips at 110. Each platform can be given a set of arbitrary limits that are set dynamically using a function call, rather than a `#define` (because there's less code to compile after the change). If your engine needs to support widely differing scenarios (perhaps indoor and outdoor scenes), this can be changed as the camera moves between them.

CAUTION

The far clip plane and fogging distance can have a negative affect on gameplay, so offer the solution to your designers, but don't implement it without discussion.

The processor can enforce other limits on your scene because it has a limit on the number of polygons that can be transformed in a given time period. This can vary according to memory, too. If you are storing and then sorting the alpha faces (because they should always be drawn back-to-front), you'll need a buffer to hold them. The size of that buffer will vary according to your platform, engine, and game, so make it dynamically configurable.

In some cases, the limits of a particular platform can demand many solutions. Every (solvable) problem in computing has more than one solution, so you might need to develop two algorithms that produce the same result. Typically, one algorithm uses a lot of memory, but is very quick. The other is incredibly compact, but runs slower. The game can then dynamically switch between them, depending on the platform, game level, or even which part of the level the engine is currently rendering.

Sometimes, it's possible to create an algorithm that works on a sliding scale, in which a specific amount of memory can be allotted and its speed will be proportional. Memory and disk caches operate like this. Within games, however, it's very difficult to find and write specific algorithms that fit this pattern. Usually two (or even three) completely different versions are hand coded and selectable at runtime. The current range of consoles has extra memory for debugging, so there's plenty of scope to experiment, profile, and choose a suitable default algorithm.

Games handle a lot of data—megabytes of it, in fact, every second. By contrast, your average word processor editing a chapter from a book might use no more than 200 KB. To achieve a good frame rate, this data must be handled optimally. Common data is usually held in caches, where caches are kept full so that the data is not thrashed to and from main memory. This requires a lot of forethought. Because each platform has differently sized caches, and different transfer rates on the bus, you must consider your data limits accordingly. For example, VU1 on the PlayStation 2 has a 16-KB data cache. If you process 32.2 KB of animation data using it, there would two complete cache fills, followed by a wasteful one copying just 200 bytes. Being able to reduce this data to 32 KB would clearly be a savings. This might mean animating fewer nodes in your character models, or governing the rules of your data assets. The change would be unperceivable to any other platform, but could save your proverbial life on others.

MODULARIZATION

Any project, large or small, is invariably created from a number of self-contained modules, each geared toward a specific job. These might be third-party libraries to parse JPG files or play movies, or custom code segments to handle algorithmic animations such as fire. Writing individual modules is considered a good thing in any development process, but it becomes crucially important when developing across multiple platforms because not all libraries make sense (or exist) on all platforms. The most obvious examples are the graphics, sound, and movie playback libraries. Each platform comes with its own libraries, and each will only compile, and be suitable, for that platform.

The project itself should be split into a large number of modules, each one capable of being treated like a black box, or Lego® brick. In the real world, every Lego brick is built with such precision, that any of the billion and one bricks now in circulation can fit neatly with any of the other bricks. Not just the bricks in your set, but any brick. With a cross-platform project, each "Lego brick module" needs to fit with every other, regardless of which country the Lego came from, or on which platform the code is intended to run because we may need to remove one brick (for example, the PlayStation 2 movie player) and replace it with another (the Xbox movie player).

Projects built from the ground up can organize these modules as they fit. Middleware users won't need to worry because these choices have been made for them. Each module should live within two separate hierarchies. First, the logical hierarchy demonstrates the module's relationship with other modules. For example, the PlayStation 2 movie player could be part of the platform-specific graphics code, which is part of the generic graphics code, which in turn is part of the core engine. Second, the physical hierarchy indicates in which specific compiler project, library, or file the PlayStation 2 movie code resides. These files need to be considered as replaceable Lego bricks. You need to ask yourself several questions to validate your reasoning: Does this code need to be replaced? How easy is it to replace? The more likely it is to be replaced, the easier that task should be.

In a single platform game, you would create an image library to load textures from the disc into the graphics engine. In the cross-platform arena, there would be several different image libraries, as each platform would work with its own special format. These libraries would probably not exist on the other platforms, and so should be considered as separate projects—even if each project only contains a single source file. This makes it easier too apply project-wide options (such as smallest code, or fastest code) to only the files that need it, because not all compile options are available on a per-file basis. Also, it's easier to replace whole projects, rather than individual source files. This can happen when a particular branch of code has been profiled (for example, the matrix multiplication code) and found to be slow on a particular platform. If your projects are all controlled from within .NET, then you can use the Exclude from Build option on those specific files. Remember that the limitations vary on a per-platform basis, and it's easier to replace a single project or file than it is to fill the source code with:

```
#if SGX_PLATFORM_PLAYSTATION2
    // do some PlayStation 2 asm
#elif SGX_PLATFORM_GAMECUBE
    // do some Nintendo GameCube asm
#else
    // do some generic C code
#endif
```

In the movie player example, code will *definitely* need replacing on other platforms, and so should be as easy to remove as possible by using a separate project. In contrast, the matrix operations in the math code *might* need to be replaced with custom assembler, so it would be best to place these functions in a separate file. Most likely, this would be a small project that is combined with the other math-oriented libraries (for example, for vectors and quaternions) to form a larger project.

As you've seen, the limitations of each platform vary, so in some cases the basic architecture might need to be modified slightly (by getting some parts to run in parallel, for instance). By modularizing the code base, you can recompile and adapt modules with a much finer granularity than you might have been able to do otherwise, making code replacement a much easier task.

If you want to use anything other than static libraries, you'll discover another problem. Dynamic libraries are very platform dependent, and usually require the function names to be exported by the linker. Windows, for example, uses `__declspec(dllexport)`. This generates a platform and compiler dependency due to the export symbol, and a potential for name mangling conflicts if the linker changes its standards. Static linking can cause bigger executables and less flexibility when it comes to changing individual modules, but in most cases static linking is the preferred solution. When it isn't (for example, level-specific code or test harnesses running on servers that cannot be shut down), you should abstract these compiler directives and hide them:

```
// for Windows
#define SGX_DYNLIB __declspec(dllexport)

// for platforms not supporting DLL's
#define SGX_DYNLIB
```

When working with middleware, these directives will be defined for you, enabling you to focus on the game modules. Alternatively, you might decide to abstract the middleware into a new module that encompass several others. This not only makes it simpler to find your way around the source (as the tree now has more branches), but also makes the abstraction easier to debug and monitor usage.

RESOURCE CREATION PATH

The whole reason behind cross-platform programming is to save you time and effort. The cross-platform plan is to write one piece of code, and get it working on four different platforms with little to no extra effort. We should extend the same courtesy to the artists and designers by providing them with a tool chain with which they can create one texture, mesh, or level that works on all our different platforms.

The differences between each platform vary in scope. Some are minor (meshes should be reduced in size), moderate (textures need to be palletized into 16 colors), or major (completely different level sections). Naturally, you should try to keep any large changes to an absolute minimum, with most of the minor and moderate changes (if not all) achievable through good tools and a data-driven engine. The basic structure of our tool chain is described in Chapter 1, "Introduction" and detailed in Figure 1.1.

Resource Detail

Whether you're creating a texture or mesh, the artist should be instructed to build it as large as possible using as much detail as he can reasonably muster, and store it in a lossless format (such as PNG). The platform-specific conversion routines will then reduce the image according to a set of rules and heuristics to ensure that a platform-friendly asset is created. This enables a 512 x 512, 32-bit texture to be created and shrunk automatically to either a 128 x 128, 16-bit texture or a 32 x 32, 4-bit texture, depending on the platform, while still retaining a high-resolution version for screenshots and magazine cover images. This can also prevent the re-creation of assets in those cases when the development cycle extends across two generations of platforms. This is rare in the console world, but mobile phone development has a continuous rate of change in which this is particularly pertinent.

The complexity of some reduction processes can be outside the general job description of a game programmer. This is never truer than in the example of re-palletizing textures. Never be ashamed to introduce third-party software into the tool chain to perform asset reduction to ensure a high level of quality across all components.

Use of Metadata

Metadata is information about data, and describes specific properties about the information in a file. Most obviously, a texture includes metadata that indicates its size and color depth. Additionally, the metadata for a texture can indicate the type of material it is intended to represent (for instance, wood or metal) so that the appropriate ricochet sound is played, and the correct bullet hole texture is drawn. The metadata can also indicate the manner in which the asset should be processed while in the tool chain—to indicate a suitable resolution for each particular platform, for example.

This data is held within the cross-platform asset, and can either be encoded from within the original application, such as Maya, or added afterwards by a custom tool. The information itself should be arranged in a hierarchy, so that a common set of parameters can be individually replaced by platform-specific versions. The tool chain must then apply this data correctly so the game and engine only see one piece of metadata in each category.

TIP

Metadata is always better than a naming convention. Not only can you store more information, but also the information is more readable and can be sanity-checked easier.

Metadata is also useful for building trapdoors into the tool chain by indicating where a new specific asset should be used in place of the automatically generated one, for example. This is a rare case and a slightly contrived example, but the word "trapdoor" was used for a reason.

File Data

The structure of these files will be identical in all cases (so we can use common file-handling code in the game), however, the low-level texture data will be tailored to each graphics driver, reducing the load time for levels. The first draft of a new graphics engine will often use the generic texture format because it provides a more immediate turn-around of assets. It also gives the graphics programmer time to study the internal texture format, making the asset converter easier to write. This may become a necessity if the internal format is undocumented.

File Store

The tool chain introduces at least two new versions of every asset in the game that can eat a significant amount of disc space, and inflict a large amount of processing overhead when the assets need to be built into a game-ready format. Although there's no good way to prevent this, you can apply some techniques to limit the number of assets that are rebuilt.

Most games are created in teams with shared networks, so you can use this infrastructure by adding a small network server to store all the assets and their converted equivalents. Grabbing a new asset then involves checking the local cache to see if it has truly been updated, and then taking the data for the platforms in which you're interested.

You can also improve your tool chain by only rebuilding assets for levels on which you are working. This requires a dependency calculator (similar to Unix `Makefiles`) to understand the level data files and which assets the level requires, but should be simple enough to implement in any case.

Disc Format

Most of the time, the disc image is built by combing all the files from a single directory on your hard drive that contains all the necessary assets. In many cases, this is not enough because the data must be explicitly ordered to get the best performance possible. This order would probably originate in the world-building tool and reflect the order in which the objects are loaded by the game.

The mapping of hard drive data to disc image isn't necessarily 1:1. For example, if the gameplay follows a fairly linear progression, but gives the player the option of turning around and walking backwards, it might benefit the game to store the level sections twice; once for forwards and once for backwards, so that the disc is only ever seeking forwards (which is usually significantly quicker). Such duplication would occur in the output phase of the tool chain, while still using a single set of assets. Chapter 5 covers the technical process behind this type of work.

Automatic Testing

The tool chain not only provides the essential link between art resource and in-game asset, but also permits an automated method of testing the noncode portions of a cross-platform game. Most notably, it can check that all the platform limits have been adhered to. This could be memory limits of the console (the Nintendo GameCube, for example, has 16 MB of ARAM for audio data), or a self-imposed memory budget for textures. These limits differ between platforms, and a good tool can take a proactive approach to enforcing them. Given a complete list of sound samples for a particular level, the tool could, for example, compute the memory required and then resample the less important samples (denoted by means of the metadata we attached earlier) to 22,050 Hz or 11,025 Hz accordingly.

Tool development of this nature is a highly specialized, ongoing field. Advanced tools can understand the graphics engine for each platform, highlight instances of inefficient geometry, or even reduce the polygon count automatically to fit within the budget.

Some graphical compression methods (for example, TM2) can exhibit nasty side effects (like purple acne). Creating tools to detect and highlight these errors will make the whole project run more smoothly by giving control to the artists that generate the assets. If their turn-around time can be reduced, then the team's efficiency will be improved, and they can validate their own work without impinging on anybody else's schedule.

GRANULARITY

Granularity is the level of detail at which a piece of code, or module, works. It could be called abstraction at a distance. Working at low granularity means you're looking at individual lines of code and single expressions. Considering a high level of granularity involves looking at the whole module. We refer to these as small grain and large grain tasks, respectively.

From a purely theoretical standpoint, every graphics engine does nothing more than draw individual polygons (with a texture, bump map, or other such material effect) onto the screen at a specific position. It would be possible to write a complete cross-platform engine on such a basis; that is, relying on a single platform-specific (small grain) `DrawPolygon` function and some simple code to *blit* the current image and then clearing the screen. But such an implementation requires a lot of low-grain work, which does not scale well. Instead, we must consider a higher granularity by handling several triangles at once, so the processing code is only loaded once for the first triangle, and kept in memory (or special registers on the graphics chip) until they have all been processed. This creates a large grain function that renders an entire mesh. Those that have written OpenGL code for Unix workstations will recognize this as the client/server architecture of the X Window™ System. Naturally, the network latency of an X server is more pronounced than loading the registers of a chip on the same bus, but the principle is identical.

You'll also need to abstract at different levels for performance and maintenance reasons. For example, the math library is a simple low-level abstraction with each function consisting of some basic C language code or a piece of optimized assembly. The latter is used for the more complex and time-heavy operations, such as matrix multiplication. However, the graphics engine will include many features (for example, pixel shaders) that cannot be abstracted in such a direct manner, or if abstracted in that way could cause performance issues on other platforms. Graphics is consequently a high-grain task. From a global perspective, the graphics API needs to give the fastest possible access to the graphics chip without revealing how it works internally. This is a tricky task, but we'll cover the specifics in Chapter 9, "The Graphics Engine." Let's look briefly at three specific examples of grain size that permeate the whole project.

Basic Datatypes

Basic datatypes are low grain because the C standard does not dictate the size (in bytes) of any particular datatype, except `char`. This might surprise those coming from a Java™ background, but C was intended to work well (but not identically) on all platforms. This means that the compiler is allowed to choose how many bytes are used for datatypes such as `int`. That number is whatever is "easiest," or more "natural," for the processor to handle. Simple `typedefs` can be used to abstract the type, and applied to every variable declared.

Memory Management

Although we have fairly standard functions in the form of `malloc` and `free` (or for those working in C++, operators called `new` and `delete`), these are not adequate when working directly with hardware, which might require you to consider special alignment issues or contiguous memory. In this instance, you can abstract the memory allocation modules, but use the returned memory pointer identically on any platform—this is considered medium grain.

Audio Code

Along with the graphics engine and other "big" concepts, audio code needs a very large grain. The primary function `PlayMusic`, for example, could play an MP3, OGG, MIDI® file, or CD music track. The format can vary according to the platform, or even sales territory, and the amount of code required to implement the function behind-the-scenes follows suit. This makes code size roughly analogous to granularity.

Many of the large-grain solutions require superfluous abstractions to maintain an equal footing with other platforms. The main render loop often requires a `BeginFrame` and `EndFrame` function to initialize various lists and flush them afterwards. These functions may remain unused on some platforms, but we include them from the start because it's easier than trying to retrofit later, when some oversight needs to be corrected. You'll see this in detail in Chapter 7 through Chapter 10.

SEPARATION AND ISOLATION

Isolation is an extreme form of modularization, and a close friend of abstraction. Previously, a good module had little dependence on others and could peacefully co-exist with them. In an isolated system, we *demand* a clear separation between a function and the code that calls it. Without isolation, our code would be littered with constructs like this:

```
#if SGX_PLATFORM_PLAYSTATION2
    GfxPlayStation2_DrawPoly();
#elif SGX_PLATFORM_XBOX
    GfxXbox_DrawPoly();
#elif SGX_PLATFORM_GC
    GfxGC_DrawPoly();
#else
    GfxWinTel32_DrawPoly();
#endif
```

Instead of the much neater:

```
Gfx_DrawPoly();
```

You can separate this code in a number of ways. We'll look at three of them, using the idea of a general-purpose graphics library as a common example.

Obvious Isolation

The easiest way to isolate the PlayStation 2 and Xbox versions of the same function is to include them in separate files, and only compile whichever one is appropriate for that particular platform. This method produces a source tree consisting of files like this:

sgx_graphics.h: Generic function prototypes and constants.

sgx_graphics_ps2.h: PlayStation 2-specific structures and prototypes.

sgx_graphics_xbox.h: Xbox-specific structures and prototypes.

sgx_graphics_gc.h: GameCube-specifics.

sgx_graphics_wintel32.h: PC specifics.

And then

sgx_graphics_ps2.cpp: Complete set of PlayStation 2-specific graphics functions.

...and so on.

Each function would then have an identical signature, regardless of the platform.

```
sgxTextureHandle sgxGfx_Loadtexture(const char *pName)
{
    /* ... */
}
```

This has many natural benefits; it's easy to write, very obvious what is going on, and unlike the following two solutions doesn't have to suffer through any indirections, which can slow the game down. They are also much easier to write and debug because of this.

On the down side, however, it can be difficult to keep all versions of the API using exactly the same set of functions. During the course of development, if one platform requires a new function that the game then uses, the other platforms then need to be upgraded at the same time. From a maintenance viewpoint, this can become a big problem.

A much smaller problem is that it's also impossible to have two different graphic managers in the game. This is of little concern with consoles, but it prevents a DirectX and OpenGL renderer from existing within the same engine because both would use identical function names. It also requires that you write some additional code to manage two different 3D scenes, such as the game world, and a render-to-texture image being shown on a TV screen.

Singletons

The *singleton* is an interesting pattern for hiding global variables and member functions inside a class that can only ever have one instance. Such members remain inaccessible (and therefore unallocated) until first used, at which point, the member remains present until the program ends or is explicitly destroyed.[3] As its name suggests, you can only create a single instance of such classes, which makes it suitable for controlling hardware in which only one set of chips exist.

```
// In singleton.hpp
class CSingleton {
    public:
        static  CSingleton *Get();

    protected:    // Cannot use private, as it prevents derivation
        CSingleton();

        static CSingleton  *sm_pSingleton;
```

```
};

// In singleton.cpp
CSingleton *CSingleton::sm_pSingleton = NULL;

CSingleton *CSingleton::Get()
{
    if (sm_pSingleton == NULL) {
        sm_pSingleton = new CSingleton;
    }

    return sm_pSingleton;
}
```

Using this implementation, an instance of our singleton class will be created when we first use the `Get` function; we can then apply this pointer to access the class's member functions. The implementation chosen here allocates the singleton dynamically using `new`. This is preferable because it allows the overridden memory allocators to be used, unlike this often-used alternative using a static variable.

```
CSingleton *CSingleton::Get()
{
    static CSingleton Var;

    return &Var;
}
```

This type of singleton, however, cannot be destroyed before the program exits.

NOTE

You can use `atexit` *to register callback functions that can be used to destroy variables when the program is about to exit. The problem with this approach is that the destruction order can vary, which is especially troublesome when two singletons have a dependency problem, or you cannot determine in which order the singletons were created.*

Singletons are very useful for implementing game components that are used across multiple projects, because no runtime memory is required unless it's actually used. If the singleton is included in its own file (and it should be, because it's a separate module), it then becomes very simple to remove the dead code from the project, should the linker not do so automatically.

One of the problems with this pattern is that if you've implemented your graphics code as a singleton, you cannot create two different graphic managers to run at the same time. However, if this becomes a problem, it's easier to adapt this class (by making it a *coupleton* through the addition of a `Get2` method) to support such a feature, than it is to amend the other patterns seen here.

Being in a class provides the usual encapsulated benefits at the expense of an indirection. Every class member call will be like this:

```
CSingleton::Get()->DoProcess();
```

The extra instructions for the function call to `Get` do not take a significant amount of time (`Get` can be inlined if you prefer), but the call to `DoProcess` does requires an internal table of indirection pointers (called a *vtable*), indicating the true location of the function. If this were written in C, it would appear as

```
pSingleton = SGX_Singleton_Get();
pSingleton->pVtbl->DoProcess();
```

Using a variable in this manner makes it impossible to guess the address of the next instruction. This means the processor's cache will not be valid, wasting time while the cache is flushed, and the correct instructions are loaded. Although the cache miss cannot be prevented with this pattern, few platforms have significant issues with them *provided* they are not called from inside tight loops. We look at a useful cross-platform variation of the basic singleton, called a *prepared singleton*, in Chapter 7, "System I/O," and highlight the general issues surrounding singletons in Chapter 11, "The Bits We Forget About."

Class Structures

Finally, we can isolate code using a simple, unadulterated class. This supports multiple renderers (unlike the other patterns) at the expense of a less elegant solution. Most notably, we need to explicitly switch between engines, and adapt the calling convention.

```
// In the cross-platform graphics.h
// This is our null driver (as discussed in Chapter 7)
class CGfxEngine {
    public:
        virtual void DrawPolygon(const GfxPoly ) {}
        virtual void DrawSkyBox(const GfxSkyBox &) {}
        // ... other functions ...
};

// In platform-specific headers, e.g., graphics_ps2.h
class CGfxEnginePlayStation2 : public CGfxEngine {
    public:
```

```
        virtual void DrawPolygon(const GfxPoly &)  {}
        virtual void DrawSkyBox(const GfxSkyBox &) {}
        // ... other functions ...
};

// In graphics.cpp
static CGfxEngine *g_pCurrentGfx;

void Gfx_SetCurrent(CGfxEngine *pGfx)
{
    g_pCurrentGfx = pGfx;
}

CGfxEngine *Gfx_GetCurrent()
{
    return g_pCurrentGfx;
}

// Followed by a wrapper function like this
void Gfx_DrawPolygon(const GfxPoly &Poly)
{
    g_pCurrentGfx->DrawPolygon(Poly);
}
```

The `Gfx_DrawPolygon` function exists as one of many wrappers that simply take the existing parameters and pass them on to the current graphics engine, using the virtual functions within `g_pCurrentGfx` to determine the correct resultant call. Adding such a wrapper for every class member in the graphics library is very time consuming and open to mistakes. This method works as a bridge pattern, however, by hiding the global variable `g_pCurrentGfx` from the end user and allowing small implementation functions inside the `CGfxEngine` driver to be controlled by large-grain functions called `Gfx_xxx`.

Divorcing Code

With so many components to a cross-platform game, it's important that you divorce the PlayStation 2 components from the Xbox, Nintendo GameCube, and PC. This is simple for the most part because most PlayStation 2-dependent code refuses to build under any other compiler. However, where the engine is also used as part of the game editor, things can become more difficult. A strict separation is required between the editor-only code and the game code. So, if code is destined for the editor (because it allows configuration, or editor-specific debug information), then sandwich it inside the following:

```
if (sgxGetSettings("RunningEditor")) {
}
```

If the code needs to be removed physically (which can frequently occur with editor-only functionality), the preprocessor must be used:

```
#if SGX_PLATFORM_EDITOR
#endif
```

If the editor is currently running under Windows, however, don't assume that it will always run under Windows and mistakenly write

```
#if SGX_PLATFORM_WINDOWS
#endif
```

because they're not the same thing. Be strict. If the feature is used for the editor, use the editor macro, and not the platform for which the editor currently works. After all, a number of the editor features could be made to work on a console, so you want to minimize the amount of fixing and back-porting.

Why would you want an editor on a console? Well, reducing the turn-around time is one reason. Also, producing a platform-specific set of parameters to balance gameplay (even if there's no save facility) will improve the workflow without having to download new code and data to the development kit. Also, editor-oriented code might later find its way into the tool chain for automated processing.

On a similar note, don't use the `SGX_PLATFORM_WINDOWS` macro when you're writing for the PC because that's not strict enough either. A PC capable of running Windows can also run Linux and BSD, or even OS/2®, CP/M™, and Plan 9™. Don't be so proud as to exclude the other operating systems from your mind. Even if you believe you'll never touch Linux in your life, call every PC build by its full name, which in most cases will be

```
#if SGX_PLATFORM_WINTEL32
// WINTEL is short for 32-bit Windows, on x86-based Intel.
// Windows also ships on DEC Alpha's, among others.
// Also consider a separate define when 64-bit Windows becomes
// available, e.g., SGX_PLATFORM_WINTEL64
#endif
```

It's much easier, and clearer, to have the correct nomenclature at the early stages and allow it to propagate, than it is to change everything later, trying to work out the correct names in retrospect.

TIP

Adopt a prefix for your macros like the `SGX_` *shown here. Some people have a penchant for using a single or double underscore prefix. This is not portable because the compiler is at liberty to use such names.*

We raise the Linux point for one specific reason: online games. The game engine invariably is the substratum of the online server, *sans* input and output methods, such as joypads, graphics, and audio. The stability of the Windows platform has never been good, and with the critical importance of dependability and scalability in the massive multiplayer arena, Linux is coming to the forefront. Even if your development team is not involved in creating the server port, someone else will be, and your maintenance programmers will thank you for thinking ahead.

In the same way, be strict concerning the separation of console code and PC-based code. If you mean console, say so. If you mean, anything except PC, then say so. The two connotations are not identical. As an example, consider in which category the automated tools fit. Can the tools be run on the console? Add comments to all platform-oriented macro definitions to indicate when and where the particular names should be used, and give examples.

Separation by Purpose

In 1994, the Sega Saturn was the first games console to apply genuine parallel processing.[4] It had eight microprocessors, among them two main CPUs, both 32-bit Hitachi™ SH2 RISC processors, running at 28.6 MHz. In practice, it was more difficult to implement the parallelism than planned, which meant most games used only the one processor, and the machine died before most programmers had begun to exploit its power.

When the Sony PlayStation 2 emerged, it followed a similar idea. It had several chips on board; some were tied to particular jobs (such as graphics or audio) and some were general purpose (the EE and VUs), imbuing it with a degree of parallelism. This time around however, the other chips were no longer an optional extra. That forced the programmers to return to the idea of parallel processing. With the success of the original PlayStation, and the hype over Sony's new machine, developers could not concede defeat and avoid the PlayStation 2 as they perhaps had done with the Saturn. The nitty-gritty of how PS2 parallelism works is shrouded by NDAs. However, we can prepare for it on current (and future) consoles by designing loosely coupled components in our game.

A loosely coupled module has little or no reliance on other modules or their data. This allows the module to privately process its data, supplying highly elegant Lego brick modules to the rest of the system. Testing is also easier because it can be done in isolation.

Loosely coupled code scales very well on multiprocessor machines because each module can be placed on separate chips and run independently. Sometimes these modules need to be rewritten in assembler for the chip in question, but because it's a module—and replaceable—it shouldn't cause any cross-platform headaches.

A typical example is character animation and skinning. In most cases, the animation data for several characters can be computed in a batched fashion at the end of each frame. This is work that can be easily offloaded to one chip, while another chip processes something else entirely, perhaps rigid body physics. The main game loop then waits for both tasks to complete, before moving onto the next frame. Ideally, both tasks should be of an equivalent duration.

Managing a loosely coupled module requires a separation between the request for an action (such as, perform 1/30th of a second of the animate) and the actual processing for that action. This requires additional parameters to store the exact details of what needs to be carried out. Following is a simplified example in which one action (animate for N seconds) is decoupled from the processing of `GetNodePosition`:

```
// In Animation.h
class  CAnimation {
    private:
        tBOOL       bDirty;
        tREAL32     fTotalIntegrateTime;
        CAnimData   AnimData;

    public:
        void IntegrateTime(tREAL32 time);
        bool GetNodePosition(tINT32 iNode, sgxVector &result);
        void Process();
};

// In Animation.cpp
void CAnimation::IntegrateTime(tREAL32 time)
{
    // No reason to dirty the data if nothing's happened
    if (time > sgxEpsilon) {
        fTotalIntegrateTime += time;
        bDirty = TRUE;
    }
}
```

```
tBOOL CAnimation::GetNodePosition(tINT32 iNode, sgxVector &result)
{
    if (iNode < 0 || iNode >= AnimData.iMaxNodes) {
        return FALSE;
    }

    Process();

    result = AnimData.NodePosition[iNode];
    return TRUE;
}

void CAnimation::Process()
{
    // Apply fTotalIntegrateTime seconds worth of anim data
    // ...

    // Reset cached values
    fTotalIntegrateTime = 0;
    bDirty = FALSE;
}
```

As you can see, we store each animate request as an accumulative total. A more complete system would also include other directives, such as animate backwards, change animation, or disable. All of which need to be stored in order, perhaps collapsing several identical options into one, for later batch processing when (or if) the need arises. These actions can all be reduced to simple codes that get executed at any time, such as the end of a frame, when the cache is full, or when it is explicitly requested with `GetNodePosition`.

On a single processor machine, these tasks are performed consecutively. The order doesn't matter because they have (or should have) no reliance on each other. Although there is a slight memory overhead in this scenario—the `bDirty` flag—you can still get performance gains by the task caching because animating a character for 1 second takes roughly the same amount of processing time as animating it for 1/2 a second. Therefore you might not need to animate upon every request. Furthermore, because a character animation is unlikely to move the object's position more than a few centimeters in any one frame, if the character is outside the view fustrum by a large amount, you don't need to animate it at all during that frame.

Loosely coupled architectures can mean developing without the most common object-oriented (OO) feature: inheritance. An animated object might be derived from a stationary object. And an animated object that emits fire could be derived from this. This approach requires that your code from one branch of the class hierarchy (for example, the animation system) needs to be available elsewhere. With a loosely coupled design, each system (the static object, the animation code, and the fire emitter) would be in separate classes in order for them to be used and run independently by the game. Each object would consequently consist of a wrapper that would control any number of these classes.

Separation by Memory

Separation by memory involves letting each module have access to its own private memory to limit bus contention. Fortunately, this is normally automatic because most consoles that can access exclusive memory usually have a specific bus between it and its processing chip (for example, between the audio memory and the sound chip).

If the main CPU wants some audio memory, it usually has to ask nicely. If the engine causes the CPU to ask for excessive data, it can saturate the bus, which negates the original benefit of having a separate bus.

Separation for the Present

When developing a game from the ground up, you must be able to add new features without breaking the code on existing platforms or interfering with the capability to compile. These new features might not yet exist (or be needed) on the other platforms—and they certainly won't do anything—but it must still compile, and shouldn't prevent data assets from being loaded. The easiest way to maintain this is to add your new function to the base class:

```
class CGenericBaseClass
{
    virtual int MyNewFunction(int) { return 0; }
};

class CXboxSpecificClass::CGenericBaseClass
{
    virtual int MyNewFunction(int);
};
```

The opposite problem also exists—when old code needs to call new code. One example of how this occurs is to think of the engine development cycle. At some point, an object needs to process its data on a new event. Let's call it "pre-alpha face render." For the rendering engine to pass that event message to a specific object requires a small hack, but we need to make it general. Without upgrading every object in the game, we can use the same mechanism of derived virtual functions shown previously. The new code calls a virtual method from the base class, and only those objects that understand the new message will process it. No other object needs to know the new message exists.

However, because there's a change in the base class, we'll need to recompile all the classes that have been derived from it. To implement a solution where that's not necessary, you can create an event system where each class has its own handler that can cope with any message. For example

```
class CGenericBaseClass
{
 virtual tBOOL EventHandler(const sgxString &Event, void *pEventData)
        { return TRUE; }
};

tBOOL
CGenericBaseClass::EventHandler(const sgxString &Event,
        void *pEventData)
{
    if (Event == sgxString("Update")) {
        // ... animate or move the object
    }
    else if (Event == sgxString("PreAlpha")) {
        // ... do stuff
    }

    return TRUE;
}
```

The event name could also be replaced with hash codes, or numeric Ids to limit the processing required.

For more complex modifications, such as collision processing between two arbitrary objects, a double dispatch method might be required. This is covered admirably (and using the collision detection example) as item 31 in Scott Meyers' excellent book, *More Effective C++*.

Separation for the Future

It's often helpful to think of your game engine like the Internet, with a client side (your Web browser, such as Firefox® or Internet Explorer™) and a server side (Apache™ or Microsoft IIS™). Regardless of what machine, operating system, or software you use, the rest of the Internet is (usually) open to you. By creating a common interface (grounded on the networking protocol of TCP/IP), everyone can talk together. The browser might be upgraded, the server could change, or the machine could change its IP address, but through a common design (of HTTP protocols, HTML standards, and domain name resolution), you can still connect to the machine you expect to, regardless of these changes.

Now imagine this as part of your API. If the engine (that is, the server) changes its prototype in any way, the generic cross-platform game code should still be able to use all the existing code without being modified. This is just as important whether the engine supports one project or one hundred, although it's naturally more important for those projects being compiled without source code, such as middleware solutions or shared objects under Linux. Several basic methods encourage this and are described in the next sections.

Ellipses

The traditional (but rarely used) ellipses method has been part of the C language for so long that it's hard to imagine life without it. Ellipsis is the official name for the "three little dots," that let you pass an arbitrary number of arguments to a function, such as `printf`. These arguments can be any type, provided at least one formally specified argument is in the function prototype. Unfortunately, there is no type checking on these parameters, and the code that reads the arguments must be able to determine their type and how many there are automatically.

Structure Sizes

The current favorite method involves passing an address of a structure. This structure can change over time, but provided the first member of the structure is consistent—by including a version Id or its size in bytes—the function can determine which version of the structure has been passed in and act accordingly. This method features prominently in Microsoft Win32 SDK.

```
SGXAnim anim;

    anim.iSize = sizeof(anim);
    InitializeAnimation(&anim);
```

C++ can provide similar functionality by using custom constructors. In the following example we can upgrade the class by adding any new members we like, provided the constructor knows about it. If the member is a class itself, *its* constructor will get called automatically. If it's a plain old datatype (such as `short`, `int`, or `long`), we have to initialize it explicitly.

```
class CAnim {
    public:
        CAnim(AnimKeyFrames *, tINT32, AnimNodes *, tINT32);
```

```
        CAnim(AnimKeyFrames *, tINT32, AnimNodes *, tINT32, tINT32);
        CAnim(AnimKeyFrames *, tINT32, AnimNodes *, tINT32, tINT32,
            tINT32);
};

// This calls the basic constructor
pA = new CAnim(pKeyframes, iNumKeyframes, pNodes, iNumNodes);

// This calls the complete constructor
pA = new CAnim(pKeyframes, iNumKeyframes, pNodes, iNumNodes,
          iParam1, iParam2);
```

Using this method, we can call any function with this class, knowing it will already be fully constructed and valid (unlike the previous version which has to patch the defaults itself). However, this is a very C++ centric solution, and it becomes very difficult to use these interfaces if it needs to be called by C code.

Succession

Instead of trying to pass all the parameters in one go, you can give each parameter its own function call and thereby establish an easy upgrade path. This technique relies on the first call to initialize the class and set up the default parameters, and each subsequent call to prepare an additional parameter. These later parameters are optional.

In C, you can do this easily by adding an extra function for each parameter, which, although long-winded, provides the necessary functionality:

```
Anim anim;

Anim_Initialise(&anim);
Anim_SetKeyframes(&anim, pKeyframes, iNum);
Anim_SetParam1(&anim, 42);
```

With C++, this can be done in a more appealing manner:

```
CAnim anim;

    anim.Init().SetKeyframes(pKeyframes, iNum).SetParam1(42).End();
```

We added an `End` member function to terminate the parameter list. This is not strictly important, but without it there's no simple way to prevent a programmer from changing the parameters already set up by calling one of the initialization functions again.

The pImpl Idiom

This final technique solves compatibility problems by hiding the implementation details behind an interface via the Bridge Design Pattern. The basic class then becomes a shell of its former self:

```
class CAnimImpl;

class CAnim {
public:
    CAnim();
    tREAL32      GetDuration();
    void         SetKeyframes(CAnimKeys *pKeys, tUINT32 iNum);

private:
    CAnimImpl    *pImpl;
};

CAnim::CAnim() : pImpl(new CAnimImpl)
{
}
```

The implementation, and consequently all its functionality, is in the second class:

```
class CAnimImpl {
public:
   // Our usual parameters and members
};
```

This not only hides the details of the implementation, but also improves compile times because the `CAnimImpl` class can be compiled independently of the `CAnim`, which is likely to be `#included` throughout the game.

DEBUGGING AND PROFILING

The best advice on the topic of debugging is simple: do some. You can trap bugs at three stages: in the programming, in the compile, and in the execution.

Programming-Based Bugs

When you are designing a new module, you should also design the test suite. Work out how you'll test the module before writing it, and make sure the tests are suitable across all platforms. This is easier said that done. Until you've written the game and can see it running across several platforms, you have little idea of where the problems are likely to be. Therefore, you need to write defensive code, and test every input parameter and every return value to every function. This can become unwieldy because the amount of debugging code increases and (in some cases) can outweigh the actual production code. Human nature also dictates that the more code you write, the greater the opportunity for bugs, including bugs in the debugging code itself.

Compiler-Based Bugs

Preventing bugs in the compile stage involves *reading* the warnings that appear, and fixing the problems correctly. If you're beginning a virgin project, you should start by switching your compiler to the highest warning level possible. If you begin work more than an hour after the start of the project, you'll want to use the second highest warning setting. The Microsoft .NET compiler, as a typical example, has a demanding set of warnings at Level 4 that are difficult to eradicate from existing code. However, the work involved will more than pay for itself in the future.

TIP

If your compiler supports it, a Treat Warnings as Errors option can keep the build looking spotless, as it forces the removal of those nagging warnings that might manifest problems later. As always, be aware that any code fix must be "correct," and does not simply involve code to placate the compiler. If the original declaration is wrong, you'll get more warnings in the future that culminate in a late night bug hunt you'd rather not have.

Avoiding bugs at this stage prevents what pragmatic programmers call the *broken window syndrome*. In an experiment in the United States, a good car was left in a bad neighborhood. It remained curiously untouched for hours. However, after someone broke a window on the car, it was plundered, abused, and burnt out within the hour. Software reflects this same broken window syndrome. As soon as the first bug appears and remains, others seem to accumulate of their own accord. You must be willing to fix your own bugs and take pride in the code as a whole. By keeping the build clean, new warnings are clearly visible in the compiler's output window, and you'll be encouraged to fix them.

Bugs can also be limited by using additional build stages, such as a compiler for another platform, as they all produce slightly different warnings. You can set up a common build machine and install compilers for every platform, and then run the code through Lint (a semantics checker).

Lint is available in free (such as *http://www.splint.org)* and commercial forms. It not only validates the syntax, but also checks for coding mistakes and potential problems. The makers of PC-Lint have produced a bug-of-the-month column (*http://www.gimpel.com/html/bugs)* for the past eight years, showing the sort of problems that Lint catches. Like strict compiler warnings, Lint errors are difficult to remove after the code has begun growing, although they are normally more useful. Nevertheless, Lint is a very useful tool to ensure that each compiler treats the code with the same respect.

Execution-Based Bugs

When debugging a game at runtime, you have nothing but your debuggers and wits to guide you. The methods for debugging are numerous, and all programmers have their own set. Some of the most important debugging methods are covered in Chapter 6; however, the most important aspect of a debugging method is to have one.

A good debugging plan is always better than a great debugger because it works everywhere. Because each platform differs from the others, they also all have different debuggers. If you come from a .NET background, you're used to the particular quirks, features, and issues of its debugger. The same is true if you've been working with Metrowerks™ CodeWarrior™, SN Systems™, or GNU (GNU's Not Unix) environments. Furthermore, the debugger's features vary depending on the platform, even within the same compiler. If your usual debugging strategy involves placing several variable watchpoints (which fire when a particular memory location changes) and waiting, then you will be disadvantaged when faced with a debugger that doesn't support multiple watchpoints. For example, the Nintendo GameCube only supports one such watchpoint.

However, you don't have to be limited to a single debugger. Both the PlayStation 2 and Nintendo GameCube have two completely different development environments: one from SN Systems and one from CodeWarrior. Debuggers function by working in tandem with the compiler, which embeds special symbol information into the executable that the debugger can read. This means it's usually impossible for one debugger to work with the executable of another compiler. However, in some circumstances (notably the SN Debugger), this is an actual possibility, without having to recompile.

If one of your supported platforms is the Wintel PC, you can debug the majority of your game code using more complex debuggers (such as Soft-ICE™ and Boundschecker™) that are otherwise available in a console environment.

You can assist your debugging efforts by adopting good code policy rules. Although these rules won't affect the code-generation process in a noticeable way, they will help you use the debugger more effectively and they occasionally make the code more readable as well. For example:

```
if (bFlagIsSet) {
    m_StatusWord |= CFG_BITWISE_FLAG_0001;
}

if (bOtherFlagIsSet) {
    m_StatusWord |= CFG_BITWISE_FLAG_0002;
}
```

We always use braces around the `TRUE` components of an `if` statement. From a debugging perspective, this always provides a separate line on which to place a breakpoint, as debuggers don't usually allow you to stop on lines such as the following:

```
if (bFlagIsSet)   m_StatusWord |= CFG_BITWISE_FLAG_0001;
```

Also, by enforcing the use of braces, errors are not introduced when new instructions are added to the code, if the programmer is fooled by the indentation. This guideline also applies to `while` and `for` loops. We present more such guidelines in Chapter 6, "Debugging," and Appendix E, "Code Guidelines."

Code-based debugging is usually a simple affair that consists of trace messages written into a window. A simple code wrapper takes a line of text that is then passed to the platform-specific trace component to output a message. The details of how this works are covered in Chapter 6. For now, just make sure that you liberally add debugging capabilities, including assertions, throughout your code.

Assertions

Assertions are sanity checks. They review the condition of the game to make sure that it still makes sense. We use assertions predominantly to check that the input parameters to each function are within a predescribed range, an algorithms result is valid, or that the data-driven resources have been built correctly. Like all debugging code, assertions are compiled out of the final executable, so you must ensure that each assertion is completely passive, having no other effects on the code. For example:

```
void CAnimation::SetCurrentKeyframe(int iKeyframe)
{
    sgxAssert(iKeyframe >= 0);
    sgxAssert(iKeyframe < m_iTotalKeyframes);
    if (iKeyframe < 0 || iKeyframe >= m_iTotalKeyframes) {
        return;
    }
```

```
    // Do stuff...
}
```

The duplicate effort in checking the parameter is one source of bugs mentioned previously. You can either omit this supplementary check, or review Chapter 6, which gives an alternative assertion macro that prevents this.

The following code shows an erroneous case, because the postincrement instruction will not exist after the assertion has been removed from release builds:

```
int CAnimation::GetNextKeyframe(int iFromKeyframe)
{
int iNext = iCurrentKeyframe;

    sgxAssert(iNext++ < m_iTotalKeyframes);    // VERY BAD CODE!!!
    return iNext;
}
```

You also can include compile-time assertions to check the sanity of your build. We'll look at these in Chapter 6.

Function Scope

Sometimes it's useful to issue trace messages when a particular function begins and ends. Trace messages are invariably slow, regardless of the platform. So although messages should be added to each major subsystem (such as graphics and audio), they should be turned off by default. To do this, you create a sliding scale of messages from "always show" to "casual information," and then set a particular threshold beyond which nothing is output.

Outside the main systems, scope messages occur most often within the initialization and I/O routines (such as the memory card or CD access) and often act as progress counters.

Resource Handlers

With the power of a data-driven engine comes the responsibility of making sure that each resource exists, can be loaded, and is valid. This is a major area of work for the tools and engine programmers, but must not be overlooked by everyone else. If the game has requested a particular texture map (for the front-end interface or heads-up display), it should check that the map is the right size and resolution (because artists make mistakes, too). The question of whether or not to continue when resources are missing or broken is a difficult one to answer; it should be determined on a case-by-case basis.

Game Logic

The whole game relies on the engine. Nothing appears onscreen without the graphics engine, nothing plays from the speakers without audio code, and nothing moves without some animation code. Much of this code has its roots in platform-specific API calls, abstracted into a common interface for the game programmers. If the enemy doesn't fall over dead, you'll need to trace the game logic to find out whether the player didn't aim correctly, the generic bullet collision code was broken, or the platform-specific animation resource didn't play. The blame game gets us nowhere; we just need messages to trace the various game states to ascertain where the problem is. Using the simple `sgxTrace` function, we could write the following:

```
void CAICharacter::GetsShot(float fDamage)
{
    sgxTrace("AI: %s was shot (damage=%f)", m_Name.c_str(), fDamage);

    m_fHealth -= fDamage;

    if (m_fHealth < 0) {
        sgxTrace("AI: %s is dead", m_Name.c_str());

        m_fHealth = 0;
        if (sgxPlayAnimation(AI_ANIM_DEATH) == false)  {
            sgxTrace("AI: No death anim for %s!", m_Name.c_str());
        }
    }
}
```

The cause and effect can be seen in code, and reflected to the trace output with simple, clear messages. If the character doesn't fall over, we can see why. It allows us to see the code path without an interactive debugger. This can be especially helpful in situations where a trace report is possible, but a debugger is not, which can include release builds.

Configuration

The development environment is complex, especially for the programmers. After a new version of the game has been released to the testers, artists, or designers, it's instantly out of date. Different machines will be set up in different ways to support the various methods of working within the team. Being able to review the game state, configuration settings, and resources present is a boon to debugging because a problem might only ever show itself on one machine. These settings can be directed into a file or saved onto a memory card, which allows the bug to be replicated on another machine. Even if this doesn't solve the problem directly, it can help narrow down the search.

Engine Statistics

Everything that can exist should be counted, stored, and traced. Collision detection calls made, polygons drawn, and the sounds currently playing are just some of the useful statistics that exist within the game. Each memory allocation should be monitored by storing such details as the filename and line number of who requested it, and how many bytes they asked for. Out-of-memory cases should certainly be traced. Cache hits (and more importantly, cache misses) from the specific hardware drivers should also be included because they will highlight the differences between platforms. Each subsystem must provide a method to supply this information to a common store. This is a branch of profiling, which is discussed next.

Profiling

The best advice on the topic of profiling is simple: do some. In the same way that you need to know what the game is doing in any particular circumstance, you also need to know how well it's doing it. This "how well" information will almost certainly differ on each platform.

Profiling code is similar to that of debugging: it will not be compiled into the final game, and so must be completely passive. Like debugging, it's prudent to test without the profiling code on a regular basis to determine the build stability, and check that no active code has crept in by mistake. Every portion of the game should have its own memory and processor time budget. The profiler's job is to accurately monitor this usage, and indicate when the budget is being exceeded.

TIP

Always profile in bulk. That is, profile the animation system with 100 characters, not 1, because this is closer to what gets handled in-game and ensures the profiler is timing the processing of the animation, and not the initial overhead of the set-up routines.

As for the question of when to use this information for optimizing the game, the answer is the same in the cross-platform world as it is everywhere else: don't optimize prematurely, and don't optimize at the end of the project. The game should run at 60 fps throughout its lifetime. As soon as it dips below this on any platform, run a profile to see where the time is going. Does it still fit within your processor budgets? Nightly builds and automated test suites are very good for keeping everyone on track here, especially because most programmers only actively develop on one platform. A regular e-mail might tell the Xbox programmers that their one-line fix actually causes a 3 fps drop on the PlayStation 2, alerting you to problems early on. Such situations are more common than you might think, and often invisible on the host platform.

PREDICTABILITY

Predictability goes hand-in-hand with debugging. In the same way that a debugging method works regardless of the debugger, so the predictability of your game should work regardless of the platform. To a great extent, this will occur naturally as part of a solid cross-platform development process. By abstracting the hardware elements away from the games programmer and presenting the elements with commonality, *very little* will be different, making the game predictable. Unfortunately, the difference between "very little" and "nothing" is too large.

These differences can come from with inside or outside the program. External influences from input devices are limited (fortunately) to the joypad, its buttons, and network traffic. Another external force comes from disc latency when streaming data, which is covered in Chapter 8, "The Audio System."

Internal influences cover differences in floating-point calculations, different representations of mathematical constants (PI might be represented at a different precision, for instance), and varied standard library implementations (such as `qsort`, as you've already seen).

Rarely is every standard library function rewritten for cross-platform compatibility. The effort involved would be too great, and in most cases, wasted. Instead, specific functions that do not demonstrate a high level of predictability need to be created manually. The biggest surprise in this area comes from random numbers.

Randomness

The random number generator (although only pseudo-random) provides incompatibilities that produce a different gameplay experience. Although not necessarily a major problem, this can make development trickier because it's easier to debug a predictable game. In fact, it's not necessary to remove the predictability for the final build because no one buys the same game for different platforms, so who's to know if differences exist or not? Also, if you've created a stable game, you wouldn't risk changing code as fundamental as the random number generator.

Using our own random numbers produces extra benefits, too. We can not only predict the distribution of numbers that we'll get (is it evenly distributed or does it follow a bell curve?), but it also guarantees the entire numerical extent will be present. When using the standard library code (which picks numbers between `0` and `MAX_INT-1`), this might not happen—ever.

The "other random number generator" must also be avoided. This is the set of random numbers created by uninitialized data. Only global and static variables are guaranteed to be zero. Local variables, and any address space that has been dynamically allocated (through `malloc`, `new`, or custom allocators) can, and will, hold garbage data. Every programmer should initialize local variables as a reflex action, either through the class constructor, or by filling it with pertinent data immediately after allocation.

The question of dynamic memory is trickier. When using dynamic memory, you must make sure that no data is ever read from a memory location without the memory location first having been written to. All memory is allocated for a reason. If it's to store 128 bytes of data, make sure it has filled all 128 bytes. If it hasn't, there's a strong possibility that something else will try to read those 128 bytes, and start behaving randomly when it gets to the uninitialized data. When we develop our memory manager in Chapter 3, we'll look at some ways to prevent problems such as this.

Trigonometry

With floating-point numbers covering such a range of values, it stands to reason they're never going to be exact. So, we have to err on the side of paranoia when using floating-point numbers in trigonometry functions (such as sine and cosine) because they need their own cross-platform implementations to prevent discrepancies in the results. One platform may answer 1.0000000, whereas another—quite reasonably—reports 0.9999999 as the correct result. These errors will only get worse as errors are reintroduced into other equations.

Input Stimuli

On a much larger scale, predictability can be used to help debugging as all the input stimuli can be captured and replayed to the appropriate managers—the joypad manager, the network manager, or the hardware manager—to reproduce an entire game. Because we've abstracted the controller code inside the engine, the rest of the game doesn't know whether the input has come from a PlayStation 2, Xbox, Nintendo GameCube, PC, or a recorded metafile.

The hardware manager is put in place to handle asynchronous events (such as reset buttons, CD errors, audio events, or empty queues) from the platform, and turn them into synchronous events. This makes sure that the precise timing of any code is identical across all platforms, and repeatable in our testing lab. This is not possible when handling hardware interrupts, but fortunately, these interrupts are platform-specific and cannot affect other platforms. Where interrupts indicate common actions (such as a CD error), they can be processed by posting an event into the synchronous message queue.

Other components that need to be predictable are hardware features and operating system limits that you cannot control. File handles are a good example. With a fixed number of file handles, you could run out of them at any arbitrary time, depending on how the game has been played. To prevent this, you need to abstract the filesystem. You then either count file handles, capping them to the lowest common denominator (to get identical results across all platforms), or you can abstract enough of the filesystem away, so that you always use one handle and never run out. The latter is naturally the better solution. Chapter 5 studies the effects (and side effects) of this solution.

TURN-AROUND

The development process is hugely complex, and we'll make no attempt to explain it here. Instead, we'll look at the two primary areas of the process that apply to cross-platform development, and how to tame them.

The first area of concern is the basic workflow issue. This ranges from coding guidelines and naming conventions, to simple things like being able to compile. Working under a single platform for any length of time can lull unsuspecting sailors into rocky programming practices. The typical cycle of "design-code-compile-test" focuses on an increasingly narrow field. After the program compiles on your platform and passes the tests on your platform, you submit your changes to source control and that's the end of the story. Unfortunately, in our environment, you must consider other platforms as well: PlayStation 2, Xbox, Nintendo GameCube, and PC. In an ideal world, you should compile and test your code under every platform before committing your changes.

In our nonperfect world, however, it's unlikely that every programmer has a fully licensed compiler for every platform, and even less likely that they have access to the hardware. Granted, with the most recent generation of consoles using Ethernet® connectivity and Integrated Development Environments (IDEs) with floating licenses, sharing development kits is more feasible than it used to be. But getting ahold of enough machines can still be troublesome. Development kits are unique pieces of technology, and as such are very limited in supply (especially with new consoles), and can take a long time to get delivered. Also, because they can cost around $13,400 each, only cash-rich companies will sign off the purchase orders in a timely manner.

One part of the repository that is frequently underdeveloped is the documentation, where part of the source tree contains a set of documents that include the coding guidelines, naming conventions, and a set of platform-specific notes. Each platform has its own idiosyncrasies and features. By creating a special file that highlights these, you can create an internal Frequently Asked Questions (FAQ) list. You can also create internal mailing lists and/or newsgroups to discuss problems, and cross-post the final answer to the FAQ as well. Documentation is often considered a big task, but if it's a collective effort, the amount of work is fairly minimal, especially because it's no more work than adding *Doxygen* comments to code (and you do comment your code, right?). The time saved certainly creates a win-win situation, especially with new hires and team education.

The second major part of the development process to look at is the turn-around of code itself. If you're working on one project, on your own, the header file that causes an entire project rebuild affects one person. When ten people are building for three different platforms, this time becomes 30 times more prohibitive. Not only that, with more platforms to develop for, there is greater potential for even more changes to that header file and more header files that might change. Therefore, we strongly recommended that you use `#if` only to determine whether code should be compiled in or out, and not to switch between features. This covers only the platform-dependent code, as the debugging and profiling code can be controlled with runtime switches.

A common use (or perhaps that should be misuse) is to use `#define` to store constants such as configuration options or debug settings. Although this is perfectly acceptable for values that are truly constant (such as PI, or the number of joypads a particular console supports), placing debugging options into common header files increases the turn-around time between making a change and testing it. The guilty code appears like this:

```
// From settings.h
#define ENGINE_DEBUG_GODMODE     0
#define ENGINE_DEBUG_INVISIBLE   1
// ... lots of other options usually appear here ...

// From game_init.cpp
Engine.Debug[ENGINE_DEBUG_GODMODE] = TRUE;
Engine.Debug[ENGINE_DEBUG_INVISIBLE] = FALSE;
```

A better solution is to provide a system of named identifiers. Using the preceding example, these might be called simply `GODMODE` and `INVISIBLE`. These strings can be hashed internally if you want to:

```
// From DebugOptions.h
class CDebugOptions {
    public:

        CDebugOptions();
```

```
        void    SetOption(const sgxString &Opt, tINT32 Value);
        tINT32  GetOption(const sgxString &Opt);
        void    Complete(void);

    private:

        tBOOL   m_bComplete;
        sgxMap<sgxString, tUINT32>    m_OptList;
};

// From DebugOptions.cpp
CDebugOptions::CDebugOptions()
{
    m_bComplete = FALSE;
}

void
CDebugOptions::SetOption(const sgxString &Opt, tINT32 Value)
{
    if (m_bComplete) {
        sgxTrace("Option '%s' ignored!", Opt.c_str());
        return;
    }

    m_OptList[Opt] = Value;
}

void
CDebugOptions::Complete(void)
{
    m_bComplete = TRUE;
}


// Example usage
Engine.DebugOptions.SetOption(sgxString("GODMODE"), TRUE);
Engine.DebugOptions.SetOption(sgxString("INVISIBLE"), FALSE);
Engine.DebugOptions.Complete();

if (Engine.DebugOptions.GetOption(sgxString("GODMODE"))) {
    sgxTrace("We're in god mode!");

if (Engine.DebugOptions.GetOption(sgxString("GODMOD"))) {
    sgxTrace("We'll see a warning message = not this!");
}
```

The function entitled Complete indicates that we have declared all our options, and any attempt to use uninitialized values will result in a warning being issued through the `sgxTrace` code. This implementation means that no header file ever needs changing, and it gives us two additional bonuses. First, we are guaranteed a complete set of valid options. Second, if we try using a PlayStation 2-specific option on the Xbox build, we'll get a warning message. Although the second reason could also be achieved by smothering every reference to Engine.Debug [ENGINE_PS2_DMA_PACKET_CHECK] with #if SGX_PLATFORM_PLAYSTATION2, we'd rather simplify the code, not complicate it.

Any programmers concerned about the wasted processor time can either cache the value in a local variable, or reread the comment about premature optimization and then move GetOption out of the critical path.

This is just one example of how the turn-around time can grow unnecessarily large. There will be others. By adhering to this, and the nine other guidelines in this chapter, you will produce a more cross-platform friendly game. Now that we've shown you the principles, we'll endeavor to examine how you can apply them into the major scenarios of game development.

ENDNOTES

1. The C standard is categorized as ISO 9899:1990, and can be bought from *http://www.iso.ch/*.
2. As a comparison, the official standard costs $273 and can be bought from *http://www.iso.org/iso/en/CatalogueDetailPage.CatalogueDetail?CSNUMBER=29237&ICS1=35&ICS2=60&ICS3=*. Whereas Amazon.com are currently selling the Shildt book for $18.99 at *http://www.amazon.com/*.
3. Several types of singleton do not fall directly into this pattern; for example, the phoenix singleton.
4. The Amiga had coprocessors, as opposed to parallel processors.

3 Memory

In This Chapter

- The Specification
- Simple Memory
- Our Own Memory Manager—Design
- Hardware Properties
- Software Properties
- Our Own Memory Manager—Implementation
- Debugging Memory
- High-Level Memory Usage
- Other Guidelines

THE SPECIFICATION

When writing a cross-platform game, we try to delude ourselves that it's the same machine underneath. We abstract the filesystem, use a common graphics API and pretend that the compiler is identical. For the most part, we do a good job. It's only when we become involved at the hardware level that we notice the veneer slowing peeling. The two basic components of the hardware specification relate to the memory and the processor. In this chapter and the next, we'll look at these components in detail to understand how they can be tamed.

As a prelude, however, you need to know about the hardware specification. From the manufacturer's viewpoint, it's a quantitative measure of memory size and processor speed; from the subjective development opinion it's a measure of how it affects us in this particular engine, or game. This information will help us dynamically tailor the individual components toward a particular platform's capabilities, or support control logic to switch between a memory-based, or processor-based, algorithm. This doesn't mean you have to write two algorithms in every case, just that given a choice, you can determine which one would be favored in any particular situation.

This information can be made available in many forms, but we'll do so by creating a class called `CPlatformHardware`. This acts as a general-purpose control panel for the engine, indicating the capabilities of the platform. Typically this would include the following:

- Platform name, location of documentation, developer Web site
- Endian-ness
- Processors/cores (number, speed, cache sizes)
- Memory (main memory, custom, access speed)
- Disc speed (seek and read times)
- Poll frequency for components (determinable by guesswork and NDAs)

Some of the data, like disc speed, might appear a little self-indulgent, but it actually provides two very useful features. First, it provides a standard location of where this crucial platform information is held. The code is trivial, and completely self-documenting, but provides anyone (junior programmers, management, and engine programmers focused elsewhere) with the full specification of the machine without having to find the appropriate manual, Web site, or PDF®.

Second, it provides a cross-platform manner by which the actual performance of the machine can be measured against expected norms. If your filesystem reports the disc speed as 120 Kbps, but the `CPlatformHardware` class tells you it is capable of 2 Mbps, this can be automatically flagged as a problem case, and the reason looked into. In single platform work, we're happy *if* this information is available. Within a cross-platform environment, it *must* be available, and capable of being used in an automated setup because we'll be testing continuously across all platforms to study the performance trade-offs between them.

Although the game can only run on one platform at a time, the tool chain will need access to several, so the implementation should make such information available for each platform. When exporting a mesh, for example, the tool can determine whether the bytes need to be swapped because of endian problems, or make sure that the accumulative count of all assets lies within the memory bounds of the machine.

The implementation of such a class revolves around the use of a singleton for each platform with a surrounding base class that will handle them all, returning a pointer to whichever data is required. We'll also add a default parameter to the `Get` member to retrieve a class pointer for the current platform:

```
CHardwarePlatform *CHardwarePlatform::Get(tPlatform Platform)
{
    if (Platform == eCurrentPlatform) {
        Platform = GetCurrentPlatform();
    }

    switch(Platform) {
        case eWinTel32:
            return CHardwarePlatformWinTel32::Get();

        case ePS2:
            return CHardwarePlatformPS2::Get();

        case eXbox:
            return CHardwarePlatformXbox::Get();

        case eGameCube:
            return CHardwarePlatformGameCube::Get();
        }

    return NULL;
}
```

We then need to produce a set of member functions for each platform:

```
const char *CHardwarePlatformGameCube::GetPlatform()
{
    return "Nintendo GameCube";
}

const char *CHardwarePlatformGameCube::GetDocsURL()
{
    return "//docs_drive/sdks/gc";
}

const char *CHardwarePlatformGameCube::GetDevelopmentURL()
{
    return "http://www.warioworld.com";
}

tREAL32 CHardwarePlatformGameCube::GetDiskAccessSpeed()
{
    return 128.0f / 1000.0f; // in seconds
}
```

```
tUINT32 CHardwarePlatformGameCube::GetDiskReadSpeed()
{
    return 20 * SGX_MEGABYTES; // bps (actual range 16-25 Mbps)
}

tUINT32 CHardwarePlatformGameCube::GetNumCPUs()
{
    return 1;
}

tUINT32 CHardwarePlatformGameCube::GetCPUSpeed(tINT32 type)
{
    sgxAssert(type==0);
    return 485; // in MHz
}

tUINT32 CHardwarePlatformGameCube::GetNumMemoryBanks()
{
    return 2;
}

tUINT32 CHardwarePlatformGameCube::GetMemorySize(tUINT32 type)
{
    if (type == eMainMem) {
        return 24 * SGX_MEGABYTES;
    } else if (type == eARAM) {
        return 16 * SGX_MEGABYTES;
    } else {
        sgxError("GC doesn't have that many memory banks");
        return 0;
    }
}
```

For a more practical version of this information, see Appendixes B through D.

The keyword here may have been hardware, but as we've said, there is also scope for introducing software limits that are based on this hardware information. A machine with a slow main processor, for example, could specify that certain elements of the AI should run every other frame. This would be balanced by a machine with a fast processor that might process all the AI, but at the expense of a nearer fogging plane to ease the graphics processing. These decisions help redress the imbalances across each platform.

We could also use this information to adjust gameplay parameters such as fogging distance. Apart from the obvious design issues that this brings up, we should be careful to specify whether or not the value is allowed to change during the course of a game. The lead programmer needs to make such decisions early to stop ill-chosen code designs from creeping into the development. You might prefer to use a separate `CGamePlatform` class for all data that can be considered dynamic throughout a game.

SIMPLE MEMORY

Memory should be so easy. From the moment the first C programmer used a pointer, memory has become so second nature that we don't give it a second thought. There are issues related to memory, however, over and above just making sure you have enough.

On any specific platform, memory is very simple. A number of the issues raised (and solutions discussed) in this chapter *could* be applied to any form of game development. It's only when we have to consider several significantly different platforms that we need to replace the phrase *could be applied* with *should be applied.*

The Issues—Datatypes

Every variable you declare, in whatever scope, makes use of memory. How much memory is used depends on the compiler and the platform. Datatypes are the simplest building blocks we can abstract, and form the basis for everything else. Each platform dictates the size of these types, and naturally enough, they differ between consoles. This means we can no longer make accurate predictions on the game's memory usage, know how long the game will run before our counters "wrap around" (is it after `0xffff`, `0xffffffff`, or even `0xffffffffffffffff`?), or accurately read a binary file from disc.

To manage this cleanly, we create a platform-specific file to contain all the datatypes. This becomes the first header file to be included from each piece of code. The datatypes on each platform are shown in Table 3.1.

TABLE 3.1 Native Datatypes Across Platforms

Platform	short	int	long
PlayStation 2	16	32	64
Nintendo GameCube	16	32	32
Xbox	16	32	32
PC [a]	16	32	32

[a] We need to be precise about which PC; this assumes Wintel 32.

It isn't necessary to quote the `sizeof(char)`, because according to the ANSI C standard, it's guaranteed to be 1 byte. No console to date has used the 6-bit byte that existed on old mainframes from 1964.

From here, we can create a file—let's call it *datatype_ps2.h*—to abstract this information:

```
typedef signed char    tCHAR8;
typedef unsigned char  tUCHAR8;
typedef signed short   tINT16;
typedef unsigned short tUINT16;
typedef signed int     tINT32;
typedef unsigned int   tUINT32;
typedef signed long    tINT64;
typedef unsigned long  tUINT64;
```

Or, if you prefer:

```
typedef signed char    s8;
typedef unsigned char  u8;
typedef signed short   s16;
typedef unsigned short u16;
typedef signed int     s32;
typedef unsigned int   u32;
typedef signed long    s64;
typedef unsigned long  u64;
```

The naming convention is up to you and your coding standards. We use the `tUINT32` variation throughout this book because it's unlikely to conflict with any existing type definitions, and the capital letters stand out. Consequently, looking at any line of the code will remind the programmer that the abstraction exists, and exists for a reason.

NOTE

The type `long long` *is not standard, although it usually refers to a 64-bit type. You can use these abstractions to your advantage by creating larger-than-standard datatypes using the compiler-specific definitions completely transparently from the end user.*

We also specify two definitions for char, because the C standard *doesn't* indicate whether this single-byte type should be signed or *un*signed. That's up to the compiler. Some compilers, such as Metrowerks CodeWarrior, allow you to change this. However, like all other types, a natural char should be avoided, and only the abstracted versions used.

Floating-point numbers don't need to be abstracted because they already have been. The use of a float already implies that we're wanting a number according to the IEEE™ 754 standard. The same is true of doubles. However, for consistency, usually two additional definitions are created using the only other suitable word for such numbers: real.

```
typedef float        tREAL32;
typedef double       tREAL64;
```

There are also two minor additions we should make: tBYTE and tBOOL. tBYTE is another form of unsigned char, but it makes more sense when working with raw data—and it's easier to type! bool, when written all in lowercase, is a standard type in C++, but not in C. It isn't a specified size, either. Some libraries include a definition of BOOL as int, while others will use a char. Either is an acceptable alternative, provided all platforms use the same. We implement a Boolean with the usually unused name of tBOOL to reference a 4-byte integer because they are used to pass results out of functions more often than they are used as data elements, and passing 4 bytes on the stack is usually more efficient than passing 1 byte.

```
typedef unsigned char  tBYTE;
typedef tUINT32        tBOOL;

// Some simple constants to replace the C++ types of
// true and false.
// Most platforms define these too, so use ifndef
// around each of them,
#ifndef TRUE
#define TRUE    1
#endif

#ifndef FALSE
#define FALSE    0
#endif
```

One additional type has already been abstracted for us, size_t. This odd, little known type is sometimes called the size of sizeof, and can hold values large enough to address the whole memory space of the target platform. This memory space is usually 4 bytes, which permits addresses up to 4 GB. Although we're unlikely to get this amount of memory in any console in the near future, the new 64-bit operating systems will undoubtedly support a larger address space (which is not the same as memory size), and consequently, a size_t that is 8 bytes wide is not unreasonable.

The instances where we need to use `size_t` are those functions that take a memory size to copy or compare, such as `memcpy`. Most programmers would normally use `int`, `unsigned int`, or both, leading to "benign" type errors and mismatched comparisons between signed and unsigned values. Again, the use of capitals should cause the type to be highlighted.

```
typedef size_t    tMEMSIZE;
```

For the most part, however, you can ignore `size_t`. Whenever you handle pointers internally, they will be automatically the correct size, and of no concern. When working on high-level game components, you shouldn't be involved with the underlying memory structure, so there's no problem there either. The only two places you're likely to use `size_t` is when writing the low-level memory manager and when trying to save pointers to disc. Throughout this chapter, we'll develop the memory manager together, so that shouldn't cause concern. We'll also look at the issues with discs in Chapter 5, "Storage."

TIP

Most loop counters use an integer to iterate over all the objects present. Although acceptable, this is technically incorrect because the theoretical maximum number of objects in memory is equal to the total size of memory (and therefore the total addressable space). Consequently, you should use `tMEMSIZE`.

The Issues—A Safety File

Now, with only the most basic of basic abstractions, we should start to create the test suite. With something so simple, there's very little to get wrong. However, when investing in an engine for the future, we should make sure that no one else is allowed to make these mistakes on our behalf, so we'll create a *safety file*.

A safety file is a simple class, or function, that tests the sanity of our build environment. Its purpose is to test the abstractions we've made, and report on any platform vagrancies that may occur. Whenever a new type is declared for the engine, we simply add another test to the safety file. Preferably, another programmer should add the test because two people are very unlikely to make the same mistake. Simply dictate the rules (for example, "`tINT32` is a 4-byte, signed variable") to two programmers. One would then create the type definition (as given previously), while the other writes the safety code as follows:

```
void SafetyCheckDatatypes()
{
    // Check for 4-byte, signed variable
    sgxAssert( sizeof(tINT32) == 4);
```

```
    sgxAssert( (tINT32)-1 == -1L);
    // Insert other types here...
}
```

On the surface, this is a very simple, perhaps even banal, requirement; however, when new platforms are added, or compilers are changed, it's comforting to know we have a safety net.

In addition to checking the datatypes, you can add functions to test for past compiler bugs, or include tricky code constructs (the STL features several of these) that past versions may have had trouble with. Although these do not need to be compiled in with every platform, by incorporating them into a common source file (and not a document hidden away on the company intranet) the lead programmer has a very simple way of checking a new compiler to see if it really does fix the problems it claims to, before launching headlong into a full appraisal of the software.

After issuing a validity check on our self-imposed limits, we can then ask the machine to list its hardware limits; that is, those limits that we're not able to change. These might include the endian-ness of the processor, the memory available, and the size of enumerations. Again, this is all sanity information, and we should know the output before we start. However, it's possible to change the endian mode on some processors, the available memory will decrease as we add more code or static variables, and enumerations might change size, so nothing is as fixed as you might first believe.

A sanity check for the processor endian-ness is straightforward, although there is no known way of using the preprocessor to determine the byte order of the machine (because it can't be used for addressing data). There is, however, some C code that will, and it's written like this:

```
/* Check endian */
tUINT16 uint16;

    uint16 = 1;
    if (*(tBYTE *)&uint16 == 1) {
        sgxTrace("Little Endian (x86, PlayStation 2)");
    } else {
        sgxTrace("Big Endian (GC)");
    }
```

We'll look more fully at endian-ness, and the issues surrounding it, later in the "Hardware Properties" section.

About Enumerations

Enumerations do not have a fixed size. Although they will always be integral, the number of bits used to hold them can vary on two parameters: the largest value present and the compiler. The first case is problematic, as this means standard code can be written in a fashion that will break certain platforms on specific compilers. Although the compilers that implement enumerations in this way will often have a switch forcing it into using 4 bytes (or whatever `sizeof(int)` is) this is not something on which to rely. Each enumeration should appear like this:

```
enum {
      tNPC_Friend,
      tNPC_Enemy,
      tNPC_Neutral,

      tLastElementForPadding = 0x7fffffff
};
```

To avoid using magic numbers (a *bad thing* in any-platform programming), we use a simple macro:

```
#define SGX_ENUM_PADDING    0x7fffffff
```

CAUTION

An enumeration can be signed or unsigned, depending on the values present, and whether the compiler is completely standards-friendly. The use of `0x7fffffff` *here ensures signed enumerations as long as no value exceeds this number.*

The Issues—The Report

Having mastered the basic types, you must now consider how they fit together—literally. When a structure is compiled, holes are automatically added between certain member variables to make sure each element is aligned on a boundary that is appropriate for the processor.

Consider the following example:

```
class PlayerData {
public:
      tUCHAR8   iInitial;
      tUINT32  iScore;
      tUINT16  iBonusesLeft;
      tREAL32  fHealth;
      tUCHAR8  iMode;
      };
```

This structure has five elements, with each variable using 1-, 4-, 2-, 4-, and 1 byte, respectively. The structure as a whole, however, requires 20 bytes, not 12. If we were to examine the memory, we would see something akin to Figure 3.1.

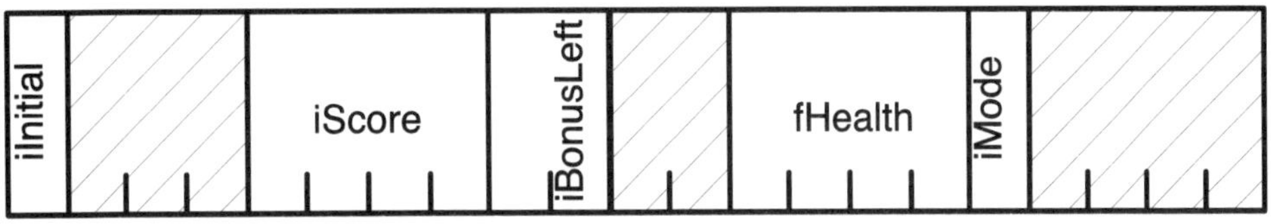

FIGURE 3.1 An example of structure padding.

As you can see, the `iInitial` member is padded to a full 4 bytes. This is not because of the character itself, but because of the element that follows it, `iScore`. 32-bit datatypes are often required to fall on 4-byte aligned boundaries, which means addresses such as 1024, 1028, 1032, and so on. Similarly, 16-bit datatypes must usually fall on 2-byte aligned (that is, even numbered) boundaries. This requirement is determined first by the processor , and second by the compiler. Some CPUs (the EE on the PlayStation 2) refuse to read or write data on nonaligned boundaries, and throw an exception if they are asked to. Other processors, such as the x86, will accept it, but only with the caveat of a performance hit, so the compiler usually aligns the integers voluntarily to 4-byte boundaries. Worse still, some processors (notably the IBM 970™) re-align the data pointer for you, and then read from that re-aligned pointer instead, which produces the wrong data.

The final character, and consequently the structure as a whole, is padded to cope with array declarations of `PlayerData`, even if none exist. Because each instance of `PlayerData` must be 4-byte aligned, it stands to reason that `iMode` must also be padded because it comes before `iInitial` in the preceding array element. If the first element is correctly aligned, every element in the array will also be so aligned.

```
PlayerData Players[4];    // Players[1] is also 4-byte aligned
```

This implies that any single instance of the variable must be identically padded.

The reason the alignment problem is hidden from most users is that the compiler takes care of these issues automatically. In a cross-platform environment, we can do the same and ignore alignment completely. Doing so, however, creates other problems to solve down the road. For example, if we wanted to save game data from the PC, and load it into a PlayStation 2, we could not use a raw format such as

```
fwrite(&Players[0], sizeof(struct PlayerData), 1, file_ptr);
```

because the structure padding would fall in different places. Instead we need to use a streamed method in which each element is prefixed with its size and type, or consider ASCII formats such as Extended Markup Language (XML). For instance:

```
<playerdata>
 <initial>S</initial>
 <score>1200</score>
 <bonuses>1</bonuses>
 <health>9.5</health>
 <mode>0</mode>
</playerdata>
```

For unification purposes, it's easier to pad each structure explicitly where the gaps appear, than to rely on the implicit padding of the compiler. This helps programmers, especially juniors, indicate where new elements should be added to the structure. In general, we need to pad the structure so that each 2-byte element appears on a 2-byte boundary, each 4-byte element is on a 4-byte boundary, and so on. This is compatible on all known platforms. After all, if a 4-byte datatype needed to be aligned on an 8-byte boundary, the simplest of arrays wouldn't work.

```
// Aligning each element on 8-byte boundaries makes no sense!
tINT32 Array[10];
```

Most people pad their structures manually to save memory, not out of fear of alignment. However, they both produce the same end result: a nice and simple, cross-platform compliant structure. Also note that using our custom Boolean type allows us to compute the structure size at compile time across all platforms.

```
// This now takes 12 bytes
class PlayerData {
public:
    tUCHAR8    iInitial;
    tUCHAR8    iMode;
    tUINT16    iBonusesLeft;
    tUINT32    iScore;
    tREAL32    fHealth;
    };
```

If there any holes, we can add our own explicit variables of the correct size, and call them `pad16`, for example.

To simplify the process of building tightly packed structures, a good process is to build the structure element by element, starting with the largest datatype, and working your way down to the smallest. This ensures that everything is packed as tightly as possible, and because the largest elements have the largest alignment requirements, you're more likely to place genuine data in what would normally become padding at the end of a structure. This produces a structure as follows:

```
class PlayerData {
public:
    tREAL32    fHealth;
    tUINT32    iScore;
    tUINT16    iBonusesLeft;
    tUCHAR8    iInitial;
    tUCHAR8    iMode;
    };
```

If you are interested in each element's position within the structure (because you're checking your alignment), you can find the offset of named variables within a structure using the `offsetof` macro in `stddef.h`. Where this is not present, you can use one of these variations:

```
#define offsetof(type, member)  ((size_t) &((type *)0)->member)
```

Or:

```
#define offsetof(type, member) ((size_t) ((char *) \
&((type *)0)->member - (char *)(type *)0))
```

Both appear to work on the current suite of compilers; however, the C programming elite frown upon both instances because neither is completely portable, and therefore are liable to fail at some point in the future. However, there's little harm in placing this inside your safety file temporarily to check the alignment of vital core components.

```
printf("iBonusesLeft is offset at : %d\n", offsetof(PlayerData,
    iBonusesLeft));
```

Sometimes you'll need to align structure as a whole by using special macros that hide the compiler-specific details. These can be used to prepare special structures that the hardware requires to be correctly aligned, or (more frequently) used to place data on a 4-byte boundary where it can be accessed faster by the processor. Most of the time, however, you should never need this in cross-platform code, and when it's used to align platform-specific structures, it should still use an abstracted name because a new compiler (or different version of the same one) might not support the same method.

Creating these macros is fairly easy because the compiler's documentation provides the information you need, but they should appear in *compiler*-specific header files and be adopted with care. .NET on Windows, for example, requires the use of a `__declspec`, making the macro appear like this:

```
#define SGX_ALIGN_BEGIN(_align)   __declspec(align(_align))
#define SGX_ALIGN_END(_align)
```

Two macros are used here because there are two possible locations for the alignment code to go: the beginning or the end. Including both at the start of development means we do not need to retro fit the `SGX_PACKDATA_END macro`.

```
#define SGX_ALIGN_BEGIN(_align)
#define SGX_ALIGN_END(_align)     __attribute__((aligned(_align)))
```

NOTE

The GNU compiler uses the `__aligned__` *keyword instead. The appendixes contain an up-to-date list of keywords.*

This produces structures and classes that appear as

```
class SGX_ALIGN_BEGIN(64) PlayerData  {
public:
    tREAL32    fHealth;
    tUINT32    iScore;
    tUINT16    iBonusesLeft;
    tUCHAR8    iInitial;
    tUCHAR8    iMode;
} SGX_ALIGN_END(64);
```

You can use these packing macros to align any structure, including those created with `typedef`. This is beneficial for high-performance types, such as vectors that profit from optimized assembler code, especially on the PS2, because this ensures that every instance of the type is correctly aligned.

```
typedef sgxVector3
    SGX_ALIGN_BEGIN(32) sgxVector3a SGX_ALIGN_END(32);
```

The problem of aligning static data is over, but you still have to contend with dynamic memory.

OUR OWN MEMORY MANAGER—DESIGN

Many games survive without their own memory management code. Most of them are PC-only games, happy to allocate memory when need be. If the physical memory is full (which, thanks to Windows, it usually is), the swap file gets called out of retirement to supply those much-needed bytes. These assumptions are invalid for us, because any cross-platform game contains at least one non-PC platform in which these rules do not apply. Three factors come into play here: the hard hardware, the soft hardware, and the soft software. Starting off, let's consider the strict (hard hardware) rules about memory:

- Fixed size
- Cannot be upgraded if the game runs too slowly
- Contains no swap file to bail you out

Next, the soft hardware properties that are liable to change between platforms are

- Endian-ness
- Alignment
- Methods of access (bus-oriented or request-oriented)

Finally, the soft software properties of the memory manager, as presented by the standard library brings up a lot of questions. How well does your vendor's implementation of `malloc` handle fragmentation? How does it compare with the other platforms? Could one platform be so badly fragmented that it's unable to allocate memory, whereas a different memory manager could? Are you sure? How do you know? We will have to abstract this completely because the standard library is so rarely standard.

HARDWARE PROPERTIES

Our design has to consider the hardware very intensely because these are the features we can't change.

Endian

The word *endian* refers to a passage in *Gulliver's Travels* in which two groups are constantly fighting over the best way to eat a hard-boiled egg. One group believes the big rounded end (big endian) should be started first, while the other group favors the small pointed end (little endian). Nowadays, the endian-ness indicates the order in which the individual bytes of a multibyte variable are stored. For example, writing the hex number `0x12345678` into the memory address `200` can appear in either of the two orders shown in Figure 3.2 and Figure 3.3.

FIGURE 3.2 Little Endian.

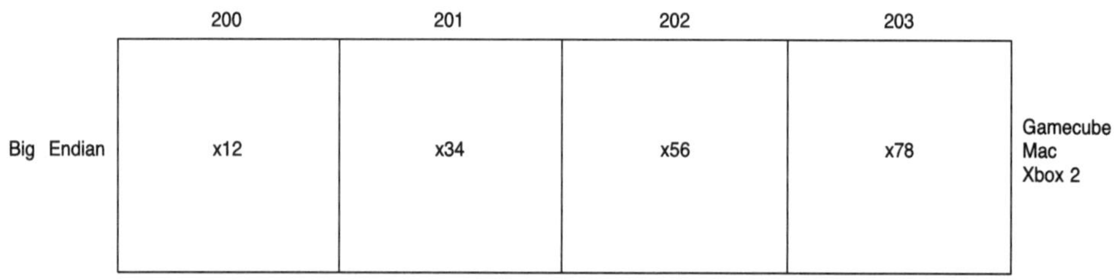

FIGURE 3.3 Big Endian.

Reading from, and writing to, memory is not an obvious problem because the compiler transparently takes care of it. Endian-ness is internally transparent on any platform. Data files are *external* components, however, and this will cause problems when the endian-ness across both machines (one reading, one writing) is not identical. Exchanging files between platforms is common in game development because most of the asset creation work is done on the PC. Mesh files are exported from 3ds max or Maya, say, in Little Endian, and need to be converted to Big Endian to be legible to some other platforms. In fact, with the current spate of consoles, only the Nintendo GameCube is Big Endian, and so endian-safe code doesn't need to be considered if there is no GameCube version. However, if a Nintendo GameCube port *is* introduced at a late stage of the project, this is the biggest single issue (of all those in this book) that will affect you. With the next-generation consoles looming ever closer, it looks to be a continued problem as the Xenon keeps the Big Endian flag flying.

The simplest way to describe the solution to this problem is *swapping*. Every variable loaded from disc (that consists of 2 bytes or more) must be swapped. The number 12 on disc may be represented as `0x000c`, but when loaded, it appears as `0x0c00`. Your list of 12 objects now appears much larger, and you will overrun memory while trying to read them. The byte order needs to be swapped for every element of every structure throughout the engine—this is a lot of work.

You can prevent the problem altogether by avoiding raw binary formats. You saw the XML example earlier, and we'll cover the implementation details of a binary serialization solution (whereby a separate class handles all the file I/O and self-describes the data) in Chapter 5. However, both self-describing formats take up more space. Although lack of disc space is not usually a problem, it can increase the time required to load the level data and use more processor time to fix the data into its correct format.

Raw formats ease both problems. You'll see methods for handling these in Chapter 5 as well. For now, we need to prepare functions that indicate (and solve) the endian problem and place them in our platform-specific header files. There is much commonality here, so we'll create two files (one for Big Endian, and one for Little Endian), and let the platform-specific header file include the appropriate one.

```
SGX_INLINE tUINT16 sgxEndianSwap16(tUINT16 var)
{
    return (tUINT16)((((var)&0xff)<<8) | ( ((var)>>8)&0xff));
}

SGX_INLINE tUINT32 sgxEndianSwap32(tUINT32 var)
{
    return ((((var)&0xff)<<24) | ((((var)>>8)&0xff)<<16) |
            ((((var)>>16)&0xff)<<8) | ((((var)>>24)&0xff)) );
}
```

We can then add our macros to indicate which version our machine uses:

```
#define SGX_ENDIAN_LITTLE   1
#define SGX_ENDIAN_BIG      0
```

And add a couple of lines to our safety file:

```
    /* Check endian */
    uint16 = 1;
    if (*(tBYTE *)&uint16 == 1) {
        sgxTrace("Little Endian (x86, PlayStation 2)");
#if SGX_ENDIAN_BIG==1
        sgxTrace("ERROR! SGX_ENDIAN_BIG macro is set");
#endif
    } else {
```

```
        sgxTrace("Big Endian (GC)");
#if SGX_ENDIAN_LITTLE==1
        sgxTrace("ERROR! SGX_ENDIAN_LITTLE macro is set");
#endif
    }
```

When you come to use this information, you have to settle on a common protocol. Will all data be saved in an identical format, and then byte swapped on load? Will separate Big and Little Endian data files be created? If you're saving from a Big Endian machine, which format should it be in? We'll answer those questions in Chapter 5. For now, we'll just write our macros in preparation:

```
#if SGX_ENDIAN_LITTLE==1
  #define sgxEndianToBig16(_v)          sgxEndianSwap16(_v)
  #define sgxEndianToLittle16(_v)
  #define sgxEndianToBig32(_v)          sgxEndianSwap32(_v)
  #define sgxEndianToLittle32(_v)
#elif SGX_ENDIAN_BIG==1
  #define sgxEndianToBig16(_v)
  #define sgxEndianToLittle16(_v)       sgxEndianSwap16(_v)
  #define sgxEndianToBig32(_v)
  #define sgxEndianToLittle32(_v)       sgxEndianSwap32(_v)
#else
  sgxCompileError("No Endian is set");
#endif
```

Some programmers might balk at such an important feature being left to the whim of an `SGX_ENDIAN_LITTLE` macro, especially when the endian-ness can be determined dynamically at runtime. Although it's possible to create a `CEndian` class to perform all of the previous tasks, because the data-swapping component of the load cycle can take a significant proportion of time, you shouldn't increase that time by using such a class to reevaluate the expression each time.

Swapping Bit Fields

Endian problems also rear their ugly heads with bit fields, because they too must be swapped. Bit fields are significantly more complex to handle because the whole bit structure is reversed. For example, take a simple structure:

```
struct BitSwap {
    tBYTE    BitField0 : 3;
    tBYTE    BitField1 : 5;
};
```

We have to manipulate this by bit twiddling the data through a pointer because the address of a bit field doesn't make a lot of sense. This results in code like the following:

```
// Having loaded a BitSwap structure into the data variable
pData = (tBYTE *)&data;
*pData = ( (*pData>>3) & 7) | ( (*pData&7)<<5 );
```

As you can see, this isn't pretty. The code certainly doesn't scale well, or lend itself to clever macro expansions and helper functions because the versions to swap three bit fields is even worse, requiring a completely different function.

It's often easier to forego the disc space, and save each bit field as its own integer. If your bit fields contain only zero or one (that is, they are individual bit fields), you can always save them by writing out a chunk of null data. The presence of this chunk indicates the bit is set, while its absence means zero. If you are using bit fields to indicate a set of flags, you might find it easier to create a separate `CBitFlags` class that handles this automatically.

Alignment

You've already seen previously how structures are padded to cope with alignment issues. Well, unfortunately we must step into this puddle once more before we can clean our boots of this matter. When working directly with hardware, you might need to have a dynamically allocated buffer aligned. This is typically present in Direct Memory Access (DMA) handlers and disk-caching APIs. The feature that uses this buffer is usually in the platform-specific portion of the code; however, it would still be beneficial to use our generic memory allocation code to keep track of the memory usage.

You can enforce memory alignment by requesting more memory than required, and offsetting the start pointer until it's aligned correctly for your purposes. To be 64-byte aligned, for example, the worst-case scenario requires that an extra 63 bytes of padding are added.

```
alignment = 64;

ptr = malloc(size + alignment-1);

// Move ptr into next 64-byte block (if not already aligned),
// or end of current block if it is
aligned_ptr = ptr;
aligned_ptr += alignment-1;

// Rewind to start of current block
```

```
aligned_ptr &= ~(alignment-1);

// use aligned_ptr...

// release memory using ptr - not aligned_ptr, remember!
free(ptr);
```

From here, you can deduce two simple rounding macros for general-purpose use

```
#define sgxAlign(_v, _align)   (((size_t)(_v)+(_align)-1 ) & \
(~((_align)-1)))
#define sgxAlignUp(_v, _align) (sgxAlign((_v), (_align)) + (_align))
```

along with the helper macros

```
#define sgxAlign16(_v)     sgxAlign(_v,16)
#define sgxAlign32(_v)     sgxAlign(_v,32)
#define sgxAlign64(_v)     sgxAlign(_v,64)
#define sgxAlign128(_v)    sgxAlign(_v,128)
```

and a simple sanity check macro

```
#define sgxIsAligned(_v, _align) (((size_t)(_v)&((_align)-1)) == 0)
```

Any custom allocator you write must support arbitrary alignment.

Notice that the fabled `size_t` is used here to make sure we don't lose any precision when we manipulate our pointers using integer arithmetic. Because we're talking about memory and `size_t` represents the maximum addressable memory, we can be certain that any results from these calculations will also reflect the whole address space.

When dynamic memory is dereferenced with pointers, there is always the potential that you'll need to read 4 bytes from an arbitrary memory location. Consequently this circumstance

```
value = *ptr;
```

might not work, and you'll have to resort to a byte-for-byte copy using an abstracted form of `memcpy`, called `sgxMemcpy`. However, this will only occur if you're trying to read raw data from disc that was saved by a machine without such a restriction (such as a PC). Be aware of such problems, but don't let them rule your life. Through good filesystem techniques, this problem can be avoided by writing the data out correctly at source (see Chapter 5).

Access

Memory can either be read through a pointer, or transferred through a DMA request. For our purposes, DMA is a platform-specific topic. You can use DMA and provide certain services to the end user transparently. Such an example is using the Nintendo GameCube's ARAM as addressable memory by using DMA and memory traps to swap memory segments between main memory and ARAM. However, this is not for the faint-hearted, and certainly not for cross-platform development. If you need to use DMAd memory then consider it as a disc, not memory, because its retrieval occurs asynchronously.

SOFTWARE PROPERTIES

In many ways, software properties are harder to deal with than hardware properties. Unlike hardware where the required properties of the game (for example, it must fit into 32 MB) are never doubted, software represents many points of views, and many different trade-offs that can be made. Although we do not attempt to provide definitive answers for questions of such a religious nature, coverage of the path is always helpful.

Fragmentation

Memory fragmentation occurs after several blocks of memory have been allocated, but only some of them were subsequently released. This leaves holes between the allocated blocks that are of varying sizes and limited use, because the still allocated memory cannot be moved, and new allocations must always be smaller than the size of the largest hole.

This then brings you back to the compiler-specific library implementation to determine *which* of these holes gets filled with which memory request, as this will indicate how long the memory will last. It's perfectly reasonable, and fairly common, to have more than 100 KB unused in the system, but be unable to allocate 15 KB, because no hole is large enough for it. Writing our own memory manager doesn't remove the problem of fragmenting dynamic memory (only lockable memory handles[1] can do that), but it does mean that the memory will fragment in a uniform manner on all platforms. This predictability is very useful because if one platform has memory issues, so will they all, and you can catch the problem earlier.

Naturally, if we never deallocate memory, then fragmentation cannot occur. This is not as impractical as you might think. If you can load preformatted level data into memory at the start of the game, then no data preparation occurs, and you avoid this typical scenario:

```
// Other data allocated here
pLoadBuffer = AllocateMemory();
LoadData(pLoadBuffer);
pGameBuffer = FormatDataForPlatform(pLoadBuffer);
FreeMemory(pLoadBuffer);
```

Notice the hole that is left immediately preceding `pGameBuffer` (see Figure 3.4).

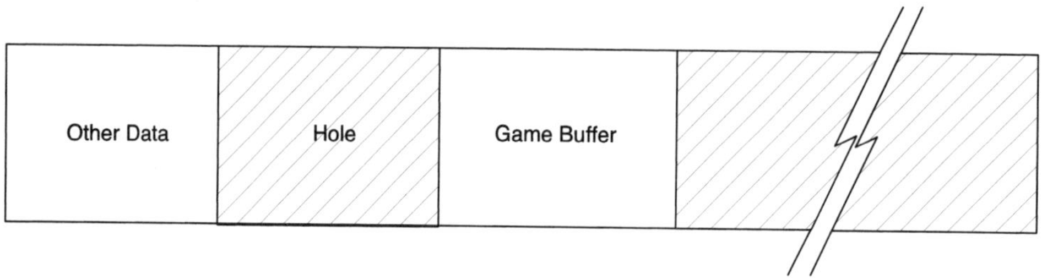

FIGURE 3.4 A fragmentation hole.

Alternatively, you can deallocate in the exact reverse order in which you allocate (see the following code snippet) to avoid the fragmentation issue. Many categories of memory allocation demonstrate how these ideas are both feasible and workable.

```
// Limiting the effects of fragmentation
a = malloc(100);
b = malloc(100);
c = malloc(100);

// Processing code

free(c);
free(b);
free(a);
```

On machines with virtual memory, such as the PC and its derivatives, the address space is much larger than the physical memory, and so is less prone to fragmentation issues. This is because new memory can be allocated virtually and mapped onto any (or all) of the available portions in physical memory.

The Standard Library

Only a handful of memory-handling functions reside in the standard library, prototyped in `string.h`. Abstracting any of these functions has become fairly rare, however, because most programmers have now relegated `memcpy` to the same drawer as `gets`, favoring `memmove`[2] and `fgets`[3], respectively.

For the purposes of debugging, however, creating wrapper functions for these memory routines is a good move, because you can monitor how much memory is being transferred each frame, check for memory overlaps in calls to your `memcpy` equivalent, and add code to check for overwritten memory. The latter is a useful, although not foolproof, method of getting around the limit of a single watchpoint on some platforms.

```
void *sgxMemcpy(void *pDest, const void *pSrc, tMEMSIZE iSize)
{
    tBYTE *pbDest = (tBYTE *)pDest;
    tBYTE *pbSrc = (tBYTE *)pSrc;

    if ( ( pSrc < pDest &&  pSrc + iSize > pDest ) ||
         (pDest < pSrc  && pDest + iSize > pSrc) ) {
        sgxTrace("sgxMemcpy overlaps! We should use sgxMemmove");
        return sgxMemmove(pDest, pSrc, iSize);
    }

    return memcpy(pDest, pSrc, iSize);
}
```

You should also abstract the other memory functions by wrapping them with your own code. You can then use common validation routines to check specific memory addresses, report on which memory blocks are getting accessed, and (in tandem with a custom memory allocator) allow you to mark blocks as read-only.

Naturally, these precautions only demonstrate their worth by reporting errors that they can see. If someone forgets about `sgxMemcpy` and uses `memcpy` instead, problems can still occur. Checking for banned functions is fairly easy (just use search and replace), and this simple abstraction is a good cross-platform-compatible step. Further leaps can be taken when platform-dependent code is introduced that traps accesses to specific ranges of addresses.

```
SGX_INLINE void *
sgxMemset(void *pSrc, int iCharacter, tMEMSIZE iNum)
{
    return memset(pSrc, iCharacter, iNum);
}
```

```
SGX_INLINE int
sgxMemcmp (const void *pSrc1, const void *pSrc2, tMEMSIZE iNum)
{
    return memcmp(pSrc1, pSrc2, iNum);
}

SGX_INLINE void *
sgxMemchr (const void *pSrc,  int iCharacter, tMEMSIZE iNum)
{
    return memchr(pSrc, iCharacter, iNum);
}
```

Usually, there's very little reason to write your own versions of `memcpy` and similar functions. If your profile shows them in the critical path, then check for any issues with the way in which you're using it first; the quickest code is the code that never runs, so you might be able to avoid the copy altogether. However, in those occasions when you do need a more optimal version (such as on the PS2 or to support SSE), you must be very wary when rewriting `memcpy`, because you'll have to manually handle the alignment problems that could be introduced.

CAUTION

Despite several clever algorithms available on the Internet, Duffs Device (a favorite of students, interviewers, and language geeks the world over), and other loop unrolling techniques might not be appropriate for cross-platform development due to inefficiencies in branch caching and other similar processor mechanisms.

OUR OWN MEMORY MANAGER—IMPLEMENTATION

Because the idea of cross-platform game development is to run the same code on all platforms, we must either make the PC appear like a fixed-memory console, or vice versa. With the exception of consoles with writable media (the current crop of which limits us to the Xbox), we cannot mimic a swap file, making the latter impossible. We must therefore resign ourselves to creating a memory-oriented sandpit for all platforms (including the PC) and using our own memory manager so that any memory requests can be directed to us. We've therefore adopted the first of our top ten tips: abstraction.

Forcing our well-endowed PC game into the memory of a shoe box is not as limiting as you might think. Remember what we said in Chapter 2: "Do not work toward the lowest common denominator." The total memory footprint on each machine will be different as all of the resources used will be correspondingly different. Think how common it is to use 4-bit textures on PlayStation 2, while our PC version uses hefty 16-bit (or 24-bit) surfaces. Such resources are allocated from a different memory pool on each platform, and do not break our rules on cross-platform development, or pollute our sandpit with unnecessary data.

TIP

Knowing the total memory size at the start of the game brings benefits in unexpected places. Apart from the fact that you'll know you can never crash because of out-of-memory problems (if it started, it will finish), developing for certain versions of Mac OS® will be easier where it's necessary to specify the maximum amount of memory you plan to use before the program is run.

So let's look at implementing a cross-platform memory manager here. Many books have been written on the topic of handling fragmentation issues and designing efficient heuristics for determining which memory hole should be filled with which allocation request. Although these topics are interesting, they are not pertinent to us. As games programmers, we don't need general-purpose algorithms that learn about the allocations asked of them. We need more specific control over the memory than a conventional memory manager provides. The heuristics could second-guess us, leaving us high and dry.

Conceptual Design

Looking in from orbit, our memory manager consists of one large chunk of memory. This chunk can be created from a single array, or allocated dynamically using the existing memory manager with `malloc` or `new`. Theoretically, we can't guarantee the alignment of this block, so we have to round up the pointer (and round down the block size) as you saw earlier. In reality, all current platforms will return a block that is 32-bit aligned, which you could also enforce by creating a large static array of `tUINT32`'s.

This super memory chunk will consist of individual blocks, each with its own header,[4] footer, and data portion. The header indicates the size of the block, whether it's in use, and who requested it. The header is owned and updated solely by the memory manager. The footer holds the alignment information (you'll see why later), and the data continues directly after this, including whatever the user sees fit to store there. Although users can surreptitiously amend this header data, they will gain nothing by doing so except a crashed machine. To detect when such an error occurs by accident, you can place markers at the end of the data block with a specific value. If this "magic" value changes during the execution of the program, you can flag a warning.

```
class CBlockHeader
{
public:
```

```
    tBYTE         m_bFree;     // using byte to save space
    tBYTE         m_bLock;
    tUINT16      _pad16;   // 2 bytes of padding

    tMEMSIZE      m_Size;      // of header+data+footer
    tUINT32       m_DataOffset;
    CBlockHeader *m_pNext;

    // DEBUG ONLY
#if SGX_DEBUG_BUILD == 1
    tUINT32       m_FileLine;
    tUCHAR8       m_FileName[SGX_MAX_PATH];       // not STL
#endif

    // More debugging help
    tUINT32                   m_CRC;
};
```

As mentioned before, this is a sample implementation. If memory ever becomes a serious issue, `m_CRC` and `m_DataOffset` could both be reduced in size. Similarly, we don't *need* `pNext` because the pointer can be found easily using the `m_iSize` parameter, so this could be removed as well. In the real world, we're unlikely to make more than 1,000 allocations in this manner, so the 4 KB we waste is more than made up for by the readability in the code. (Consider the byte for `m_bFree` as a moment of weakness.)

NOTE

Inside the memory manager, we need outright control of the memory, which precludes our use of the STL.

You create the initially empty block (encompassing all memory) with

```
CMemory::CMemory(void *ptr, tMEMSIZE size, tUINT32 align)
{
    m_Alignment = align;
    m_StructAlign = sizeof(tMEMSIZE);
    m_PaddedHeaderSize = sgxAlign(sizeof(CBlockHeader),
        sizeof(tMEMSIZE));
    m_pAllocatedBlock = ptr;
    m_AllocatedSize = size;

    // We can use ReInitialise to clear the entire memory
    // block, without separately invoking all the destructors
    ReInitialise();
```

```
}

void
CMemory::ReInitialise()
{
    // Create default block, stretching across all memory
    m_pFirstBlock = (CBlockHeader *)m_pAllocatedBlock;

    CreateBlock(TRUE, m_pFirstBlock, m_AllocatedSize);
    m_pFirstBlock->SetDebug("Main block", 0);
}

tBOOL
CMemory::CreateBlock(tBOOL bFree, CBlockHeader *pHeader,
    tMEMSIZE total_size)
{
    pHeader->m_DataOffset = pHeader->CalcDataOffset(m_Alignment);

    if (pHeader->m_DataOffset >= total_size) {
        sgxTrace("There's no room left to split the block");
        return FALSE;
    }

    pHeader->m_bFree = bFree;
    pHeader->m_bLock = FALSE;
    pHeader->m_Size  = total_size;
    pHeader->m_CRC   = 0;

    tBYTE *ptr = (tBYTE *)pHeader;

    ptr += pHeader->m_DataOffset;
    ptr -= sizeof(CBlockFooter);

    CBlockFooter ft;
    ft.m_PadSize  = pHeader->m_DataOffset;
    ft.m_PadSize -= sizeof(CBlockHeader)+sizeof(CBlockFooter);
    ft.m_Magic    = SGX_MEMORY_MAGIC8;

    sgxMemcpy(ptr, &ft, sizeof(CBlockFooter));

    return TRUE;
}
```

The use of a `CMemory` class is not just C++ advocacy; it's an indication that there can be several different mini memory managers within the game, each one allocating memory from its own private stash. This enables you to create explicit memory budgets for each subsystem (for graphics, audio, and so on), which will be strictly adhered to because each subsystem only has knowledge of its local memory manager. In the cross-platform world, this becomes even more useful than elsewhere, because you'll want the basic game components to be identical on each machine (so they deliver the same gameplay experience), but you'll need more memory for the graphics and audio subsystems because of the differing overheads on the various consoles. Allocating memory to these particular subsystems is a job for the main program, which sits in platform-specific world:

```
tBYTE *ptr = new  tBYTE[SGX_GRAPHIC_MEMORY];
CMemory GraphicsMemory(ptr, SGX_GRAPHIC_MEMORY, 8);

// Game loop

delete ptr[];
```

Allocating Memory

Allocating a block of memory is done simply by looking through the list of chunks for one that is unused and that, when combined with the size of the header, is large enough to hold the data. We then cut this block in two, creating one used half (for the new data), and one unused half. We can either pick the smallest block that is suitable (so we waste the least space), or the largest free block present (enabling a better fit for any larger blocks that appear). Either method is acceptable. It's a mathematical impossibility to produce an algorithm that will be optimal in the general case. We'll adopt the former.

Every allocation creates a memory structure as shown in Figure 3.5. You've already seen the header, but between it and the user's data block is some padding and footer information. These two elements, when combined, ensure that the data block is aligned correctly for the user. The footer holds a magic number (to check for data overruns) and indicates how many bytes of padding were needed to correctly align the data block. This requirement stems from the fact that the header can usually be aligned to 4 bytes (or `size_t`), but the user's data can often be aligned to 16-, 32-, or even 128 bytes. This means the amount of padding used in any particular instance will vary according to the memory address of the header. Because the padding between header and data can vary, we can't work backwards to find the memory location of the header, given the data block pointer.

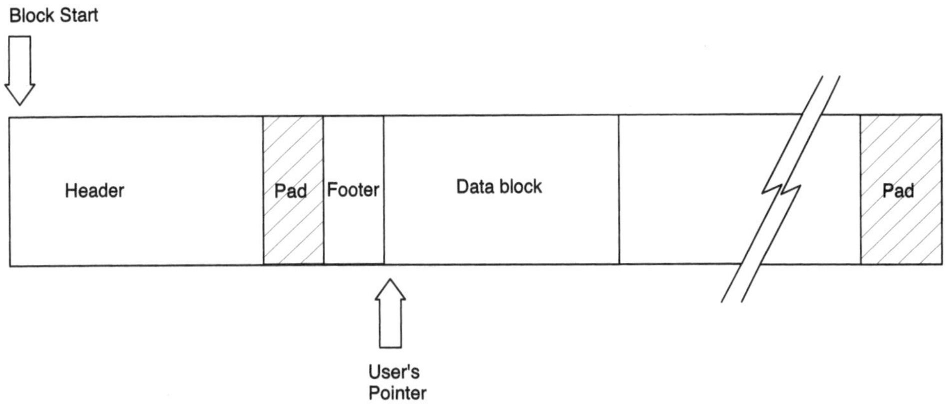

FIGURE 3.5 The memory header block.

```
class CBlockFooter
{
public:
    tBYTE m_Magic;
    tBYTE m_PadSize;
};
```

Note that the footer is placed immediately before the data block, and might not fall on an aligned boundary. Therefore, we need to make sure this data

- Consists of single bytes (which are always aligned to byte boundaries)
- Is copied to a correctly aligned structure before use, as demonstrated in the `CMemory::CreateBlock` function

The end user never needs to know about the padding, alignment, or memory blocks—the game code only deals in data pointers. `CMemory::Alloc` returns a pointer to the data and `CMemory::Free` receives the same pointer back. The data knows nothing about itself. Only the header does. We use this padding information to seek out the header block, so we can access it. If the potential alignment exceeds 255 bytes, then we have to upgrade the `tBYTE` into a `tWORD`.

In the rare case that no memory is left, we have to return the infamous `NULL` pointer or throw an exception. Returning `NULL` is safer; exceptions are rarely caught because they're underused and misunderstood. After all, how many of your fellow workers understand why you shouldn't throw exceptions in destructors?[5]

```
void *
CMemory::Alloc(tMEMSIZE size, const char *pFName, int line)
{
CBlockHeader *pNew;

    pNew = GetFreeBlock(size);

    if (pNew) {
        pNew->SetDebug(pFName, line);
        return pNew->GetDataPtr();
    }

    return NULL;
}
```

NOTE

To see why we use the standard integer type for the line number, see Chapter 6, "Debugging."

The caller might not expect the console to run out of memory (because the memory size is fixed, and the game worked last time), but it should be able to cope in most runtime situations[6]—as it should with any error code that gets returned from the operating system, be it faulty joysticks, broken discs, or memory problems.

```
CBlockHeader *
CMemory::GetFreeBlock(tMEMSIZE size)
{
CBlockHeader *pHeader = m_pFirstBlock;
CBlockHeader *pNewBlock;
tMEMSIZE total_size;

    while(pHeader) {
        if (!pHeader->m_bFree) {
            continue;
        }

        total_size = pHeader->GetBlockSize(size, m_Alignment,
            m_StructAlign);

        if (total_size >= total_size) {
            pNewBlock = (CBlockHeader *)(((tBYTE *)pHeader) +
                total_size);
```

```
            if (CreateBlock(TRUE, pNewBlock,
                pHeader->m_Size - total_size)) {
                pNewBlock->m_pNext = NULL;

                CreateBlock(FALSE, pHeader, total_size);
                pHeader->m_pNext = pNewBlock;
            } else {
                // No room to split block - give it all of it
                CreateBlock(FALSE, pHeader, pHeader->m_Size);
            }

            return pHeader;
        }
        pHeader = pHeader->m_pNext;
    }

    return NULL;
}
```

Garbage Collection

When no more memory can be found, we have one trick that may be performed before returning an error: garbage collection. The memory manager scans the entire chunk looking for any consecutive memory blocks that can be combined into one larger block. We can collect garbage at any time (and it's one of our housekeeping features mentioned previously), but the most common times are immediately after releasing some memory, and whenever there's an out-of-memory condition.

```
void CMemory::GarbageCollect()
{
CBlockHeader *pHeader, *pNext;

    pHeader = m_pFirstBlock;
    while(pHeader) {
        pNext = pHeader->m_pNext;
        if (pHeader->m_bFree && pNext && pNext->m_bFree) {
            pHeader->m_Size += pNext->m_Size;
            pHeader->m_pNext = pNext->m_pNext;
        } else {
            pHeader = pNext;
        }
    }
}
```

For example, if `Alloc` fails, we can persuade it to collect garbage, thereby giving the memory allocator a second chance before returning `NULL` to the user. Our function is then as follows:

```
void *CMemory::Alloc(tMEMSIZE size, const char *pFName, int line)
{
CBlockHeader *pNew;

    if (!(pNew = GetFreeBlock(size))) {
        GarbageCollect();
        pNew = GetFreeBlock(size);
    }

    if (pNew) {
        pNew->SetDebug(pFName, line);
        return pNew->GetDataPtr();
    }

    return NULL;
}
```

Naturally, if we collect our garbage after every memory release, the extra collection in `Alloc` is redundant, so we have to choose which method to employ. The "collect on allocate" approach ensures our allocator runs as fast as possible throughout the normal situations of the game itself, slowing down only when it runs out of memory. In contrast, garbage collecting after every release takes more time overall, but it does so consistently, so you'll never get a sudden slowdown due to memory allocation problems. This is usually a better solution because it's done in constant time and reduces memory fragmentation. It also avoids the cache misses that can occur if you coalesce the memory blocks during the allocation phase.

Releasing Memory

Freeing memory consists of two steps: 1) find the block and mark it as free and 2) join it with a neighboring free block to make a larger one, if it's available. Because this block may be after, *or before*, another free one, you can't reliably coalesce these blocks with a cut down garbage collector, such as the following:

```
    pNext = pHeader->m_pNext;
    if (pHeader->m_bFree && pNext && pNext->m_bFree) {
        pHeader->m_Size += pNext->m_Size;
        pHeader->m_pNext = pNext->m_pNext;
    }
```

Because we also need to repeat this process with an `m_pPrev` pointer that we don't currently have, we need to either upgrade the header block or call our existing `GarbageCollect` function.

The code for releasing memory is straightforward; we just need to mark the block as unused:

```
void CMemory::Free(void *ptr)
{
CBlockHeader *pFreed = GetHeader(ptr);

    sgxAssert(!pFreed->m_bFree);

    pFreed->m_bFree = TRUE;
}
```

It's up to the platform-specific component to release the super memory block using `delete` or `free`, as detailed previously.

NOTE

`Free` *is well understood to take a pointer to a memory block. If you don't mind working against this convention, you can change the prototype to read* `Free(void *&ptr)`. *The use of a reference allows you to reset the original pointer variable to* `NULL` *automatically, eliminating most double-free bugs.*

You can replace any, or all, of this implementation with code that you've written yourself, or downloaded from the Internet. Web sites and FTP servers are awash with implementations that focus on speed, tight packing, small blocks, and large blocks. Whichever version you decide to work with must support the two most important memory requirements for cross-platform development: arbitrary alignment and a compatible endian. A lot of good information is available at *http://www.memorymanagement.org*, which also covers cyclic blocks and binary buddies.

DEBUGGING MEMORY

Of the many debugging facilities we may want to add, *magic numbers* are the most frequently used. These magic numbers sit at one end of the user's data, or sometimes both ends, and do nothing. If the user overwrites this magic number, then something has gone wrong, and the magic no longer works. The numbers should therefore be checked before every allocation, and every free. Although this only gives you a vague idea of who corrupted the memory, it does allow you to stop the game running so you can review the memory chunk in the debugger. If the headers are badly corrupted, it's impossible to allocate, or free, any more memory without doing further damage to the program.

Another type of magic number comes in the form of block validation. You saw an example in Chapter 2, "Top Ten Tips," where problems could arise if you started to use uninitialized data; you've now seen the cause. Adding a simple `sgxMemset` to the allocation routine will help, but certainly isn't foolproof.

```
void *CMemory::sgxAlloc()
{
// ... other code ...
#if SGX_DEBUG_BUILD
    sgxMemset(pNew->GetDataPtr(), size, 0xCD);
#endif
}
```

You can then check that any routine that allocated 100 bytes of memory actually used all 100 by running a simple validation check over the memory:

```
void CMemory::Validate(void *ptr)
{
#if SGX_DEBUG_BUILD
CBlockHeader *pHdr = GetHeader(ptr);
tBYTE *ptr = (tBYTE *)ptr;

    for(tMEMSIZE i=0; i < pHdr->m_Size; ++i) {
        if (*ptr++ == 0xCD) {
            sgxTrace("Data byte %i (%x) has not changed", i, ptr);
        }
    }
#endif
}
```

If the program wrote `0xCD` into its memory as part of the normal output (which is rare, but possible), the validation routine would produce a false positive: an error where there is none. A false positive would also be produced if the program intentionally never made use of its full memory space. This error can be very annoying, especially if the trace stops the program from running. Ultimately, there can never be any completely foolproof way of preventing this, so any validation routine used must be unobtrusive, but visible. The ultimate goal of a validation system is to choose a random enough pattern that it can be detected by the validator, but not one that is likely to occur naturally during the game.

The secret word is random. Writing a series of random numbers into the data block should reduce the number of false positives to a bare minimum. This works because our random number generator isn't random at all[7], so we can pick a unique starting seed by using the memory address of the data and be assured that the random number sequence will be identical in both cases.

```
void
CMemory::WriteValidation(void *ptr)
{
CBlockHeader *pHdr = GetHeader(ptr);
tUINT32 OldSeed = sgxGetRandSeed();   // don't disrupt the normal game
tBYTE *ptr = (tBYTE *)pData;

    sgxSetRandSeed((tMEMSIZE)pData);
    for(tUINT32 i=0; i < m_Size ; ++i) {
        *ptr++ = (tBYTE)(sgxRand() * 0xff);
    }
    sgxSetRandSeed(OldSeed);
}
```

Additionally, you can add a lock-unlock pair to the memory block. When a data block has been locked, we consider it read-only and unavailable for use. The locking routine creates a checksum for the entire data block, and stores it in the header. If, when released, the checksum differs, we know it has been corrupted and we need to restart the debugger.

```
void CMemory::LockMemory(void *ptr)
{
CBlockHeader *pBlock = GetHeader(ptr);

    sgxAssert(pBlock->m_bLock == FALSE);
    pBlock->m_bLock = TRUE;

    // Compute a simple CRC
    pBlock->m_CRC = pBlock->GetChecksum();
}
```

You might also want to extend this read-only idea by adding checks to the `sgxMemcpy` and `sgxMemmove` functions. The simple code for each of these features is covered in Chapter 6.

You can add as much detail to the debugging tools as necessary to catch the bugs you have at the time because it's an ongoing process. Normally, what's been presented here will be enough. There are always some situations that won't get caught (for example, a memory block that is only concerned with zero and non-zero values, and treats `0xCD` as valid data), but that's life.

Profiling Memory Usage

Many features can appear in the memory chunk manager. The simplest to provide are usage statistics, which might include

- Largest memory block allocated
- Total memory allocated
- List of all allocations
- Maximum memory used

Maximum memory used is important because it indicates how much memory the game needs—our true memory footprint. During the initialization, some memory will no doubt be allocated and then freed. If this amount exceeds all future allocations, the total memory usage reported at the end of the game will not provide a true picture.

The chunk manager can be proactive, too. It could do the following:

- Prevent any further allocations after the game has started.
- Modify the "find free block" algorithm to suit the game needs.
- Profile memory usage to find the most common block size, for example.

The code for such features involves nothing more a few loops, some storage variables, and about half an hour of programming time.

Allocation Wrappers

Now that we have a good set of functions working, we're going to change them by creating an `sgxAlloc` macro. Macros are expanded in the code itself, which gives us a great opportunity to use the predefined terms `__FILE__` and `__LINE__`. These represent the filename and line number in the source code where they are used. If we pass these to our `Alloc` function, we can easily report exactly who was allocating the large memory blocks. To fit in with our naming convention, we'll use the following:

```
#define SGX_ALLOC(_SIZE)   Alloc(_SIZE,  __FILE__, __LINE__)
#define SGX_FREE(_POINTER) Free(_POINTER)
```

HIGH-LEVEL MEMORY USAGE

Memory is a three-part problem in two halves. The first, writing a manager, has been completed. We next need to introduce a clean and sensible way to use it. For engines and games written in C, this is remarkably simple. A global search and replace for `malloc` and `free` is all it takes. C++ programmers, on the other hand, must work a bit harder.

The `new` operator isn't just the C++ way of saying `malloc`. It is, after all, an operator, not a function, so there must be more to it than that. Primarily, `new` also calls the constructor of a class and so takes on a new importance. Search and replace won't help you this time, because `new` has many different syntaxes, and not all of them like being changed. Instead, you'll have to rewrite portions of the code to take advantage of the custom allocator, and replace `new` manually. Fortunately, help is at hand, because C++ allows you to override the `new` operator to call customized functions.

```
// Overloading new for all instances of the class
class CGraphicsEngine {
public:
        void* operator new (size_t size);
        void  operator delete (void *ptr);

static  void  SetMemoryHandler(const CMemory &mem);

private:
static  CMemory *m_pMemory;
};

void* CGraphicsEngine::operator new(size_t size)
{
    void *ptr = m_pMemory->Alloc(size, "Overloaded new", __LINE__);
    return ptr;
}

void CGraphicsEngine::operator delete(void *ptr)
{
    m_pMemory->Free(ptr);
}

void CGraphicsEngine::SetMemoryHandler(const CMemory &mem)
{
    m_pMemory = &mem;
}

CMemory *CGraphicsEngine::m_pMemory;
```

It's also possible to overload the global `new` and `delete` operators. These operators automatically affect every allocation in the game not already covered by their own code. However, this is not recommended because it can change the behavior of library code (and external code) that you don't have source for.

Application Memory Usage

Having your own memory allocators is a good start, but it's just that—a start. In the same way that a loop construct like `for` can have different applications, memory can be used in a variety of ways. For example, part of the engine might allocate memory once at the start of the game and never release it, while other algorithms might allocate and deallocate memory repeatedly throughout their lifetime.

Under some environments, we can trust the supplied memory manager to cope with all these situations. When running cross-platform, these environments will change and the effects will differ, especially when memory is tight. One platform might be able to allocate a large block, whereas another cannot simply because of its previous choices in where to allocate previous memory requests. This can occur when some code (such as the graphics engines) allocates common structures (such as an active sprite list) in a platform-specific area.

By extending the programming metaphor of "say what you mean," we can implement specific memory handlers for the different memory purposes, create cleaner (more obvious) code, and make sure each platform acts identically.

The categories of memory allocation are:

- Static block
- Heap memory
- Temporary (scratch) memory
- Cyclic buffers
- Memory pools
- Stacked allocations
- Dynamic memory

If the memory for each category were to be allocated from `SGX_ALLOC` (which it generally will), we can introduce useful functionality that will be common for all platforms without reinventing any other wheels. Such code introduces a second layer of abstraction into our memory manager. We can therefore use cyclic buffers, say, on all platforms very easily. From a game programming point of view, we can use our deductive knowledge to choose the best category of memory allocation for the algorithm in question.

Next, we'll look at each category in turn, explaining what each means, and how it helps you.

Static Block

The key word here is *block*—singular—not block*s*. Static block is one large block, allocated at the start of the game, and used for any memory requests that will not be deallocated individually. In this way, everything can be released with one call, saving a significant amount of overhead from the point of view of class destructors and the expense of memory headers. Looking at our `CBlockHeader`, every allocation requires 20 extra bytes (or around 280 when the debug filename is used). Although this overhead will be reduced in our release candidate (to perhaps 8 bytes, plus the padding which is always required), it is still present.

Our static block is therefore put to best use when allocating a lot of small blocks of memory within the engine. This might be object structures or lists of adjacent sectors in the scene graph. The latter case is well suited to static blocks because the number of adjacent sectors would vary tremendously—probably ranging in number from 1 to 30 or more—and remain unchanged throughout the level. Traditional arrays would be useless (or wasteful), and individual sector allocations would be too bulky.

There are two sides to the implementation story. The first, and easiest, is the abstracted allocator. Here we simply retain a single pointer indicating the next portion of memory to use. This can be incremented, and padded, according to the requested memory size (as shown in Figure 3.6). The second side is more difficult, and is the computation of the static blocks initial size. If we're using it to store the scene graph, as suggested previously, then we need to know the size of all this data in advance. For lazy programmers, this would involve a rough guess, and a backup plan. Such a plan would usually involve modifying the `AllocateSectorList` function from

```
return NULL;
```

to

```
return AllocateFromSomewhereElse(size);
```

For the more precise programmers who realize how precious memory is, this number will need to be calculated when the level is saved and prepended to the level data. This usually involves a series of very simple loops, adding up all the static components of a level. This has one obvious problem: this total becomes outdated very quickly if portions of the engine change or features are added or removed. Although this can be minimized through the use of `sizeof`, any external data lists will have to be updated too.

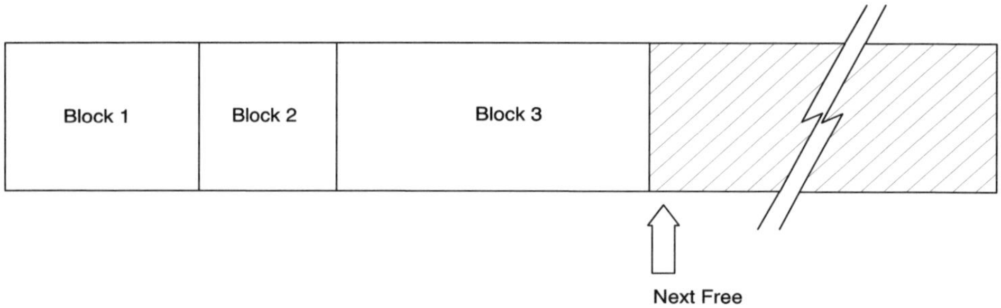

FIGURE 3.6 Static memory block.

A subtler problem can result in the computation of this size when the host platform building this level data is not identical to the target platform. This is not through differences in structure padding because you've learned how to deal with that, but occurs when the size of particular structures are not identical because, for example, the DirectX driver includes its vertex buffer. In these cases, the wrong amount of memory will be allocated. There should be very few (if any) of these, but occasionally they creep in.

No easy global solution exists for this problem because it occurs on a case-by-case basis. One usable solution involves a trick using padding. These structures should contain, as their last element, a `void` pointer. On most platforms, this element will be unused, and can either be written off as collateral damage (preferred), or omitted through a little extra magic:

```
// PC-based level exporter code
class sgxMyStruct {
    // normal stuff
#if SGX_PLATFORM_WINTEL32
    void *padding;
#endif
};

// Calculate size of structure (on the PC, which has the
// extraneous padding element)
sz = sizeof(sgxMyStruct);
if (TargetPlatform != CHardwarePlatform::eWinTel32) {
    sz -= sizeof(void *); // padding element not needed
}
static_block_size += sz;
```

For those platforms that need additional elements, we reuse this padding pointer to reference some legitimate data that has been allocated in another block. The total size of both blocks being calculated with

```
// Platform independent modifier
sz = sizeof(sgxMyStruct);
#if SGX_PLATFORM_WINTEL32
    // Add space for a supplementary structure, as pointed
    // to by sgxMyStruct::padding
    sz += sizeof(sgxMyStructWinTel32);
#endif
```

After loading this data into the engine, we can simply rewire the padding pointer, which can be renamed to something more suitable for the particular application, and continue as normal.

Heap Memory

Heap memory is, in essence, no different from the traditional memory allocator we've already written. It's also the simplest to use. The reason for its inclusion here is to keep a level abstraction layer across the memory manager. By preventing the end user from accessing the global `CMemory` instance directly, we have greater control over the game and its resources. This can be extended further by abstracting the allocation according to the subsystem, which you'll see later in the "Using Allocation Within Subsystems" section.

Consequently, this is the only allocation function that can "create" memory. All the others must request some existing memory and reformat it to make it useful in some other fashion.

Temporary Memory

Temporary memory is intended for large memory blocks, and sometimes called *scratch* memory. Instead of allocating a block of memory and releasing it at the end of the function, a single block is created at game start and made available to whoever requires it for a specified (but fixed) period. It is a long-term solution because the block itself can be a megabyte (or more) in size and remains active throughout the entire game, but it saves users from creating their own workspace buffers that lie dormant for most of the time.

The most common time for scratch usage is during initialization at the start of the game. During this time, a lot of data is loaded into buffers, and then passed on to various components in the game. Sometimes this data needs to be formatted in a particular way, such as occurs with mipmap creation or texture swizzling, before the data is stored in its final buffer.

The terminology here doesn't involve "allocate" or "free," but "lock" and "unlock." Once locked, no one else may request use of the memory. After the routine has finished with the memory, the memory is "unlocked," and it becomes available to everyone else. Every lock must have a corresponding unlock, and every lock *should* unlock before calling any other functions; this isn't always possible, so full coverage tests must be done. This ensures that it's impossible for one function to leave a lock on the scratch pad when another function (called from the one above) attempts to lock it and fails. This is known as a *lock contention.*

> **NOTE** *If the same scratch is to be used by different threads, it can be difficult to prove that there will never be lock contention. Instead, you should either limit which modules and threads may use this temporary memory, or create one scratch block per thread.*

The amount of scratch memory usually varies between platforms. This is no reflection on the inability of the engine programmers to conform to the other platforms, but the main usage of scratch lies within the load and initialization procedures where large amounts of memory are consumed (especially for sound and vision, as these will prepare platform-specific assets that cannot be unified). Because the amount of temporary memory is usually determined by the platform-specific startup code, platform-independence isn't a concern, so we can adjust the scratch size to match our requirements.

We still need to consider this point, however, and add one additional piece of functionality to the lock function that indicates how much memory we intend to use. This serves two purposes for you. First, you can assert whenever this value exceeds the available space in the buffer. Second, you can monitor the usage and decrease the space allocated to it accordingly. You can also add useful debugging information into the code by writing some magic bytes at `requested_size+1`, and check that they've been untouched when the scratch is unlocked.

After the game starts, the biggest user of this temporary memory will probably be the movie playback code or the animation system. There may some additional whole-screen effects that use it as a drawing surface, but this is less likely because the newer consoles like to control the surface memory themselves.

In some instances, you might need to create two (or more) separate blocks. These blocks are useful when loading unformatted data into memory to eliminate contention when one routine is trying to decompress the data stream and another, separate process is trying to format it for a particular chip. Working with several temporary blocks is more difficult, but not impossible if it's done carefully. The guidelines are:

- Make sure every buffer has a particular name, and designate which subsystems may use which scratches.
- Monitor its usage across all platforms to ensure minimal wastage.
- Allocate the memory for every buffer in one contiguous block, enabling several temporary blocks to be locked together. Special cases (for example, movie decompression) might require more memory than any single buffer can hold.
- Double check that you actually need the memory before locking it. Would a small static buffer work? Can you unlock it before calling any child functions?

The lowest level engine components—filesystem, main graphics pipeline, audio buffers, and so on—should never use a common memory buffer. The lower the level of component, the more likely it is to conflict with a higher-level component that's already locked the buffer. The problems involved in resolving contentions are easy when only one other potential routine is attempting to lock the buffer; but too problematic in general when any number of routines might attempt to because you need to know who *might* have already locked the buffer at any time. Simply put, any system that needs continuous or frequent access to a buffer, or needs to maintain data consistency within a block, should use its own memory.

Cyclic Buffers

Cyclic buffers consist of a fixed number of memory pigeon holes, each holding an identical (and fixed) amount of memory. Every time an allocation is made, it comes from the next pigeon hole—whether it's free or not.

Cyclic buffers have similar benefits to a static block as very little overhead exists because no housekeeping information is kept within the memory, but it also has the added bonus that a `NULL` pointer will never be returned. As a downside, however, because the buffers are of fixed size, it can be very wasteful if you need to store different types of objects within the buffer.

Cyclic buffers are perfect for scaling cross-platform games, because the code works naturally with whatever size buffer you have. There's no difference in the handling code for 100 objects or 1,000 objects. If you're running out of memory on one platform, you can lower this number. If you have space left over, you can improve the richness of your world by increasing it. For this reason, cyclic buffers are only good for the "unimportant" parts of the game, such as bullet holes, blood splats, and smoke effects. The meaning of the word "unimportant" in this context can be quantified to include all nongameplay oriented features. It applies to those effects that, if they weren't there, they wouldn't be missed.

Determining what features are unimportant is a problem for the game designers, and in some cases a problem for you, because you'll need to code special instances where, for example, smoke is unimportant in all cases, except in level 12 where smoke signals are a clue as to the felon's hideout. In such cases, you'll need to use slightly more advanced allocation methods, which could include the implementing memory pools. You would also need to choose an alternative solution if you were required to control the decay of any particular object, for example, vapor trails or particle systems. Memory pools (discussed shortly) may be better in these instances.

Implementing a cyclic buffer is easy, and works very quickly as each entry can be dereferenced as an array element. Taking the bullet hole example, we would create a buffer holding the maximum number of entries (as determined by the platform), and define a structure to hold each bullet hole.

```
class BulletHoleData {
    tBYTE bUsed;
    /* ... other parameters ... */
};

ptr = CyclicBuffer4Bullets.GetPtr();
num = CyclicBuffer4Bullets.GetNum();

for(i=0;i<num;i++) {
    if (ptr[i].bUsed) {
        // process bullet hole
    }
}
```

The internal processing code for a cyclic buffer also follows on from ideas within the static block code, with a single pointer referencing the next available element (as shown in Figure 3.7). The only difference here is that after the data chunk has been exceeded, it wraps around to the start.

The implementation given previously is realistic because at most stages of the game the buffer will be full of data, and so no time is wasted iterating through the entire list. Even when it's not (such as the start of the game), there's such a small

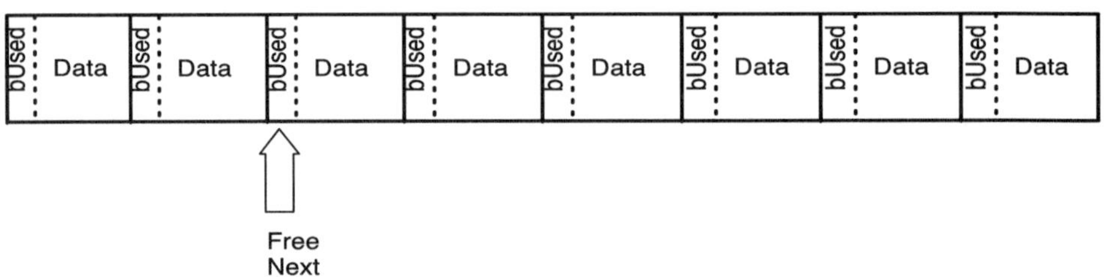

FIGURE 3.7 Cyclic memory.

time hit in checking a single `bUsed` value (compared to the work of processing and rendering a bullet hole) that it'll never show up in your profiles.

Memory Pools

A memory pool is an advanced version of cyclic buffers, where each element in the memory pool can be allocated and deallocated independently. It has the advantages of dynamic memory, with the compactness and low overhead of static blocks or other fixed-sized buffers. For these reasons, memory pools are also very useful in the cross-platform environment, as the pool can be scaled to fit the target machine.

Memory pools should be used wherever control is needed over the particular elements within it. This would include particular systems in which specific elements would fade out and die at arbitrary times. These *can* be implemented using cyclic buffers, but at the expense of extra processing because the particles in question could be removed from the cyclic list without warning.

Unlike cyclic buffers, however, all the memory allocated by a pool must be explicitly deallocated. This means there's a very slight overhead in storing a pointer to your data in the pool, and the possibility that no memory will be available for it. Again, when this is a fundamental part of the gameplay, you should use heap memory instead.

Because all the data in a memory pool (detailed in Figure 3.8) is contiguous, it can still be treated like a cyclic list, if necessary, using the code given previously. However, because a pointer is returned that (if valid) is guaranteed to exist until you release that memory, it's more common to use memory pools over cyclic lists.

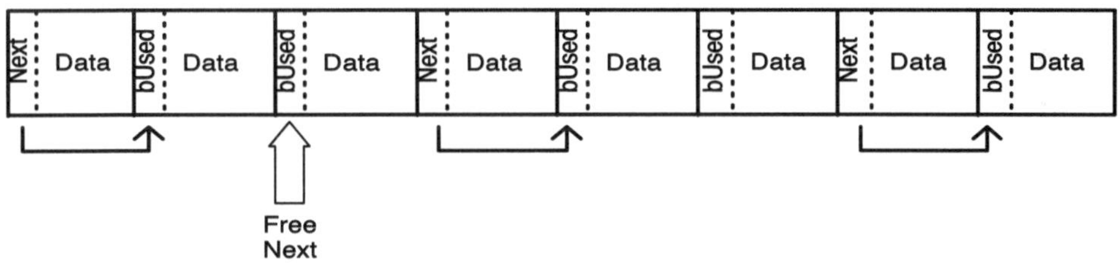

FIGURE 3.8 Pool allocation.

Stacked Allocations

The stack in question is a traditional first in, last out (FILO) affair and works very well at avoiding memory fragmentation. This category also has echoes of the static block you saw previously. Again, whenever we allocate memory we increment the single pointer to provide a new, untouched, portion of RAM. However, this time, we can only deallocate the very last thing we allocated. Consequently, this method will never have defragmentation issues, and only requires 4 bytes of overhead per allocation.

You can use this method to provide more complex temporary buffers, handle resource assets, and cope with the "Global versus Game" problem discussed in an upcoming section. By controlling your own memory stack, you can also compensate for a fairly minimal processor stack by storing function parameters in your memory instead. Consider the following recursive code:

```
void
FindBestAction(CMiniMaxState &state)
{
    if (state.m_CurrDepth == state.m_MaxDepth) {
        return;
    } else {
        CMiniMaxState new_game(state); // copy ctor

        for(int action=0; action < state.GetNumActions(); ++action) {
            new_game = state.ApplyAction(action);
            new_game.m_CurrDepth = state.m_CurrDepth + 1;

            FindBestAction(new_game);

            if (new_game.GetScore() > state.GetScore()) {
                state.m_Action = new_game.GetAction();
                state.m_ActionScore = new_game.GetScore();
            }
        }
    }
}
```

The amount of recursion required here is immense, but typical. Collision checking, scene graphic rendering, and AI all use deeply recursive algorithms. By moving the data from a process stack into a memory stack, however, we can ensure cross-platform compatibility when the depth of recursion gets too large for some platforms.

TIP

Holding stack data in your own memory also allows you to process very time consuming recursive algorithms across several frames because the stack information does not get destroyed. AI path-finding routines fit very well into this category.

Because we can create an instance of `CMemory` with any piece of legitimate memory, we can also create a temporary `CMemoryStack` class inside a temporary memory buffer, which keeps us from wasting space on rarely performed operations.

```
CAction
NewFindBestAction()
{
CMemoryStack *pStack;
CMiniMaxState intial_game_state;
CAction action;

    pStack = (CMemoryStack *)CMemoryTempBuffer::GetLock();
    pStack->PushNew(initial_game_state);
    NewRecursiveMiniMaxTest(pStack);

    action = pStack->GetTopPtr()->m_Action;

    CMemoryTempBuffer::Unlock();

    return action;
}

void
NewRecursiveMiniMaxTest(const CMemoryStack  *pStack)
{
CMiniMaxState *pParameters = pStack.GetTopPtr();

    if (pParameters->m_CurrDepth == pParameters->m_MaxDepth) {
        return;
    } else {
        for(int action=0; action < pParameters->GetNumActions();
           ++action) {
            CMiniMaxState *pNewParams= pStack->PushNew(*pParameters);

            pNewParams->ApplyAction(action);

            FindBestAction(pStack);

            if (pNewParams->GetScore() > pParameters->GetScore()) {

                pParameters->m_Action = pNewParams->GetAction();
                pParameters->m_ActionScore = pNewParams->GetScore();

                pStack->Pop();
```

```
            }
        }
    }
}
```

As well as providing a cross-platform compatible stack, this has the additional debugging feature of being able to test for stack overflow, instead of just suffering the crash when it happens.

Dynamic Memory

The dynamic memory handler we're suggesting here is something of a pariah. Although it has its own memory, it doesn't really handle any allocations on its own, but instead uses the services of the categories we've already discussed. The basic philosophy is to use the dynamic memory handlers for the majority of pregame and in-game allocation (which will still occur if you use STL) as an abstraction layer for the heap. Instead of owning a single block of memory, we'll create several. Along with the standard heap, we'll also create memory pools of 16-, 32-, 64-, and 128 bytes in length. The size of each pool is game-specific, but because it's not platform-specific, it earns its place here. Any allocation made to the dynamic memory class will get passed to the most suitable block it owns, and which still has space available.

So should a small amount of memory be requested, say 10 bytes, we can allocate one entry from the 16-byte pool. This only wastes 6 bytes, and would be preferable to the 20 bytes we waste when allocating dynamically from the heap. If there is a request for 26 bytes, we can use the 32-byte pool, and so on. If there isn't an appropriate pool, or the one in question is full, we can either employ the next size up, or revert to using the heap.

The demarcation between pool sizes is your own free choice, and there are several variations on this theme. If one of our frequently used structures is 40 bytes, we could create a pool for that instead. If more than 20 bytes are going to be wasted in any pool allocation, we could revert to the heap, knowing its overhead is smaller. Whatever decisions are made, they should be done at a global level, where differences in platform cannot affect the memory placement. Determining the number of wasted bytes in your memory manager is possible, but you shouldn't use it to determine game control unless you're certain there are no external influences. That could include platform-specific elements in the memory manager, such as DMA packet information or a fluctuation in the size of `MAX_PATH` used by the allocator's filename.

The relationship between these memory categories can be represented diagrammatically as shown in Figure 3.9.

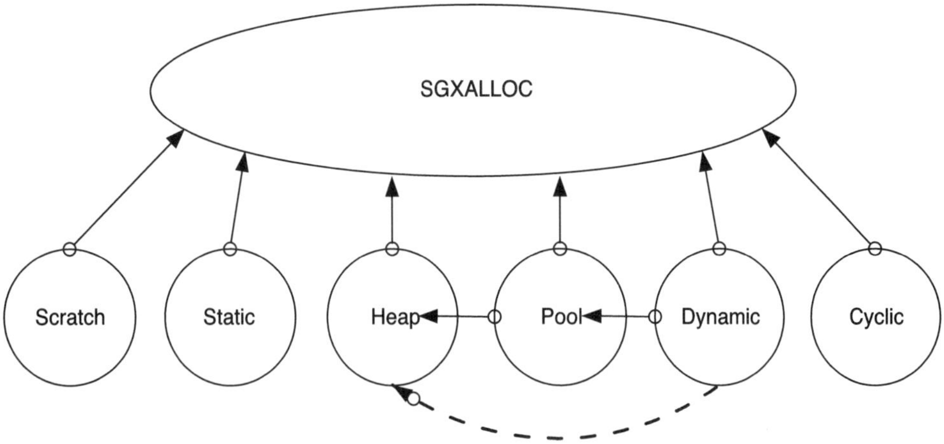

Figure 3.9 Relationship between allocators.

Adopting such systems ensures that we never truly allocate new memory after the game has started. This is a very good state to be in for two reasons: 1) it prevents crashes due to memory allocation and 2) it's easier to port a zero-allocation system (such as this) to an allocating one than vice versa.

Using Allocation Within Subsystems

Each memory handler we create should be isolated according to the subsystem. Often, in game development, each section of the game will have a particular budget. AI, graphics, and audio, for instance, will all have limits on how much memory and CPU time they may use. These subsystems can provide their own allocation routines. This makes it easier to track who has eaten all the RAM, as each subsystem is given their own memory block. The engine then takes control of the global memory, making it impossible for any other system to steal memory, unless it gets ahold of the subsystem's own personal pointer.

There will be several wrappers of this type, to cover each category of memory allocation. However, this does provide a simple method of preventing unwarranted allocations (perhaps of the static block) from those subsystems that should not need them.

```
void
CAISubsystem::Initialise(CMemory &mem)
{
tBYTE *ptr = (tBYTE *)pPrivateAIMemory;
tUINT32 memory, block;
```

```
        memory = mem.GetLargestFree();

        block = memory/10;
        m_pStaticBlock = new CMemoryStatic(mem.ALLOC(block), block);

        block = memory/20;
        m_pStaticBlock = new CMemoryCyclic(mem.ALLOC(block), block);

        block = memory/50;
        m_pStaticBlock = new CMemoryPool(mem.ALLOC(block), block);

        // Whatever's left can go to the heap
        m_pHeapBlock = new CMemoryStatic(mem.ALLOC(mem.GetLargestFree()));
    }

    // An example of the AI-specific allocation functions
    void *
    CAISubsystem::AllocHeap(tMEMSIZE size, const char *pFilename,
        tUINT32 line)
    {
        return m_pHeapBlock->Alloc(size, pFilename, line);
    }
```

This code involves a basic wrapper around the allocation code, like this:

```
#define aiAllocHeap(_size) \
CAISubsystem::Get()->AllocHeap(_size, __FILE__, __LINE__)
```

Note that `aiAllocHeap` must use a macro to retain the value of `__FILE__` and `__LINE__`. Without these, debugging becomes more difficult because all the memory helper functions (such as `ListBlocks`) appear to come from a single line, somewhere in `CAISubsystem`'s `AllocHeap`.

For those still wary of the overhead of singletons or additional function calls, you can use a global variable for the AI's heap block (say, `g_AIHeapBlock`), at the expense of security, as it's no longer possible to prohibit use of the memory.

The final step here is to provide a `free` function. With a little extra logic, you can provide an auto-sensing function that releases memory from whichever manager it was allocated from. This is useful when code is in development, although it can be a little slow.

```
void CAISubsystem::Free(void *ptr)
{
    if (m_pHeadBlock->IsPtrValid(ptr)) {
```

```
            m_pHeadBlock->Free(ptr);
        } else if (m_pCyclicBlock->IsPtrValid(ptr)) {
            m_pCyclicBlock->Free(ptr);
        } else if (m_pMemoryPoolBlock->IsPtrValid(ptr)) {
            m_pMemoryPoolBlock->Free(ptr);
        } else if (m_pStaticBlock->IsPtrValid(ptr)) {
            sgxTrace("Can only free stack block in one go");
        }
    }
```

Global versus Game

One important use of these (new) functions is to make the distinction between game memory (holding the level data and engine structures), and global memory (for the menus, frame buffers, and anything else that must always be present). A separate memory block should be created for both portions and be used independently when loading textures, for example.

```
LoadTexture("frontend1", GlobalBlock);
...
LoadTexture("levelimage1", GameBlock);
```

By considering the frontend as a subsystem, we can allocate all its memory from a static block that is never deallocated, while all the game-related memory is held separately. This has two major benefits over the use of general-purpose heaped memory. First, it means that the game can be checked for memory leaks at the end of each level or game, because a simple call to `GameBlock.ListBlocks` shows which in-game objects haven't freed their memory upon the rallying cry of "end game."

Second, it means that once tested, the game does not need to deallocate memory when the game ends because the entire block can be re-initialized *en masse*. This saves the processor from having to deallocate each block in turn, saving both the overhead in destructors, and the housekeeping duties of the memory manager. With the number of allocations often made within a game, this can be a significant time saver.

The global versus game split often includes the following areas:

Global

- Driver data (including initialization and housekeeping data, frame and Z-buffers, audio mixing buffers)
- Generic resources (HUD, the player)
- Menu resources (graphics, sounds, text)

- Save game image (for transferring data between game levels because all game data is lost)

Game

- Level-specific data (scene graph, resource assets, sounds)
- Game state data (particles, bullet holes)
- In-game allocations (the STL)

Games using a continuous terrain, where each section is loaded asynchronously, need additional divisions between memory. Here the split is more likely to be:

- Global (as listed previously)
- Game framework (showing how each level section fits together)
- Level data x N (dependent on game design)

However, the actual structure of asynchronous loading is beyond the scope of this book.

OTHER GUIDELINES

Before leaving this section on memory, we should outline a few basic pointers on general programming style with respect to memory.

The Stack

The first area to consider is the beloved stack. This is an effect of the compiler. Not only is the stack size likely to be different between compilers, but the amount of stack used with each function call will also vary, as will the call depth, because the PlayStation 2 graphics API is unlikely to have the same hierarchy as that of the Xbox. This makes it very difficult to guesstimate a comparative amount of stack for each platform. The general rule of thumb is to use the default—unless that doesn't work, in which case, increase it to whatever size you need, but no more. This magical size can be determined by placing the stack at a fixed address, filling the potential stack space with null characters, and then periodically scanning this block (from the bottom to the top) for any nonzero data. A simple debug macro can be created to perform this check, and placed throughout the code. It may also be added as part of a trace message or assertion.

Local Buffers

Don't allocate large strings or memory buffers on the stack as this can introduce bugs because they are consequently easier to overrun. Typical uses include trace messages, or output buffers for building filenames into character arrays; which coincidentally would usually detail the location of the bug—if it hadn't already been corrupted by the stack overflow. If you need a large working area, consider using the temporary buffer. If this isn't available or you're only considering using 100-5,000 bytes (when locking a 2 MB buffer would be considered wasteful), then you could implement the buffer as a static variable. You also could use a global, which is declared above the function, and include an explanatory comment. Mark it so that it appears like a mini-scratchpad buffer.

CAUTION *If a static or global buffer is chosen, be careful when the code utilizes threads; such methods will fail if the function needs to be re-entrant. We'll cover this in full, including threading, in Chapter 4, "The CPU."*

By Value or By Reference?

Use references if possible. Better still, use constant references. This applies in cases where a value is passed through to a function, and when a pointer is normally used.

```
void DoSomething(int a, int b)
```

should become

```
void DoSomething(const int &a, const int &b)
```

In some instances, notably PlayStation 2, many CPU cycles can be saved by using `const string &`, instead of `string *`, just because of the way the compiler handles it. Furthermore, as C++ programmers will tell you, passing classes by value is expensive as a temporary variable is constructed (and later destructed) when passed into a function. This also applies to data returning from a function, like this:

```
// Don't do this
SomeDataStruct DoSomethingElse()

// Do this
DoSomethingElse(SomeDataStruct &)
```

You'll see other instances of references and pointers, and how they can introduce (and prevent) bugs in Chapter 6.

Recursion

Don't overdo the recursion. From the moment you learn about recursion (usually by writing a factorial program), the solution to so many problems should become clear. Although there's no problem using recursive solutions in games, it must only be employed with careful thought. Ask yourself how many iterations of this function will normally occur? How many *could* occur? Is there a difference between these numbers? Are the exit conditions secure enough?

The processing required for a recursive solution is little different from that of an iterative one. However, the stack usage will be wildly different. Unless you're confident about the situations in which it will be used (and most game recursion comes from sorting, collision detection, and AI path-finding) and have tested all situations (and by *all situations*, we really do mean *all*) in which they might be used, it will probably be safer to implement the algorithm using iteration, or with the `CMemoryStack` class we discussed earlier. All recursive algorithms can be implemented iteratively.

From a security viewpoint, it's unlikely that you'll know which level or path-finding route will use the deepest level of recursion, so you should monitor this closely to prevent stack overflow. It can be done quite simply with a global variable and a counter:

```
int g_FunctionRecurseDepth, g_FunctionRecurseDepthMax;

void Function()
{
    if (g_FunctionRecurseDepth++ > g_FunctionRecurseDepthMax)  {
        g_FunctionRecurseDepthMax = g_FunctionRecurseDepth;
    }

    // do something, which may involve calling Function() again

    g_FunctionRecurseDepth–;
}
```

There are also techniques involving scope traces, which we cover in Chapter 6.

Local Variables

Be sure to initialize your variables. Not really the right time to say it, but it still needs to be said. Uninitialized variables are not guaranteed to be assigned any useful value by the compiler. The sole exceptions are global and static variables that will be zero according to the ANSI standard. Everything else will reflect whatever was in memory at the time. Fortunately, most compilers will warn about "use before assign," so take heed.

Intelligent Buffer Usage

Think in cyclic buffers. Game consoles, in common with other embedded systems, have a fixed memory. So begin to think of solutions that utilize cyclic buffers. Bullet holes and blood splats are common examples here. Understand the difference between cyclic buffers and memory pools, and use the correct one. If in doubt, use a pool.

Minimize Dynamic Memory

Ideally, we should allocate everything at game start, and nothing thereafter. That way, you'll know that after the game has loaded, it cannot fail to play through because of memory issues. You might also elect to "close" the memory allocators after the game has loaded. This would apply to the static and dynamic categories, and can be implemented at any level of the system, or in individual subsystems. The initial game start allocation should also include a little extra memory for level transitions and any additional "Now Loading" resources that are not part of your global allocation.

CAUTION

If you can carry objects between levels, the second part of that level might require more memory when played in situ *than it does standalone during testing.*

ENDNOTES

1. This is where you don't return a pointer to memory; you provide a handle. This handle is then converted to a pointer on demand, which gives the memory manager an opportunity to move the data to a different memory location, without changing the handle. Normally, you *lock* the handle to retrieve a usable memory pointer.
2. `memcpy` has undetermined behavior when the memory regions overlap. `memmove` does not.
3. `gets` retrieves a string, but does not check that the buffer is large enough to contain it. In console development, however, the use of `stdlib` functions, such as `fgets`, are forbidden by the powers that be.
4. We could create a separate table for the headers, but we'd never know how big such a table should be because it would be fixed in advance with the maximum number of separate allocations allowed. It's better to allocate

space for the memory manager's housekeeping tasks from the memory it's dealing out to others.

5. When an exception is thrown, the stack unwinds to destroy any data objects on it. If you're in a destructor when you try to do this, you get a cyclic problem because the destructor was called as a consequence of another exception and the process will hang.
6. The basic initialization doesn't need such checks, as failure at this time usually represents something catastrophic that we cannot recover from anyway.
7. It's pseudo-random. This has more benefits than problems as it ensures predictability. We look at this more fully in Chapter 6.

4 The CPU

In This Chapter

- The CPU
- Time Slicing
- CPU Scalability
- Parallel Processing
- Avoiding the Whole Problem

THE CPU

The CPU is a necessary evil of computing. No matter how fast it is, or how well it performs, it will always be too slow. What's more, it's impossible to hide the fact. You can always abstract the filesystem, change your graphics library, or use new audio code. But, at the low level, there's always the same chip, doing the same job, in the same amount of time. That is true for one CPU, two CPUs, or an entire farm. The amount of processing is fixed.

Getting the game to run as fast as possible is a common aim of all developers. Hitting the magical 60 frames per second (fps) is accompanied by smug self-satisfaction, a smiling producer, and a choir of angels. Achieving that goal is usually the result of late nights, pizza, and an intimate knowledge of the profiler. With a cross-platform title, however, these rules do not apply. What is fast for one machine might be slow for another. The Xbox, for example, has a single main processor, whereas the PlayStation 2 splits its processing over several processors. To optimize for PlayStation 2, therefore, requires a paradigm shift that affects the way the whole engine works. You must think of all the chips as a whole, how best to utilize them individually, and how to make full use of the data bus between them.

Later in this chapter, we'll look at several ways to split the main game into task blocks that can be farmed out to other chips. First, however, we need to consider the main processor and how to use it. Even when you only have a single CPU, you can still make gains by splitting the code into smaller chunks and processing them separately. With the game code in sections, it's easier to time-slice the code, introduce threading, or prepare it for the move onto two or more separate processors. Threading and parallel code will become significantly more important in the next generation of consoles, so a little preparation now will not only save processor time in the short term, but reduce the porting effort in the future, when your game works cross-platform between the PC, Nintendo GameCube, PlayStation 2, Xbox, and the yet-to-be N5™, PS3™, and Xbox 2™.

Timer Resolution

Measuring time is one of the easiest things to do. Every platform provides at least one method of checking the time. Whether it's a clock showing hours, minutes, and seconds, a "time since epoch," or "time since switched on," there's always some method of finding out how long a piece of code takes. Consequently, we can write our game code to compensate, regardless of the processing it needs to do. The clearest (and most necessary) example of this is in the main game loop.

If the game is running at 60 fps, we'll process the game logic and draw a new screen 60 times every second. This means each combined pass of "update" and "draw" can take no more than 16.6 ms. If the game always runs faster than this, we need to add a slight pause before continuing. If the game runs slower, we have to skip a frame.

Some APIs provide an alarm or timer mechanism, allowing you to trigger events after a specified time period. Such functions have limited use because the resolution of these timers has an unacceptable margin of error. In the Win32 API, for example, a `WM_TIMER` message can be sent to your main window (up to) 100 times every second. This is fast enough for most games, but the message is only guaranteed to appear within 10 to 15 ms (55 ms on older Windows 95 and 98 machines) of its predicted time, which is a significant proportion of the 16.6 ms each frame takes to process.

To combat this, we won't work with an external event process; instead, we'll resort to our own loop that will process the data as fast as possible.

```
while(!bExitGame) {
    UpdateGame();
    DrawGame();
}
```

The compensation we mentioned earlier exists because we cannot *guarantee* the 60 fps target on every frame. Modern games are incredibly complex. They have more variables, more possible scenarios, and more unknowns than any other software on the market, so it's impossible to test every variation. There might be a difficult jump that only some players can make which positions him onto a high wall looking out across the whole level. One particular maneuver might cause six NPCs to wake up, instead of four. In each case, there will be more processing than was anticipated, and the game will slow down. We can't prevent these situations from happening, but we can limit their effect on the game.

The trick here is to measure the time that each frame takes, and apply that back into the system.

```
tREAL32 current_time, time_elapsed;

current_time = CGameClock::Get()->GetTime();
time_elapsed = current_time - last_time;

ProcessGameComponents(time_elapsed);

last_time = current_time;
```

The time (measure in seconds) is passed onto the rest of the game. This changes the meaning of "game tick" from a very definite "one movement per frame," to "N seconds of movement per frame," which makes the game much easier to write (because a second is a standard unit, like meters). The game is also less prone to timing variants between platforms because they're all compensated for in the same fashion. If one frame takes a long time to process, a large `time_elapsed` value will be passed to the game on the next frame, causing characters to process a larger chunk of their animation, or move the bullets farther. Now, regardless of the platform, any slack in timing gets picked up by the main game loop. All this requires that each game object (be it an NPC, bullet, or special effect) be written to use this value:

```
void CGameBullet::UpdateComponent(tREAL32 time_elapsed)
{
    vPosition += vSpeed * time_elapsed;
}
```

Some portions of the game will ignore `time_elapsed`. These portions are limited to anything that interfaces with time in the real world, and not the stunted time we deliver to update the game components. This would cover the following:

Audio Engine: Needs to feed the audio chip with data whenever possible.
Graphics Engine: We still need to draw the game screen each frame, regardless of its duration.
Input Library: Grabbing joystick movements should occur every frame, although the application of rumble (which is gameplay-based) will apply `time_elapsed`.
Disc Handlers: Data streaming from a disc works to its own timetable, not yours.

A platform-specific update will also handle any specific technical requirements (such as open disc covers) that are not handled by the other components.

NOTE

The `time_elapsed` *value in our engine will always be greater than zero because it isn't possible to execute code in no time. There will always be one entire screen drawn every frame, so the minimum* `time_elapsed` *will be large enough to show up, regardless of the quantization of the processor's clock. However, there is good cause to design the game components to accept a zero value in the* `UpdateComponent` *function. This will help support additional game features such as the (perhaps overused) bullet time effect. It also makes it easier to unify the start game procedure because the first frame can be given an* `Update(0)` *that will prepare any resources that have been setup, but not actually process any of them. If you adopt this route, just remember to avoid dividing by zero.*

This solution provides as solid a clock as possible across each platform. So no special code needs to be written for the particular console in question. This certainly saves you from the myriad timer solutions under Windows, which include *Multimedia Timers* (with an accuracy of 1 ms, but can provide no more than 16 timers to your process), *Waitable Timers* (intended for thread synchronization), and *Queue Timers* (lightweight kernel objects that reside in *timer queues*).

Processor Yield

So far, our solution will work in most cases where only one thread is running on the *platform*. Should there be a second thread belonging to you—or anybody else—it is unlikely to ever get processing time, as our code never gives it an opportunity to do so. This includes all games running under Windows because the operating system (OS) is also a program with its own threads that need processing time.

Yielding control back to the OS can solve this problem. Many functions do this automatically, such as those involving file I/O, but there is also one function that does nothing else but yield control. On Windows, this function is called `Yield`. Periodic use of this function allows the processor time to breathe, giving the OS a chance to handle its housekeeping chores. By abstracting this function with our own, `sgxYieldWait`, we can pause for N seconds on any platform (spinning or yielding, as appropriate) to complete our frame-handling code.

If you only need the thread to breathe once per frame, you can get the main thread to wait on a semaphore at the end of each update. The vertical blank interrupt handler triggers this semaphore.

Programming the Clock

The implementation of CGameClock is not quite a straightforward abstraction of the PC's QueryPerformanceFrequency as you might initially think, because it doesn't always need to return the time. This clock is counting *game* time, not real time. In this role, the clock can be stopped, started, reset, and even slowed down, as seen in the bullet time effects of games such as Enter The Matrix, Max Payne™ and Die Hard™: Vendetta.

To achieve this functionality, we use the platform-specific main loop to inform our clock about the passing of real world time. The game clock then applies this information to decide what the equivalent game time should be, and what values to pass onto the game components during the next update cycle. For example:

```
game_time_elapsed =
    CGameClock::Get()->ApplyRealTimeToClock( OS_GetTime() );

UpdateAllGameComponents(game_time_elapsed);
```

Our basic clock then no longer needs to understand anything about the platform, or hide any platform-specific functions inside it. This means the clock is completely cross-platform, and all the extra functionality can be added once.

An example of this functionality is the use of constant time. If the game is processing N seconds worth of data each frame, it's highly likely that frame 11 on the PC will be different from frame 11 on the PlayStation 2. Not through any particular fault of our own, just that the accumulation of time will differ slightly. This in itself is not a problem, because our game code will compensate for the differences. But during development, there are other tasks to attend to—like debugging. If we're storing all the keypad presses (see Chapter 7, "System I/O") for a playback mode, then the time at which they're pressed is crucially important. If a slow disc takes an extra 0.01 seconds to provide our streamed speech, then it could appear as if the press was in frame 10, not 11. This could literally be a matter of life and death for the NPC under test, so we need to feed the clock specific timing values.

Similarly, if we're capturing successive frames for compilation into a video sequence, we want 60 fps, regardless of the actual frame rate. So, again, we have to ignore the real world clock, and use our own numbers. Finally, if the game begins to slow down (for whatever reason), don't let it slow down too far, because this can cause a snowball effect. Consider a frame that took 0.02 seconds to process. The next frame, to compensate, processes 0.02 seconds of AI, animation, and physics. This extra work might cause the frame to take 0.03 seconds. This is then applied to the next frame, which in turn takes 0.04 seconds to process, and so on. There are two elements to this problem: cure and prevention. The cure is to clamp the clock time, so that it never processes more than, say, 1/15th of a second's worth of data in any one frame. The prevention is to use constant-time algorithms. That is, the time taken to process 1 second's worth of game data, is (approximately) equal to the time taken to process 2 seconds. Most components in the game, such as animation, will work this way naturally. The biggest offender in this area is usually the collision of physics-based objects. Not because it's more complex to process them across longer periods of time, but because more collisions are likely to occur within it, and the processing time of the physics engine solver increases according to the number of objects and collisions it has to handle. We look at solutions to this in the "Time Slicing" section later in this chapter.

TIP

The physics and collision code often needs to be run faster than the actual frame rate to avoid numerical instability. It should have a maximum time step value and needs to be called enough times to eat up the entire `time_elapsed` *value.*

This gives our game clock four basic modes of operation. The implementation of which is very simple:

```
tREAL32
CGameClock::ApplyRealTimeToClock(tREAL32 current_time)
{
tREAL32 time_elapsed;

    time_elapsed = current_time - last_time;

    switch(m_ClockMode)
    {
    case CLK_REALTIME:
        time_elapsed *= m_FractionalSpeed;
        break;
```

```
    case CLK_AS_GIVEN:
        time_elapsed = m_GivenTime;
        break;

    case CLK_CONSTANT:
        time_elapsed = m_ConstantPeriod;
        break;

    case CLK_CLAMPED:
        if (time_elapsed < m_ClampedMax) {
            time_elapsed = m_ClampedMax;
        } else if (time_elapsed > m_ClampedMin) {
            time_elapsed = m_ClampedMin;
        }
        time_elapsed *= m_FractionalSpeed;
        break;
    }

    last_time = current_time;

return time_elapsed;
}
```

This is supplemented with basic support functions:

```
void
CGameClock::SetModeConstant(tREAL32 fps)
{
    m_ConstantPeriod = 1.0f/fps;
    m_ClockMode = CLK_CONSTANT;
}

void
CGameClock::SetModeClamped(tREAL32 min_fps, tREAL32 max_fps=60)
{
    m_ClampedMin = 1.0f/min_fps;
    m_ClampedMax = 1.0f/max_fps;
    m_ClockMode = CLK_CLAMPED;
}
```

Adding the start and stop clock functions (which requires holding the real time at which the clock gets stopped) is left as an exercise for you.

Programming Timers

If you want to include your own alarm or timer mechanism in the game, it's best to implement it manually using the same `time_elapsed` variable we've calculated for processing the game components. In this instance, the rationale is not concerned with timer latency, but with resources. Because the API will probably implement timers using a hardware interrupt, the maximum number allowed depends on the platform. That is obviously a no go area; however, creating a simple array allows an arbitrary number of timers in the system, and one timer is consistent across all platforms.

```
// As called from the main loop
CEventTimer::Update(tREAL32 telaps)
{
    if (m_bRunning) {
        m_fTime -= telaps;
        if (m_fTime < 0) {
            CMessageQueue::Get()->AddMsg(this, eTimer);
        }
    }
}
```

By queuing the event messages, you can also change the traditionally asynchronous behavior of timers. They will now appear in the same order across all platforms even if the time elapsed value changes, as the message queue gets filled and consequently dispatched in the same order as the global object list.

Programming Profilers

If the main loop is the only place we need to handle time, then our job is done. We've already seen that we can pass our time elapsed parameter to all the game components, so it would appear that the job is done, except for one situation: profiling.

Profiling requires access to a high-resolution timer throughout the entire lifecycle of the game, so you'll need an additional method of retrieving the time aside from the main game loop. For this, you need nothing more than a quick scan of the API to find an appropriate timing function, and a small abstraction layer on each platform. Still with Windows, you could achieve this by pairing `QueryPerformanceFrequency` and `QueryPerformanceCounter`.[1]

```
class CPCHighTimer : public CHighTimer {
public:
    CPCHighTimer();
```

```
    virtual void      Start();
    virtual tREAL32   GetTime();

private:
    LARGE_INTEGER     m_Frequency;
    tREAL64           m_FrequencyTime;

    LARGE_INTEGER     m_Start;
};

CPCHighTimer::CPCHighTimer()
{
    // period is the number of counter increments that
    // occur over 1 second
    if (FALSE == QueryPerformanceFrequency(&m_Frequency)) {
        sgxTrace("Cannot query performance timer.");
    } else {
        m_FrequencyTime = (tREAL64)m_Frequency.QuadPart;
    }
}

void CPCHighTimer::Start()
{
    QueryPerformanceCounter(&m_Start);
}

tREAL32 CPCHighTimer::GetTime()
{
LARGE_INTEGER curr;
tREAL64 t;

    QueryPerformanceCounter(&curr);

    t = (tREAL64)(curr.QuadPart - m_Start.QuadPart) * 1000.0;
    t /= m_FrequencyTime;

    return (tREAL32)t;
}
```

This returns the time using milliseconds as its standard unit, because this granularity is available on all current platforms and is accurate enough for the large-grain profiling we're likely to be doing. It also breaks from tradition of only ever using standard units (like seconds) because the numbers we're expecting will be in order of microseconds, and therefore more useable in this form.[2] However, by using floating-point numbers, we can use more decimal places, which provide the time in microseconds, too, for the small-grain profiling that will occur in the future.

TIP

We use standard units, such as seconds and meters, throughout the game engine to ensure that everyone understands what "time" is measured in, and to make calculations easier and quicker to perform because conversion isn't required. Multiples should only be used where there is a significant loss of precision, such as in the nanosecond or microsecond range. In which case, multiples should be clearly labeled.

TIME SLICING

Time slicing is a method of cooperative multitasking that allows several pieces of code to execute on a single processor without using threads. Time slicing diverges from the conventional idea that the entire game is processed every frame, as such a large body of processing does not scale well in an ongoing, or cross-platform, development environment. Most of the code *doesn't* need to be run every frame—the AI thinking code is one example. If you're running short of time, you can suspend the AI processing and return to it on the next frame, or the frame after. At the high level, this can work on entire components (such as AI), or at a lower level, you can isolate the various tasks within a particular module. Let's take the AI as an example.

Within any particular frame, each AI character is likely to do many different things, as shown in Figure 4.1.

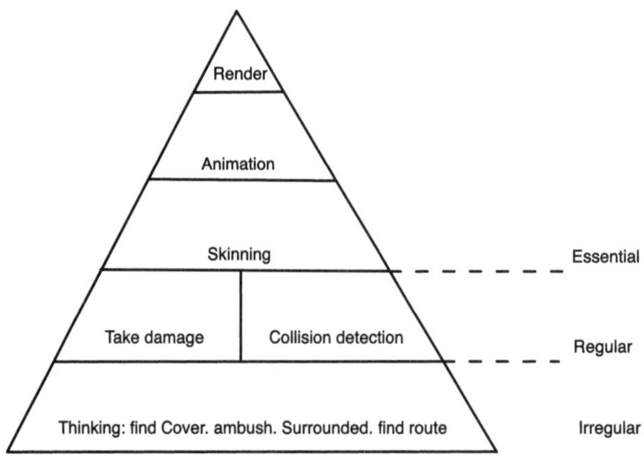

FIGURE 4.1 Typical AI tasks.

Now, an inherent level of detail (LOD) is present. Those elements at the top must be done every frame, while the others (like thinking) could survive on one update every five frames, or whenever processing time is available. One of the most processor-heavy tasks the AI will generally perform is path finding. This can be spread across 60 different frames, reducing the time used at each instance to virtually nothing. In the real world, 60 frames is only one second out of the player's life, so the player is very unlikely to notice.

Character skinning is a special case. It is placed on a par with animation in the diagram because without it, the body will contort and look obviously wrong. The only way a player can believe the character is intelligent is by observing his actions. By actions, we're looking at the animations. If the animations are good, smooth, and nonjarring, the character will appear natural. If you're running with level of detail (LOD) on your meshes (and if not, why not?), then the lower levels might not require skinning.

The LOD can also be determined by taking hints from other parts of your game. For example, if the engine didn't draw a character during the last frame, it can use a lower level of processing (or perhaps be ignored together).

Every time-sliced subsystem (AI or graphics, for example) should handle its own timing between child components. This is more effective than using one global time-slicer because there will be special cases in which the game logic needs to reprioritize portions of the code. One such case might be the introduction of a set-piece scenario. If a scene introduces five new characters to the world, but time slicing caused their release to be staggered, that scenario would fail because it would no longer be synchronized. The cardinal rule of "gameplay is king" trumps the rule of "keep it at 60fps." True, the game might run slow for a frame or two (it might not if the other subsystems are time slicing correctly and compensate for this), but the player is usually forgiving about slow-downs...especially if it's only occasional, and/or there is an obvious reason why it is happening.

These subsystems can even be time sliced among themselves, as shown in Figure 4.2.

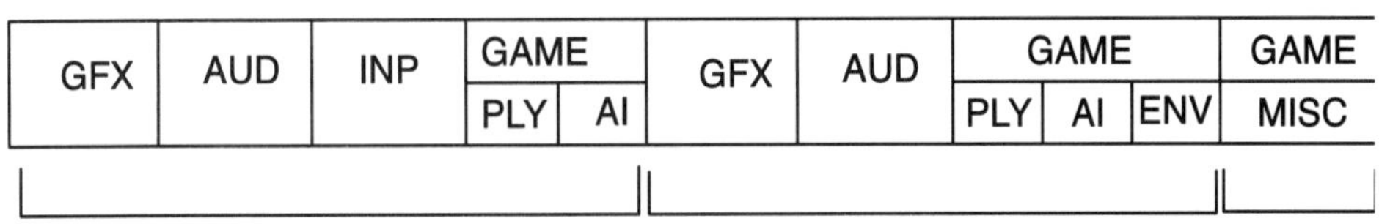

FIGURE 4.2 Time slicing the complete engine.

Each portion of the game logic can be implemented in a variety of ways relating to how often it will be processed. This breaks down into three categories:

- Process always
- Process every N frames
- Process every frame if possible

In theory, there's also a "do every N frames, if there's time," but this is seldom used because it doesn't map onto any particular problem. The patterns that should be employed for any particular subsystem can be categorized as described in the following sections.

Process Always

A lot of the engine code fits under this category. The graphics and audio rendering certainly need to be updated every frame; otherwise, both screen and speakers will be void of information. Without it, the graphics and audio will not synchronize correctly.[3] The joypad also fits in here. Not because it's a processor hog, but because it's part of the console's input interface that connects with the user. This needs to feel responsive at all times because without it, the player no longer feels in control of the game.

Typical I/O features that need this immediate response are:

- Controllers (reading joypads)
- Reset button handlers
- Disc cover alerts

However, even these features are not set in stone. The controllers, for example, are usually supplied with a vibration feature. This effect is used to shake the pad slightly when you're hit by a bullet or rocked by an explosion, and achieved by means of a small motor in the controller. This motor takes a short while to start up and a short while to wind down. Depending on your point of view, this might make it a perfect candidate for processing every frame (to get the wheels in motion as soon as possible), or every other frame (if it's going to take 1/10th second to stop the motor, waiting another 1/60th second isn't going to be a problem).

Similar logic can be brought into play when handling the reset button: the human mind cannot react quicker than 1/10th second, so we only *need* to respond every six frames. However, a technical requirement might force you to poll it more often.

In the real world, you are likely to find that many of the housekeeping functions (such as reset buttons and controllers) are so cheap that the overhead of time slicing them costs as much as it does to process them in full. That is because such functions just test a flag, set a bit on the I/O chip, or have been optimized to be that cheap because they need to be called every frame.

A lot of gameplay code also fits into this section. The player, most obviously, but also anything that moves fast, such as bullets and any other objects that can affect the player (or other objects that are also processed every frame), such as elevators, mirrors, and moving platforms. This can have a knock-on effect as more objects get processed at full-speed because of their interactions. Fortunately, the subset can be limited because many objects only have a secondary interaction with the player, as you'll see next.

Process Every N Frames

This applies to anything with a secondary interaction in the game world. These are objects that affect the game in an important, but not real-time, way. An opening door, for example, might take 1/2 second to open. If it does that over 15 or 30 discrete steps, it's usually of little consequence, especially when it's moving slowly—provided it still takes 1/2 second to open.

This category also includes anything that should appear like clockwork, including moving physical objects and some special effects, such as a pulsating light.

What cannot be included are any effects that are related to the position of the camera because that changes every frame (it's attached to the player which moves every frame). So any billboard images (a.k.a. forward-facing sprites) for smoke, fire, or other such particle effects cannot be included in this category. For finer grain control, the positioning of these effects would still occur on each frame, but the animation itself could be limited to every other frame. In these cases, the dividing line is fuzzy. Taking this idea further, a special effect could be split into the following parts:

- Update the position of graphical elements.
- Render.
- Update the boundary for collision or visibility checking.

So although we have a dependency (the boundary information requires the new position), the importance of the boundary calculation would be considerably lower and so get time sliced, and processed on alternate frames.

Process Every Frame if Possible

The phrase "if" makes this a very indeterministic section. All the code that adopts this method, therefore, should be similarly indeterministic, such as AI. In all parts of an AI system, the processing needs to take place as soon as possible, but not necessarily immediately. If an NPC sees the player in frame 1, but doesn't start the animation until frame 3, no harm is done. Even if the player manages to notice the time difference, it can be explained away because the character is a low-level grunt who's a bit slow, anyway. For situations where the character gets shot, then the bullet processing code will put the NPC into an "alert" state, and move this AI's processing to the head of the time-slice list, which we can do easily because the game (as opposed to the engine) controls the timing control.

Certain special effects fit into this category too, but only those that are indirectly controlled by the player. A light switch, for instance, hides the action of the switch from the light bulb, and so the code to change the lighting in the appropriate area can take two frames if necessary. On the other hand, a pulsating light is a regular, clockwork event, and so would not work in such an indeterministic manner. Instead, this would be processed every N frames, as mentioned in the previous section.

Side Effects

In some cases, the corollary of processing code in one category will cause side effects in another. This should only ever happen in one direction, from low frequency to high frequency. So for example, the high-priority pulsating light might cause an NPC to spot a lurking player on this frame or the next, because the NPC's thinking has been time sliced to a lower frequency. Note that the light would still cause the player's shadow to get updated every frame.

If you ever find that the components induce a dependency in the opposite direction (that is, an event happens every frame, but won't get processed until a different "every N frames" component is ready), then you need to rethink the time slicing for both sections of code, and reorder if necessary.

The functionality implemented in each category should be distinct from the time-slicing method employed because some modules will move between categories during the course of development. In some rare cases, they might move between platforms. However, it's more likely that the frequency will change, so an "every frame" routine ends up being invoked "every three frames." Implementing this is very simple as the subsystem can ask the `CGamePlatform` class how important this feature is, and adjust itself accordingly.

```
class CTimeSliceableObject { ... }
class CNPC : public CTimeSliceableObject { ... }
class CGruntNPC : public CNPC { ... }

// Initializing subsystems
void
CAISubSystem:StartGame()
{
tINT32 iTimeSlice = CGamePlatform::GetTimeSliceNPCGrade();
```

```
sgxVector<CNPC *>::iterator it;

    // for each NPC
    for(it = m_NPCList.begin(); it != m_NPCList.end(); ++it) {

        // nongrunts will perform all their processing every frame
        m_TimeSlicer.RegisterEveryFrame(it);

        // grunts are time-sliced
        if (it->IsGrunt()) {
            m_TimeSlicer.RegisterEveryNFrames(it, iTimeSlice);
            m_TimeSlicer.RegisterWhenTimePermits(it);
        }
    }
}

void
CAISubSystem:UpdateGameComponents(tREAL32 time_elapsed)
{
    // if no special cases...
    m_TimeSlicer.UpdateComponents(time_elapsed);

    // ...otherwise we must control it directly
    m_TimeSlicer.UpdateEveryFrame(time_elapsed);
    m_TimeSlicer.UpdateEveryNFrames(time_elapsed);
    m_TimeSlicer.UpdateWhenTimePermits(time_elapsed);
}

//
// For the individual NPCs
//
void CGruntNPC::UpdateEveryFrame(tREAL32 time_elapsed)
{
    CNPC::UpdateEveryFrame(time_elapsed);
    DoMovement();
    DoAnimation();
    DoSkinning();
}

void CGruntNPC::UpdateEveryNFrames(tREAL32 time_elapsed)
{
    // this telaps is the time since the last
    // call to 'UpdateEveryNFrames'
    CNPC::UpdateEveryNFrames(time_elapsed);
```

```
        DoDamageCheck();
        DoCollisionDetection();
    }

    void CGruntNPC::WhenTimePermits(tREAL32 time_elapsed)
    {
        CNPC::WhenTimePermits(time_elapsed);
        DoThinking();
    }
```

Notice that we call our functions `UpdateEveryFrame` and `UpdateEveryNFrames` to emphasize the distinction. Note also that the implementation of `CAISubSystem::UpdateGameComponents` makes three passes on the objects. This is essential to make sure that we don't run out of time processing the nonessential components before we've finished the "always" objects. Similarly, we process those marked "every N frames" before those that are happy with processor time when available, since the "every N frame" objects have been chosen to be periodic functions, while the rest are suited to an "if there's time" mentality.

Optionally, you can also specify a timeout, ensuring that even these objects get processed at least five times a second, for instance. This should cause a minimum of disruption because the current generation of engines assume everything will get processed every frame.

TIP

The housekeeping header that prefixes each time-sliced piece of code should be as small as possible, so it can be skipped over without killing the cache.

CPU SCALABILITY

For all the good work you and your programming team do with respect to time slicing and optimization, there will always be code that needs to run every frame. This constitutes a fixed amount of processing that needs to be carried out across all platforms. Maintaining a balance between them all is tricky, but four main techniques can help you make full effective use of the CPU, regardless of the platform.

Lowest Common Denominator

Lowest common denominator, as we mentioned in Chapter 2, "Top Ten Tips," is the traditional method of scaling the product by limiting the game to the capabilities of the lowliest platform currently under development. This method is largely ineffective because of the wide disparity between the individual hardware components. However, when combined with other methods (such as the extra burn technique, mentioned shortly), it can make good use of the target machine.

The smallest common component of most games is in the event loop and message passing system. This is insignificant in terms of processing, and so should never be on your critical path. However, this component can provide a simple lowest common denominator for your engine. Components then can be added to your core (on the main CPU) until the first platform shows signs of strain, at which point all further code is set to run on one of the additional processors.

Scale Back

The scale back method takes the existing engine and limits the processing burden by removing code or data. This can be done by optimizing individual routines, but more usually involves limiting the amount of objects processed each frame. A particle system, for example, might lower its limit of 2,500 particles onscreen to 2,000. Or the maximum number of bullet holes might be cut for one particular platform. In extreme cases, you might be able to reduce the number of NPCs onscreen at once, but check with your designer first.

Some scenarios might require you to re-create particular data assets using fewer polygons or textures for each platform. This will occur in normal circumstances anyway, because each asset will be converted to platform-specific versions for speed and efficiency, but you might need to extend this functionality by adding new metadata into the tool chain.

In all cases, you should be looking to adopt efficient algorithms. Those marked as `O(n)`, for example, take twice as long to process if there are twice as many entries. If you can't scale back the number of processing components in the algorithm, you can then look at changing the algorithm itself to `O(log(n))` or `O(1)`. Often, this requires more memory, and so those trade-offs occur on a platform-by-platform, and case-by-case, basis. Additionally, you could split the processing across two or more frames using time slicing.

Level of Detail (LOD)

In many traditional development environments, LOD is used to replace large meshes with low polygon versions when that particular mesh is a long way from the camera, where such precision would be invisible and result in wasted processing. The cost in this approach is the additional development time (on the part of artists, more than programmers), and extra memory required to store alternate versions. To create a rich environment onscreen requires a lot of detail that can only be generated through LOD techniques, so the extra resources are considered acceptable losses.

The same technique has been used with textures for years, where they are called *mipmaps*. Here the texture map consists of several versions of the same image, each intended for viewing at different distances. However, aliasing artifacts that occurred in the rasterization process made the adoption of mipmaps necessary, not the greed for processing power.

At a more general level, however, LOD can be applied to an individual algorithm or data set. For example, if a billboard sprite is only one or two pixels onscreen, it could be rendered with a shaded polygon, thus saving time for the texture upload. The Inverse Kinematics (IK) component of the animation system could be limited to the main characters, and those less than 20 meters in front of the camera. The distance at which such detail is omitted varies between both platforms and games, and would be included as part of the `CGamePlatform` class.

NOTE

When making distance-based LOD decisions, remember that an object 100 meters away appears very large onscreen if you provide a telescope, binoculars, or a sniper rifle in your game.

Extra Burn

Finally, with the game running to a base specification, you can add ingredients to the mix according to the spare cycles of each processor. In this way, you can achieve maximum use of the platform.

You can burn extra processor cycles in many ways. You can add new, or more elaborate, special effects by using more polygons in the rendering process, creating larger textures, or employing three-pass rendering for some materials. Also you can scale up the processing on your objects in the same way you scaled down earlier. In a similar fashion, you can vary the LOD distances to improve the visual impact of the game by using the better quality meshes for the nearest objects, as opposed to increasing the number of meshes onscreen.

PC games probably have the biggest amount of extra processing to burn, especially if the game originated on consoles. The standard method here is to provide an "Options" page in the frontend menu, and let the user control various special features, such as foliage, pixel shaders, or anisotropic filtering. This not only provides a means to scale up on the PC, but also allows users to adapt the game to match the capabilities of their particular machine. This achieves our goal of complete scalability very simply by putting the onus on the player, which in the world of PC gaming is acceptable.

In all cases, the extra processing is applied to the engine component of the game—typically graphics—because the gameplay and AI have always been so finely tuned that allowing the NPCs to think an extra step ahead could drastically change the gameplay.

PARALLEL PROCESSING

Parallel processing is the art and science of running two pieces of code together at the same time. On the face of it, this is a simple proposition. After all, Windows lets us run lots of pieces of code at the same time when it multitasks different programs, such as our e-mail client and our Web browser. Parallel processing differs from this situation, however, because the code being processed in parallel belongs to the same program and uses the same data.

This increases the potential for unseen problems as two independent parts of the program try to access the same data. Questions like, "Who holds the canonical version of this data?" are no longer straightforward because one component might be changing the data, while the other is trying to read it. The paradigm shift to parallel processing is as great as from porting C code to C++, so don't underestimate the time scales.

In this section, we'll consider all three aspects of parallel development. The first, hardware determination, affects the mechanisms by which code and data is set up to run on the processor, or processors. The second, software patterns involved in the distribution of tasks apply our code to various portions of the hardware. The final aspect concerns the caveats involved in the low-level implementation of our parallel code.

Parallel Determination

Within the current range of platforms, we have three basic methods of parallelism to consider. These are governed by the processors in the hardware and cannot be changed, although we can always drop "down" to a lesser solution. For example, the machine may support multiprocessing, but we might only use a multi-threaded solution. It's unusual to do this, however, because the battle for the next generation of games will be fought and won on their capabilities to exorcise every ounce of power from the machine through parallelism.

Multi-threaded

Traditionally, multi-threading is where several pieces of code are handled by one processor. Such pieces of code are called *threads*, and are lightweight processes that inherit the global variables of whichever process spawns them, and proceed to execute their own code, usually designated in a single function. This is the simplest form of parallel processing and can even exist on machines with only one processor because the OS controls each thread, giving it a small period of time before swapping it out and letting another thread process its code.

In more recent OSs, these threads can be distributed across as many processors as exist in the machine. This is not to be relied upon, however, and with the exceptions of filesystem and debugging threads, a multi-threaded development has little-to-no use within the games arena. This is because whenever the frequency at which tasks are switched exceeds 100 Hz, their benefits evaporate, and they become a hindrance to good performance. They do still have a use for teaching the mechanics behind thread programming in a more limiting environment, and for background tasks and routines that spend more than 95% of their time inactive.

Hyper-Threading

Hyper-threading refers to a single physical processor that is made to appear like two logical ones, and stems from the Intel P4 family of processors, incorporating the NetBurst™ microarchitecture. By appearing as two processors, one thread can be run on each to increase the processing power, while still accessing the same memory space. Creating optimal hyper-threading solutions involves a careful use of the caches because they are located on the physical chip, and consequently shared between logical processors. In contrast, the instruction pointers, return stack prediction and *Instruction Translation Lookaside Buffer* (*ITLB*), are all replicated, so the traditional rules apply.

More information about hyper-threading technology is available from *http://developer.intel.com/technology/hyperthread*.

Multiprocessor

As the name suggests, multiprocessor refers to separate processors that exist to run their own code, while still having access to common data. You'll recognize this as the description of the PS2,[4] where each processor is a custom chip running its own code. In the future, these chips are likely to be more generic processors with competent C and C++ compilers, allowing for a more general approach to parallelism. PCs with multiprocessor support are no longer particularly expensive, so they provide a low barrier to entry into the world of multiprocessing systems. However, they require a large OS (such as Windows) to run alongside your program and because the processor assignment is done at the process level, it's not always clear as to where your code will run.

No matter which approach the hardware manufacturers have taken, those of us playing the software game can adopt a unified approach to this problem. We just adopt the ideas from our time-slicing code and split our game code into sections to determine which portions can be run in parallel, and which cannot.

After we've considered this paradigm shift, the move to a multi-threaded system is much simpler. Not because the code is easier—it isn't—but because it employs the same process of looking subjectively at your engine. You must be able to say where the interdependencies lie between components, and determine what code can be run in isolation. All of this must occur before you begin the implementation. The days of ad hoc code and design are behind us now. We need to look forward. We need to *design* the code, and look at the factors that determine where the code should be physically processed, and how.

NOTE

Any part of a program that can be executed concurrently with other parts is termed a thread, regardless of the architecture on which it is running.

Parallel Distribution

Whether we're executing the player code, running an animation, or processing the audio, any piece code must run on a processor. Which processor, however, can vary. For each module we must consider the following processor and memory questions:

Processing Questions

- P1: Does it need the functionality of a custom chip?
- P2: Does it need to communicate with other processes during execution?
- P3: Does it depend on another process to complete first?

Memory Questions

- M1: Does it use main memory?
- M2: Does it use custom memory (for example, the Nintendo GameCube ARAM)?
- M3: Does it use both main and custom memory?
- M4: Does it read from memory?
- M5: Does it write to memory?

The answer to each question gives us a clue as to how each particular module should be implemented. For an explosion effect, for example, we would answer yes to P1 (access to the graphics chip), possibly to P2 (to cause damage to the player), and no to P3. The answers to M1, M2, and M3 usually stem directly from the processing questions, and cannot be changed without affecting the algorithm. The use of a custom chip[5] automatically qualifies it for access to custom memory; possibly in addition to main memory if it needs to communicate with other processes. We can determine an effective method of parallelism using Table 4.1.

TABLE 4.1 Options of Parallelism

	Yes	No
P1	Modular parallelism	Pipeline/farmed/fine grain
P2	Pipeline/farmed	Fine grain
P3	Pipeline	Farmed

In all cases, every machine will have a primary CPU (because there is only one entry point to your program: `main`), so the game loop will sit on this primary CPU and spawn separate threads onto the other processors. The type of work, the method by which the processor will be parallelized, and the specifics of your hardware will determine which processor is used. Because the hard work involved is in implementing the algorithms, the practical question determining which of the, say, six chips we should put our code onto is comparatively easy and governed by the type of parallelism employed.

Thread Creation

The first task in any thread-based system is to create the threads. This code requires a simple abstraction of whatever functions the standard API provides for us. Generally, each thread will be spawned with a function pointer and data parameter, although we'll add one additional parameter to indicate the logical processor[6]. Most of the time, this parameter will be unused, but it future-proofs the interface with a minimum of work.

```
typedef void (*cbThread)(tUINT32 iParam);

tBOOL
sgxSpawnThread(cbThread pThreadCode, tUINT32 iParam,
        CScheduler::tCPU iCPU);
```

An important implementation-oriented trade-off should be considered here, because the overhead in spawning separate threads is considerable, especially when compared to the execution time of the code you're likely to be running. Instead of spawning separate threads when they are needed, it's preferable to create them at the start of the game, and apply code as required. A typical mechanism would involve *worker threads*.

Each worker thread can be in one of three different states:

- Stopped, but waiting to start
- Running
- Exiting

The way to apply a piece of code to a worker thread is by sending an event message to it. This communication method is no different from those you've probably witnessed before in Windows. The main difference here is that the message we send does not need to be copied, because the address space of the message sender and receiver are identical. One possible implementation for our worker thread would appear like this:

```
void
WorkerThread(tUINT32 UserData)
{
void (*pCallback)(tUINT32 param);
tUINT32 Param;

    while(TRUE) {
        if (sgxGetMessage(&pCallback, &Param)) {
            (*pCallback)(Param);
        } else if (sgxGetTerminateMessage()) {
            return;
        }
        sgxYield();
    }
}
```

Fine-Grained Parallelism

This is a method whereby each thread executes the same code, but using a different set of data. It can also be referred to as *data parallel.* The classical example here is a particle system, where each processor handles a fixed number of particles concurrently with the others (see Figure 4.3).

This type of parallelism is easy to implement because the processor code is identical to the single-threaded version, and because each chunk of data is distinct from the others, there is no message passing between processors, or any dependencies from other portions of the data set. Each processor being independent of the others makes this a very scalable algorithm. You can run this on 2, 3, or more processors without having to know in advance how many there are. You can even change that number on-the-fly should you need to.

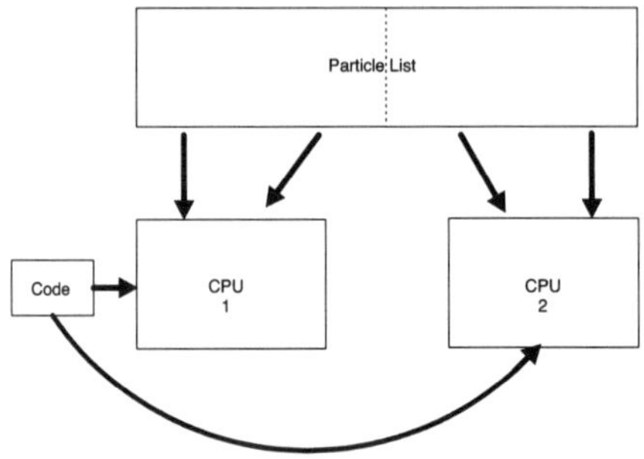

FIGURE 4.3 Data parallel.

```
class CParticleData;

num_particles = pParticles->GetTotal();
num_cpu = CPlatformHardware::Get()->GetNumCPUs();
load = num_particles / num_cpu;

for(cpu = 0; cpu < num_cpu; cpu++) {
    first = cpu * load;
    last = first + load - 1;

    sgxApplyThread( ParticleSystemUpdateFn, SGX_PROCESSOR_1 + cpu,
        (tUINT32)CParticleData(pParticles, first, last));

}
```

Unfortunately, while the coding is simple, finding game components that fit into this category is not. Very few pieces of game logic are truly independent. For instance, each object in the physics engine needs to interact with other physics objects, and the renderer needs to feed data to the graphics chips in a specific order. Although the communication is not a bad thing in itself, interacting with other components means you have two options: either your processor will stall until the response has been given, or you need two copies of the data so that you can process one while distributing the (unchanging) data from the other. This acts like a double-buffered display in the graphics engine. This dependency limits the parallelism you can achieve, but it has a more profound effect here because we know it's possible to get an efficient, and predictable, response from a fine-grained system.

Typical adoptees of fine-grain parallelism include animation and skinning, because in all cases the process is completely independent of anything else, and the amount of processing is not trivial.

When the amount of processing, per object, is very small, and there are only a few objects to process, it's better to use modular parallelism so that they can be handled in bulk.

Modular Parallelism

Modular parallelism separates the game code into modules that have some element of commonality, such as world furniture (like doors and windows), but are completely independent of other game code (for instance, AI). Each thread then executes the entire module as if it were in a single-processor machine. This usually involves executing a large amount of code, but helps to minimize intercommunication between threads as communication is generally slow.

To a certain extent, the modular approach is akin to the workings of the PlayStation 2 because each subsystem is written for a specific chip, given to it for processing. The skinning might occur on the VUs, for example, while the AI is handled by the EE.

Determining which processor should run which code has no obvious solution. Sometimes the decision is made for you because some chips are better targeted toward certain tasks, or they might need to be specifically programmed in assembler. Any chip with fast mathematics processing (such as the VUs on a PS2) is a suitable target for animation or skinning code, for example. This can be complicated by any code that has a dependency (for example, the skinning system relies on a completed animation) and so must be run in sequence. Any code that has *two* dependencies obviously can only be run after both have completed.

Furthermore, you can use several methods to assign code to a processor. The method is determined by the code in question, and the design of the game. The two methods we'll discuss here are pipelines and worker farms.

Pipelines

Pipelines are similar to those found in graphics programming, and consist of a number of predefined code modules that take data, process it, and pass it along to the next module (see Figure 4.4).

A single task is divided according to the separate steps within it. This could apply to the physics engine as a whole, as a separate processor handles each step (equations of motion, collision, and so on) before passing its result onto another. As each piece of pipeline code handles the communication between itself and the next processor, no overall controlling CPU is needed. The main CPU initializes the pipeline at the start of each frame, and then participates in the processing itself to avoid wasted cycles. If the processors involved are general purpose, however, you won't always make good gains by implementing a pipeline due to the extraneous time involved in communicating.

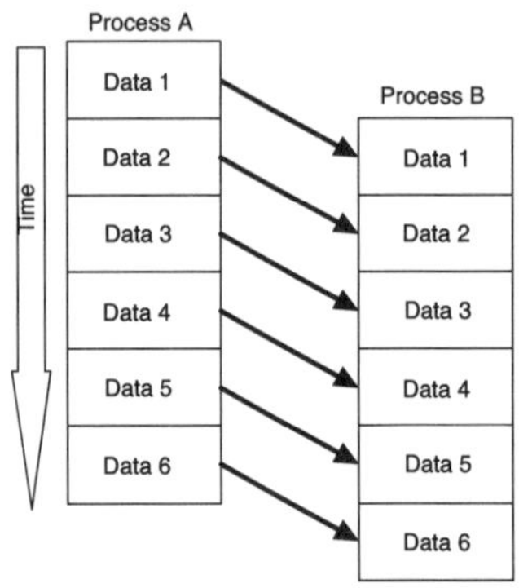

Figure 4.4 A pipelined architecture.

Farming in Parallel

An alternative method uses the farming metaphor. The main CPU takes a list of tasks, and farms them out to whichever processor is idle. This works better with larger objects that perform more processing, because the overhead in providing new code to each CPU can be large.

The main consideration is to provide enough work for the main CPU. Otherwise, its power is wasted because it's either performing housekeeping tasks for the other processors, or it's waiting for them to perform. Although the main CPU can process tasks of its own, it must still be responsive to the other (possibly faster) processors to prevent them from being starved of work. The rule of thumb is that a slow CPU can manage the housekeeping, basic polling (discs, reset button, and so on), and not much else; a fast CPU is better destined for pipelined or fine-grained solutions.

In all cases, communication between modules is necessary, as is some measure of dependency. Our solution to this is to require that every module is registered at the start of the game, replete with its list of dependencies.

```
RegisterModule("animation", ProcessAnimationCallback, 0L, NULL);
RegisterModule("skinning", ProcessSkinningCallback, 0L,
     "animation", NULL);
LockModuleList();
```

We could then write a scheduler that looks at each module in turn, and executes the next code block with the callback given on the next free processor whenever one becomes available for work. That is, we *could*. But having such a general-purpose system means that the code we're calling has to be equally general purpose, and capable of surviving in any situation. However, the fact that you're reading this book probably means you're writing a game. And a game is a very specific piece of software. It's two years of work, in return for one month of shelf life. Adding generality to the modules increases the development time for very little gain, and if you're keeping the basic engine for several games, you'll want to couple them closely to improve performance. In which case, it's more beneficial to profile the major components, and manually determine their deployment across processors. On a smaller scale, however, the individual calculations of, say, the animations would still be farmed out, but to a smaller selection of chips, and the animation system as a whole, would run alongside other code.

Determining which pieces of code can, or should, work alongside one another is determined by your engine, game, and platform. You've seen several examples already. The platform changes are not abstractable in the traditional sense of the word. You'll need to write a platform-specific function that determines how and where each module is to be run. But with each module preregistered, this is fairly simple. The techniques for running different code on different chips are also platform-specific, but you can abstract that by extending the concept of threads. Again, this is fairly simple as you saw with the particle system example. The main problem in developing parallel software is with the implementation. Our design and knowledge of each module saves a lot of the initial work, but the real devil is truly in the details.

Parallel Implementation

Although the details of thread creation are hidden behind NDAs, we can still draw up a series of guidelines for multi-threaded programming because it's a well-understood discipline outside our field. Using threading libraries such as *pthreads*, Win32 threads, or *OpenMP*, we can gain some experience of the issues we'll encounter without having to wait for the next generation platforms.

Reentrant Code

Reentrant code refers to something that can be called and executed at the same time by two different threads without any unwanted side effects. On the surface this might appear absurd, because the code operates on completely different data in each case, and would naturally be reentrant. However, each thread still has access to common data, even when the particular class instance differs. This is most obviously caused by static and global variables, because many people are not averse to using static buffers to save stack space (as have we), especially for generating filenames or building debug strings. For example:

```
char *
GetFilenameForNPC(int iNPC)
{
```

```
static char buff[256];

    sprintf(buff, "GAME_NPC_LEVEL_%s_NPC_%d", g_LevelName, iNPC);
    return buff;
}
```

And there's nothing wrong with that,[7] until the code becomes threaded, that is. At which point, nothing can stop one thread executing the `sprintf` statement, and before the calling function gets to use the filename, another thread overwrites that same buffer by using a separate call to `GetFilenameForNPC`. Or perhaps the level is changing; the first NPC is loaded with the old level name in error before the global variable, `g_LevelName`, gets changed, and the second NPC is loaded with the new level name. Granted, global variables have generally been expelled by the Programming Monks of the Structural Order, but it's not an atypical situation.

This problem can even occur in single-threaded code. The frontend system, for example, will generally only ever run on a single thread, but if it ever uses the `GetFilenameForNPC` function, then it's unwittingly opening itself up to abuse from another thread if that code is not reentrant.

The natural solution is to allocate memory from the heap, but that can be expensive. We could allocate something from the stack, but that causes problems with return codes and limited stack space. The solution (or *a* solution) is to use *cyclic buffers*. Here we have, for example, four separate buffers in which to place the result. We then return one, and move on to the next to store the following result.

```
char *GetFilenameForNPC(int iNPC)
{
static char buff[4][256];
static int curr = 0;
char *pResult;

    pResult = buff[curr++];
    if (curr > 3) {
        curr = 0;
    }

    sprintf(pResult, "GAME_NPC_LEVEL_%s_NPC_%d", g_LevelName, iNPC);
    return pResult;
}
```

The number of buffers should, in the worst-case scenario, be equal to the number of threads present in the system. On an Xbox 2, this would probably involve six buffers (three processors, each with two separate cores). You'll usually have enough memory for this, although in practice, it's very unlikely you'll exceed four buffers in any code, especially when handling files, which is an inherently sequential operation.

CAUTION

If new threads are added in the future, this code might break. This can be countered by asserting the buffer size with `sgxMaxThreads` *or by allocating the memory using frame reclaim.*[8]

You can prepare for the next generation of consoles by adopting thread-safe code early, which provides the added functionality of permitting

```
sgxTrace("First group of NPCs are %s, %s and %s",
    GetFilenameForNPC(0),GetFilenameForNPC(1),GetFilenameForNPC(2));
```

without the usual gotcha.

NOTE

An alternative solution is to pass a suitable buffer into `GetFilenameForNPC`*, thereby avoiding the threading problem at this level.*

Remember to use the special multi-threaded libraries when working with threads. The option for Developer Studio is shown in Figure 4.5.

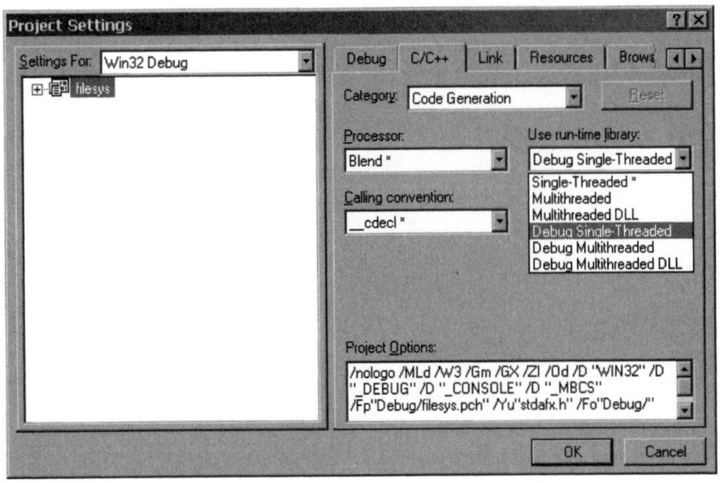

FIGURE 4.5 Using multi-threaded libraries within Microsoft Developer Studio.
Screen shot reprinted by permission from Microsoft Corporation.

Threadsafe Code

This encompasses a wider horizon of ideas than reentrant code, but without reentrant functions, it's almost impossible to write anything that is threadsafe. Here, *threadsafe* means the whole module (which can mean the entire code base) will work without side effects, regardless of which threads are active at any time.

When events happen in sequence, there's usually no problem because we've been using the same programming idiom for years. But when the concept of threading appears, two pieces of apparently unconnected code could execute on separate processors, and in any order. Worse still, they could execute at the same time, and corrupt each other's data or introduce contention. Imagine the scenario shown in Figure 4.6.

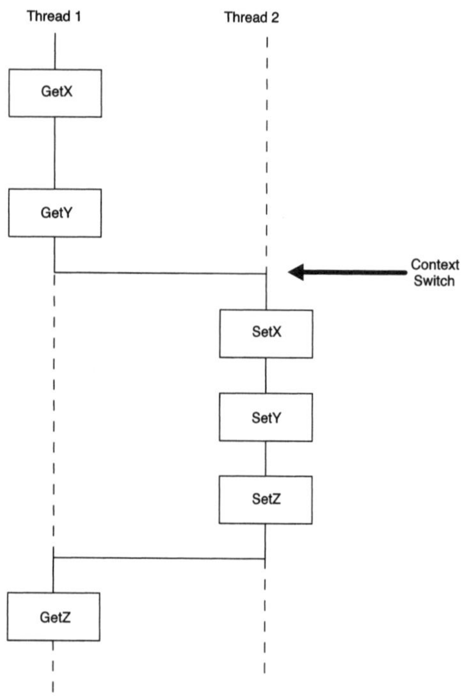

FIGURE 4.6 Data corruption through threads.

Our second function is now working with data that is not only wrong, but corrupt. Incorrect data might cause the NPC to be drawn 5 cm to the left. Corrupt data could introduce null vectors (0,0,0), denormals, infinities, or other such morbidities into the chain where previously they never occurred. This is one of the traditional problems that has no cure, only prevention. We need to indicate to the processor in question that we need exclusive access to a particular piece of data.

Our solution is a *mutex*, which stands for mutually exclusive. It consists of two small function calls that straddle a block of code. The first says "I am doing something important to XYZ, don't let anyone else touch it," while the second says "I have now finished with XYZ." Every function that now wants to use XYZ must also place a mutex around its *critical section* of code. When the first piece of code wants to enter this section, it checks the mutex, notes that it is unlocked, and enters, locking the door behind. When the second piece of code arrives at the mutex, it notes that the mutex is locked. At this point, that thread sits and *spins* in an endless loop waiting until the mutex is unlocked by the other thread.

This requires that the mutex is only used for as short a time as possible because it prevents other threads from executing at maximum efficiency. You should be very careful to ensure that every function releases its captured mutex because deadlocks can occur when two functions have each captured one mutex, and require the mutex that the other function holds in order to continue. This has strong echoes of the principles behind locking scratch memory from Chapter 3, "Memory."

TIP

The memory manager should always be written threadsafe because corruption here can permeate every subsystem in the game.

Great care should also be taken to only use mutexes where necessary, because the locking mechanism can be expensive, especially when communication needs to take place between different chips that consequently utilizes the bus. In some cases, the bus will be monopolized for the duration of such communications, meaning the platform will be unable to continue with any further processing.

TIP

Try not to use mutexes on the critical path as this may idle the chip completely, meaning nothing further will get done until the mutex has been unlocked.

Mutexes are a voluntary technique on behalf of the programmer that prevents conflicting pieces of code from executing; mutexes have no control over the data being protected, nor the means to prevent data from being corrupted by overrunning arrays or forgotten mutexes.

```
// At start of game (platform-specific)
CMutexWinPC g_MutexUsingXYZ;

// During game (general code)

// Inside some critical function
g_MutexUsingXYZ.Capture();
```

```
        x = pMatrix->GetX();
        y = pMatrix->GetY();
        z = pMatrix->GetZ();
    g_MutexUsingXYZ.Release();

    // At end of game (can be implemented with general purpose
    // mutex clean up code)
    g_MutexUsingXYZ.Destroy();
```

`g_MutexUsingXYZ` in the preceding example is a global variable that keeps track of who (if anybody) has claimed the mutex. All truly threaded platforms will contain their own functions and types for handling mutexes. We simply wrapper that in our structure, which can also aid debugging by holding the file and line number of the last captured mutex.

We could also expand this structure to hold engine-specific details about the mutex, such as the time spent spinning waiting for a release, or the memory location of the data itself. This can then be used to implement processor-specific traps on these memory locations to trigger alerts if the locations are accessed without permission.

The implementation of the mutex-locking function must be handled with supreme care, which means using the one that exists for your specific platform. Here's one such abstraction using the *pthreads* library:

```
void CMutexPthread::CMutexPthread()
{
    if (pthread_mutex_init(&m_Mutex, NULL) == 0) {
        //ok
    }
}

void CMutexPthread::Capture(const char *pFile, int line)
    if ( pthread_mutex_lock(&m_Mutex) == 0) {
        m_pCurrentFile = pFile;
        m_CurrentLine = line;
        return;   // success
    }
    // Gulp! Failed
}


void CMutexPthread::Release()
{
    if ( pthread_self() == m_Mutex.owner ) {
```

```
        pthread_mutex_unlock(&m_Mutex);
        m_pCurrentFile = NULL;
    }
}

void CMutexPthread::Destroy()
{
    pthread_mutex_destroy(&m_Mutex);
}
```

The full implementation involves a multilayered abstraction with a common base class so that other platforms can share the *pthread* implementation:

```
class CMutex
{
public:
    virtual void Create()=0;
    virtual void Capture(const char *pFile, size_t line)=0;
    virtual void Release()=0;
    virtual void Destroy()=0;
};

class CMutexPthread : public CMutex  { pthread_mutex_t m_Mutex; }
class CMutexWinPC : public CMutexPthread  { ... }
```

Be warned that a mutex implementation is available that removes all platform dependencies, but it should be avoided because it's stability is impossible to guarantee. Assuming the `m_Mutex` variable in question is volatile,[9] see if you can spot the mistake.

```
void BadMutex::Capture()
{
    while(m_Mutex) {
        /* spin and do nothing until the variable is reset */
    }
    m_Mutex = 1;   // claim mutex for ourselves
}

void BadMutex::Release()
{
    m_Mutex = 0;
}
```

The logic of this code is accurate. It does the same job as our *pthreads* version. However, the problem stems from the likely compiler output that, in pseudo-assembler, would look like this:

```
capture:
   cmp m_Mutex, 0  // assume we have direct addressing
   bne capture
   ld m_Mutex, 1
```

As you can see, a single instruction gap exists between checking the value of `m_Mutex`, and setting it to 1. During this time, it's possible for another thread to note the value of `m_Mutex`, see that it's available, and capture it for itself. Both pieces of code now believe they have exclusive rights, whereas neither do. The OS-specific libraries (which pthreads use) have mutex code that uses special *atomic* instructions, which perform the previous operation in a single step.

This gap of one cycle might not seem like much, but when the code is run many thousands of times during a game, on several different threads, it only needs one cycle to crash the computer, and the laws of averages says that it will happen at some point during development. Murphy's law says it will happen during testing, and it won't happen when you try to debug it.

For the preceding `GetFilenameForNPC` function to be truly effectively, you need to be paranoid and surround the `curr++` line with a mutex.

```
SGX_NPCFilename.Capture();
    pResult = buff[curr++];
    if (curr > 3) {
        curr = 0;
    }
SGX_NPCFilename.Release();
```

An alternative to a mutex is a *semaphore*. This performs the same job as a mutex, but allows more than one piece of code access to the restricted block. How many more is up to you when you set up the semaphore. You can think of a mutex like a binary semaphore, only allowing access to one thread at a time. A multilayered abstraction is consequently possible here, because after we have an implementation for a semaphore, other synchronization objects, such as mutexes, can be implemented by means of a semaphore.

Threads and Singletons

Despite their power and elegance, singletons begin showing signs of strain when used in a threaded environment. For the singleton to be completely threadsafe, every function must avoid static and global variables, but as the singleton is a glorified global variable, this can be very tricky. The first problem occurs when we initially create the singleton:

```
CSingleton *CSingleton::Get()
{
    if (sm_pSingleton == NULL) {
        sm_pSingleton = new CSingleton;
    }

    return sm_pSingleton;
}
```

Should one thread be suspended immediately after the if line, and before the new `CSingleton` object is created, a second thread can arrive, realize that `sm_pSingleton` is `NULL`, and create a second object. This not only creates two objects, but also causes a resource leak because only one memory location exists in which to store the object.

Instead, we need to apply two checks using a technique called `Double-Checked Locking`. This is where `sm_pSingleton` is checked twice; the first caters for those cases where the singleton exists, and is very quick (but flawed). The second uses a mutex to safely create the object without being interrupted.

```
CSingleton *CSingleton::Get()
{
    if (sm_pSingleton == NULL) {
        g_MySingletonMutex.Lock();

        if (sm_pSingleton == NULL) {
            sm_pSingleton = new CSingleton;
        }

        g_MySingletonMutex.Unlock();
    }

    return sm_pSingleton;
}
```

This still has one potential problem in that the `sm_pSingleton` variable, the weak spot in all this work, can be held in a register or not written back to memory immediately. This can be minimized by storing the `sm_pSingleton` variable in a volatile variable.

Because the volatile type can prevent some special compiler optimizations, it's best not to use it in all cases. Instead, create an abstraction for it, which can be removed when threaded code is not required:

```
#define SGX_VOLATILE     volatile
```

The implementation of functions within your singleton should apply the normal rule of multi-threaded development that we've already discussed.

CAUTION

Check your compiler documentation to determine when `volatile` *will perform the job you require of it.*

Naturally, this problem can be avoided in its entirety if all singletons are explicitly initialized before use. This is best achieved by creating each singleton sequentially on a single thread, often within `main`. We look further at singleton patterns in Chapter 7, "System I/O," and cover this idea again in Chapter 11, "The Bits We Forget About."

Thread Communication

Aside from mutexes, most threads need to communicate at some point. This is necessary, but discouraged, because for one thread to send a message, another has to receive it, which introduces a delay into the system. This requires one thread to wait for the other, causing the same problems we saw with mutex communication.

In most cases, threads won't need to communicate between themselves (only to their master) and so this problem is avoided. Where this is not possible, it's best to place the message controller on the main CPU. This can then act as a holding queue for the messages between threads. Because the `main` thread will be doing no real work, it can process and dispatch messages very quickly, removing the latency that would otherwise be present.

The implementation of a message queue is very straightforward, and involves nothing more than a simple mutex around the queue handler.

Callbacks

So far, we've referred to a callback function as one that is intended to trigger new code after a previous event has completed. For most people, the traditional pointer-to-function metaphor will suffice in the cross-platform world, as it does with a single platform. However, when additional processors are involved, it might be necessary to trigger a callback on a specific CPU. This requires some additional work; namely, the replacement of our simple function pointer with a more complex mechanism, such as a class reference.

```
typedef void (*cbFunctionPtr)(tMEMSIZE);

class CCallback {
public:
    cbFunctionPtr       m_pFunction;
    tMEMSIZE            m_Data;
    CScheduler::tCPU    m_CPU;

    CCallback(cbFunctionPtr ptr);
};

CCallback::CCallback(cbFunctionPtr ptr)
{
    m_pFunction = ptr;
    m_Data = 0;
    m_CPU = CScheduler::eAnyCPU;
}
```

This simple extension allows the primary constructor to handle function pointers as normal, while enhanced constructors can accept a specific CPU to process the callback. This can then be passed to the CPU scheduler to dispatch the function accordingly. Naturally, the enumeration of CPUs will have both platform-specific (`eEE`), and generic (`eMainCPU`) names to abstract the details. However, in many cases, this will only occur in platform-specific code.

This is a general technique for handling callback functions, although it will be particularly pertinent when we discuss asynchronous loading in Chapter 5, "Storage." For clarity, however, all other callback examples will use the traditional pointer-to-function method.

Memory Access

We end this section on thread implementation with a warning about memory. It concerns a trick sometimes used in C to reference arrays:

```
tUINT32 my_array[16];
tUINT32 *pCleverArray = &my_array[-1];

    pCleverArray[1] = 0;
```

Here, `pCleverArray[1]` is the first element of `my_array`, and is equivalent to `my_array[0]`. Negative array indices can also be used to make memory-walking algorithms easier. Both should be avoided. Referencing arrays outside their bounds causes undetermined side effects. One platform might work as you expect, while another might not. When threaded code is used, the data referenced by such a pointer could fall outside the memory bounds allowed to that thread, as in Figure 4.7.

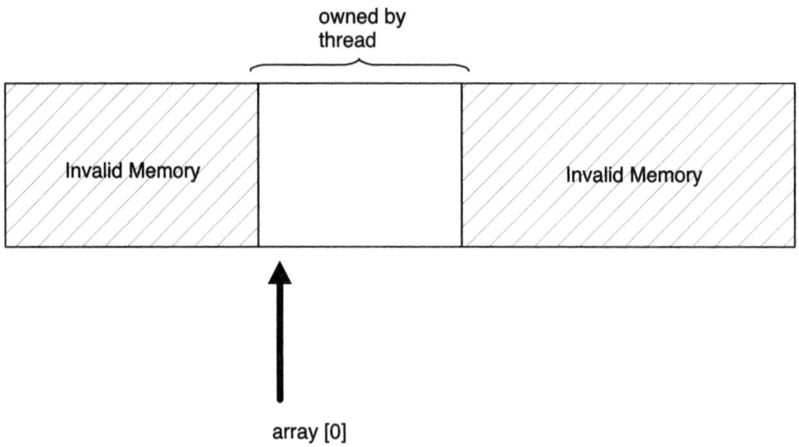

FIGURE 4.7 Memory bound errors across threads.

This is likely to cause an exception and halt the machine. Discovering this type of bug is difficult because its presence depends on the memory location of the data involved. To prevent it from happening, just don't use `-1` as an index.

TIP

Overreaching your allotted memory can manifest problems in other areas, too. Consider code to invalidate a cache that marks the memory from `start` *to* `start+sizeof(struct)`*. This invalidates 1 extra byte of memory. Although this might be considered nothing other than suboptimal, it can (and will) cause hard-to-spot crashes when the cache is part of the hardware on, say, a PS2.*

Task Scheduling

Having now written our game components in a thread-friendly, processor-agnostic fashion, we have the task of combining them into a platform-friendly manner. This is moderately easy, however, no simple cross-platform solution exists. The game needs to be run several times, profiling the performance in all situations to get an idea of how long the various tasks take. This can be represented as fractions of the total time, and employed into a block diagram as shown in Figure 4.8.

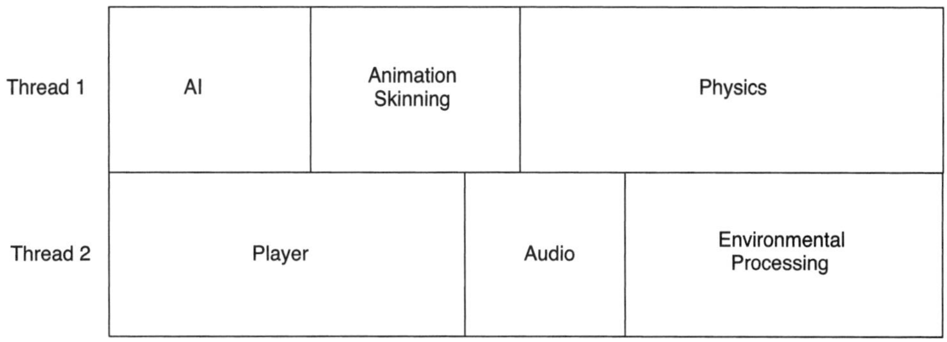

FIGURE 4.8 Combining threads.

To create this diagram, use pieces of cardboard, a pair of scissors, and a large table. Cut longer rectangles for tasks that take longer, and fatter rectangles for those that can run across several processors and shuffle them. The first cards can be placed in slots where the console forces the choice of processor onto you (for example, the VUs on the PlayStation 2). Then, build up the table based on those features that can occupy several processors, followed by those with dependencies. Repeat this for each processor, and then code the rules into your basic module scheduler.

Although a more adaptive solution can be found by writing a more complex scheduler, it makes debugging significantly more difficult because the goalposts move whenever the scheduler reorganizes the order of the tasks. This is something to avoid unless you have significant experience in the field. Also, the static assignment of code to processor limits the amount of thrashing that the processor caches have to do, enabling better performance. This becomes more critical in the hyperthreading environment where careful cache use is vital to good performance.

Determinism

Although it's essential that most of your engine components are threaded, for the most part your gameplay code will operate as a single thread. Those parts that do run concurrently will either be engine components, or be fairly simple and have little or nothing to do with each other. This is not due to a technical problem, but a staffing one. The adoption of the techniques discussed previously will be slow. Writing any form of threadsafe and reentrant code is difficult, and writing a real-time application such as a game is more so, because the processing order for the objects will no longer be predictable. Threads might cause function A to be followed by B during one frame, while the other 59 frames have B running before A. Even after locking variables with mutexes, other problems can still occur. You'll need a highly skilled programmer with a lot of time to track down subtle ordering bugs that could occur in such circumstances.

Consider this scenario: If your player has 100 health and is about to lose 10 points from a bullet, and 10% from an explosion, what will his final health value be? If the health is always modified in the same order, that as given here, then the answer will be 81—100 - 10 = 90, 90 - (10% of 90) = 81. But if each operation was done in a separate thread where the execution order was reversed, the result would be 80—100 - (10% of 100) = 90, 90 - 10 = 80. Any game player who's survived half a level on 1 point of health will tell you that this is a matter of life and death—literally.

The question that is usually leveled is one of game design, not implementation, because these particular problems cannot be solved at the low level of coding, memory locking, and so on. Every platform reacts differently, and to make them appear otherwise is foolish. Adopting a high-level approach, and changing the way your player damage code works is the better solution. And that solution is to make those gameplay-critical components execute consecutively in a single thread.

Of course, the game designer might determine that, in reality, this difference is not important and the randomness of the damage factor will hide any such discrepancies. That's their call. Provided we know the problem, and the ramifications of the solution, we can code safely for all platforms.

AVOIDING THE WHOLE PROBLEM

If, after following all the guidelines here, your code is too slow, then you have nothing left to do but repeat the cycle of profile and optimize. However, we can issue some facetious advice on how to make your game run consistently at 60 fps.

From day one, never let the game run slower than 60fps—on any platform.

If your first level (consisting of one NPC in an empty room) runs at 60 fps, you have a perfect start. From then until the end of the project, you should continually check the frame rate. Do this every day, week, or month. Do it automatically with tools. Do it by playing the game. As soon as the frame rate drops on any of the platforms, find out why. Are there too many NPCs onscreen? Is the geometry too complex? Are the effects too expensive? You should then endeavor to fix the problem before work continues. This is very important on consoles with a high level of granularity with respect to frame rates because under 60 fps, some consoles—notably the PlayStation 2—will not render at 59 fps. They drop to the next fraction, which is 30 fps. From here, people will think it still looks okay and they'll not notice any further performance drop until the game hits 29 fps. At which point, the ship is sunk as the screen updates at a pitiful 20 fps.

NOTE

Nothing is particularly bad about a game at 30 fps on most consoles. However, continually switching between 30 and 60 is to be avoided at all costs, so you might want to lock the frame rate to 30 fps until you've had several frames running at 1/60th second, and can be sure you'll maintain 60 next time around.

The same is true of memory, of course. Keep checking it. Development kits usually ship with extra memory to hold the symbol table, and extra debugging information. Don't become complacent about this RAM. It's on loan. You have to give it back on the consumer model. Remember this if you're developing on the cutting edge.

If you're working with the next generation consoles and don't yet have hardware, but are using a similarly spec'd PC,[10] make sure your machine emulates the memory footprint accurately. Use a custom memory manager and massage the numbers if necessary to get an accurate reflection of your game. There's little worse than getting your game to run on a console, only to find your memory estimates are 2 MB out, and not one level will fit.

Naturally, this is easy to say in retrospect with a finished engine, but you can still maintain a good frame rate without a finished engine, or even hardware. One such technique is called *state commit*. This is where the game runs entirely at its own pace. Whenever a discrete amount of processing has occurred—an AI character has been updated for example—the AI commits all its state data into the system, making this information public. The AI code then continues processing using its own private copy of data until it's in a suitably state to commit again. In this way, the engine can take a snapshot at any time and it will have a completely consistent game state, enabling it to hit 60 fps all the time. The implementation for this is tricky because determining suitable commit points is difficult, and finding the extra memory for these state commits can be expensive.

A simpler technique is to employ the same profiling and monitoring techniques you've seen earlier, so you can spot when the AI uses more than its allotted processing time. Although not a true reflection *of the console*, it's a good reflection *of the code*, and that's cross-platform.

ENDNOTES

1. The multimedia timer, `timeGetTime`, has millisecond accuracy and resolution, but has been shown to be less accurate with later OSs, such as Windows 2000. `QueryPerformanceFrequency` directly references the clock on the chip, and is (sort of) OS-independent and a much better choice for PC-

based development. The "chip" in question refers to any Pentium® or AMD®-based processor. Curious readers may care to consider RDTSC, the Pentium instruction that stands for "Real Time Stamp Counter."

2. This is much the same reason most electronic engineers talk about microfarads, even though the standard unit of capacitance is the farad.
3. In the real world, visual and auditory events are never synchronized because the speed of light and the speed of sound are significantly different. An explosion 330 meters away, for example, will be heard 1 second after it becomes visible. Although realistic, this conflicts with the player's perception of reality and so is rarely employed in games or films.
4. To a certain extent, the Xbox is also a multiprocessor system, but very few people program it as such.
5. Although the processing might require a custom chip in some cases, perhaps to do hardware lighting, the library functions called from within that code will be general purpose, and the platform-specific detail abstracted away.
6. If we have three processors, each with two cores, we would want to distinguish between all six of these logical processors when generating the threads. Only when assigning code to them would the physical processor be a concern because that's when the caches need careful consideration, as we mentioned with hyper-threading.
7. Except you cannot call it twice before a sequence point.
8. Frame reclaim is where a block of memory is put aside solely for transient allocations made during a frame. Allocations from this block are made as normal, and last until the end of the current frame. At which point, the entire block is released *en masse* (like the game memory we saw in Chapter 3) and reused for the next frame.
9. This keyword forces the compiler to refetch the value of a variable whenever it's used, preventing it from being held in a register and consequently not getting updated if the memory location changes. Its primary use was in memory-mapped devices.
10. Before the original Xbox development kits were available, Microsoft was rumored to have shipped standard PCs with an equivalent graphics card, sound card, and processor. Although it's possible to adopt this technique on other consoles, it can be difficult to measure the actual performance of an unknown processor using only its clock speed as a guide.

5 Storage

In This Chapter

- The Four Corners of Storage
- The Problems
- The Data Conversion Process
- Designing a Filesystem
- Filesystem Implementation
- Handling Physical Devices
- Creating Back Doors

THE FOUR CORNERS OF STORAGE

A cross-platform storage system has four interconnected components that all have a symbiotic relationship with one another:

Data: The individual bytes containing a game resource asset, such as a texture or character mesh. This can include platform-specific data and generic data.

File: The means of packaging the game asset. It includes parameters about the data as a whole, such as its size.

Filesystem: The manner in which files are made available to the game and presented to the programmer. It handles the directory structure, and controls the external properties of a file, such as its name.

Hardware: The physical media that stores the data, such as a disc, memory card, or even the RAM.

These four sections are roughly analogous to the sections within this chapter. We start by looking at the raw game data to find out how to handle it effectively for the filesystem and hardware, while maintaining a level of platform independence.

Next, we'll look at the filesystem in general, including how to abstract the hardware away from the end user. Finally, we'll study the hardware to determine how it affects us.

Throughout this chapter, we'll use the abstract notion of a file. It's no different from a file you would use with any standard OS. Nor is the class, CSGXFile, any different from what you would expect to find in any standard API. So although we'll use this class throughout the chapter, no particular functionality is implied. The class is there primarily as a placeholder until we describe the filesystem in which it resides.

THE PROBLEMS

While data remains in memory, its format doesn't change. The problems with the data's endian and size are all but over after they're residing in RAM. When dealing with a single platform game, there's no problem with getting that data into memory, as any data we write out will be read back using the same set of library functions, running on the same machine. All file operations will work transparently without any extra work on our part, and either the compiler, the library, or both will shield us from any platform-specific quirks (such as alignment issues). These issues suddenly emerge when opened up to a cross-platform environment.

The problems originate from the practice of data-driven development. In this case, doing something "the right way," increases our workload. In a data-driven environment, every resource and step of game logic is not coded into the application, but held externally and processed in an ad hoc basis. In addition to creating a greater flexibility, it minimizes the size of the executable, and provides a faster turnaround during development.

Consider a simple piece of OpenGL code. The examples given in most books and magazine articles demonstrate using OpenGL by creating an array of vertices and faces that is not dissimilar to this:

```
sgxVector VertexList[] = {
    { -1,  1, -1, },
    {  1,  1, -1, },
    {  1,  1,  1, },
```

```
    { -1,  1,  1, },
    { -1, -1, -1, },
    {  1, -1, -1, },
    {  1, -1,  1, },
    { -1, -1,  1, },
};

sgxQuadFace FaceList[] = {
    { 0, 1, 2, 3, },    // top
    { 4, 5, 6, 7, },    // bottom
    { 0, 1, 5, 4, },    // back
    { 3, 2, 6, 7, },    // front
    { 0, 4, 7, 3, },    // left
    { 1, 5, 6, 2, },    // right
};

void DrawCube()
{
    glEnableClientState(GL_VERTEX_ARRAY);
    glVertexPointer(3, GL_FLOAT, 0, (void *)VertexList);

    for(int i=0;i<6;i++)
    {
        glBegin(GL_LINE_LOOP);
            glArrayElement( FaceList[i].v1 );
            glArrayElement( FaceList[i].v2 );
            glArrayElement( FaceList[i].v3 );
            glArrayElement( FaceList[i].v4 );
        glEnd();
    }
}

void DrawScene(void)
{
    glClearColor (0.8, 0.8, 0.8, 0.0);
    glClear(GL_COLOR_BUFFER_BIT | GL_DEPTH_BUFFER_BIT);

    glMatrixMode(GL_PROJECTION);
    glLoadIdentity();
    gluPerspective(60, 1/1, 0,1000);
    gluLookAt(0,0,250, 50,0,0, 0.0, 0.0, 1.0);

    glMatrixMode(GL_MODELVIEW);
    DrawCube();
```

```
    glutSwapBuffers();
}

int main(int argc, char *argv[])
{
  glutInit(&argc, argv);
  glutInitDisplayMode (GLUT_DOUBLE | GLUT_DEPTH);
  glutInitWindowSize (500, 500);
  glutInitWindowPosition (100, 100);
  glutCreateWindow (argv[0]);

  glDepthFunc(GL_LEQUAL);
  glEnable(GL_DEPTH_TEST);

  glutDisplayFunc(DrawScene);

  glutMainLoop();

  return EXIT_SUCCESS;
}
```

Sample code such as this compiles, runs, and functions in exactly the same way on any GL-compatible platform you can find. However, the data involved never leaves the application. Nor does any external data enter it. As we've mentioned, these transitions cause the problems, and any significant difference in hardware or OS will cause the program to exhibit less than perfect results.

Some example code *will* demonstrate a data-driven approach, and might be considered a cross-platform solution. This might involve loading an ASCII text file containing the array data that we had hardcoded in our previous example. This would consist of the same list of points and faces, and would be loaded (probably through `fgets`) into memory, before being parsed into arrays. Not even this is completely cross-platform because the filename might be case-sensitive on certain machines, and if subdirectories are used, there's also the problem with differences between filenames such as *images/texture1.png* and *images\texture1.png*. A cross-platform library is a good first move, but not an all-encompassing game plan.

With these problems waiting to trip you up within the first couple of steps, the reasons for abstracting the data storage mechanism are obvious. In a simple case, we could wrapper the standard library calls (such as `fopen` and `fread`), modify the directory slashes (from `/` to `\`, or vice versa), and change case according to platform. But more than this, we'll also need to prepare the data specifically for the platform, too. Consider our OpenGL example again. Our basic quad requires 64 bytes in memory. If that were stored in plain ASCII on disc, it would occupy about 120 bytes (depending on the precision[1] used). If our game used recognizable creatures instead of amorphous floating cubes, we could be looking at 6,000 polygons apiece. Even after combining the common edges, this could still amount to 240 KB of memory for a binary version, and more than 480 KB for an ASCII version. And that's not counting the processing time to parse the text file or build the arrays. So, we definitely need to use platform-specific resources in our game. We can provide that data in two ways:

- Use identical data for all platforms, and convert it upon load.
- Use platform-specific data, and convert offline before loading.

Either solution will work, and both have been employed in shipped games from the past few years. However, when given a choice, the second option is preferable, and will become the norm in the future.

At first glance, this might appear counterintuitive, especially given the title of this book. We have looked at several ways of keeping data identical across platforms, and have discovered several metaphors and patterns for writing adaptive code. So much so that a convert-on-load approach would appear to be the simplest solution. Indeed, the creation of platform-specific data would appear to *add* problems because of the increased turn-around as both export and import portions of the code must be developed and tested in tandem and seamlessly combined.

There are several reasons for creating platform-specific data:

- Decreasing load time
- Using different data
- Using similar data
- Working with different discs

Decreasing Load Time

Load time depends on the effort you put into the formatting: are you just preswapping individual data elements, or are you prebuilding a complete 20 MB chunk of level data? At the very least, the level data should be preswapped; otherwise, every byte has to be examined, swapped, and, in some cases, swapped back again, before the code can continue.

Using Different Data

Probably, and almost definitely, each platform will use a different resource for the same object to cope with the chasm between memory footprints. The most obvious example is with textures. The PS2, for example, makes thorough use of 4-bit textures. These images have been created automatically by tools such as Photoshop®, the GIMP™, or ImageStudio™ to achieve the best results possible with 16 colors. The eye of a human artist then is required to check them for unsightly dithering artifacts and decide whether a new texture should be explicitly created and used instead.

Using Similar Data

In addition to the wholesale changes made to the data resources, there will also be some minor additions made for specific platforms. Again, we draw examples from the PS2 arena where the standard audio format, VAG, does not include the sample duration. Even though this can be approximated from the number of samples and the average compression ratio, an accurate value needs to be stored alongside the data to enable features such as "notify me when you've finished" to work correctly. These features would work naturally on platforms using formats such as WAV, which already include this data.

Working with Different Discs

Although every current console supports a minimum of 650 MB disc space (which may not even be contiguous), many game developers find that's not enough and require compression, or resort to larger formats such as DVD. The storage space differs wildly as each manufacturer designs its console to different ideals. Most adopt a conventional DVD disc, and support a total of 4.7 GB. Nintendo, on the other hand, seeks to use its own proprietary formats, enforcing a different (and arbitrary) 1.5 GB storage limit.

Being able to shoehorn your game data into this available space can be quite a task. Squashing the data footprint may occur naturally by using different data formats, using file-level compression, or deploying alternative storage methods. For example, what was held on the disc as red book audio, might now be compressed into MP3 or Ogg Vorbis format, and streamed from the disc as data instead. Disc space is one of the unavoidable hard limits (along with processor power). In such cases, the resultant code will need to be changed, but (as we'll see in Chapter 8, "The Audio System") the underlying storage format should not affect the game programmer.

THE DATA CONVERSION PROCESS

Naturally, there's a lot to think about when building a platform-specific format for your data. At the start of the development cycle, you can forget about most of it, as you would normally begin by converting the data on the target machine itself. This is a practical consideration that enables programmers to get resources into the game much quicker in the short term, and limits the number, and location, of potential problems. After the data can be handled effectively on the target machine, and the programmer has a better understanding of the console, the conversion process can be honed more efficiently offline, especially given that the processor power of the desktop PC (or artwork-conversion server) will invariably dwarf the games console. Naturally, this has a greater resonance when working on the engine side than the game side.

The implementation of these conversion routines should be as simple as possible, and avoid the use of any platform-dependent functions, as this will impede its removal from the game code, and increase the development time when such code has to be rewritten in order to be placed into the tool chain at a later date.

Changing the data format in this way need not break backward compatibility, however, because we'll build our data so that it is upgradeable—we'll show an example of versioning later in this chapter. A compatibility method must exist, regardless of which one, as new formats and options will be added throughout the life of the data, and we need to avoid continuous code and data rebuilds.

All conversion methods have three components: the source (or raw) data, the conversion process, and the destination (cooked) data. In our case, the conversion process will have several variations—one for each platform—and a base class. The base class will hold the generic resource data that exists on all platforms, and might appear like this:

```
class CSGXGameMesh {
    sgxString       m_Filename;
    tUINT32         m_ReferenceCount;
    CPlatformMesh  *m_pData;
};
```

From here, we can derive new classes for each platform, and one special one for the generic data. This ensures that unnecessary data isn't kept within those classes that do not need it.

You can then create the individual platform-oriented classes using the following implementation rules:

- The in-game structure must be as fast as possible. This means that after conversion, the in-game structure will require minimal *patching up* (that is, rewriting pointers).
- The in-game structure must be as small as possible.
- All conversion code must be modular so it can be removed from the game, and the *cooking* can be done externally.

- Ultimately, conversion should only occur within the tool chain (usually on a PC), so speed here isn't important.

Adopting the class as shown previously, we can reference `CSGXGameMesh` throughout the code in a general-purpose fashion. No function, outside of the game engine, ever needs to understand the platform-specific data because it's unable to do anything with it. Any generic code that requires information about the mesh (such as a polygon count for handling level of detail) can query virtual methods to retrieve it.

The load procedure, in its simplest form, can handle raw and precooked data with a simple header preceding the main data:

```
void
CGameMesh::Load(CSGXFile &File)
{
tINT16 converted;

    File >> converted;
    File >> m_Filename;   // common data

    if (converted == 0) { // this is an unconverted mesh
        CGenericMesh *pData = LoadMeshData(File);
        m_pData = new CPlatformMesh;
        ConvertMeshData(m_pData, pData);
        delete pData;
    } else if (converted == 1) { // this is fully compliant mesh
        m_pData = LoadMeshData(File);
    }
}
```

The conversion (a.k.a. data munging) routine usually consists of simple functions, copying data from one place to another, and depends entirely on the data formats you are using. There's no great mystery to the functions, but they do require patience, as errors can be subtle. After the conversion routine has been proven to work, it can be moved offline into the tool chain very easily. At which time, the load routine simplifies to a single line:

```
    m_pData = LoadMeshData(File);
```

This creates a workable import/export facility for our game. It may work across several platforms, but not all of them. And it certainly isn't upgradeable for new mesh features or functionality. To do that, we need to extend the generic format using a technique called serialization.

Serialization

The natural instinct when it comes to packaging data is to store everything in one large file of cooked data, instead of several small files. By everything, we mean *everything*; the textures, animations, level vertices, and much more. This means that the data will be stored on consecutive disc sectors, which reduces the seek time between each successive file load. This time is significant on DVD- and CD-based media.

NOTE *Some filesystems have a limit on the maximum size of any individual file. To be safe, any size that doesn't fit in a signed integer is probably too big. The Win32 API gives details on its solution to the 32-bit limit, but it's best to avoid it altogether if possible.*

Using a single file also reduces the effective size of the whole data, because a 1 KB file can occupy 8 KB of disc space. The amount of wasted space varies between disc formats because of the disc's *cluster size.* Each cluster on a disc can only hold one file, or one part of a single file. You cannot store two files in a single cluster. Therefore, any file smaller than the cluster size will waste space. This example file would waste 7 KB of disc space.

In return for saving disc space, there is an additional expense with the new code that we must develop to create a combined block. After all, every element inside the raw block needs to be extracted and handled individually before saving a cooked version. Datatypes, for example, need to be swapped when moving between Big and Little Endian machines, and some data will be ignored on particular platforms. The save routine could consist of various export functions, such as this:

```
void
ExportVerticesToGamecube(const CSGXFile& File,
    tUINT32 iNumVertices, sgxVector3 *pVert)
{
tUINT32 iTemp;

    iTemp = sgxSwap32(iNumVertices);
    File.Write(&iTemp, sizeof(iTemp));

    for(i=0;i<iNumVertices;i++) {
        sgxVector3 v = pVert[i];
        sgxSwapVertex(v);
        File.Write(&v, sizeof(v));
    }
}
```

This saves out a small compact version of the data, both in terms of code size and volume of data on disc. Even when we consider a second export function to handle nonswapped data, and a second `ImportVertices` function, the code footprint will still be fairly minimal.

Unfortunately, this provides no scope for debugging. One block of raw data will look very much like another. There is no clue whether the data under the current pointer is 8, 16, or 32 bits wide. Exporting more complex types, such as STL `maps`, requires extra work, but is still obscured by appearing as streams of raw binary data.

Maintenance is also a problem, as there isn't any simple way to keep both `Import` and `Export` functions in sync. The addition of another element in the `sgxVector3` structure (perhaps to add vertex coloring) will break the exporter, the importer, or both (and probably in a way that isn't obvious).

We might be able to afford the disc space to write out all this data in plain ASCII (perhaps using XML), however, not only are these files 50-500% larger, but also they require significant extra processing to parse the text because we've resorted to raw data—not cooked. We should always be considering binary files to keep the load times to a minimum[2] because although the addition of binary metadata still adds an overhead to the total size, the processing overhead will be much lower, and it will be easier to remove for the final release build.

To handle cooked binary files, we'll employ a technique called *serialization*, which includes metadata for each element. This metadata includes the element's type and size, and we can add this at all levels of the import/export cycle, right down to the individual integers. In doing so, we're no longer handling binary files, as would be handled by the traditional `CSGXFile`, but we're creating our own structure within the file, in the same way that other programs create their own file formats on disc. Although we could extend the `CSGXFile` class to include metadata methods to handle the serialization, a new class will isolate the base file underneath, allowing us to specify and change the serialization format as time progresses and platform modifications dictate.

```
class CSerializeFile
{
    // ... other stuff ...
    CFile    *m_pFile;
    // ... other stuff ...
}
```

Let's begin with some basic file-handling routines. First, the save code:

```
CSGXSerializeFile&
operator<<(CSGXSerializeFile& File, tUINT32 &val)
```

```
{
    sgxAssert(IsSaving());
    File.m_pFile->WriteString("int32");
    File.m_pFile->WriteConstant(sizeof(val));
    File.m_pFile->Write(&val, sizeof(val));
    return *this;
}
```

And then an equivalent load routine:

```
CSGXSerializeFile&
operator>>(CSGXSerializeFile& File, tUINT32 &val)
{
    sgxAssert(IsLoading());
    sgxString str;
    tUINT32 size;

    File.m_pFile->ReadString(str);
    sgxAssert(strcmp(str, "int32")==0);

    File.m_pFile->ReadConstant(size);
    sgxAssert(size==sizeof(tUINT32));

    File.m_pFile->Read(&val, sizeof(val));
    return *this;
}
```

This has two obvious problems. The first is that a lot of extraneous information is included that we need to remove from production builds, and there's no easy way to do it. Second, a lot of custom code must be written for each type. As the number of classes grow, this will become very difficult to maintain. Let's consider these points in order.

Debug Levels

We have two options for handling this, depending on how flexible we need the debug information to be. Will we, for example, need to load debug data in the release version? Or vice versa? And, perhaps more importantly, will we need it at this low level?

The answer is usually no. Loading and saving individual integers only becomes a problem during initial development, and in very rare cases afterwards. All other file problems can normally be detected at a much higher level when, for example, the `CPlayer` class tries to load the data for a `CNonPlayerCharacter`. We can therefore implement two instances of `operator>>` by switching in a low-level debug macro.

```
#define SGX_FILE_LOWLEVEL_DEBUG   1
//...
CSGXSerializeFile&
operator<<(CSGXSerializeFile& File, tUINT32 &val)
{
    sgxAssert(IsSaving());
#if SGX_FILE_LOWLEVEL_DEBUG==1
    File.m_pFile->WriteString("int32");
    File.m_pFile->WriteConstant(sizeof(val));
#endif
    File.m_pFile->Write(&val, sizeof(val));
    return *this;
}
```

If you need greater control over the debug information during runtime, it's easy to add a control element to the `CSGXSerializeFile` class that will add or remove this information on request. You then simply add a file header using the `CSGXSerializeFile` constructor indicating whether this file *in its entirety* has debug information, and if so, how much. For fine-grain control, you can add this header to specific classes (for example, the scene graph) and change debug level midway through loading or saving. This also eradicates the turn-around time involved in recompiling the source.

Limiting Maintenance Code

We can cut the amount of extra work required by using two features of the C++ language: *Run-Time Type Information* (RTTI) and *templates*. Those still using C can achieve a similar effect with:

```
File.m_pFile->SaveConstant(sizeof(val));
```

Optionally, you might also want to include a text string (such as ">>") to indicate the demarcation between types.

RTTI is a way to determine the actual type of a variable while the program is running. It exists on all compliant compilers, although it might need to be turned on in the compiler options as shown in Figure 5.1.

RTTI works by storing small pieces of metadata—that can be understood by the type library—alongside the variable. If this idea seems familiar, that's because RTTI has done all the work we would have had to do to change `int32` into something more general.

To use RTTI, we need to include `typeinfo.h`, and use the `type_info` class:

```
CSGXSerializeFile&
operator<<(CSGXSerializeFile& File, tUINT32 &val)
{
    sgxAssert(IsSaving());
    File.m_pFile->WriteString(typeid(val).name());
    File.m_pFile->WriteConstant(sizeof(val));
    File.m_pFile->Write(&val, sizeof(val));
    return *this;
}
```

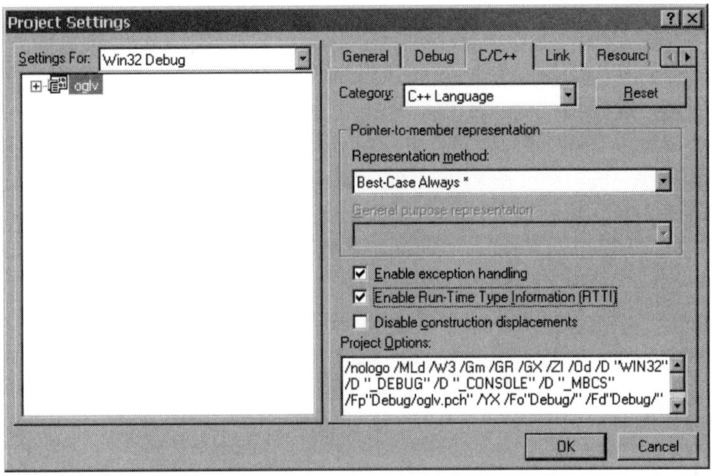

FIGURE 5.1 Enabling RTTI in Microsoft Developer Studio.
(Screen shot reprinted by permission from Microsoft Corporation.)

CAUTION

Although `type_info::name` *is always a string, the standard doesn't indicate which string it should be. The result is not* persistent, *and it can even vary during the course of a program. We can therefore only use this information as a debugging tool to indicate to a human which type follows. Consequently, we cannot trigger assertions on faulty datatypes as reliably across platforms as we could if we had programmed the strings manually. The size of the type is still available although not as foolproof, but still suitable for the low-level driver.*

We have now eliminated all our type-specific information, enabling us to replace each function with a single template:

```
template<class T>
CSGXSerializeFile&
operator<<(CSGXSerializeFile& File, T &val)
{
    sgxAssert(IsSaving());
    File.m_pFile->WriteString(typeid(val).name());
    File.m_pFile->WriteConstant(sizeof(val));
    File.m_pFile->Write(&val, sizeof(val));
    return *this;
}
```

CAUTION

Each class has its own RTTI data, while each instance of that class has a pointer to it in much the same way as the `vtable` *works. In fact, compilers usually implement RTTI as another entry in the* `vtable`. *What this means (and the language specification bears this out) is that we're only guaranteed accurate RTTI information if at least one virtual function is within the class because that is the trigger for creating a* `vtable` *in the first place.*

Now that we're able to save information to disc, we have to make sure that the information can be understood and correctly parsed by the game. Having unified the export code into a single template, we've lost the ability to use different functions for endian swapping. This is vital functionality we definitely need to get back.

Endian Issues

Just looking at the functions used to swap 32 bits of information from one endian to another (Chapter 3, "Memory") should illustrate how expensive it is to process. If your engine loader has to swap every piece of data as it is read in from the disc, your load time will increase dramatically. To combat this, we'll adopt the (more than) reasonable approach that all data will be saved in the same format as the engine intends to use it. That is, all data swapping will take place in the exporter.

Because of all the groundwork we've done previously with the overloaded `operator<<`, we know that each type will be written out individually, but the template hides certain details from us, and it requires some messy code to determine which `sgxEndianSwap` function needs to be used with which `type_info`.

Instead, we can replace the rather impersonal `write (&var, sizeof(var))` code with an overloaded operator, and add the endian-swapping functionality to our `CSGXFile` class. This overload tells us what type we're dealing with and prevents mistakes with mistyped arguments being passed to `Write`. If the type in question has no overloaded operator, we'll have to create one, but because that's a compile-time problem, we'll learn about our omission quickly.

```
CSGXFile&
CSGXFile::operator<<(tUINT32 &val)
{
    sgxAssert(IsSaving());

    tUINT32 swp = val;

    if (m_bSwapEndian) {
        swp = sgxEndianSwap32(swp);
    }

    Write((tBYTE *)&swp, sizeof(swp));

    return *this;
}

CSGXFile&
CSGXFile::operator>>(tUINT32 &val)
{
    sgxAssert(IsLoading());

    Read((tBYTE *)&val, sizeof(val));

    if (m_bSwapEndian) {
        val = sgxEndianSwap32(val);
    }

    return *this;
}
```

From here, we can then add a method to both the `CSGXSerializeFile` and `CSGXFile` classes to indicate whether the data should be swapped, or not.

```
void
CSGXFile::SetTargetPlatform(CHardwarePlatform *pPlatform)
{
    CHardwarePlatform *pCurrent = CHardwarePlatform::Get();

    if (pCurrent->GetEndian() != pPlatform->GetEndian()) {
        m_bSwapEndian = TRUE;
    } else {
        m_bSwapEndian = FALSE;
    }
}
```

This member function will be invoked after the file is created (or opened for reading), and the `m_bSwapEndian` property is then used with every invocation of `operator<<` or `operator>>` as part of the `file` class.

Unfortunately, this does involve a little extra work. The work's not hard or complex, but every type in the game needs to undergo this process. Whereas previously the save code would have been templated or macro-ized, we now have to break out each instance into its own explicit function, and swap the data manually. A potentially hopeless scenario has been avoided, however, by using the function-overloading capabilities, so we know that every type will be correctly saved and swapped. The mismatched types that were so prevalent with `fprintf` are consigned to the past.

The C language doesn't actually allow you to create new types,[3] so the amount of work for this should take no more than an hour (less if you copy the versions we've provided for you). Every type, user-defined or not, can only constitute one or more of the following:

- `char`
- `short`
- `int`
- `long`
- `float`
- `double`

Single bytes (whether alone or as strings) do not need swapping, so the code remains unfettered by endian-swapping macros. The types known as `short`, `int`, and `long`, already have their macros, and are easy to integrate with `CSGXFile`. Doubles are, or at least *should* be, unused, because of the processing hit they take on some platforms. Although there is no difference between signed and unsigned types, we still need an appropriate function for the overload. In fact, the only gotcha is likely to be `floats`. In this case, we need to pretend the 4 bytes representing our number is, in fact, an integer and can be swapped as one. This requires a simple bitwise copy from one memory address to another.

```
CSGXFile& CSGXFile::operator<<(tREAL32 &val)
{
    sgxAssert(IsSaving());

    float swp = val;

    if (m_bSwapEndian) {
        register tUINT32 t = *(tUINT32 *)&swp;
```

```
        *(tUINT32 *)&swp = sgxEndianSwap32(t);
    }

    Write((tBYTE *)&swp, sizeof(swp));

    return *this;
}

CSGXFile& CSGXFile::operator>>(tREAL32 &val)
{
    sgxAssert(IsLoading());

    Read((tBYTE *)&val, sizeof(val));

    if (m_bSwapEndian) {
        register tUINT32 t = *(tUINT32 *)&val;

        *(tUINT32 *)&val = sgxEndianSwap32(t);
    }

    return *this;
}
```

Unifying Load and Save

So far, we've provided operator overloads for both load and save. Although this isolates the low-level file handling away from the objects that use them, it features heavy redundancy by forcing us to have two separate, near-identical, functions. Maintaining such code is a breeding ground for platform-specific problems. It's better to have a single control function that can invoke either the load *or* save code, which is what this simple template does:

```
template<class T>
CSGXSerializeFile&
CAAPI operator|(CSGXSerializeFile& File, T& var)
{
    if (File.IsSaving()) {
        return File << var;
    }
    else if (File.IsLoading()) {
        return File >> var;
    }
    return File;
}
```

The implementation, as you can see, is straightforward. Note that we've opted to overload `operator|` to provide this functionality. This is another Unix throwback, because the bar symbol (`|`) means *pipe*, which provides a method to send data between files and processes. Users of the Boost library will probably have noticed similarities by now, and our avoidance of `operator&`.

CAUTION

This particular implementation is not const-safe because the unified `operator|` *only requires the* `const` *qualifier in one step— the save. None of the* `operator<<` *functions in this chapter used* `const` *for that very reason. In the real world, you can use* `const` *and* `const_cast<T &>(var)`, *but that would just clutter the example.*

We can then invoke the serialization code with a common function such as:

```
void
CEngine::SerializeVertices(CSerializeFile& File)
{
    File | m_iNumVertices;

    if (File.IsLoading()) {
        m_pVert = new sgxVector3[m_iNumVertices];
    }

    for(tUINT32 i=0;i<m_iNumVertices;i++) {
        File | m_pVert[i];
    }
}
```

Note the use of our templated `operator|` to handle all datatypes without explicit code. This is an improvement. Also, note the rather ugly `if (File.IsLoading())` in the middle of the code. This is *not* an improvement.

In its present form of "count and pointer," there's no easy way to unify both halves of the storage equation, as the loader always needs to allocate memory for the new data. However, the method we've employed isn't particularly attractive anyway because we have two separate pieces of information (the data and a description of its size) to describe one concept (some vertices). Every item we save needs to be *self-describing*. In the same way that our RTTI code described the size and format of the data that was to follow, our vertices should describe how many there are, and in what format.

At first glance, this seems to imply another class containing both elements. However, that would still suffer from the same problem—a special case to allocate memory when loading. What we need is a way to move the allocation code out of the general class handlers and into the loading routines. A quick look at the operator>> code, however, indicates that we need to know specific details about the class that's calling it to determine the number of elements. This is simply moving the problem from one function to another.

The problem stems from the simple fact that the data format is split in two halves, so we need to combine them. The way to accomplish this is by using STL—specifically, an STL vector of sgxVector3s. By creating an operator<< for an STL vector *as a whole*, we can export its size and data in one function. Then, by implementing this as a template, we have no direct involvement with any specific class, just the vector container. Provided all such classes are derived from a common base (for example, CSerializeable), we have a catch-all should we need to use virtual methods to handle any specifics within a particular class.

```
class CSGXSerializeable{}
class CSGXSerialVector : public CSGXSerializeable{}

// Saving code
template<typename T>
CSGXFile&
operator<<(CSGXFile& File, sgxVector<T>& val)
{
    tUINT32 size = (tUINT32)val.size();

    File << size;
    for (sgxVector<T>::iterator it=val.begin(); it!=val.end(); ++it){
        File << *it;
    }
    return File;
}

// Loading code
template<typename T>
CSGXFile&
operator>>(CSGXFile& File, sgxVector<T>& val)
{
tUINT32 size;

    File >> size;
    val.clear();
    val.reserve(size);

    for (tUINT32 i = 0; i < size; i++) {
        sgxVector<T>::iterator it = val.insert(val.end(), T());
        File >> *it;
    }
```

```
        return File;
    }
```

CAUTION

Notice that we still use the overloaded `operator<<` *to perform the writing, not* `WriteRaw`, *because the data inside the vector may not be a primitive (such as* `int`*), and still need to be swapped. Using* `operator<<` *causes it to be done automatically.*

Remember that all STL containers engaged by your engine will also need an equivalent treatment. Meaning, you might need handlers for `vectors`, `sets`, `maps`, `deques`, and `lists`, if they're used. We've written these functions as part of `CSGXFile` instead of `CSGXSerialize` to give them the maximum exposure within the game.

CAUTION

Smart pointers are sometimes smarter than the average compiler as it's possible that the compiler will not find a correct version of the `operator |` *when one is in use. With these compilers, an explicit function is required.*

Extensibility and Future-Proofing

Adding version information into a file format becomes significantly easier when there's a simple way to read and write data; otherwise, you'll find yourself with versioning information to describe the version. With our common serialization function, we can insert versioning information to both importer and exporter by adding a simple number to the head of each block. We can now look at adding version information at various levels.

For the Whole Class

This involves marking each class with a single version Id that switches between various manifestations of the code. It's probably no different from the design that exists on most single-platform games.

```
void
SerializeVertices(CSGXSerializeFile& File)
{
tUINT32 version = 3;

    File | version;

    switch(version) {
        case   3:
```

```
                File | m_Vertex;
                File | m_Normal;
                break;

            case    2:
                File | m_Vertex;
                break;

            case    1:
                sgxError("We do not support this version anymore");
                break;
            default:
                sgxError("Bad version number");
        }
    }
```

The implementation may vary, such as the use of drop-through case statements to save the duplication of large chunks of code, but is fundamentally identical to any other versioning system. This works well in the short term when only a few extra properties are added, but as the objects grow (with new platform-specific or common features), the serialize functions can become cluttered. Occasionally, you'll need to do some spring cleaning. The technical situation is very simple because you just cut large sections of the code out of the function and recompile. From the standpoint of the development team, you'll need to coordinate with the producer as to when this should occur. He should make sure that all level data is exported again, ensuring that it has the most recent version numbers for each object. If you are concerned about losing code, you can place those older versions into a separate function called `LegacySerialize`.

TIP

We start our versioning at 1, not 0, because it's less likely to appear by accident in an incorrect file.

When new versions of the data are introduced, any extra elements, such as `m_Normal`, must be correctly initialized to sensible defaults through the constructor. Otherwise, those elements not saved in the original file will contain uninitialized data, and will likely result in a crash. The default constructor should always be implemented to ensure a valid object. Avoiding such a constructor should be the exception, not the rule. An example of such an exception would be classes that are on the critical path or those that are usually used extensively within the engine, such as world data vertices.

The Vector Exception

Vectors are unlikely to have runtime constructors because of the time overhead in creating them. If the constructor was called on each of 100,000 vertices within a game level, the constructor would write around 1.2 MB of data to memory. The vertices loaded from the disc would then rewrite this data, doubling the thumb-twiddling time before the game starts. There are a few solutions to this:

- Use structures, or classes, consisting solely of *plain old data* (*POD*), that is, without virtual functions, and reference them by pointer. This eradicates the use of constructors because the data can be loaded into a block of memory, and a `pFirstVector` pointer can be set up to it. Individual objects, *per se*, are not created. Unfortunately, it isn't possible to set up a private constructor to enforce this, and it's very difficult to prevent globally allocated objects while still permitting objects to be created on the stack (as would occur with local variables).
- Use a constructor only during the debugging builds of your game. Traditionally, a constructor is used to create a perfectly valid object for use within the program. In our arena, it's more usual to create an *invalid* object by, for example, setting `x`, `y`, and `z` to a signaling NaN (Not a Number). In this manner, every platform (technically speaking, every platform that adopts the IEEE 754 standard) will throw an exception when invalid data is used.
- Use a constructor to initialize the most recently added member variables, but remove them all for the final build. This enables old data to be loaded without change thanks to a combination of the constructor and existing file data. Before the final version is shipped, a data format lockdown should take place, so all data can be rebuilt in the latest version and the constructor removed.
- Don't have a constructor at all. This can be problematic as the initial vector will contain random data based on what was previously stored there, making the results indeterminable between program runs, and making it more difficult to debug.
- Use inplace allocation for the memory blocks of vectors, and a traditional constructor for local variables.

The second option (using a constructor only during debugging) is the preferred situation in most cases, whereas the last option (using inplace allocation) gains momentum for experienced developers with more specific needs.

CAUTION

The PowerPC™ 970 is not IEEE 754-compliant, and doesn't throw exceptions. This is a design decision based around the interests of speed, and therefore has no workaround.

CAUTION

SSE is very slow at processing quiet (that is, nonsignaling) NaNs and denormals. Only VTune™ (currently) is able to pick them up. Unlike the PowerPC problem, they can be suppressed by manipulating the control flags.

For Portions of the Class

Replacing smaller portions of platform-specific data is more difficult because we need to handle nested `version`-like variables, and so the depth of `switch` statements will increase. Instead, it's preferable to encapsulate any such instances within their own classes, so all the data can be serialized in one block and versioned as a whole, using the method described previously for complete classes.

If, for example, our `sgxVector3` class was to be extended with an additional element across the whole engine, then upgrading each module that featured vertices (meshes, scene graphs, and so on) would become a maintenance nightmare. Instead, we should encapsulate the vertex data, the new properties, and its (now required) versioning information in a new class (called, say, `CVertexList`) and write a specific serialize function for it:

```
void
CVertexList::Serialize(CSerializeFile& File)
{
tUINT32 version = 2;

    File | version;
    switch(version) {
        case 2:
            File | m_VertexProperties;
        case 1:
            File | m_Verts;
            break;
        default:
            sgxError("Bad versioning data on %s", typeid(*this));
    }
}
```

From here, it's a simple matter to overload the binary `operator|`, enabling this function to be called as if it were any other type. Any piece of substantial code, especially those with platform-specific components, should be given its own serialization function in this manner.

Every method given thus far assumes that all data will be mirrored; that is, what leaves the host exporter is always the same as required by the target platform. That should be true in all general cases, except when platform-specific data is required.

Introducing Platform-Specific Data

As you saw at the beginning of this chapter, some objects require supplementary details for specific platforms. Although we can't avoid this, we need to minimize the amount of platform-specific code we write. That is, we need less of this:

```
if (File.IsSaving()) {
    if (bExportingGamecube) {
        File | GCVertexData;
    } else {
        File | VertexData;
    }
}
```

And more of this:

```
File | VertexData;
```

This is an achievable goal, but only on some levels. After all, it's impossible to handle different data using the same code—at the low level, at least. The code to save a vertex, for example, contains a line that reads:

```
File << x;
```

This has no choice but to save the floating-point number in `x`. However, by working on the level above that, a vertex does have the option of adding extra data into the save file:

```
CSGXFile&
operator<<(CSGXFile&File, sgxVector3 &v)
{
    File << v.x;
    File << v.y;
    File << v.z;

    if (File.GetPlatform() == CHardwarePlatform::tPlatform::ePS2) {
        File << v.idx;
    }

    return File;
}
```

Likewise, the game engine that uses the vertex class can have its own platform-specific code marked in a similar way. This may be a workable solution, and it's moderately well structured from the view of keeping the data contained and close to the I/O system. But it does branch away from the unified load and save routines we've worked so hard on, as we need to implement similar code for both `operator>>` and `operator<<`.

Using Derived Classes

One solution is to use the `virtual` keyword, and the serialization class we've already written. By creating two classes, one generic and one platform-specific, we can use the `vtable` as a giant `switch` statement to reference the appropriate function. So, we have a generic engine class, such as:

```
class CEngineData : public CSGXSerialize {
public:
    tUINT32                  m_iArbitraryNumber;
    sgxVector<sgxVector3>    m_VertexData;

    virtual CSGXSerializeFile &Serialize(CSGXSerializeFile &File);

};
```

And a derived PS2-specific version:

```
class CPS2EngineData : public CEngineData {
public:
    tUINT32                   m_OnlyOnPS2;

    virtual CSGXSerializeFile &Serialize(CSGXSerializeFile &File);

};
```

So now, any common code can use its `CEngineData` pointer to reference the correct load and save routines, without having to worry about the platform:

```
CSGXSerializeFile &
CPS2EngineData::Serialize(CSGXSerializeFile &File)
{
    tUINT32 version = 1;

    CEngineData::Serialize(File);

    File | version;

    switch(version)
```

```
        {
        case    1:
            File | m_OnlyOnPS2;
            break;
        case    0:
            sgxError("Unknown version");
        }
        return File;
    }
```

We call the parent class before reading our own version tag. This is not essential, but makes it easier to trap bugs because if the parent class breaks the file format, `CPS2EngineData` *will read a version tag from an incorrect file address. This will produce an unknown version message, letting us know the problem occurred before we read the* `version` *variable. However, if this number was read (and written) before the parent block, we would have a correct version and corrupt data, which might lead us to suspect the* `CPS2EngineData` *class.*

Although this solution looks much cleaner, it isn't suitable in all cases because there's still some conditional code to determine the correct type. To use the virtualized functions, we need a pointer to the correct type. This means our `if-then` construct will appear around the initial allocation of this engine, as opposed to the data it contains.

```
CEngineData *pEngine;

if (CHardwarePlatform::Get()->GetCurrentPlatform() ==
        CHardwarePlatform::tPlatform::ePS2) {
    pEngine = new CPS2EngineData;
} else {
    pEngine = new CEngineData;
}

pEngine->Serialize(serial);
```

This is a good method for large, top-level classes—usually engines. The overhead, in terms of code and extra formatting data, is fairly low, but it does require a mechanism for creating the specific structures. Classes such as engines and their kin fit naturally into this category because they're often creating within the platform-specific code areas anyway, or through an object factory that might be as high in the code's food chain as `main.cpp`. In many cases, the creation of a PS2-specific engine class naturally invokes a PS2-specific vertex class, and a PS2-specific texture class, meaning that we don't need any other specific code within the basic engine. For lower-level control, however, we need an alternative solution.

Using Chunked Classes

The important thing to realize about platform-specific data is that most of it isn't actually platform-specific. Generally speaking, none of it is. That is, the *data* can be loaded onto any platform where there's code to read it; we just intend to limit the *use* of that data to specific platforms.

Knowing this, we can ask our PC to export data in a format suitable for each platform using the same code that the PS2 will use to load it. Because the PC will not be using this data, it doesn't matter whether its `CEngine` class holds information that it can understand or not. We can then reapply a versioning scheme on the platform-specific class that gets serialized with the normal data. The version method we've used so far is adequate, despite the unflattering maintenance code that is necessary to surround each "is the data for this platform" block. However, there's always room for improvement, so instead, we'll use a chunk system. A chunk system writes each block of data out with a special header. This header is in a common format and describes the next block in terms of its contents and size. Upon loading, the chunk code can look at this header and determine whether it makes sense to load it. If not, the chunk code reads the size from the header, skips over the block in its entirety, and continues reading. Chunks can be nested if required, whereby the skip process will omit that chunk and all its children. It's similar to a binary version of XML.

For our system, we'll implement the chunking code in its own class, derived from `CSGXSerialize`. Any data that wants to use chunks can then derive from that instead, while still having full access to all the functionality of `CSGXSerialize`. We'll implement all the chunk header handling code in this class to keep the basic code in `Serialize` to a minimum—which was the reason for moving it there in the first place.

Each chunk consists of the header and some data. The data is whatever our platform-specific class needs to save, and can be handled by the unified `Serialize` function. The header will be a simple combination of the size and an identifier to describe the platform. We'll use the enumeration from `CHardwarePlatform`.

Reading this data is very simple, and looks like this:

```
CSGXSerializeFile &
CSGXSerializeChunk::ReadData(CSGXSerializeFile &File)
{
    tUINT32 Platform;
    tINT32 Size;
```

```
        File | Size;
        File | Platform;

        if (Platform == CHardwarePlatform::Get()->GetCurrentPlatform()) {
            // Valid on this platform, so read it
            Serialize(File);
        } else {
            // Skip over the chunk header
            File.Seek(Size, CSGXDeviceBlockState::tSeekFrom::eCurrent);
        }

        return File;
    }
```

NOTE

We use a signed value for the seek offset so that we can rewind the pointer easier.

The writing, on the other hand, requires one extra piece of magic, `GetSeekPos`. This new function destroys the illusion that `Serialize` writes the data in a purely serial fashion. It doesn't. For that to work, we would need to know the size of the data being written at the same time as we wrote the header. Knowing this would require extra coding, extra CPU time, or both.[4] Instead, we can misdirect our audience by using the underlying file handle to query the current file position, so we can rewind to it later when we have the correct size.

```
CSGXSerializeFile &
CSGXSerializeChunk::WriteData(CSGXSerializeFile &File,
       CHardwarePlatform::tPlatform iPlatform)
{
    tUINT32 ChunkSize = 0;
    tDISC_SIZE StartPos, HeaderSize;

    StartPos = File.GetSeekPos();

    File | ChunkSize;
    File | iPlatform;

    if (File.m_pFile->GetTargetPlatform() ==
            CHardwarePlatform::Get(iPlatform)) {
        ChunkSize = File.GetSeekPos();
        HeaderSize = ChunkSize - StartPos;

        // We're exporting for this platform
        Serialize(File);
```

```
        // Calculate the size
        ChunkSize = (tUINT32)(File.GetSeekPos() - ChunkSize);

        // Now rewind the pointer, and fill in the size
        File.Seek(StartPos, CSGXDeviceBlockState::tSeekFrom::eBegin);
        File | ChunkSize;

        // Now back to where we left off
        File.Seek(StartPos + HeaderSize + ChunkSize,
            CSGXDeviceBlockState::tSeekFrom::eBegin);
    } else {
        // No data to go here.
        // Just save an empty chunk
    }

    return File;
}
```

We have adopted a very specific form of chunking here. Each chunk can only save platform-specific data, and will only load data for the platform on which they're currently running. In the real world, chunks cover a much larger terrain. Even in games, there might be cases (notably Xbox and Xbox 2) where we'll want the same chunk saved out for two identical platforms. This extension is not covered here, although it would be fairly easy to do by expanding the chunk header to contain a list of supported platforms.

Creating Chunked Classes

From here, anything derived from our magical `CSGXSerializeChunk` class (say, `CPS2Data`) can simply call the `ReadData` and `WriteData` functions to be provided with all the functionality they need. The appropriate locations from which to call these functions are the overloaded file I/O operators << and >>, because every type requires its own version.

```
CSGXSerializeFile&
operator>>(CSGXSerializeFile&File, CPS2Data &v)
{
    v.ReadData(File);
    return File;
}

CSGXSerializeFile&
operator<<(CSGXSerializeFile&File, CPS2Data &v)
```

```
{
    v.WriteData(File, CHardwarePlatform::tPlatform::ePS2);
    return File;
}
```

Now, whenever an instance of `CPS2Data` is serialized, the appropriate operator will be called and the data gets written to disc with a chunk header indicating for which platform it's intended.

The Export Process

We have now completed the cross-platform components of our system, and just need to add the topmost layer; that is, the code that interacts with the platform itself. On export, this will consist of the PC creating an appropriate file, setting it up ready for the platform (to affect the endian-ness), and writing data to it. This data might need to be converted into the platform-specific version first, but this is code we have (or *should* already have) written. We're implementing it here by means of a copy constructor.

```
void
ExportData()
{
    CSGXFile file("/win/engine", "rw");
    CSGXSerializeFile serial(file);
    CEngineData data;

    // Get data (could be from anywhere)
    BuildEngine(data);

    // Convert it
    CPS2EngineData *pPS2 = new CPS2EngineData(data);

    file.SetTargetPlatform(CHardwarePlatform::Get(
        CHardwarePlatform::tPlatform::ePS2));

    // Save it
    pPS2->Serialize(serial);
    delete pPS2;
}
```

We only need this platform-specific code to generate a PS2 engine file on disc. We can then create a near duplicate function to export Xbox and GameCube data.

For the loading process, we can use exactly the same `Serialize` function, ensuring a safe future for our data and the lead programmer's sanity. Because the data has been designed (that is, preswapped) for our platform, we don't need to explicitly set up the target platform for our file class, and so can use the much shorter version:

```
CSGXSerializeFile file("/win/engine", "r");

    pEngine = new CPS2EngineData;
    pEngine->Serialize(file);
```

In this case, notice that the win directory is an example showing the location of our data. The directory can, in fact, be on a CD-ROM, DVD, or ZIP file.

Removing Dead Code

For the most part, platform-specific code allocates only platform-specific data. The PS2 engine, for example, allocates the PS2 scene graph classes, instead of the generic versions. And, in turn, allocates a PS2 vertex class instead of the generic one, and so on. This eradicates the clumsiness of

```
#if SGX_PLATFORM_PS2
```

throughout the code, and ensures that data is only accessed through the appropriate virtual methods, as the programmer cannot be sure at which type the `sgxVector3` points. As a consequence, PS2 data structures, although present on all platforms, do not cause an increase in the memory footprint of other code.

In some cases, however, it's unavoidable to include platform-specific data inside common structures (although the motives might be questionable). In these instances, there will be an additional memory overhead as each platform suffers both the platform-specific, and generic, data. Because this is a rare case, an occasional `#if` is forgivable, and the platform-specific datatype can be changed according to the platform.

```
#if SGX_PLATFORM_EXPORTER || SGX_PLATFORM_PS2
    typedef struct {
        // some data
        } sgxPS2Data;
#else
    typedef char sgxPS2Data;
#endif
```

The same macro construct will be required around generic code that handles the structure and the elements within it; however, because we can't condone such methods, we won't provide any examples.

Profiling Data

For additional functionality, we can also add debugging support by reporting the file size and comparing it to the memory size available for a given level, as returned by the `CGamePlatform` class we created in Chapter 3.

```
pPlatform = CHardwarePlatform::Get(iPlatform);
pGame = CGamePlatform::Get(iPlatform);

filesize = CSGXFileSystem::Get()->GetFileSize("/win/data1");

if (filesize > pGame->GetLevelMemory()) {
    sgxTrace("This level appears to be too big for the %s",
        pPlatform->GetPlatform());
}
```

We can also use this idea to guesstimate the total load time for the level:

```
pPlatform = CHardwarePlatform::Get(iPlatform);
pGame = CGamePlatform::Get(iPlatform);

loadtime = pPlatform->GetDiscAccessSpeed() +
    filesize / pPlatform->GetDiscReadSpeed();

if (loadtime > pGame->GetMaxLevelLoadTime()) {
   sgxTrace("This level should load in %f seconds", loadtime);
}
```

The trace messages can instead be directed toward your game editor, and the information can be shown graphically in a dialog box to aid artists and designers as they work within their budgets.

Introducing Platform-Specific Resources

Unlike game-oriented data, resources such as textures and sounds are usually held in separate files that are loaded upon request. This makes it significantly easier to load specific versions for each platform, as each variation is an individual file that can be built and rebuilt without affecting the whole game. Each game object that requires the resource then simply exports a unique identifier (usually a filename) for it, and waits for the filesystem to load the data. The engine then interprets this data in a platform-specific manner, and returns a base class pointer, as shown in Figure 5.2.

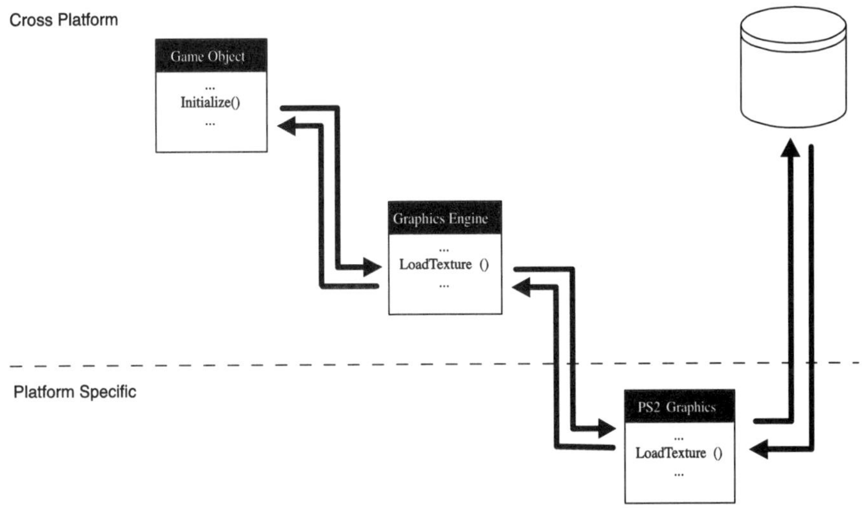

FIGURE 5.2 Handling platform-specific external resources.

At a later stage, these resources can be moved from their individual files into a single all-encompassing disc image to save seek time. When being built into a single file, these resources can be saved following the object class that requested it or at the end of the file, in which case, each request needs to be queued and loaded in batch.

Serializing Class Hierarchies

So far, we've produced a workable method to serialize single classes into, and out of, memory. As most games now employ C++, these classes are likely to form part of a hierarchy. Although it's simple to add a serialize call to each object's parent class, it's not so simple to handle changes in class hierarchy.

Fortunately, such occurrences are rare, and being a cross-platform title shouldn't change their scarcity. This doesn't make the code less important, however, as one class reading the data of another will, at best, crash the machine immediately, or at worst, introduce invalid numbers into rarely used components that crash the machine at a later stage after all evidence has been removed.

TIP

If you limit yourself to one class per file (and there's no reason why you shouldn't), then a simple macro at the top of each file will ease the process of moving class hierarchies. The `PARENT` *macro can be used throughout the file in place of the real parent class name. So, if the parent does change, the majority of your code needn't.*

We therefore need a method whereby hierarchy changes are noted and ignored, preventing problems from going unnoticed on any particular platform. The way to do that is, as you might have guessed, with versioning and chunks. When the hierarchy changes, a new chunk is introduced that reroutes the code path to the appropriate parent, avoiding the old class. The class itself is still valid because despite not being loaded, it has valid data assigned to it by the constructor.

The class-handling code is identical to the chunks we've implemented already for platform-specific data, although this time the data is cross-platform and available to all. Instead of using a simple integer to indicate the platform, we need a more complex type to reflect the class itself. Classes are interesting beasts because there are likely to be many of them, and some will come and go during the course of a project. Although a simple integer lookup table can work (with a global index of valid identifiers), it's often preferable to use a *GUID*.

GUID (Globally Unique IDentifier) consists of 128 bits, arranged as a structure of four elements:

```
typedef struct {
    tUINT32 Data1;
    tUINT16 Data2;
    tUINT16 Data3;
    tBYTE   Data4[8];
} sgxGUID;
```

The precise values are generated by the Windows program, GUIDGEN, which comes as part of the standard environment in Microsoft Developer Studio (although it's also available separately from the Internet). The uniqueness of the IDs comes from a number of factors, such as the time, the IP address of the current machine, and the MAC (Media Access Control) address of the network card. Although MAC addresses can be changed, network cards need not exist, and time is common around the world, the chance of any two developers getting the same GUID are so remote that it's not worth considering.

The output from the GUIDGEN program comes in many forms, depending on the type of development you are doing. Our cross-platform work requires the third option, as highlighted in Figure 5.3, which generates a simple piece of C source. We can then modify this to use the cross-platform structure shown previously, and give it a suitable name.

```
// {C05D5392-D807-48e4-8645-1971AC968978}
static const sgxGUID PlayerClassChunk =
{ 0xc05d5392, 0xd807, 0x48e4, { 0x86, 0x45, 0x19, 0x71, 0xac,
    0x96, 0x89, 0x78 } };
```

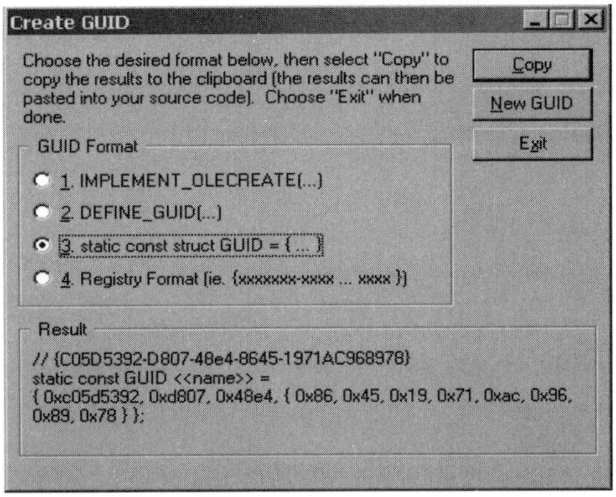

FIGURE 5.3 The GUIDGEN program. (Screen shot reprinted by permission from Microsoft Corporation.)

We then add suitable code to load and save this data, and a routine to compare it (element for element) with another GUID, and we're ready to use them on all our platforms.

Managing this situation gives us two basic choices: 1) let each class determine whether its parent class marries up with the chunk on disc, and so control the loading process or 2) let each class handle itself. Either way is fine, but to be consistent, we'll adopt the method chosen previously for the platform chunks; that is, give control to the chunks themselves. The rest of the code requires the services of the copy and paste brigade, so it's not featured here.

Object Creation

Handling these objects is all well and good, but creating them can be another story. Given a GUID, for example, how would you normally create an object of the correct type so it can be loaded seamlessly into memory? Usually, you need some means of tying the GUID to a specific class. The problem stems from the inability of C++ to construct a specific object at runtime—the binding must occur during the compile stage.

Aside from large convoluted switch statements, the best way is to use a design pattern known as an *object factory*. We've already touched on a simple variation of this when we used a derived class to hold PS2 engine data and its custom vertex information. The solution is for every object to provide a mapping between GUID and its own special callback function (which does the specific allocation). This map is then stored as part of the load manager for all the objects, so each GUID taken from disc can be matched to a specific callback that generates the object. This avoids switch statements, prevents duplicate IDs from being used, and eliminates the need for any centralized administration of GUIDs.

Interdependent Objects

Every game is greater than the sum of its parts. Every object, be it an NPC, a door, or the player, increases its playability factor when it interacts with other objects in the world. Internally, these interactions are usually handled by means of pointers between objects; which, on their own, are useless when it comes to disc storage. We therefore need to replace each pointer with a unique identifier that works across platforms, and across the divide between memory and disc. Several possibilities are available, and one is right for your game.

Numeric ID

Numeric ID is easy to understand and cross tabulate, and forms the basis of many systems. A unique number is stored as part of the object structure, and instead of saving a pointer, this number is saved. The first object created is given the number 1, the second uses 2, and so on. Whenever a level is saved, the current counter is stored alongside the other data so IDs can carry on from where they left off last time. This method remains simple because you don't have to keep track of deleted objects in an attempt to reclaim numbers. 32 bits gives you access to more than 4 billion unique objects—something that won't wrap around in the near future, even if you add one object every second for the next 136 years.

This method can only work as demonstrated when a maximum of one person is permitted to work on a level at any given time. If two people are able to add objects into a level at the same time, their IDs will be identical for any new objects created. Only workflow and tools can prevent this problem, either by prohibiting two people from adding to the level (the other may still be allowed to edit existing data), or by having a "level merge" feature built in to the editor. This latter feature is usually more trouble than it's worth, though, because any interconnections between objects also have to renumber themselves.

When this ID number has to be unique across the game and not just a level, the most significant byte can be amended to represent the game section. This will be true when several mini-levels are loaded at once and treated as one, as they are within asynchronous games that feature huge cityscapes, for example.

Names

Because most (if not all) of the objects in a game are created within a user-friendly editor, a name is given to each of them for reference by the artists and designers. Although the extra space taken by a string might be considered expensive, most are less than 12 characters long and with around 1,000 objects per level, this amounts to only 8 KB of extra data than if we had used 4-byte integers. This size obviously increases if the full resource path is used, or if the object name includes decoration, such as the level name.

For prudent developers, text strings can be converted into hash codes (2 bytes *might* be sufficient, but 4 is certainly recommended) before being exported. However, although the chances of a collision are very rare, they can happen, so you'll still need to run a quick check over your data before exporting.

TIP

Hash codes are one-way functions that prevent you from retrieving the human-readable name from a hash code, such as 0x9f73ba94. Therefore, make sure you also export a dictionary to map between them when opting for this solution.

The Pointer

Yes, believe it not, the numeric value of the pointer can also work, but not in the same way as it does when in memory. When each object is exported, 4 bytes must be prepended to the data stream to indicate its memory location in the exporter. A dictionary is then added to the end of the file, listing these pointers and the object associated with them.

This is not as friendly as using a name because the user cannot control it. But the object pointer will be unique within the exporter and available for use without any extra processing. It is also more difficult to debug, however, because no recognizable text strings appear in the file, and (more importantly) the identifiers for each object change whenever a level is reexported.

Patching Pointers

Regardless of the on-disc storage method, we'll still require some means of matching pointers in memory to IDs from disc. For this example, every game object will be supplemented with unique numeric IDs.

On Save

Before the game is saved, we must run a `PreSerialize` call on every object. At which point, all the object pointers are converted into their respective IDs and written back into the object pointer.

```
void CEngine::PreSerialize()
{
    sgxVector<CGameObject*>::iterator it = m_GameObjects.begin();
```

```
        for(;it!=m_GameObjects.end();++it) {
            (*it)->PreSerialize();
        }
}
```

This destroys the integrity of the game data, so we must iterate through our objects using a separate list of pointers, and not the ones contained within the objects. We are using an engine-based list held within `m_GameObjects`.

A typical `PreSerialize` call for each object would then appear like this:

```
void COurGameObject::PreSerialize()
{
    m_pObj1 = (CGameObject *)m_pObj1->m_ID;
    m_pObj2 = (CGameObject *)m_pObj2->m_ID;
}
```

These ID values are then serialized—like normal by the `Serialize` function—when the time comes. After saving, the IDs are converted back into real pointers by a subsequent `PostSerialize` call, which is identical to the procedure we carry out when loading (detailed next in the "On Load" section).

CAUTION

You must always convert IDs back to pointers, even if you intend to exit the application immediately after doing so. Destructors will invariably attempt to dereference the pointers to either reduce reference counts, or free up child resources. Dereferencing integers usually crash the machine.

Additionally, note that there's no shame in using a union to hold *both* the pointer and the identifier because no one will ever see them in the same room together.

On Load

Having loaded our IDs into `CGameObject` pointers, we must endeavor to convert them back into genuine pointers, reflecting the state of our memory. This is a two-stage process. Our first step is to build a dictionary that connects the object IDs with their new memory pointers. The second is to rewrite the object pointers (currently holding integral IDs) to dereference valid objects.

Building the dictionary is a simple iteration through the object list to match their pointers (provided by the engine's object factory) with their IDs (as serialized from disc).

```
void CEngine::BuildDictionary()
{
    sgxVector<CGameObject *>::iterator it = m_GameObjects.begin();

    m_GameDictionary.clear();
    for(;it!=m_GameObjects.end();++it) {
        m_GameDictionary.insert
                (DictionaryMap::value_type((*it)->m_ID, *it));
    }

}
```

This procedure can be optimized slightly by adding entries to the game dictionary as they are loaded. Other solutions, such as serializing the dictionary with the game and using pointer offsets to reference the objects, are left as exercises for you.

After the dictionary has been built, we can write our `PostSerialize` function very simply indeed:

```
void COurGameObject::PreSerialize()
{
    m_pObj1 = CEngine::Get()->GetDictionaryObject(tUINT32(m_pObj1));
    m_pObj2 = CEngine::Get()->GetDictionaryObject(tUINT32(m_pObj2));
}
```

The Dictionary

The implementation shown in the previous section uses an STL map to hold our dictionary. A typical access function would be written like this:

```
CGameObject *CEngine::GetDictionaryObject(tUINT32 id)
{
    DictionaryMap::iterator it = m_GameDictionary.find(id);

    if (it == m_GameDictionary.end()) {
        return NULL;
    }

    return it->second;
}
```

It may be quick, but requires memory over and above that required for the game. Because this is usually around the 64 KB mark, it's not a major concern. However, if memory is tight, but processor speed is plentiful, you can reference the dictionary on-the-fly by polling each object and comparing its ID with the one you're seeking, removing the need for an external dictionary `map`.

If the implementation requires speed, however, then a `map`-oriented dictionary is much better because the search time is no longer linear. In fact, it's only linear if we have one object seeking out the ID of one other. If every object in the game is looking for an ID, we have a squared relationship. So 100 objects would require (a maximum of) 100 * 100 checks, whereas 1,000 objects (which is more realistic) needs 1,000 * 1,000. These numbers get very big, very quickly.

A map, on the other hand, can remove half the search tree at every step, so it's a much better implementation—if you can spare the memory. But 1,000 objects will only take 8,000 bytes on all current platforms (4 bytes storing the pointer, and 4 to hold the ID), and that amount of memory is normally salvageable from elsewhere, especially since this information is transient and of no use after the pointers have been rewritten. Therefore, this data can be loaded into a memory block, used, and dumped without leaving any of the holes we saw in Chapter 3. Additionally, we can choose to hold this information in a temporary buffer.

NOTE

We call our patch up function from an object loop, not part of the serialize code. This ensures that every object in the game has been correctly prepared before the save begins. Otherwise, this would cause problems where objects had mutual dependencies (such as doors and door frames or AI grunts and their commanders) or the ordering of the conversion did not match the order of the game objects.

Duplicate Code

One issue you may have spotted—apart from the verbosity of the conversion functions—is that we have two references to `m_pObj1`. This redundancy is asking for trouble with mistyped variable names, so we need to replace it.

One suitable method is to provide a single conversion function, `SerializePatch`, which processes the data for both pre- and post-serialize. We can switch between the two conversion routines by passing a function pointer to handle the patching:

```
void COurGameObject::SerializePatch(cbPtrConversion cbFn)
{
    (*cbFn)(&m_pObj1);
    (*cbFn)(&m_pObj2);
}
```

This requires that our conversion functions look like this:

```
void CGameObject::Ptr2ID(CGameObject **pptr)
{
    if (*pptr)
    {
        *pptr = (CGameObject *)(*pptr)->m_ID;
        sgxAssert(*pptr);
    }
}

void CGameObject::ID2Ptr(CGameObject **pptr)
{
    tUINT32 id = (tUINT32)*pptr;

    *pptr = CEngine::Get()->GetDictionaryObject(id);
    sgxAssert(!*pptr || (*pptr)->m_ID == id);
}
```

This method also works if the object pointer and ID are held in different variables; we just need to modify our conversion functions to accept two parameters.

From here, we have methods for handling all the data within our cross-platform game. We now move onto the next section, where we transfer this information to, and from, a disc.

DESIGNING A FILESYSTEM

The filesystem exists to abstract the physical properties of the disc away from the files that reside upon it, and the software that uses them. It can describe both the manner in which files are arranged on the disc, and the hierarchy itself. For every file and directory on the disc, the filesystem has its own structure detailing its size, location, and other properties.

Every computer and current console has a filesystem. A PC running Windows is using *FAT32*, *VFAT*, or *NTFS*, whereas the Xbox hard drive uses a custom variant called *XFAT*. The PS2 CD- and DVD-ROM discs use the *ISO 9660* standard, whereas Nintendo has opted for a proprietary format in the guise of GD-ROM. Each filesystem is different from the others in terms of limits, capabilities, and features, but all employ a typical design of nested files and directories, as shown in Figure 5.4. Like the processor speed, this is something we cannot abstract because it's ingrained into the silicon of the disc controller hardware. However, we can *hide* this information by creating our own filesystem on top, requiring that all file requests go through us first. This essentially allows us to store a file within a file (or many

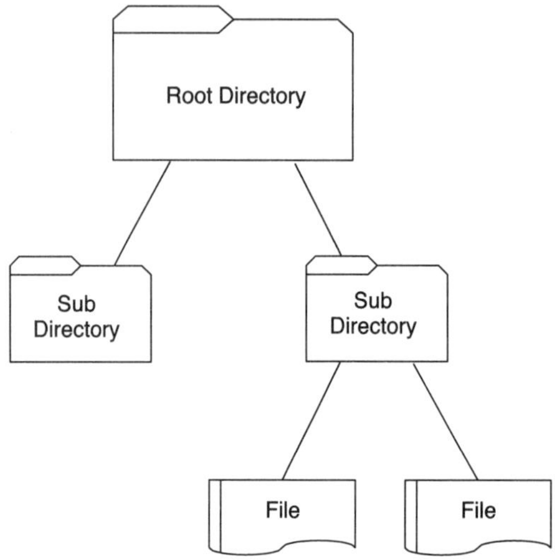

FIGURE 5.4 A typical filesystem hierarchy.

files within a file) on the real disc, giving us full control of the properties of each file and facilitating a cross-platform filesystem.

Having our own filesystem creates benefits in other ways. During the development of a cross-platform game, it's usually necessary to load files from the PC's hard drive, instead of the console's disc. This offsets the savings of extra CD burning and development turn-around time, against the costs of the multiple code paths that are required to handle the different filesystems. By requesting data through our own filesystem, the CD to hard disc changeover can take place easily, without the need for large-scale modifications throughout the code.

Also, by replacing the low-level disc-handling code with a module to handle a memory card, we can use the same filesystem layout, and therefore the same file-handling code, to create our save game files too. This allows memory card data to be written out to a hard drive instead for later debugging with virtually no extra code.

Considering the future, note that the filesystem need not be local. By implementing the *HTTP* (*Hypertext Transfer Protocol*), we can read (and write) information to a Web server as easily as we can the memory card or disc. This could be our own servers for PC-based massively multiplayer online games, or those of a commercial nature, such as Xbox Live™.

To aid the development process, an *SMB*[5] (*Server Message Block*) server can be implemented as this would allow us to load game resources across a network to the console directly. This can then be used to dynamically change assets while the game is still running, giving the best turn-around time for which we could hope.

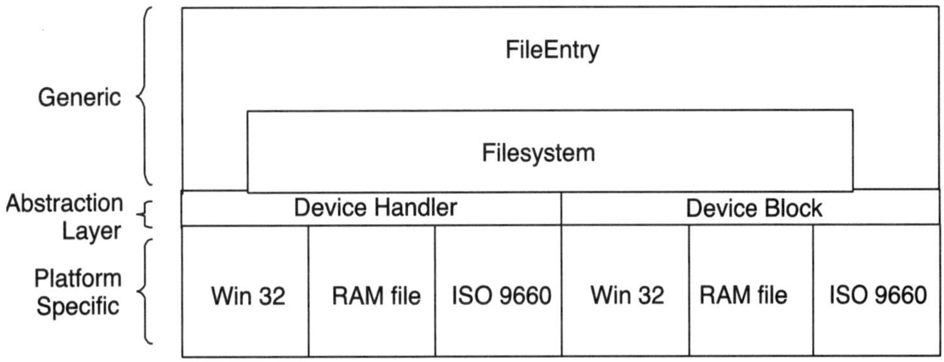

FIGURE 5.5 Filesystem architecture.

The architecture of our filesystem appears as shown in Figure 5.5, with the fully abstracted file elements at the top, and the hardware-specific handling functions at the bottom.

At first glance, it might appear a little heavy handed to be building a completely new filesystem just to add support for a couple of quirky features we might never use. Perhaps we should simply wrapper the platform-specific I/O calls as we suggested at the start of the chapter to remove the differences of directory delimiter (/ or \), case, and directory name.

However, even for today's systems, the standard filesystem is not always capable enough and requires hiding. The best argument in this category is the PS2 and its adoption of ISO 9660 because it has limits that are not capable of supporting the massive games we're now developing.

ISO 9660

ISO 9660 is the format used for storing data on a CD-ROM or DVD-ROM. It was the internationally approved and standardized version of the existing *High Sierra* format that had been created in 1985, with the HS specification itself being published on May 28, 1986. Because the standard was essentially designed by committee, several factors govern its ideas. This may also explain the decision to create three different levels for the standard:

Level 1: This restricts filenames to eight characters for the name, and three for an extension. These are known as 8.3 filenames and are much the same as those under MS-DOS™. Furthermore, the filenames themselves can only use uppercase letters, numbers, and the underscore character. Finally, but perhaps less importantly for games development, it only supports eight levels of nested directories.

Level 2: Same as level 1, but the filenames can consist of up to 31 characters.

Level 3: Permits the fragmentation of files and is used primarily with CD-Rs.

Of the three choices, Sony opted to use level 1 which, as you can see, is the ISO 9660 standard in its basic form.

NOTE

The longer filenames currently in use on CD-ROMs generally come courtesy of the extensions known as Joliet and Rock Ridge.

By creating our own filesystem, we can store one file on the CD-ROM called `DATA.BIN` that combines all our other files, along with their associated attributes. This data would normally be present within the disc's filesystem and include items such as size, filename, and directory path. Because we're creating our own filesystem, this information has to be held and maintained by us. By placing it inside `DATA.BIN`, it can be held in our own format using our own naming conventions, so we're no longer constrained by 8.3 filenames, uppercase characters, or eight directory levels—provided, obviously, that we're prepared to implement such features.

Having established that a custom filesystem is required—on at least the PS2—we can consider whether to exercise this prerogative on the other consoles. We could, after all, abstract the file I/O code away from all platforms, but wrap the ISO 9660 format itself (and not the whole filesystem) in extra swaddling to avert the aforementioned problems.

Extending a custom filesystem to work across two platforms is no more difficult than writing it for one. That is to say, the solution scales well. The extra work involved on a per-platform basis is not that great, but we earn a greater flexibility and commonality across the board, so this the recommended approach.

Disc Size

The ISO 9660 standard only indicates how the data is to be stored on the disc. It doesn't indicate how much data can be stored there. This is obvious from the fact that DVD-ROMs use the same system as CD-ROMs, and that it's possible to purchase CD-Rs in 74- and 80-minute versions. When building assets for each platform, we need to consider this limit because we don't have the luxury of using longer CD-ROMs if necessary—we have a fixed size.

When developing cross-platform games using the same (or similar) data, you will be expected to store all 30 levels (each clocking in at 20 MB), alongside whatever cut-scenes and streaming audio is required in the same amount of disc space. This is not workable in an obvious manner because some discs are bigger than others. In these cases, a custom filesystem would help because you could write a filesystem device that performed decompression on all the data read from the disc on-the-fly. This would be completely transparent to the end users because the only data they ever receive is from your filesystem, fully decompressed.

It might also be technically possible to implement your own *Rock Ridge* extensions to the CD-ROM of a console. Even if we had such an implementation, NDA's would prohibit its publication here.

Layout

Layout concerns how the filesystem appears to the end user and what properties it possesses, such as the directory hierarchy. Because we already have to re-invent the filesystem to achieve cross-platform compatibility, we'll save ourselves some time by not designing a completely new layout; instead, we'll take many ideas and notions from the most common filesystems in use today—notably `VFAT` from Windows, and `ext2` from Linux.

Hierarchical

Almost everyone would agree that a hierarchical structure is a good thing, so we then have to consider how to use that structure. This includes questions such as:

- What is the root called?
- Should we use `/` or `\` between directory names?
- How deep can directories be nested?
- What characters should we allow for filenames? What about spaces?

All these considerations are fairly arbitrary, and have no bearing on the overall architecture. The only real prerequisite is that tree branches are easy to replace so that `host0` can become `cdrom0` on the PS2, for example.

The solution we'll adopt has its origins in Unix. Starting with a root called `/`, we'll create all other files in directories beneath it through a system of *mount*s. Mounts are locations within the filesystem where particular devices are added and treated like any other file. Consequently, these devices can also be opened and read like a file or traversed and enumerated like a directory. For those not conversant with Unix, let's walk through a simple example.

Consider a file in our filesystem called `/memory`. This file sits in the root directory, but has been mounted using the memory device. This means that any accesses to the file called `/memory` gets routed to the handling code of the memory device. So any read from this file is, in actuality, reading straight from memory. Similarly, writing into this file will change the memory, and any file seeks will change the memory location that is being read from, or written to.

This `/memory` file doesn't have to constitute the memory of the entire machine, as that would be very unsafe, but it can be a small purposeful block that is later copied to the memory card, or used as a way of storing the game state at various check points.

Directories work in a similar manner. When we mount a directory into the filesystem, the device adds each file and subdirectory into the hierarchy, along with some specific information (such as the *real* filename on disc). Whenever the filesystem is asked to access these files, the device is given back this specific information to create a genuine file handle that can then be used to read the data.

TIP

We have chosen to use the forward slash (/) here because it not only follows the Unix metaphor, but also doesn't require itself to be escaped within text strings (unlike the backslash \).

To perform the `host0/cdrom` trick mentioned previously, we must make sure that our implementation allows us to mount different devices into the same place. This should be straightforward, provided we can close any files that are still open inside the previous directory before we *unmount* it. Bear in mind that unmounting can occur during the game, as a directory called `/game/level` might hold only the data for the current level, and change fairly frequently.

At a minimum, we'll have a device to handle our CD-ROM (of whichever persuasion it is), a memory block (or RAM disc), and the PC's hard disk. Platform-specific devices also need to be added, but they are not discussed here. Advanced users (that is, Linux geeks) may care to provide other devices for the filesystem. We have suggested some later in this chapter, in the "Filesystem Additions" section.

We can express the hierarchy for our game by any types we want, but to ensure flexibility across all platforms, we'll use dynamic memory. This removes the arbitrary directory limits imposed elsewhere, as these are harder to overcome than the softer limits such as memory. (We can always reduce another texture or audio sample if we run out of memory.) From a practical consideration however, it's a good idea to limit the amount of files present in the root directory, moving them instead to a subdirectory of it, as this makes it easier to move entire hierarchies and remount them elsewhere. This is also true when there's just one file. It follows the traditional idea in C programming, where `main` should only include one function that in turn runs the game. One suggestion is shown in Figure 5.6.

Figure 5.6 shows that we have a copy of the disc's physical structure available (under `disc`), and details of the devices attached to the machine (such as joysticks

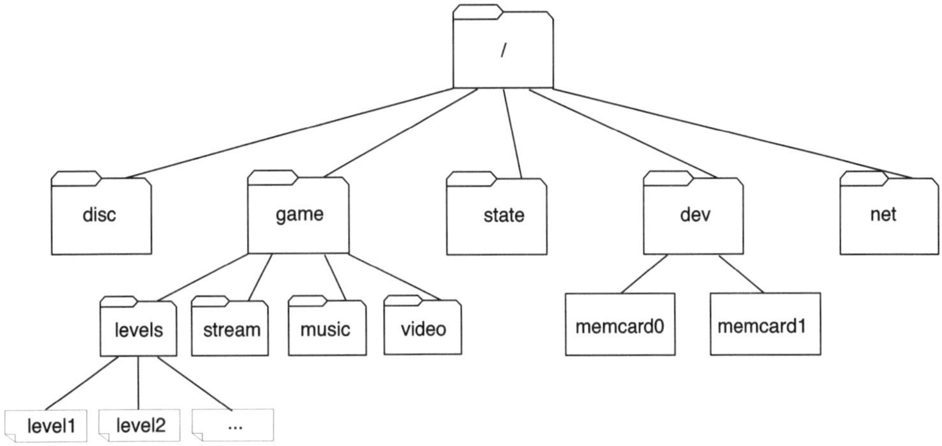

FIGURE 5.6 Basic hierarchy.

or memory cards). The `state` directory is intended to contain save game files of the most recent check points within the game, while `net` is a future-proof mechanism to let us talk to other machines without networking code infiltrating the game directly.

Every element within the file hierarchy can be a directory or a file. Accessing a file should trigger code that actually does something, such as loading data or sending a network packet, while the directory is simply a means of getting there. New devices are always mounted to a directory.

From here, we can see a practical case (a memory card) of where it will be necessary to mount the same device in more than one place. This means that the same file could be visible with two separate paths; from an implementation viewpoint, this means that `static` and `global` variables (including singletons) should not be used.

Case Sensitivity

Case sensitivity is a thorny issue, and despite the focus of Unix-centric ideas in this chapter, we'll adopt a case-*in*sensitive filesystem. This is not a personal preference, but a practical one. It's difficult to maintain the many thousands of resources present within a game, and this can become worse if `9mm_pistol` and `9mm_Pistol` don't equate to the same file. Because the target audience for the filesystem is not restricted to the programming staff—both artists and designers will be creating and naming assets, remember—we should cater to them by adopting something of which they have more experience. This is probably the Windows case-insensitive filesystem.

FILESYSTEM IMPLEMENTATION

With so many elements constituting our filesystem, we need somewhere simple to focus our initial implementation efforts so that we don't suffer from too many dependency problems. That place is the directory structure.

Our filesystem holds the complete directory structure in memory with a `CSGXFileEntry` class to describe either a file or a directory. This structure is completely cross-platform, although we'll need some device-specific information to fully describe the file to the device-specific file-handling code. We need to hide these details away, so we create an abstract class (called `CSGXDeviceBlock`) that is used to reference all this device-specific information pertaining to a particular file. It does not, in itself, have any form of implementation, because we're just using it as a placeholder.

Directories, on the other hand, exist solely within the filesystem so we can traverse them from within our code, without resorting to platform-specific I/O calls that may have undetermined delays as the API queries the disc. When mounting a directory into the filesystem, we therefore need to manually create subdirectories within the filesystem to mirror the hierarchy.

Our first draft would appear like this:

```
class CSGXFileEntry
{
public:
    CSGXFileSysData      m_Data;
    CSGXDeviceBlock     *m_pBlock;

    CSGXFileEntry       *m_pFirstChild;
    CSGXFileEntry       *m_pNextSibling;
};
```

Our filesystem uses many `CSGXFileEntrys` to build its hierarchy of files and directories. The latter, as described in the class, points to its first child entry, while each child points to their next sibling. This ensures we have a constant number of pointers within each file entry, which makes memory management easier. The trade-off between time and memory should tilt in favor of memory because the time aspect is fairly inconsequential as file I/O is significantly slower than any CPU-bound task.

Root is also a directory, but handled as a special case because it doesn't have a device attached to it. The filesystem handles this explicitly, so we can create a very simple filesystem with a single `CSGXFileEntry`:

```
CSGXFileSystem::CSGXFileSystem()
{
    m_CurrentPath = "/";
    m_pRoot = new CSGXFileEntry("/");
}
```

From a development perspective, `m_CurrentPath` makes life much easier for programmers because they can use the relative path or individual filename to access files. This is naturally much shorter than the full path, and can usually be seen in its entirety when watching the variable in the debugger. The filesystem code should include a function to build a full path internally, depending on whether a relative or absolute name is given.

```
void
CSGXFileSystem::GetFullPath(sgxString &fullpath,
        const sgxString &path) const
{
    if (path[0] == '/') {
        fullpath = path;
    } else {
        fullpath = m_CurrentPath + path;
    }
    // We could also add further validation here
}
```

We should call this function on every file operation to ensure that we have a complete path, regardless of whether it exists or not. This becomes one of our internal utility functions, along with `GetFileEntry`, which will traverse the full path, as given, in an attempt to find the `CSGXFFileEntry` for the file or directory in question. The implementation of this is also fairly straightforward.

The other important utility function we need at this time is `CreateFileEntry`, which finds the parent directory of the potential new file and adds an entry underneath. Again, the implementation is simple, and uses the `GetFileEntry` function we've already written.

```
CSGXFileEntry *
CSGXFileSystem::CreateFileEntry(const sgxString &parent,
        const sgxString &name)
{
    CSGXFileEntry *pParent = GetFileEntry(parent);

    if (!pParent) {
        // Cannot create file, since parent doesn't exist
        return NULL;
```

```
    }

    CSGXFileEntry *pThis = new CSGXFileEntry(name);

    // Append latest entry to start of list
    pThis->m_pNextSibling = pParent->m_pFirstChild;
    pParent->m_pFirstChild = pThis;

    return pThis;
}
```

Now that we have good control over the directory tree, we just need to populate it by mounting devices onto it.

Filesystem Devices

In this section, we'll briefly look at three different devices that represent the basic cases you'll come across. Others can be added at your leisure. However, they all come with the same apparatus; a means for mounting (and unmounting) themselves, and a set of methods to open and close the individual files they contain. The example devices are:

Memory files: A block of memory is read/written as if it were a file. Suitable for memory cards and save game states.

Disc hierarchies: A copy of the file structure present on the hard drive or CD-ROM is re-created in RAM, with references to the external files still on disc. We'll demonstrate an implementation using the Win32 API and a class called `Win32Disc`.

ZIP files: An amalgamation of several files, encased in a single unit for storing on an ISO 9660 disc. The "zip" moniker can be misleading because it's not necessary to compress these files. They can be stored, uncompressed, as a single contiguous data stream. The code for fully implementing a ZIP-friendly file filesystem is extensive, and isn't quoted here. For more information about file formats, visit *http://www.wotsits.org* or one of the many other Web sites with material on this topic.

Creating a Device

The `CSGXDevice` class (and those derived from it) refers to the device as a whole. When writing the `CSGXDeviceWin32Disc` device, for example, it details the device from the root of the Windows directory structure. Before mounting a device, however, we need to create it.

```
CSGXDeviceWin32Disc windisc("c:\\gamedisc");
```

This would invoke the constructor:

```
CSGXDeviceWin32Disc::CSGXDeviceWin32Disc(const sgxString &path)
{
    m_Root = path;
}
```

We don't need to do any further processing here because the directory `C:\gamedisc` could be mounted into several points in the hierarchy. Consequently, we'll scan the directory when the device is mounted, and add the new `CSGXFileEntrys` accordingly.

TIP

If your game does extensive device mounting, you can save time during the game by building the hierarchy at this stage and copying it into the tree upon mounting. Naturally, there is a memory overhead for holding duplicate copies of the hierarchy.

In contrast to all this, a memory file would only need a pointer referencing the start of the memory block, and an indication of its size when creating its device. A memory card would be similar. However, a memory card may require additional code to initialize it, so that would also need to be included here.

Mounting a Device

Now that we can create devices, we need some way to mount them onto the filesystem. The code that does this varies depending on whether we are mounting it as a file (as with memory) or a directory. In both cases, we can use a virtual member function

```
tBOOL
CSGXDevice::Mount(CSGXFileEntry *pEntry, const sgxString &root);
```

to spawn a tree from the root node given by `pEntry`.

Most of the time, you won't be adding single files to the filesystem; you'll be adding entire subtrees. This involves adding file entries underneath the given `pEntry` one per directory and one per file. This is not difficult because our underlying class structure and abstracted memory allocation covers the issues of interplatform resourcing, while the abstracted filesystem removes the dependency on platform-specific API features and data formats.

The mounting process *does* need to create new file entries underneath the existing mount point when replicating the directory hierarchy in memory, as it appears on the disc.

This is a big win for us because it makes basic file queries, such as "does this file exist," virtually instantaneous. Instead of just being consigned to the "nifty optimization" code pile, this has a crucial role to play in cross-platform work. Notably, it eliminates the time difference that exists when seeking for files. This becomes important in some games that load specific resources on a level-by-level basis. For instance, the default HUD graphics are stored as `hud_gfx.png`, but a special day-glo version used for the cave hunting level is called `hud_gfx_cave.png`. Checking at level start for `hud_gfx_<level_id>.png` on the physical disc will cause more interplatform discrepancies than a quick search of memory.

From the user's perspective, mounting a device is very simple:

```
CSGXFileSystem::Get()->Mount(windisc, "/disc");
```

Instantly, the method of mounting different devices into the same hierarchy becomes clear. This is then coupled with the device-creation code and placed in the platform-specific `main.cpp` file before calling the generic game code. Then, any code can reference files in the abstracted `/disc` directory without knowing its underlying implementation.

The implementation involved in mounting isn't difficult either, because the device and filesystem work in tandem, doing whatever components are easier for them. However, most of the hard work is done by the device-specific code. From the filesystem's viewpoint, it only needs to create a new directory for the mount to live, and pass control off to the device.

```
tBOOL
CSGXFileSystem::Mount(CSGXDevice &Device, const sgxString &location)
{
    CSGXFileEntry *pMount = MakeNewFileEntry(location);

    if (!pMount) {
        sgxTrace("Could not create mount point at %s", location);
        return false;
    }

    // attach to device
    sgxString fullpath;
    GetFullPath(fullpath, location);

    pMount->m_pFSDevice = &Device;
```

```
        return Device.Mount(pMount, fullpath);
    }
```

You probably noticed the new `m_pFSDevice` element introduced here. This is a convenient pointer that lets us refer to the device directly. This pointer saves us traversing the tree whenever we need to make a request of the device, as we would when creating a new file on it.

The device then does the work of enumerating each file in the directory. This must be platform-specific because the API for doing this varies by platform. This example uses the Win32-specific `FindFirstFile` and `FindNextFile` functions:

```
tBOOL
CSGXDeviceWin32Disc::Mount(CSGXFileEntry *pEntry,
        const sgxString &rootmount)
{
    WIN32_FIND_DATA finddata;
    HANDLE hFind;
    sgxString search = m_Root + "/*.*";
    CSGXFileSystem *pFS = CSGXFileSystem::Get();

    hFind = ::FindFirstFile(search.c_str(), &finddata);
    if (hFind == INVALID_HANDLE_VALUE) {
        return false;
    } else {
        // Scan directory for files
        do {
            if (finddata.cFileName[0] == '.') {
                // Ignore all 'dot' files
            } else if (finddata.dwFileAttributes &
                    FILE_ATTRIBUTE_DIRECTORY) {
                // Ignore subdirectories (possible future
                // expansion task)
            } else {
                CSGXFileSysData FileData;

                FileData.m_Name = rootmount + "/" +
                                    sgxString(finddata.cFileName);
                FileData.m_Filesize = finddata.nFileSizeLow;

                pFS->CreateNewFile(FileData);
            }
        } while (::FindNextFile(hFind, &finddata));

        ::FindClose(hFind);
```

```
    }

    return TRUE;
}
```

For every file in the system, we use `CreateNewFile` to add a suitable entry to the filesystem. This reacts in the same way that `Mount` does. That is, it does some (minimal) housekeeping tasks of its own, and passes control directly to the device to create a device-specific file block:

```
CSGXFileEntry *
CSGXFileSystem::CreateNewFile(const CSGXFileSysData &FileData)
{
    sgxString basename;
    sgxString parent;

    GetBaseName(basename, FileData.m_Name);
    GetParent(parent, FileData.m_Name);

    CSGXFileEntry *pNewEntry = CreateFileEntry(parent, basename);

    if (!pNewEntry) {
        return NULL;
    }

    CSGXFileEntry *pParentEntry = GetFileEntry(parent);

    pParentEntry->m_pFSDevice->CreateNewFile(pNewEntry);
    pNewEntry->m_Data = FileData;
    pNewEntry->m_Data.m_Name = basename;

    return pNewEntry;
}
```

Our Windows device would function like this:

```
CSGXFileEntry *
CSGXDeviceWin32Disc::CreateNewFile(CSGXFileEntry *pNewEntry)
{
    // The real Windows path can be deduced from the parent's full
    // windows path very easily.
    sgxString winpath = m_Root + "\\" + pNewEntry->m_Data.m_Name;
    pNewEntry->m_pBlock = new CSGXDeviceBlockWin32Disc(winpath);
    pNewEntry->m_pFSDevice = this;
```

```
    return pNewEntry;
}
```

Creating the `CSGXDeviceBlockWin32Disc` block is critical because it must contain all the information necessary to handle a file at any later stage as no other information will be present. For Windows, we just need its full path because that's all we would ever pass to the Win32 function `CreateFile`. A memory card device, however, might need additional handles.

TIP

In `CreateNewFile` *and all other library functions, we capture the error at the lowest level and report it at the highest. This is good practice in all development as it stops purious error messages by engine code that might not be true errors as far as the user is concerned. A cross-platform project has more of these layers and could create even more spurious messages.*

Holding our mounted filesystem in memory doesn't occupy as much space as you might originally think because we don't need to mount the contents of the entire CD at once. Each level will probably remain in its own directory, so we can save memory there, while the streamed data (the vast majority of files if your game has a lot of speech) will probably never be mounted.

Scanning the CD-ROM disc structure can be a very costly procedure, as the OS has to read information for every file on that portion of the disc. So instead of reading this at game start, we can prebuild the data using our PC-oriented tool chain and export it into a file, ready for preloading by the game.

Mounting a File

Now that we've completed our mounted filesystem, repeating the process to mount an individual file like the memory device is trivial. After all, we've already incorporated the code into our directory mount code. The only difference is that the filename doesn't need to be stored because the name (such as `/memory`) is already held in the `CSGXFileEnry` node.

```
tBOOL
CSGXDeviceMemory::Mount(CSGXFileEntry *pEntry, const sgxString &root)
{
    pEntry->m_pBlock = new CSGXDeviceBlock;
    pEntry->m_Data.m_Filesize = m_Size;
    return TRUE;
}
```

We need to create a basic `CSGXDeviceBlock` here, despite the fact it will never be used; we have all the data we need after all. However, that pointer indicates that we're dealing with a file as opposed to a directory, so it must point to something.

File Handling

Now let's look at the mechanism for reading a file because most media is read-only, although it could equally be used for writing data. For each file that a device handles, there are two components: a static part and a dynamic part. The static part details the file as it exists on the disc, and as the name suggests, doesn't change throughout the lifetime of the game. The static part is referenced directly from the filesystem and includes the filename and file size, as stored in the `CSGSXFileSysData` class.

The dynamic portion (which we call the *state*) represents a particular instance of an open file. This acts like an `HFILE` handle in Win32 or `FILE *` from the C standard library. There is a many-to-one relationship between dynamic and static file blocks because the same file can be in use by several parts of the game, each with its own handle. We'll use the abstract class `CSGXDeviceBlockState` as a base for these dynamic handles.

To tie the `CSGXDevice` and `CSGXDeviceBlockState` classes together, we hand control for opening the file to the device code. This is because each device has a limit on the number of files that can be opened at once. Naturally, this limit varies according to platform, so we might want to use `CSGXFileSystem` to place a cap on the number of files that can be opened.

Determining a sensible number for such a limit is very difficult, however, and has been omitted in our implementation. The difficulty comes from the game itself, and the device used. If the disc layout contains just one ZIP file containing all others, for instance, then we only need one file physical handle to rule them all. Our logical handles can manage each instance within that one file. However, if we were mounting the same data from a hard drive instead, and each file was stored individually, each file would require a separate handle. We'll therefore let the device limit the file handles as it sees fit. If we run out, then we'll adopt a ZIP file for that particular platform. In the real world, however, this should rarely happen provided you close all your files behind you.

TIP

This is one instance where a paranoid use of lowest common denominator really can work. Knowing that the lowest number of available file handles across all your platforms is 12, for example, you can prevent any file handle-based problems by having no more than 12 ZIP files on your disc. One physical file handle is assigned to each ZIP file at game start, and released on exit.

Now that you've seen the theory on what a device has to do, you can make the first steps to implementing it.

Sample Implementation–Memory Files

The creation of a RAM file needs nothing more than a pointer to some data to represent the file, and an indication of how large the data block is. When combined, this information represents a memory device that we can mount into our filesystem.

```
tBYTE            OS_MemoryCardBuffer[4096];
CSGXDeviceMemory MemCard(OS_MemoryCardBuffer, 4096);
```

When opening and closing this memory file, we need to do nothing more than set the current "file" pointer to zero:

```
CSGXDeviceBlockState *
CSGXDeviceMemory::Open(CSGXDeviceBlock *pBlk,
        const sgxString &access)
{
    CSGXDeviceBlockStateMemory *pState =
        new CSGXDeviceBlockStateMemory;

    pState->m_CurrOffset = 0;
    pState->m_pMemDevice = this;
    return pState;
}
```

As you can see from the completed code, the block state also needs to remember the current device by storing it in `m_pMemDevice`. This additional step is required because each instance of the open file needs to determine the size of the memory file, and its base pointer. The `Open` member function is the last time a file has access to this information before it is created. This is intentional because it gives complete control to the way in which the `Read` and `Write` routines work, such as this:

```
tMEM_SIZE
CSGXDeviceBlockStateMemory::Read(tBYTE *pDest, tMEM_SIZE size)
{
    tMEM_SIZE readbytes;

    if (m_CurrOffset + size > m_pMemDevice->m_Size) {
        readbytes = m_pMemDevice->m_Size - m_CurrOffset;
    } else {
        readbytes = size;
```

```
        }

        sgxMemmove(pDest, &m_pMemDevice->m_Ptr[m_CurrOffset], readbytes);
        m_CurrOffset += readbytes;
        return readbytes;
    }
```

The two important areas to note are:

- The use of our wrappered `sgxMemmove` to avoid alignment problems and enable easy debugging.
- The careful checking of the memory bounds. Reading beyond the end of a file will normally fail because it's protected by the low-level file library, and its corresponding `read` function will return an error code that we can use. But exceeding the bounds in the privileged realm of a computer's memory will likely result in a crash, because no error codes are provided.

In really bad situations, accessing beyond the valid bounds of memory can cause a security issue, as it's possible for hackers with too much time on their hands (hi guys!) to rewrite portions of the game code for nefarious purposes (such as installing Linux) as they did with 007: Agent Under Fire.

Sample Implementation–Disc Drives

The code for handling a disc is similar to the memory file, but not any more complex. The primary difference is that we have to create a block state that holds the current file handle that is API specific. In this example, we're using the Win 32 API.

```
CSGXDeviceBlockState *
CSGXDeviceWin32Disc::Open(CSGXDeviceBlock *pBlk,
    const sgxString &access)
{
    CSGXDeviceBlockStateWin32Disc *pState =
        new CSGXDeviceBlockStateWin32Disc;
    CSGXDeviceBlockWin32Disc *pBlock =
        static_cast<CSGXDeviceBlockWin32Disc *>(pBlk);

    if (access == "rw") {
        pState->m_hFile = ::CreateFile(pBlock->m_Filename.c_str(),
            FILE_WRITE_DATA, FILE_SHARE_READ, 0, OPEN_ALWAYS,
            FILE_ATTRIBUTE_NORMAL, NULL);
```

```
    } else {
        pState->m_hFile = ::CreateFile(pBlock->m_Filename.c_str(),
            FILE_READ_DATA, FILE_SHARE_READ, 0, OPEN_EXISTING,
            FILE_ATTRIBUTE_NORMAL, NULL);
    }

    if (pState->m_hFile == INVALID_HANDLE_VALUE ) {
        return NULL;
    }

    return pState;
}
```

This `m_hFile` handle can then be used as it would normally be in any other Win32 application, wrapped by the usual suspects of file operations, such as `Read`:

```
tMEMSIZE CSGXDeviceBlockStateWin32Disc::Read(tBYTE *pDest,
    tMEMSIZE size)
{
tMEMSIZE size2read = size;
DWORD bytesread;

    ::ReadFile(m_hFile, pDest, size2read, &bytesread, NULL);
    return bytesread;
}
```

The other functions, such as `Seek` and `Write`, also follow this method.

TIP

We explicitly use global scope functions here as a matter of course because in areas like this, we'll probably have a conflict in function names.

ZIP Files

A device based around *ZIP* files is something of a half-way house. Like a disc drive, a ZIP file creates a full directory structure of `CSGXFileEntrys` within the filesystem—although in this case, every entry points to the same physical file on disc. But conversely, it also has similarities with memory files, because much of the data is held internally.

To control the files efficiently, we can use the device itself to hold an array of handles (one for each mounted file) that are passed to the individual file blocks for processing. This also shifts the onus of "how many file handles do we need" from the file open code to the mount code, which happens less often, making it easier to track down problems.

Creating a suitable ZIP file is as easy as using Windows; however, although using a commercial package such as WinZip is certainly cheaper (in terms of development time) than a roll-your-own solution, it does have one flaw that needs to be ironed out.

The ZIP format, as it stands, places the directory list at the end of the file. This means that the mounting code starts at the beginning of the file, seeks to the end, reads the table of contents (TOC), and seeks back to the beginning. This wastes a lot of unnecessary time and can be solved by either creating a separate TOC file on the disc or by preprocessing the ZIP file to add a duplicate TOC at the beginning of the file.

TIP

Always use the minimum number of `seek` *calls when loading as this is usually the slowest of all file access methods.*

In concept, a ZIP is no different from any other type of packed file, such as *tar*. Indeed, the original *Quake 3* PAK files were nothing more elaborate than ZIP files. However, the ZIP format is used in a lot of cross-platform code that is already available, and will support compression out of the box. This latter point is becoming more important as the first playable version of the game comes together, and disc space begins to looks tight.

Filesystem Shortcuts

Readers of high-brow computer literature—that is, big heavy books—will notice that many corners have been cut when developing this filesystem. That is because we can. Our filesystem does not need to worry about fragmentation, sector sizes, or disc limits. Unmounting a filesystem will only occur when all the resources have been cleaned out of memory, so there's no tricky "Unable to unmount" problems to consider. And, we have little use for symlinks, pipes, or character devices.

Most of these shortcuts are possible because we're only dealing with the replication of an existing, and fixed, filesystem. Even the ability to save files to disc has been severely simplified. If you want to implement an all-encompassing (but more difficult) solution, allow us to suggest *BSD*™.

BSD (Berkeley Software Distribution) encompasses the original extensions to AT&T®'s Research Unix OS. It covers an entire OS, including the filesystem, and is available on the Internet under a very generous license. Essentially, it can be used for any purpose, commercial or otherwise, without payment, royalties, or fees. In other words, any programmer can port the BSD filesystem to each of the various consoles. This would then allow a single image to be used for every platform. Just add a custom bootloader and watch the magic unfold. It's like a highly technical version of one massive ZIP file covering the whole disc.

Filesystem Additions

For those that prefer an easier task, you can incorporate several filesystem devices without too much work. Some will be useful to you, and others won't, but we'll suggest them anyway.

`null`

`null` is a dummy file that is mounted in place of another and swallows all data that is written to it. Every operation succeeds, and every write claims to happen. Although in reality, nothing is ever changed. This could be used to calculate the memory required for a file buffer, before it's actually created.

proc

proc is a filesystem of read-only files that holds information about the current state of the processor or game. It could retrieve the throughput of the processor cache or return the number of polygons rendered during the last frame. This is especially good for homesick Linux users, but ultimately less useful than `CGfxEngine::Get()->GetPolyCount()`. It may have a brighter future on networked games as a means of creating pipes between machines.

decrypt/encrypt

If your game is appearing on the PC or PS2 (both of which have easily accessible disc formats), you might want to create a filesystem that decrypts all the data that comes from the disc. This could be done wholesale, or be limited to particular directories where sensitive data or code is kept, like the level data, resource distribution files for a real-time strategy game (RTS), or external pixel shader code.

HANDLING PHYSICAL DEVICES

Like processor speed, the disc drive is a fixed commodity and its properties cannot be avoided. What we cannot hide or abstract, we have to contend with. The following is a set of basic characteristics that exist across platforms. All that varies are the platform-specific numbers attached to each one.

Time to determine file properties: For instance, the disc's size and whether it exists or not. Our filesystem avoids this by storing the disc hierarchy in memory. Some consoles do this, too.

Time to access first file: This latency is governed by the disc starting to spin, and the head moving to the correct location. Fast Constant Linear Velocity (CLV) drives have large latencies due to the time it takes to change the disc's spin speed between inner and outer edges.

Disc read speed: This can vary according to the position of the files on the disc on Constant Angular Velocity (CAV) drives. A simple 24-speed CD-ROM can easily achieve 1.8 MBps at the center of the disc, and more than 3.6 MBps at the outer edge.

Latency to access second and subsequent files: This can differ from the initial file latency problem because the head may not need to move, and the disc would already be spinning.

We can ignore the time that the disc spends to wind down from this list because that can occur while we continue executing the game.

These criteria might be focused toward CD-ROM-based media, but they are also applicable in other situations, such as HTTP. Accessing data across a network has a latency and a variable throughput rate that is analogous to the seek time and read speed of a CD-ROM. Because our abstracted filesystem makes it easy to access data from an external server, we only need to program for an *asynchronous* file idiom to be cross-platform compatible for varying speeds of disc. Not only this, but we'll also be future-proof for networking applications.

Asynchronous Loading

Asynchronous loading is the process of loading data independently of the request, and is also said to be *nonblocking*. The function call requesting the data returns immediately and the program continues as normal. Behind the scenes, however, the filesystem queues the file request and loads the data at the next opportunity. When complete, a callback is made to inform the program that the data is ready, at which point it can patch up pointers (as you saw earlier with `PostSerialize`) or load more data. At no point, does the main program stop running or need to process other file operations, because this is all done independently—usually on a second thread. As mentioned previously, this is a good idiom to follow because it copes with any speed of access, including speeds that vary or fluctuate.

Every OS that supports threads is capable of loading data asynchronously. All that changes is the amount of work required by us to abstract the specifics.

The End Users Interface

The common interface is fairly simple because it's analogous to the more usual synchronous file-handling functions we've seen a thousand times before.

```
CSGXFile::CSGXFile(const sgxString &Name, tBOOL bAsync=FALSE);

void CSGXFile::Read(void *pData, tMEM_SIZE Size,
    pASYNCCALLBACK AsyncCallback, void *pUserData);

void CSGXFile::Close(pASYNCCALLBACK AsyncCallback, void *pUserData);
```

The most noticeable difference here is that we don't return a status from the `Read` or `Close` functions because we're only queuing the operations that we can't indicate any form of success or failure at this time. Some implementers might prefer to return a handle indicating the queued request so that we can poll it later. There's nothing wrong with such an approach.

We *can* retrieve a success (or otherwise) message when we open the file because that can be determined immediately. Our filesystem holds details about every file in memory, remember, so we don't need to spend (synchronous) time waiting for that response.

The callback function is a necessary evil here. Necessary because we need to know when the data has arrived, so we can process it, and evil because the callback must always be a global function or a static member function within a class. To maintain our `this` pointer, we should use functions like this:

```
// Any code inside SomeClass using a callback needs to pass this
// as there's no class instance associated with static members.
pFile->Read(&data, 100, StaticFn, (void *)this);
```

And write the function like this.

```
// This function must be static
void SomeClass::StaticFn(void *pUserData)
{
SomeClass *pThis = static_cast<SomeClass*>(pUserData);

    pThis->ReadHasCompleted();

}
```

TIP

Whenever you use callback functions, there should always be at least one additional parameter apart from the function name. This is to ensure the callback has an intimation of the data that it's required to process, once called. Two parameters are often preferable, but one (of `tMEMSIZE` *or* `size_t`*) is always the bare minimum because anything can be passed in one parameter—even if it's a pointer to a structure containing two elements.*

Which Functions Block?

The file-loading code might not be the only blocking function present. Some platforms also block when opening the file or querying the file size. Determining which functions will block is platform-specific, and only determinable by experimentation or documentation. The rule of thumb is that if the OS has to read data from the disc (be it from the file itself, or the platform's FAT equivalent), then that function will block. Some platforms cache this data locally, or hold the FAT in memory and are nonblocking. Our abstracted filesystem should eliminate most of these blocking cases (such as the size or its existence), while all other blocking functions will be abstracted by our filesystem, and the request will be queued.

The Manager Interface

Despite appearances, an asynchronous file operation should only load one file at a time. This is because each file is placed at a different location on the disc. Loading two files at once is detrimental to performance because the disc head moves backwards and forwards repeatedly between blocks. Instead, each request is queued and serviced in sequence by a manager class that mimics the order in which the game works. One request might constitute a file read, moving the file pointer or closing the file.

```
class CAsyncRequestData {
    tASYNC_CMD  m_Command;

    // Data for reading
    void       *m_pDestMemory;
    tUINT32     m_Size;

    // Data for moving file pointer
    tUINT32     m_Position;

    // Generic
    CPlatform   *m_pPlatform;
    void        *m_pFileHandle;

    // Callback
    CBFN_ASYNC   m_pCallback;
    void        *m_pUserData;
};

CSGXAsyncManager::AddRequest(const CAsyncRequestData &Request)
{
    m_Requests.push_back(Request);
}
```

Every frame, during the update cycle, must poll the status of the most recent file read. If it has finished, we can invoke the callback function and process the next request. If no files are being processed during that frame, we can check the request list, and start the first pending request, should it exist. For example:

```
CSGXAsyncManager::Update()
{
    if (m_ProcessIsReading) {
        if (IsReadingComplete()) {
            m_Requests[0].InvokeCallback();
            m_Requests.pop_front();
            m_ProcessIsReading = FALSE;
        }
    }

    if (!m_ProcessIsReading) {
        ProcessNextRequest();
    }
}
```

The General Case

At a basic level, most APIs provide a function to perform an asynchronous read, giving you the option of specifying a callback. All the current consoles also have their own functions to do this, either through a callback or by polling the request handle whereby you can retrieve the `OS_IsBusy` status on every frame. Windows 2000, XP, and NT require an additional step. After opening the file, you must create a *Completion Port*, but it serves the same purpose, namely to provide an indication of when the file operation has finished. In either case, the abstracted interface you create will appear identical to those using it, and these platform-specific details will be hidden.

The Legacy Case

Three flavors of Windows, namely 95, 98, and Millennium (ME), do not support completion ports. However, if you need to support these OSs, asynchronous file handling is still possible by creating your own thread. This is a worker thread as you saw in Chapter 4, "The CPU," and does nothing but wait for requests from the main thread to load data, or open and close files.

```
// We're using Windows typedefs to match the Windows examples
// which makes it easier to acknowledge what is happening
// here since this code will match any samples we've
```

```
// debased.
DWORD WINAPI Win95WorkerThread(LPVOID pParam)
{
CAsyncManagerWin95 *pAsync =
        static_cast<CAsyncManagerWin95*>(pParam);

    while(TRUE) {
        switch(pAsync->GetStatus()) {
            case ASYNC_IDLE:
                break;

            case ASYNC_DO:
                pAsync->SetStatus(ASYNC_READING);
                pAsync->ReadData();
                pAsync->SetStatus(ASYNC_IDLE);
                break;

            case ASYNC_READING:
                // Cannot get here, but stops compiler warnings
                break;

            case ASYNC_EXIT_THREAD:
                ExitThread(0);
                break;
        }
        // We must not occupy all the processor time by spinning
        sgxYieldWait(0);
    }
    return 0;
}
```

Requests are inserted into the request queue as normal through `CAsyncManager` and picked off by the thread when it's ready to process them. Note that the functions to `Get` and `Set` the status must be protected with mutexes internally to prevent them from causing any of the problems outlined in Chapter 4.

NOTE

Any use of threads requires a multithreaded library. The configuration for Windows was shown previously in Figure 4.5.

Although this solution is for the problems of older Windows machines, the solution could also be adopted with moderate ease to other consoles and OSs. This would certainly limit the amount of new code that needed to be written. However, using the API's own functions (such as completion ports in the case of Win2K) is more efficient because the OS will react faster to the messages than we can, creating a lower latency.

Closing an Asynchronous File Load

The final stage is to provide a simple set of methods to destroy everything asynchronous. This will be used at the end of the game, and between distinct sections of gameplay, perhaps when discs are swapped. In these situations, any data that is queued for loading is wasted because it gets deleted immediately after load. This data can also cause timing issues because the loading normally clashes with the subsequent cut-scene that is typically loaded in these situations, causing disc contention.

Synchronous Loading

Also known as *blocking* I/O, synchronous loading has been with computer programmers since the days of punched cards, and with us since the start of this chapter. After a load request is made, the computer does nothing else until this data had arrived, at which point, the function returns with a value to indicate its success.

A Basic Abstraction

We've already created a perfectly good synchronous filesystem, replete with cross-platform abstractions, so we are not about to create another. Instead, because we must deal with asynchronous file handling too, we'll revisit the code and make some alterations to cope with the problems.

First, each file handle can be considered synchronous or asynchronous. This would mean wrapping every function in swaddling and switching between the two versions. Although not difficult, it's certainly not elegant.

Second, this would *require* us to run a second thread, because while a blocking function is running, nothing else can. However, while we're loading a game level, for example, it's impossible to look at the state of the reset button, determine whether the disc cover has opened, or ascertain if any of the other requirements that might exist on your console of choice have occurred. Even drawing a progress bar can become a little tricky.

Although in theory we could just split each file read up into several small blocks (performing the required checks between each one), it won't work in practice because if the disc cover is opened halfway through reading a block, the function cannot return until the cover is closed. We can't inform the user that the cover is open until that block has finished. So, we definitely need a second thread. Although this is a viable solution, it's not the best.

A Blocking Wrapper

Now that we've spent the time and energy to write an asynchronous file system, we might as well use it. And we can always use it for blocking I/O. Quite simply, we send a request to the filesystem for data, and manually spin until the callback is triggered:

```
void
BlockingReadData(CSGXFile &File, void *pData, tUINT32 size)
{
    tUINT32 Token = 0;

    File.ReadAsyncData(pData, size, BlockingCallback, &Token);
    while(Token == 0) {
        sgxHandleConsoleRequirements();
        sgxYieldWait(1);
    }
}

void
BlockingCallback(void *pUserData)
{
tUINT32 *pToken = (tUINT32 *)pUserData;

    *pToken = 1;
}
```

With some additional coding, we can simplify this process by removing the need for the callback function by adding an `IsComplete` query state function to `CSGXFile`.

NOTE

The mutex blocks around the writing of `pToken` *have been omitted from this example for clarity. In this particular instance, it doesn't matter if we process one extra iteration of the loop or not, however, it might give a false sense of security when we come to write another, similar, case.*

The `sgxHandleConsoleRequirements` function can be redirected to the platform-specific code that determines which elements are vital for continuous checking and which are not—for example, handling the reset button or the disc cover open. Because these cases are special to each platform, a specific function will be written to handle them, and render the appropriate message to the screen.

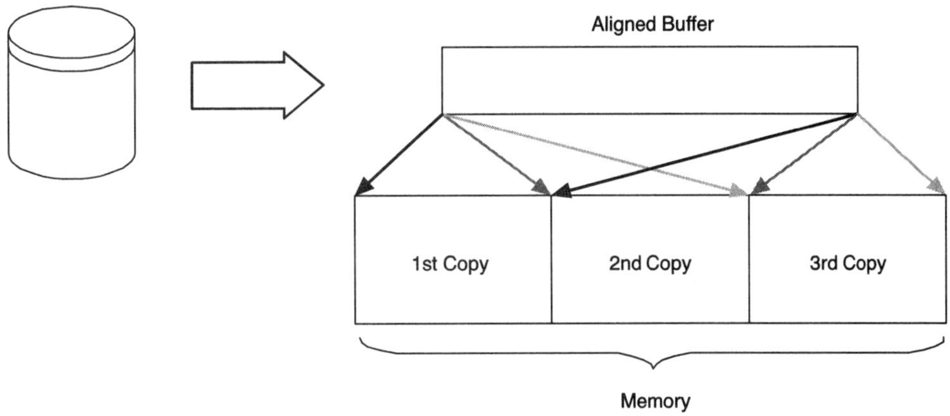

FIGURE 5.7 Loading aligned data.

Block Sizes and Caching

Throughout this section, we've considered the simplest of disc systems—the one that works as we expect it to. However, all computers work as *they* expect to, according to a set of designs and rules to which we must adapt to make them work as *we* want. This creates some additional complications.

Aligned Buffers

Some platforms only read data into aligned buffers. While the rest of memory enjoys a 4-byte requirement, handling data from the disc might involve an alignment of 128 bytes or more. This means we need an additional buffer for loading, as shown in Figure 5.7.

This is achieved in the low-level platform driver, where every request from the user is split into blocks. Data then flows from the disc into the specially aligned buffer, and is copied out into the user's memory.

```
SGX_PACKDATA_BEGIN(128)
tBYTE ms_AsyncBuffer[SGX_ASYNC_BUFFER];
SGX_PACKDATA_END(128);

// Replace the load request with several smaller ones

size_left = Request.m_DataSize;
do {
    AlignedRequest = Request;
    AlignedRequest.m_pBuffer = ms_AsyncBuffer;
    AlignedRequest.m_DataSize = SGX_ASYNC_BUFFER;
```

```
        AlignedRequest.m_pCallback = NULL;

        if (size_left > SGX_ASYNC_BUFFER) {
            size_left -= SGX_ASYNC_BUFFER;
        } else {
            size_left = 0;
            AlignedRequest.m_pCallback = Request.m_pCallback;
        }

        CAsyncManager::AddRequest(AlignedRequest);
    }
    while(size_left > 0);
```

Additionally, some consoles only read from the disc on cluster boundaries. This requires a similar mechanism.

This method also assists development on those platforms that require all disc operations to load into contiguous memory. Exactly the same loop is required; we just need to change the `ms_AsyncBuffer` buffer to one allocated in the correct manner for the platform.

The size of this buffer is platform-specific, and resides in the global portion of the memory (see Chapter 3 for a discussion on "Global versus Game" memory). The buffer can be any size you have available for it. General-purpose temporary memory, despite its transient nature, is not usually suitable here because it prevents any number of calling functions from using it. Furthermore, you're likely to find many people wanting to load (non inplace) data into the very same temporary buffer during this process, so it's best to avoid such memory blocks.

TIP

If you have to poll for the reset button during the game, this loop can help determine a suitable size for the block size. If your platform can load 2 MBps, and you need to respond to button presses within 1/10th second, then the block size is a very obvious 200 KB.

Caching

Our serialization method from earlier in this chapter, although powerful, does have some performance problems when used on its own. It is, after all, a process whereby bytes are loaded individually, and their contents are used to determine how many further bytes to load.

Cross-platform disc caches are difficult to create because every system has its own way of referencing files on the disc, making it harder to know which file would be loaded next, and preventing us from beginning a preload into memory.

Instead, we can adopt one of two different methods, both of which scale well. The first one is to forget about the problem, and let the console worry about the cache. This is not always available, but will generate good performance increases when it does.

The second involves creating a look-ahead cache for the current file, not the disc. This is implemented as a third layer in-between the filesystem and the device. Because a file is loaded in parts, the first request for data is usually followed by a second request for the data that immediately follows it. This makes for a very easy predication algorithm as the look-ahead cache can automatically fill itself on each request with the next consecutive piece of data. This always holds true because you'll never need to seek backwards in the file when loading.

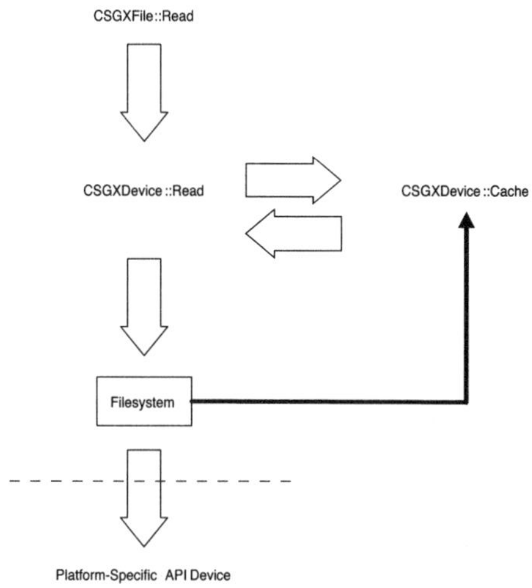

FIGURE 5.8 Adopting a cache.

In all cases, it's quicker to request a single 100 KB chunk from the disc than loading 100 1 KB blocks. It also provides the opportunity for the disc head to seek elsewhere (for example, a streamed movie or sound) without thrashing between your file and another.

TIP

A single stream is usually enough for game data, with all the other streams given over to multimedia content.

The cache architecture is shown in Figure 5.8.

This file-oriented cache can be as large, or small, as you like. In truth, it needs to be as large as you *need* because there are requirements on all platforms to load the game within a specific time, so you'll need to increase the size of the cache until you reach that target. The rules for profiling also apply here: start with the game loading in a suitable timeframe, and stop growing the level when it exceeds its temporal budget. This ensures that we adopt a "ship any day" policy.

Additionally, if the target appears elusive, you might need to combine several files into one (as we did earlier with ZIP files) to cut down on the seek time, and improve the chance of cache hits when loading. Although we don't know what the next file will be, we do know the file is likely to be in the cache because it's part of the same ZIP file we're currently reading. With a little extra work, you can create the ZIP file in such a way that each file within it is stored in the same order that it will be loaded. This can be managed by writing out a log file from a typical game run that is then post-processed into a ZIP file by the offline tools. The look-ahead cache will not only have the next part of the current file in its memory, but will have the next file, too.

The General Case

Write as much code to work with asynchronous file handling as you can. As threading becomes more prevalent, process requests will be sent to different CPUs (not just to disc controllers) and their results will be passed back asynchronously. Starting now will not only make this transition easier, but also provide a means of streaming data from other sources in an identical fashion. These sources could enable a pain-free jump to network programming, a means of handling the memory card, or a method to implement virtual memory.

Currently, only the GameCube has sufficient external memory (in the form of ARAM) to make virtual memory a fast enough possibility. But because this memory is attached to the audio chip and not the processor, it has to be transferred to main memory through DMA (Direct Memory Access) calls. This also responds in an asynchronous fashion, enabling the same code that streams data from the disc on one platform, to stream information from ARAM on another.

CREATING BACK DOORS

Despite all the polite software engineering terminology and methods we use, there will always be hacks. These back doors are necessary because the gaming field needs direct access to data at times, and any other formal method would be too slow. Typical situations for this live in the audio and video arenas. Audio streams are often used for speech and music that are too incidental to the game for them to be held in main memory all the time, and movies often play cut-scenes that would be too bulky to handle in any other way. If all our data is hidden behind abstractions, accessing this data could become more troublesome.

Going Around the Problem

Go around the abstractions and cross-platform niceties we've put in place. It doesn't break with tradition because the code in question, say movie playback, will be platform-specific anyway and its use will usually be limited to cut-scenes. We can create a `Suspend` method to relinquish any exclusive locks the engine may still hold, and process as if it were a single platform game.

The only instance where we need to be more careful is when the movie playback is integrated with the gameplay. In these situations, it might be possible to run out of file handles on one particular platform, but not another because we'll be accessing the filesystem in two different ways. This problem can be solved by using the cross-platform component of the movie playback to open the file twice: once through the normal filesystem, and again by the back door inside the playback code. In both cases, we must remember to close both files after the movie has finished. Our filesystem will then know about this extra file handle and not permit other files to use it, which ensures that there are enough file handles in general.

In some (extremely rare) situations, where the movie playback code expects exclusive access to the file it will be reading, it might become necessary to create a dummy file alongside our movie. We can perform the same operation as described previously, except it operates on a dummy file such as `mymovie.mpg.dmy`, keeping the number of file handles in use artificially high.

Knowing the Device

Although we have endeavored to keep the secret identity of our filesystem from the end user, we can't obscure it totally because we must be able to determine the media type from which we're loading, as this may determine which modules should be loaded to support the platform fully. PS2 programmers working with the Input Output Processor (IOP)—this means you.

A ZIP Warning

Although ZIP files are a necessity for PS2, the compression option should be limited to your own data files. Most third-party libraries (including Jason Page's excellent first-party code, *MultiStream*) expect to get a raw, uncompressed, data stream. This is mostly true of audio and video libraries, and cases where data is DMAd from disc. If you are only offering them compressed data, a lot of messy code will be necessary to rectify this problem. The best solution is to leave the zipped data uncompressed—either for the whole game (making it easy to debug file dumps), or for just the necessary data. Libraries will generally take one of three approaches.

- They handle the entire disc I/O themselves using the platform's own SDK or their abstracted version of it.
- They use a callback that you provide to fill a specific buffer with data.
- They request an already opened file handle (and offset within the file) where they can retrieve their data using the API's I/O functions.

In the first case, you have no choices, and must provide the files separately on the disc. They can be mounted into your custom filesystem (so you have access to them), but you must not control the file by requesting an exclusive lock on it, for example. Although it's annoying to program special case scenarios for these libraries, it's primarily detrimental to PS2 games where ZIP files are essential. Fortunately, most library vendors have acknowledged this problem (especially with their PS2 code) and won't use their own I/O exclusively. If that isn't the case, think very carefully about using that library; it might be better to switch vendors.

The second case is naturally the best because it fits directly into our cross-platform filesystem without change. Because you are supplying data, not file handles, you can even keep the data compressed on disc.

Finally, the half-way house solution, as adopted by the likes of *MultiStream* is a capable solution that works well, although it does require some platform-specific code (which is usually in the platform-specific driver anyway, so no harm is done there) to provide the file handle and offset.

ENDNOTES

1. To accurately represent a floating-point number requires more than 20 characters when written out in full. If floats ever need to be written in text, then either accept the loss in accuracy (which is not generally recommended for graphics) or store them as 4-byte hex numbers (representing the exact IEEE bit patterns) that can be imported directly into memory.
2. The player is not the only one expecting the game to load fast between levels. Most console manufacturers have requirements for maximum load times.
3. It only allows you to create synonyms for existing types.
4. One possible solution, which minimizes duplicity, requires the creation of a null file type. This allows you to read and write as much data as you like, despite the fact that the information is never stored anywhere. Instead, it

just keeps track of the current (imaginary) file pointer so you can determine how many bytes were "written" for that chunk. You can then call serialize again with a genuine file reference, and perform the actual file writes.

5. The SMB protocol is currently used for Windows file sharing, but is a well known standard. Open source code exists in the form of the Samba project, which can be used to allow a Linux machine to participate in a Windows network without any problems. This code could be ported to any of the consoles to provide this functionality for the tool chain.

6 Debugging

In This Chapter

- Basic Requirements
- Debugging Methods
- Implementing Debugging Code
- Output Targets
- Making Data Readable
- Maintaining Consistency

BASIC REQUIREMENTS

Although a solid design and good programmers are the cornerstones to any development practice, the debugging process is one you'll approach time and time again. Code is written once, read twice, and debugged forever. Because of its importance, you should adopt the best practices for debugging.

The debugging process applies in three instances: before the coding (design), during the coding (implementation), and after the coding (testing). At each stage, the bug hunt becomes progressively more involved, and usually more costly to fix.

In this chapter, we'll consider the latter two stages, study methods for writing cross-platform code that prevent bugs, and (for when that fails) trace the program while it is running, irrespective of the hardware or debugger.

DEBUGGING METHODS

The methods we'll look at here could apply to game development on any platform. There's nothing magical about ideas such as "initialize your variables." The methods discussed serve as a good primer, if nothing else, and gets everyone reading from the same page. You should find that preventing bugs in a single instance also prevents them in general and across platforms.

Coding Style

Every company has its own set of coding guidelines. For the most part, whatever has been laid down should be adopted. The following sections are suggested variations to ease the debugging phase of cross-platform game development.

Use of Scope

The opening brace indicates a statement block that allows new variables to be created at a different scope. This permits the following:

```
for(int i=0;i<10;i++) {
    int i=5;

    sgxTrace("i=%d", i);
}
```

This loop runs 10 times, as expected, but does not produce the incrementing output we expect because the second occurrence of `i` is at a different scope. However, this can cause the debugger (and the human using it) to get confused between the two variables, as there is no clear way to distinguish between them.

Some compilers produce a warning on such code. Others won't, so don't wait for the warnings to appear; otherwise, someone using a different compiler (such as your PS2 programmer) will hit problems for unexpected reasons.

On a similar theme, don't reuse an old variable name in a new situation because it too causes comprehension problems.

Order of Expressions

Despite having all the rules of precedence built-in to the language, we should add extra brackets for clarity as it provides a safety blanket for those difficult to track down bugs where "the compiler must be wrong."

There are a couple of traditional examples to quote here.

```
if (count % 4 == 0)
```

This often-quoted problem occurs because the modulus operator (`%`) has a lower precedence than the comparison and so it evaluates last, behaving as if we'd written:

```
if (count % (4==0))
```

Another bug-prevention method involves reversing the expression, so instead of

```
if (x == 42)
```

we write

```
if (42 == x)
```

which prevents the classic "single equals" bug if one of the `=` symbols is omitted. After all, `x=42` is valid, but `42=x` is not. Although, naturally, this doesn't help in the case of `x == y`.

Additionally, when testing the zero case (that is, `x == 0`), it's usually better to write

```
if (!x)
```

instead, because this removes the possibility of mistyping the double equals entirely.

Initializing Variables

Make sure all local variables are all initialized to zero or some other pertinent value. The same is true with dynamic allocation, where it's normal to fill the uninitialized memory with easy-to-spot data, such as signaling NaNs. Local variables used without initialization are often warned against in the compiler, but you can't rely on that.

When dealing with classes, a constructor is always called, even if it's the default constructor where nothing happens. In fact, the compiler automatically writes and calls six different functions for every class you create (default and copy constructor, destructor, the assignment operator, and two address-of operators). It's then up to the optimizer, or linker, to remove them. Use the constructor—that is its job, after all—to make sure you have a perfectly valid object every time.

TIP

You can prevent the default constructor from being called by making it private. This ensures that any class you create must be given valid data through a customized copy constructor. Note that you should always create a default constructor if you also write a nondefault one—although some compilers are lenient and do not require this.

Initializing objects through a constructor might appear to be a time sink, but in reality so little of the main game loop is spent initializing objects that you shouldn't worry about it until the profiler tells you otherwise. (There is an antithesis to this called the vector exception, which you saw in Chapter 5, "Storage.") As always, write the code in a safe and structured manner first and optimize later in only those areas that need it.

Use of Macros

Much has been written about the correct use and creation of macros as if they are fraught with danger. Not because they are ill-conceived in any particularly way, but because macros have been used for many tasks that were not originally intended. Once a means of using `TRUE` instead of `1`, macros have since been used to implement everything from debugging routines, to complete functions and compiler-based assertions.

For most programmers, however, the walk away from the C language toward C++ has not caused every new path to be trodden. Macros are *still* overused, and, naturally, the bugs they cause are still present.

Inline Functions

In C++, inline functions can replace the majority of macros currently in use. Adding such a function requires the keyword `inline` to be placed before the function name. This is part of the language, and therefore available on all our platforms. However, we'll abstract this away into `SGX_INLINE` and `SGX_FORCE_INLINE` so we can remove `inline` for test scenarios and uniformity. This second macro replaces the compiler extension of `__force_inline`, or similar, for those situations that really need the optimization.

```
#define SGX_INLINE          inline
// Replace __force_inline with inline if unsupported
#define SGX_FORCE_INLINE    __force_inline
```

NOTE

The `inline` keyword has been part of the standard since C99, which is the one used here. However, it has been given as an extension for many years and is consequently well supported.

Both of these macros are only *hints* at the compiler to inline; the compiler is not obliged to do so. You might need to further massage the project settings to encourage the compiler to inline them for you. Therefore, the inline functions should be used as a note to yourself, which produces self-documenting code.

If you need to force the inline issue, then you can create a separate file called `math.inl`, and write all your functions there. This file can then be `#included` in the header by compilers supporting inline, and in the source by those that don't. This prevents two function bodies from conflicting in the linker.

TIP

Make sure all inline functions are declared before use; some compilers will not inline them otherwise.

Templates

A *template is* a C++ feature that you saw extensively in Chapter 5. Templates allow you to replace macros with equivalent functions using a replacement type. Many macros work because no inherent type information is included within them. The populist example is of `min` and `max`.

```
#define min(a,b)    ( ((a)<(b)) ? (a) : (b) )
#define max(a,b)    ( ((a)>(b)) ? (a) : (b) )
```

A template provides a mechanism whereby separate functions are produced for each different type with which the code is called. Provided you're not using macros like `min` and `max` to compare objects of different types (and you never should be), a template function works wonders.

```
template <typename T>
const T sgxMin(const T &v1, const T &v2)
{
    if (v1 < v2) {
        return v1;
    } else {
        return v2;
    }
}
```

Enumerations

Despite existing in the C language for many years, enumerations appear to have taken a back seat when compared to a list of `#defines`. Switching to `enums` not only makes the code easier to write, it gives some scope for type correctness, and provides the debugger with more information with which to work.

As you saw in Chapter 3, "Memory," we must also make sure the last element is `0x7fffffff`, or at least its linguistically friendly, `SGX_ENUM_PADDING`.

If You Must Use Macros

This should apply more to engine programmers because their code will be on the critical path more often, but if you *must* use macros at least follow the traditional rules. This will ensure that no compiler-specific issues arise from their use. And a compiler-specific problem always manifests itself into a platform-specific problem.

First, use a lot of brackets. Use at least one around each argument of the macro, plus one for the expression as a whole to make sure the precedence is maintained for any expression that is applied to it. Furthermore, never use the same variable twice because any self-modifying expression used in conjunction with the macro will result in compiler-specific results. This typical example

```
#define SQUARE(a)    ( (a) * (a) )
```

results in errors with expressions like

```
wrong = SQUARE(iCount++);
```

because the macros expands to

```
wrong = ( (iCount++) * (iCount++) );
```

This is unexpected, and the result will almost certainly differ between machines. Be wary of math routines that are written as macros to achieve their speed, as they can easily fall foul of this problem, especially when two identical arguments are given by the programmer.

TIP

A good rule of thumb is that if you can call a macro with something like `iCount++` *or* `a + b`*, and there are no side effects, you have a reasonably robust macro.*

Where two instances of the same variable are required (and you're not ready to use inline functions or templates), you should employ the `do-while` trick. This technique avoids the problem we've already seen by creating a separate *scope* in which new variables can live. These local variables can then be reused without damaging the input parameters.

```
#define sgxNormalize(v) do { tREAL32 d=sgxAbsV3(v); \
    sgxDivideV3(v,d); } while(0)
```

This technique is not without its issues, however, because a function call should evaluate to an expression, whereas the `do-while` loop is a statement; this is formally incorrect because an expression can be considered a statement, but not vice versa. This construct has other problems too insomuch as we can't `return` a value from it, but if we cannot use `inline` or `template` functions, then this is the safest method for creating a macro.

Naming Conventions

Be sure to choose a naming convention, preferably with some scope for expansion in the cross-platform arena.

Some code will only compile on certain platforms, but to distinguish between code that will and code that won't, it's so much easier to read the name than to search for its definition. Something as simple as a platform prefix is enough.

```
PS2_GetNumMemoryCards();
```

You might also find it convenient to differentiate between the Xbox and DirectX builds because despite their heritage, significant differences exist between them that need to be considered.

Don't Modify Parameters

Any parameter that is passed into a function by value becomes a local variable. Although you can change its value as often as you like, it's not a good idea. This is because some debuggers show the call stack by dumping the memory contents of the stack, and not the values passed to the function. If the value on the stack is now a local variable, it will get changed as the function executes. A simple function such as

```
tUINT32 CountEnemyNPCs(tUINT32 iTotal)
{
tUINT32 iCount = 0;

    while(iTotal–) {
        if (pNPC[iTotal].IsEnemy()) {
            iCount++;
        }
    }
    return iCount;
}
```

can cause puzzled looks. Imagine the code seems rather sluggish, and the debugger is paused inside this function. The value of `iTotal` might appear to indicate that only 10 objects were prepared for processing, and we're just about to start (or have just started) iterating around the loop. In which case, you're very likely to think, "We've only just started running this loop. This cannot be the problem." And, you'll move on. What has actually happened is that it's already processed the first 100,000 erroneous entries, and there are now just 10 left to go. C++ users can prevent this problem from ever occurring by using `const` here, with the following prototype:

```
tUINT32 CountEnemyNPCs(const tUINT32 iTotal)
```

The `const` keyword will warn, at compile-time, about any attempt to change the value of `iTotal`.

We get a bigger win when applying this idea to larger datatypes. Vectors, for example, can regularly pass 12 bytes or more to every function that uses them. Replacing them with a constant reference instantly maintains the integrity of 24 data bytes within the debugger, and *usually* improves the execution speed because the references are generally passed into the function through the registers, as opposed to the stack. So instead of doing

```
tREAL32 sgxDotProduct(sgxVector v1, sgxVector v2);
```

you should do

```
tREAL32 sgxDotProduct(const sgxVector &v1, const sgxVector &v2);
```

This stipulation also means that the results of any validation performed on the input parameters have to be nondestructive as well. We say "*usually* improves the executions speed" because processors with vector units (such as SSE and VU0) provide a counterexample, but this is usually limited to the platform-specific portions of the low-level drivers.

Debugging Methodologies

One of our top tips from Chapter 2, "Top Ten Tips," was that a good debugging method can win out over a great debugger. In additional to the prevention techniques you've just seen, there are also the curing processes of how to actually use the debugger.

All the ideas presented here do not require any particularly debugger or platform and can be applied in any situation.

Source Control

Only people building engines with stone wheels and coal burners will fail to see the benefit of source control as part of their standard build process. But having source control isn't just a way for your manager to keep an Orwellian eye on your progress; it can also be a lifesaver when it comes to debugging because it allows you to revert to previous versions that did work and trace the progress of the bug. For this reason, it's best to check in a lot of very small changes, as opposed to a single large one.

If you're working on code in isolation away from the main development team, you can set up your own private area for source control. This enables you to make a lot of check ins without polluting the main branch of the repository. You can then integrate these changes back to the main branch when you've fully written and tested the code. Most source control programs support this workflow method; what differs is how well they manage it, and how much processing and disk space it requires.

On the micro-level, the undo buffer of your text editor provides a minimal form of source control that allows you to see your previous attempts at implementing a solution. This is not recommended as a replacement for source control, but rather a temporary complement so that you can review the changes and thinking that led to the current implementation over the past couple of hours. As a warning, however, remember that if you undo a lot of work and (accidentally) add a single character to the editor, it will no longer be possible to redo the changes back to the original state.

Binary Split

Binary split helps track down problems to a small area of the source by eliminating half of the code at each step. It can be used to track down problems such as memory corruption, badly performing algorithms, and erroneous data. If you're familiar with the binary search algorithm, you already understand how this works. If not,the process is as follows:

Knowing the bug exists somewhere between the start and end of the code, place a breakpoint (or output a trace message) half-way through. The bug now exists in the first, or second, half of the code and your trace message will intimate which. You then consider the faulty half of your code as if it were the whole source, and place a breakpoint halfway between the new start and end, and so on. Repeating this step will eventually resolve itself to one line that causes the problem. Because the search area halves each time, this technique scales well. One bug in a linear 4 billion-line program (not that you'd write such a beast) can be found in, at most, 16 steps.

The difficultly comes in determining a half-way point, but this can be eased by making an initial step that considers each subsystem separately: the draw loop, the update loop, and so forth. So, for example, having found the corrupt memory location (by watching the machine crash at least once before, say), we can monitor its state on either side of the update loop. We can also place checks around the update and draw calls of individual objects to concentrate our initial search because the biggest difficulty in finding the half-way point stems from the vast number of loops that are usually present in code.

Stepping Stones

The stepping stones method is a largely preventative measure that requires a debugger with a single step facility. On the first test run of a new routine, the code is stepped through line by line, from the beginning to the end, which forces the programmer to watch the code path unfold, and the variables change accordingly. This is very interesting to watch, as the expected behavior does not always present itself. It can be a time-consuming task, but it encourages more thought during the original implementation, and is a more sure-fire preventative method than just running the game "to see what happens" and then fix accordingly.

Use Disassembly

Disassembly should only be employed as a last resort, or when you already know where the problem lies and cannot work out why the code is faulty. The basic premise of this method is that not even compiler writers are flawless, and in some cases, the compiler (or its libraries) may be at fault. Most debuggers will let you step through the disassembled code and watch the registers change accordingly. Although much of it will look incomprehensible at first, after a short while, it will begin to make sense. After all, it's always easier to read code than it is to write it.

IMPLEMENTING DEBUGGING CODE

Even with a series of good metaphors and debugging stratagems, we still need *something* to aid us during debugging. The debugger will help us, but controlling it is a very selfish operation because whenever we're in the debugger looking at variables or checking the call stack, the game isn't running—only the debugger is. This applies to all software running on a single thread. For a runtime commentary on the game, we need to write some additional debugging code.

For the most part, this code will be written through macros because it's much easier to remove any code they reference from the nondebug builds. In release builds, for example, the pseudo-function we've been using so far, `sgxTrace`, might exist as:

```
#define sgxTrace    sizeof
```

This replaces the original function call with a bracketed expression that gets evaluated at compile time. Because the results of this expression are not stored anywhere, the optimizer dutifully removes it. Such debugging functions/macros would be wrapped with the cross-platform compatible macro, SGX_DEBUG_BUILD, creating the fully-fledged form of

```
#if SGX_DEBUG_BUILD
    #define sgxTrace     sgxOutputTrace
#else
    #define sgxTrace     sizeof
#endif
```

But this trace macro is only the start. Like most of the game, debugging is a multilayered problem. Initially, we need a method to output a string, any string, to the debug window. This is followed by the more complex routines that take arguments, allow message filtering, and perhaps log the messages into an external file.

Trace Messages

The most common way to retrieve information about the running program, apart from looking at the screen, is through *trace messages*. This text-only form of computer communication began with source code littered with `printf` calls, all intending to track the progress of the program under test. We haven't moved that far.

Of the many methods we'll be employing in this chapter, we must first determine how to write trace messages to the output. This will vary according to platform, but will invariably consist of a single function call that writes a `char *` string to the debug window; a suitable trace function (such as `OutputDebugString`) will usually have been provided by the API. For consoles, this debug window may be a separate application running on the host PC that retrieves messages through the serial port or across the network. .NET users have their own integrated message window, although *any* message sent to a debug window is generally slow, regardless of platform or architecture.

```
void sgxOutputTraceMessage(const char *pMessage)
{
    OutputDebugString(pMessage);
    OutputDebugString("\n");
}
```

This version (for the Win32 API) exists in its own file, and sits alongside files for each of the other platforms where any idiosyncrasies of the trace function can be catered to—like the one shown here where `OutputDebugString` doesn't add a carriage return. Although this might appear to provide less functionality than the original, the only feature we lack is the ability to print progressive text into the debug window. This is no severe loss because we (should) have an onscreen load bar for the data preparation phase, and a game that executes so fast that such text would be pointless during runtime.

To supplement this single cross-platform prototype, we have a unified header file that covers a number of similar routines that exist as cross-platform code. These routines use *ellipses* to provide a `printf`-style interface to the rest of the game.

```
void sgxOutputTrace(const char *pMessage, ...)
{
    static char buffer[1024];

    va_list va;

    va_start(va, pMessage);
    vsprintf(buffer, pMessage, va);
    va_end(va);

    sgxOutputTraceMessage(buffer);
}
```

Believe it or not, these two functions form the backbone of our entire cross-platform trace system. We can provide many more tracing mechanisms by extending and adopting this code.

CAUTION

Remember to adopt the threadsafe idioms for production code, as shown in Chapter 4, "The CPU." Such devices have been omitted here for clarity.

Trace Levels

The ease at which messages can be added to the source is very often its undoing. Every programmer adds a couple of messages to report the progress of his own code, but no one ever takes them out. It's not uncommon to suddenly find 100 new trace messages scrolling past after a new build. Like warning messages in the compiler, this makes it more difficult to spot the important, new messages that you're interested in. We should therefore create mechanisms to limit and control these messages.

The methods you employ can be as simple or as complex as you're willing to write. We'll look at several ideas here.

Warning Levels

The warning levels method grades each message on a scale from 1 to 5, with 1 being ordinary informational messages and 5 being fatal errors. This breaks down to the following:

5 Fatal Error: For drivers or OS components that cannot be initialized. There is no way to continue.

4 Error: General problems, such as lack of memory, where the situation can recover, but only at the expense of some functionality.

3 Warning: When size limits are reached and emergency steps are being taken, for example, flushing caches and buffers.

2 Message: One-off pieces of information about the game, such as how many NPCs have been created, the amount of memory used by the graphics engine, or the time taken to load the current level.

1 Information: Casual, transient, information, such as game and engine state changes.

We can represent these warning messages in code with the following:

```
#define SGX_ERR_FATAL       5
#define SGX_ERR_ERROR       4
#define SGX_ERR_WARNING     3
#define SGX_ERR_MESSAGE     2
#define SGX_ERR_INFO        1
```

By extending our trace functions to include the warning levels, we can control the verbosity of our output by comparing the trace level with a predetermined limit, set by a simple call to:

```
SetTraceLevel(SGX_ERR_MESSAGE);
```

In addition to these error levels, we can add two special meta-ranks:

```
#define SGX_ERR_REPORT_NONE  6
#define SGX_ERR_REPORT_ALL   0
```

We can then indicate what level of messages we're interested in, and the trace function will act across the entire application. The only decision we then have to make is whether we'll include all messages *up to* this severity or ignore those *below* it. Our implementation considers that fatal errors and the like are so important that we (nearly) always want to see them. Therefore, a trace level of `SGX_ERR_MESSAGE` means everything at the message level and above. For those that read C code more efficiently than natural language, this would read:

```
void sgxOutputTrace(tINT32 idx, const char *pMessage, ...)
{
    if (idx < g_iTraceLevel) {
        return;
    }
    // ... normal output code
}
```

TIP

For those working closely with QA, a separate trace level called `SGX_ERR_BUGID` *should be added. This trace can exist at any level, and provides an easy way for people to see which bugs are believed fixed, and an even easier way to remove spurious trace messages after the fix has been verified.*

Filenames and Line Numbers

Filenames and line numbers information are very useful to have. When a trace message is given, knowing which particular function has changed the game state is often more useful than the fact that it has been changed. For this reason, and many others, it's beneficial to have access to the filename and line number of the code that generated the trace message. The preprocessor is very considerate in this regard as it provides two macros that indicate both properties. These can obviously only be used within macros because the only location that emits messages would otherwise be limited to `trace.cpp`, line 32. We consequently have another good reason to keep the user-focused `sgxTrace` routine a macro.

The macros in question are called `__FILE__` and `__LINE__`, which produce a character string and integer, respectively. Using them within our `sgxOutputTrace` function is not straightforward because macros are not permitted to take multiple arguments, nor can they use ellipses.

So instead of adding these arguments to the end of a line, we must add them to the beginning, creating a prototype like this:

```
void sgxOutputTrace(tUINT32 idx, const char *pFile, tMEMSIZE iLine,
    const char *pMessage, ...);
```

Our `sgxTrace` macro redirects our code to the function that supports ellipses, and then we have a macro to replace the string with additional parameters for trace level, filename, line number, and then the message text. The macros that make the magic work are:

```
#define SID_FATAL(Msg)       SGX_ERR_FATAL,__FILE__,__LINE__,Msg
#define SID_ERROR(Msg)       SGX_ERR_ERROR,__FILE__,__LINE__,Msg
#define SID_WARNING(Msg)     SGX_ERR_WARNING,__FILE__,__LINE__,Msg
#define SID_MESSAGE(Msg)     SGX_ERR_MESSAGE,__FILE__,__LINE__,Msg
#define SID_INFO(Msg)        SGX_ERR_INFO,__FILE__,__LINE__,Msg
```

This causes our trace invocation to look like this:

```
sgxOutputTrace(SID_INFO("State change: %d => %d"), iPrev, iState);
```

Additionally, we can create a default trace macro for the one we use most often to cut down on those all-important keystrokes:

```
#define SID(Msg)             SID_WARNING(Msg)
```

Our new `sgxOutputTrace` function would appear like this:

```
void
sgxOutputTrace(tUINT32 idx, const char *pFile, tMEMSIZE iLine,
    const char *pMessage, ...)
{
    static char buffer[1024];
    va_list va;

    if (idx < g_iTraceLevel) {
        return;
    }

    sprintf(buffer, "%s(%d): ", pFile, iLine);

    va_start(va, pMessage);
    vsprintf(strchr(buffer, '\0'), pMessage, va);
    va_end(va);

    sgxOutputTraceMessage(buffer);
}
```

The format used for the filename/line number combination is very important, because the debug window often has a miniature parser that "does something" with strings formatted in a particular way. The format given here causes .NET to jump to the file (and line) in question when you double-click on it.

Using an `sgxTrace` macro is not merely a convenience when calling the function, it also helps remove the trace code when building final release versions. Setting the trace level to `SGX_ERR_REPORT_NONE` may stop the messages from being output, but it does not stop the code from being compiled in, as the optimizer cannot determine whether the trace messages will be used. This data compromises filenames and comment strings, and can amount to a significant portion of your memory.

This gives us a complete, usable trace system, but only in general. We now need to consider the module-specific instances.

Submodules

Within a game—any game—we'll have a number of modules. There might be one for AI, one for audio, one for graphics, and so on. If their trace messages are all vying for the attention of the programmer, something will get missed. It might be something benign, but if deadlines are looming, Murphy's Law dictates that the "missed" something will be important. To combat this, we should implement a filter that works according to module. This can be in addition to, or instead of, the warning scale we've already implemented.

Splitting messages according to modules also reflects the team dynamic, as one programmer is normally assigned to each subsystem. This allows them to read their own messages, without being bombarding by those of other programmers.

The code for a module-oriented trace is very simple because we've already written exactly the same thing for the global case with `sgxTrace`. We can simply copy and paste the `sgxOutputTrace` and `sgxOutputError` functions into a class definition, say `CTraceModule`, and create an instance of this class inside each module in the game.

The identical code now residing in `CTraceModule` and `sgxTrace` can be remedied easily.

Going Global

There's nothing wrong with considering our entire game as a module, and using a pseudo-module to capture all its trace messages. It certainly cuts down on duplicate code, and the additional memory and processor speed overhead in using the class is negligible.

The implementation for such a class requires its own singleton (because it no longer lodges in somebody else's class), and an alternative macro for `sgxTrace`, like this:

```
#define sgxTrace    CGlobalTrace::Get()->OutputTrace
```

We can then move our other generic trace functions across to the class like this:

```
void CTraceModule::SetTraceLevel(tINT32 iLevel)
{
    m_iTraceLevel = sgxRange(iLevel, SGX_ERR_REPORT_ALL,
      SGX_ERR_REPORT_NONE);
}
```

to create a fully featured trace system.

Ellipses as Parameters

So far, we've added functions without worrying about duplicate code. Every trace function that handles ellipses incorporates its own trinity of `va_start`, `vsprintf`, and `va_end`. This might appear like a candidate for its own function, enabling us to pass the ellipses as a parameter in its own right to some other function, but there's no portable way to achieve this in C or C++. Some vendors supply functions like `vsnprintf` with their libraries to achieve this end, but this is not recommended.

TIP

Throughout this chapter, we've used the standard C type of `char`*, and not our predefined, cross-platform types of* `tUCHAR`*,* `tCHAR`*, or even* `tBYTE`*. This is not to say that such matters are unimportant where debugging is concerned, but the parameters we would normally pass to these functions are standard C strings, like "*`Changing AI state now.`*" These get evaluated by the language as* `char *`*, which may differ from the current platform's* `tCHAR` *type. So by using* `char` *throughout the module, we don't have any warnings about type, and can eliminate the need for extensive casting.*

Running with Threads

The biggest time sink with trace messages is usually the time it takes to communicate with the host PC or debug window. As the communication takes place, small delays often appear onscreen, and the game suddenly jitters and drops one or two fps from the display. To avoid this problem, you might want to run the low-level `sgxOutputTraceMessage` function in conjunction with a thread. The `sgxOutputTraceMessage` function then stores the messages it receives from the main game thread, while a second worker thread (running at a lower priority) takes messages at a convenient time and dispatches them to the debug window.

Limits and Static Counts

The creation of a new scope allows us to create new variables, too. One interesting application is to create a trace macro with its own `static` variable. This will create a new variable for every trace message in the system, the value of which will remain throughout runtime. Granted, this may add several kilobytes to your debug-only memory footprint, but it will enable you to stop individual trace messages after, say, 100 of them have been output.

Some messages, like "`Mesh has 50000 polygons, slow render ahead!`" might be considered a good sanity check for the engine and artists, but when a particular boss requires it, the continuous stream of messages is annoying and obstructive. In these cases, a limited trace that ignores all future messages might be a better answer.

```
#define sgxTraceLimit(limit, trace)     do { \
  static tUINT32 n=limit; \
  if (n && n--) { trace } \
} while(0)
```

This only works as a macro, because otherwise you would be limited to 100 trace messages, *in total*—not per type.

Because of the limitations with macros and variable arguments, we have to include the entire trace implementation as a single parameter to `sgxTraceLimit`. This might look unwieldy as the invocation appears as:

```
sgxTraceLimit(100, sgxTrace(SID_INFO("Overtly large polygon!")); );
```

But in reality, this allows us to reuse the macro for assertions or errors—and there are several other ways in which this idea can be explored. For example, you can reverse the test so that after five successive assertions, the macro will run an alternative piece of code causing the processor to halt, and forcing the programmer to fix the problem before he can continue.

Function Entrances and Exits

Of the many useful types of messages we can retrieve, an indication of which function is being called is one of the most important. This is often used when attempting to narrow down the location of a bug through a binary split.

The prototype of each function is different, so we can't create a macro to declare the function *and* issue a trace message at the same time because, as we've already discovered, macros do not take multiple arguments. Instead, we need to adopt a more sedate approach, and manually insert trace messages into the code.

```
void ProcessGruntPathFinding(CGruntNPC *pNPC)
{
    sgxTrace("FN: Enter 'ProcessGruntPathFinding'");
}
```

This, unfortunately, is the easy part. Adding its counterpart upon exit is more trouble, especially within larger functions that have more branches and exit points. Adding trace messages on every exit can be laborious and error-prone, so we need to adopt an automatic way of issuing them. The only trick we have requires C++.

Using the C++ Destructor

Instead of manually tracing the entrance and every exit of a function, we can let the compiler do the hard work for us by using the class destructor. The simple constructor code makes a copy of the function name at the start and keeps it while the variable is in scope. When the destructor gets called, we simply emit the exit message.

```
class CScopeTrace
{
public:
    CScopeTrace(const char *pFunction)
    {
        sgxTrace("FN: Entering '%s'", pFunction);
        m_Function = sgxString(pFunction);
    }

    ~CScopeTrace()
    {
        sgxTrace("FN: Exiting '%s'", m_Function.c_str());
    }

private:
    sgxString m_Function;
};
```

The mechanism we now have in place can be expanded in many different ways, and in other scenarios to suit your needs. Perhaps you'll query the clock to report timing data and act like a small profiler. Or perhaps the `CScopeTrace` class will maintain a `static` member variable to indent each function name according to the call depth. Or, finally, perhaps you'll add the originating filename and line number into the message.

One thing that should certainly happen is that we wrapper the creation of the class in its own macro. This will ensure an easy upgrade path when, or if, we get around to coding such features.

```
#define SGX_SCOPE(fn)     CScopeTrace scope(fn)
```

can become

```
#define SGX_SCOPE(fn)     CScopeTrace scope(__FILE__, __LINE__, fn)
```

without anyone realizing. It also creates an easy removal path when we build the final release.

Walking the Stack

The ability to view the call stack is available in almost every debugger known to man, so determining the code path is easy when you're inside one. Normally that's enough, but being able to determine which function called you during runtime without a debugger can be very helpful too. If, for example, you know there's a problem in the `FireMissile` function, but *only* when it's called by the player code, a traditional debugger is not much use. One solution is to prepare a global variable before calling `FireMissile`, like this:

```
g_CallingFromPlayer = TRUE;
FireMissile();
g_CallingFromPlayer = FALSE;
```

We can then trigger an `sgxTrace` message in those problem instances by using this variable. This can become outdated very quickly, though, and certainly doesn't scale well if we need to consider other functions.

Instead we want to be able to trace the call stack manually and determine the calling function from inside `FireMissile`. This isn't easy, and certainly isn't possible in a portable, cross-platform fashion, so in many cases, the preceding code is the best we've got.

By now, however, most of your game should be compliant enough that you can find problems on one platform by using a debugging session on another. If this is true, you can use the Windows tool called *Extended Trace,* which walks the stack from inside the program and outputs the information. This tool can be modified to create some very useful runtime debugging routines. You can download Extended Trace from *http://www.codetools.com/debug/extendedtrace.asp*. An additional tool to dump stack information from a WinTel32 machine can be found at *http://www.codeproject.com/tips/stackdumper.asp#xx324128xx*. This tool can be adapted to create code that accepts a function pointer and halts when it appears on the call stack.

```
sgxBreakFunction(PlayerFunctionThatCallsFireMissile);
```

We can achieve platform-specific variations of this function thanks to the simple memory layout of most consoles. The details are available with a disassembler and a little patience, although NDAs prohibit their inclusion here.

Checking Alignment

Any class allocated from dynamic memory or created through a factory object will, by its nature, be aligned according to the needs of the platform; however, raw data read from the disc will not. However, this should happen infrequently because our serialization code in Chapter 5 will prevent it. But pointers can go awry and sometimes raw data is necessary, at which point, the alignment problem resurfaces. Prevention is always better than cure, but when prevention isn't possible, we need to detect the misalignment before it crashes our machine.

One method is to overload the basic operators so that whenever they're used the `this` pointer can be integrity checked.

```
sgxVector3 operator +(const sgxVector3 &rhs)
{
    sgxAssert(this);
    sgxAssert(sgxIsAligned(this, 4));
    return sgxVector3(x+rhs.x, y+rhs.y, z+rhs.z);
}
```

This works because the vtable holds the function pointers for all instances of the class and so is not affected by broken individual pointers. However, when an attempt is made to access a member of the class, the `this` pointer is used to find it, and so references the invalid memory. This will throw an exception. These assertions alert you to that fact ahead of time.

Handling Errors

When a trace message reports an error, it's sometimes a good idea to suspend the program from running, so you can check the stack, variables, and memory contents in an attempt to solve the problem. Halting the processor can be done in a trivial cross-platform manner:

```
void sgxHalt()
{
    // Use {} instead of ; to avoid warnings
    while (1){}
}
```

Console manufacturers will indicate if any API-specific halt functions are available to freeze the state of the hardware. Being able to halt the processor with a specific assembler instruction should prevent it from causing any further damage to itself, or the rest of the code, allowing for better forensics. This code should be removed before release because it would fall foul of the technical requirements.

NOTE *We have placed this in its own function so it's obvious from the call stack that the program has stopped because of an explicit* `sgxHalt` *instruction, and not because of a nonterminating loop or other such issue.*

`sgxHalt` can then be used as part of the trace call or `sgxError` function, which may act like the `SID_ERROR` level.

Triggering Breakpoints

For some messages, we might prefer to trigger a breakpoint rather than halt the machine outright. Triggering a breakpoint is certainly less permanent. Managing this feat requires some platform-specific code to replicate the effect of the debugger. Under the WinTel architecture, for example, we need to write:

```
#define sgxBreak()    __asm { int 3 }
```

Other platforms will require a rummage through the processor's instruction set to find the appropriate instructions that NDAs prohibit us from disclosing here. However, first check instructions utilizing the words *break* or *interrupt*.

Note that introducing assembler instructions into the program stream is a *compiler*-specific chore, not a platform-based one, because the mnemonics can change between them. So `__asm` in the previous code would normally be replaced with `SGX_ASM`, which should appear in our compiler-specific header file.

Assertions

One of the best uses of `sgxBreak` is within assertions. As we saw in Chapter 2, assertions are lines of code that trap error cases that should not happen within a program, and are intended as sanity checks during runtime.

The most often-used examples of assertions are input parameter validation and return value checking because both error cases are caused by the program. In each instance, an expression is evaluated, and the program continues unabated if it evaluates to true. That is, you have asserted that the function parameters are true, and you want to continue running the function.

```
sgxAssert(idx >=0 && idx < m_MaxNodes);
```

If that isn't the case, then the assertion will fire, and you'll be presented with the error. In our case, this will call `sgxBreak`, dropping us back into the debugger so we can isolate the cause of the bug. Alternatively, we could open a Windows message box, halt the processor, write the message into the trace window, or all the above.

```
#define sgxAssert(expr)   do { if (!(expr)) {    \
sgxTrace(SGX_ERR_ERROR,__FILE__,__LINE__,#expr); \
sgxBreak(); } }while(0)
```

These assertions should be removed in release versions by switching the macro to an empty expression as usual.

```
#define sgxAssert(expr)   sizeof(expr)
```

Because of this, no active code (that is, anything that changes a variable or machine state) should be included within the assertion because it will disappear in release. So

```
sgxAssert(pEngine = CreateEngine());
```

should be replaced by

```
pEngine = CreateEngine();
sgxAssert(pEngine);
```

This can often be the cause of sudden fatal crashes in release builds.

After coding an assertion, we should still consider handling the error safely. Although the case *should* never happen, if you're as paranoid about development as most programmers are, you'll still supplement the assertion with:

```
if (idx <0 && idx >= m_MaxNodes) {
    return NULL;
}
```

CAUTION

Excessive runtime checking can lead to a bug known as "running so slow that the game becomes unplayable," so you might want to remove the checks completely in the final release version and low-level functions and tight loops to prevent performance issues.

Assertion Validation

As we saw in Chapter 2, assertion validation in itself can lead to bugs in the debugging code, as both requests have to be kept in sync. But because the assertion is evaluating the expression anyway, we might as well use the (faulty) result. You may, therefore, rewrite the macro to exit the function automatically on failure. We've called ours `sgxAssertRts`.

```
#define sgxAssertRts(expr, rval)   do { if (!(expr)) { \
sgxTrace(SGX_ERR_ERROR,__FILE__,__LINE__,#expr); \
sgxBreak(); \
return rval; \
} }while(0)
```

Because we still like the checks done in release builds, we need a special version of this macro that will only include the conditional check.

```
#define sgxAssertRts(expr, rval)   do { if (!(expr)) { \
return rval; } }while(0)
```

In reality, an assertion that returns should involve two versions: one to return a value and another to just return. From a best practices perspective, however, any function that can fail should have an error return code. Any function with an assertion is, by its action, telling you that it can fail, and so should return an error. Furthermore, if this (or any other error) then goes unchecked, that too can be considered a bug.

Assertions with Messages

Return values are not the only extensions we can add to the assertion macro. The trace message that is written out on failure is simply a repeat of the faulty expression, as this is the only information we have at the time. However, it's not very easy to read, and if the assertion is going to stop the program from running, we want a better reason than `pEngine->iNode < pAnimation->iRefCount`! To this end, we can extend the macro to include a text description written *in* English by the original programmer to describe the problem in real terms, why it happened, and how to fix it. As this adds yet another set of macro variations, it can often be preferable to include such information as a comment within the source code.

However, one clever means of achieve this feature without an extra variation is to include the description within the expression. Because a string evaluates to a nonzero value (its address in memory), we can also write:

```
sgxAssert(pNode && "Cannot handle NULL pointers");
```

Compile Time Assertions

One additional assertion macro you should create is the compile time assertion. As the name suggests, this evaluates the condition during compilation and terminates the compile if it fails. Stopping the compiler is a simple case of forcing it to compile a piece of syntactically correct code that could not possibly be valid, such as a negative array size.

```
#define sgxCompileAssert(exp) typedef char COMPILE_ASSERT[(exp)?1:-1]
```

This assertion is limited to the subset of evaluations that can occur at compile time, such as `sizeof` and constant mathematics. Compile time assertions are generally used to check for type conformity in and across various modules, such as:

```
sgxCompileAssert(sizeof(ThisVertex) == sizeof(ThatVertex));
```

This particular implementation can only be used once at any given scope. You can therefore extend the macro by supplying a unique identifier to each instance:

```
#define sgxCompileAssert(ver,exp) \
typedef char COMPILE_ASSERT##ver[(exp)?1:-1]
```

Alternatively, you can incorporate several tests into one. For example:

```
sgxCompileAssert(sizeof(ThisVertex) == sizeof(ThatVertex) &&
                 sizeof(ThisVertex) == sizeof(AnotherVertex));
```

Memory

The C language, because of its low-level approach, encourages direct access to memory. After all, we are given pointers to use instead of references. But while this provides an unrivaled power and means of control, it also leads to a type of bug virtually unknown (or impossible) in other languages, such as Java. The memory corruption bug is the scourge of C programmers the world over. Game developers, because of the sheer amount of memory they process each frame, suffer this more than most. In Chapter 3, we looked at several ways the memory manager could help limit these problems through magic numbers (placed at either end of the allocated data block) and data locking. Now let's consider some other methods to prevent these problems.

Memory Corruption

There's an art to tracking down the precise moment in time that corruption occurs. We have to backtrack and find that moment to set things right.

In some cases, we can detect memory corruption before it occurs. Sometimes we can detect it before it causes any (major) damage, and sometimes we cannot detect it until it's too late, and it *has* caused some damage. Which scenario occurs is due to luck.

Before It Occurs

This is a little white lie, as you cannot detect the corruption before it occurs. However, what you can do is detect it before the next instruction occurs and that's just as good.

This requires the ability to monitor the whole memory, and know what area is valid for any particular write operation. In the world of games development, this is almost possible in a cross-platform environment, but very tricky and immensely time consuming.

The development task splits into two: PC and console. On a PC, Windows stores all the code and data into memory pages. Attempting to write into a code page or a data page we don't own will cause the OS to raise an exception and halt the program. This is mostly triggered by writing data to a `NULL` pointer, which generates a "general protection fault." Writing into data pages we *do* own is valid and escapes without warning. However, this is not discerning because it makes no distinction between the area of memory we're intending to write to and the rest of that code page. That data may relate to a completely different part of the program, and be even more difficult to track down.

On a console, you can exercise greater control over the memory because it all belongs to you. You no longer need to differentiate between your data and someone else's; however, now there's the possibility of corrupting your code, instead. The situation is identical to the PC situation discussed previously, and requires a manual implementation of the page-locking solution. This is achieved by platform-specific calls to locked portions of memory, which raise an exception in the same way that Windows does.

In either case, your debugger might support watchpoints. These are breakpoints that can be set to fire whenever a memory location is written to. However, the size of the memory that can be watched, and the number of different watchpoints you can place, is limited by the hardware. So don't become reliant on them. If the bug occurs on all platforms, it's certainly recommended to run the game elsewhere, making use of other debugging features and tools.

After It Occurs

Having resigned ourselves to the fact that we will most likely catch problems after they occur, we can set about trying to narrow down the location, and trap them as soon as possible.

We can limit the amount of checking necessary by intelligently considering where such memory overruns are likely to occur. Within the C language, this is usually through overrunning arrays and *gatepost* errors. Gatepost errors are sometimes known as *off-by-one* errors, where the actual loop or calculation is off by one. This can occur within a loop that checks for `<= 10`, instead of `< 10`, for example.

Another frequent problem occurs when trying to write into memory we've already released. By adopting the .NET approach, and setting such pointers to `0xDDDDDDDD`, we should be able to trap them more easily because accessing this memory location will raise an exception.

When these techniques fail and we're still unsure of the precise line that corrupts our memory location, we have to resort to the binary split and *brute force and ignorance* (*BFI*). By noting the memory location that is in error and its value, we can then add a small chunk of code, similar to the following:

```
static tUINT32 SafeValue = 1;
// ...
static tUINT32 BrokenValue = 0;
static tUINT32 *pBrokenMemory = (tUINT32 *)&SafeValue;

// Update object

if (*pBrokenMemory == BrokenValue) {
    sgxBreak();
}
```

This code is completely cross-platform, and can sit permanently in any part of the main loop without side effects (save the *very* minor performance hint). Being in the main loop means it will get called several thousand times per frame, so we should be able to narrow down the corruption to a single object.

Despite the problems and annoyances with some console development environments, they have one very strong selling point: they debug consoles. Consoles have a fixed memory configuration, so if a problem occurs at memory location `0x92a72b` this time, it will occur there next time, too, and on any other consecutive run—providing nothing else changes. To prevent anything from changing, the broken memory detection code you've just seen can (and should) remain present until the final release.

In actuality, most Windows builds also have the same memory location between successive runs, but this is less guaranteed, and certainly more irksome if you rely on it and the location later changes.

When the corrupted memory location changes on each execution (or is likely to change), you have to consider what the memory location refers to, and watch that instead. So if you know the problem lies with the 12th AI character losing its state, you can simply get the AI module to register this address with a separate function that will keep track of the memory location automatically.

```
static sgxVector<CWatchLocation> g_WatchLocations;

void sgxDebugRegister(void *ptr, tMEMSIZE size)
{
    g_WatchLocations.push_back(CWatchLocation(ptr, size));
}

void sgxCheckForOverwrites(void *ptr, tMEMSIZE size)
{
     tBYTE *pStart = (tBYTE *)ptr;
     tBYTE *pEnd = pStart + size; // actually one byte beyond the end

     sgxVector<CWatchLocation>::iterator it = g_WatchLocations.begin();

     for(;it != g_WatchLocations.end(); ++it) {
          if ((pStart < (*it).pWatchStart && pEnd > (*it).pWatchStart)||
             ((*it).pWatchStart < pStart && (*it).pWatchEnd > pStart)) {
              sgxTrace("Memory overlap! 0x%x (%d)", ptr, size);
          }
     }
}
```

This list of memory locations can also be checked by the wrappered `sgxMemcpy` and `sgxMemmove` functions you saw in Chapter 3.

```
void *sgxMemset(void *pSrc, int iCharacter, tMEMSIZE iNum)
{
     sgxCheckForOverwrites(pSrc, iNum);
     return memset(pSrc, iCharacter, iNum);
}
```

Note that when debugging with raw memory across platforms, the endian-ness of the machine affects the value of your broken data. So if the memory debugger shows `0x1234` for the PC problem, you'll need to set the GameCube watchpoint to `0x3412`. Fortunately, these are rare cases.

TIP

The trick using static variables is very flexible. It can also be used to switch in new pieces of code on-the-fly when experimenting with different algorithms or tuning a game to find the right set of parameter weights. This is a reasonable cross-platform solution to the lack of edit and continue on most console development systems.

In some cases, errors only manifest themselves after a long time, in which case, an error message will be meaningless for the first 1,000 times, and be so tiresome to read that it will probably be turned off. Tracking these problems can sometimes be done through the debugger. But, as always, where the platform tools do not support this, we have to manually create a trick of our own. We can use our old friend, the `static` variable.

```
#define sgxBreakAfter(count) do { static tUINT32 curr=0; \
if (++curr > count) sgxBreak(); } while(0)
```

TIP

Although the `static` variable trick is very attractive, all instances of them should be added before the game is run because Microsoft Developer Studio does not support their inclusion through an edit and continue.

Prevention

Prevention is always better than a cure, however, prevention is significantly more difficult for memory corruption problems. Short of wrapping every pointer write in a function call that checks its bounds, preventing memory problems is unlikely to happen. Instead, consider these solutions.

Use References

Most of the time pointers are not needed, as references work equally well. Many large and well-respected languages work very well without pointers. References can be faster, too. References can be used in almost every case that was once the bastion of pointers. Only those function calls that may reasonable accept a `NULL` pointer as a valid parameter cannot be directly replaced with references.

Use STL

Although STL doesn't eliminate pointers, it does limit their exposure by hiding them from view. However, as end users we don't have to worry about overwriting memory because the only pointers we get to see are marked as iterators, and always point to something useable—even if that something is `end()`, which is also useable, but not available for dereferencing.

Use Arrays

Your first instinct might be to cough and splutter at the thought of arrays, but within a game, we don't need dynamic memory because our basic memory constraints have been handed down to us. Instead, we can create all the data we need in the tool chain and load it as a single block. Or we can allocate our data as a single block at the start of the game, and use placement `new` to create objects within that block. From there, we can limit ourselves to class references that only modify member functions. Additionally, we can overload `operator[]` to test the array bounds. This range check has a negligible affect on speed, particularly when the array size is known at compile time and can be supplied as part of a template. For example:

```
template <typename T, tMEMSIZE SZ>
class sgxArray
{
public:
    T &operator[](tMEMSIZE idx) {
        sgxAssert(idx>=0 && idx<SZ);
        return array[idx];
    }
private:
    T array[SZ];
};
```

This can be instantiated with code such as

```
sgxArray<tREAL32, 16> array;
```

which can then be extended to allow the dynamic resizing of arrays, such as is available from STL.

Dummy Data

In addition to ideas you've already seen in Chapter 3 about writing dummy data into newly allocated and recently released memory, you can adopt a similar idea with pointers. When a pointer becomes unused, we can assign it the value of `0xDEADDEAD`, for example, to help trap errors that would otherwise be masked by checks such as

```
if (!ptr) return;
```

because the validation check would succeed, but the first dereference would fail.

Class Integrity

Every class, or structure, should have a way of testing its own integrity and therefore determine whether it has been corrupted. Such checks fall into two categories: those that use existing data and those where new data is added for the sole reason of performing the check.

A check with existing data might compare a pointer and its associated counter; if the counter is 0, then the pointer should be `NULL`, for example. Conversely, if the counter is not 0, then the pointer must be valid for `N` objects. A call to the memory manager will confirm whether this pointer does indeed reference a suitably large memory block.

Adding data explicitly for integrity checks is less prevalent, but just as easy. As an example, we could create a count of all the NPC statistics (for example, health and stamina) and store the sum in a new member variable. Such information can be removed from release versions in the same way as assertions.

CAUTION

Do not use data from external sources to perform class integrity checking unless you can guarantee they are constant and will not change, as this will create false positives.

OUTPUT TARGETS

Of the more difficult bugs to track down are those that disappear as soon as you start looking for them. These are *Heisenbugs*, named after the Heisenberg Uncertainty Principle.[1] The addition of a breakpoint can often be enough to eliminate the faulty behavior. Worse still, a simple trace message can not only eliminate the bug, but prevent it from ever returning. This is a situation that would normally be greeted by cheers, if it wasn't for the fact that you know the bug's still in there, and you no longer have any way of tracking it down. This variation is called a Schroedinbug.[2]

Such things happen because the machine has changed in some subtle way. And that subtle way will probably vary between computers. So let's look at some of the side effects that can be caused by trace messages, and some ways to narrow down the problem across any platform.

Time Delay

The simple act of creating a string might be enough to raise the time elapsed value for that frame from 0.05 to 0.050001. Something that could have a wide reach if an animation triggers an event, for example.

Because we are able to force feed our game loop, we can manipulate the figures so we only get a constant 60 fps.

Flushes

If the messages are to appear on an external device, such as a disc, debugging window, or a host PC, there will be a large number of steps in the process that could cause various caches to flush; such as instruction, data, or disc. Writing a message to the hard drive could cause the disc cache to empty, meaning the next load will be slower than usual. Or the dirty data that your game was still (erroneously) using will be removed, and you'll get a correct version with the next read. This is a very common cause of bugs on the PS2 because you (the programmer) have direct control over many caches and scratchpads that have been kept opaque on other platforms. Many PS2 bugs can be fixed, or caused, by flushing a cache or invalidating too much of it, respectively.

Sending to Host

Even in normal operation, there can be a noticeable time lag between the message being sent and the message arriving in your debug window. If whatever handshaking protocols are required by your development kit suspend the console while this happens, the time delay will be significantly increased. It might even be long enough to lose an entire frame.

On a multitasking OS, this time delay might cause another program to be given an extra slice of processing time, at which point, any number of caches and OS data stores could be modified. As mentioned previously, we can create a worker thread to dispatch these within a separate time interval that minimizes the problem.

Bugs in the Compiler

Most trace functions, including our own `sgxTrace`, uses variable arguments to process the output message. Handling this requires a lot of registers and is difficult to optimize effectively, and so normally causes a register spill that results in no optimizations. Consequently, when this code is removed, the compiler has more opportunity to optimize—and get it wrong. Instead of removing the trace function entirely, retest your game by commenting out the driver-specific component, leaving the `va_arg` code intact.

Bugs in the Debugging Code

These range from the ridiculous to the sublime. In the obvious case, check that any debugging output is actually correct. Compare the variables given in your trace window with those shown in the debugger, and double-check the ranges of any comparisons performed. Also, make sure that the trace level is likely to output all the messages you expect.

In rare cases, the existence of another function on the stack could modify the state of memory to move whatever variable was getting corrupt to a different location, causing another (possibly less problematic) value to get corrupted instead. Even an overrunning debug text string could rewrite the erroneous data into something valid.

Reproduction Bugs

If your first errors are reported when you enter your name as "Billy Bob III," but half-way through testing, you just type "A" (to get to the bug quicker), you will change the state of the game. Overrunning `sprintf`s can very easily corrupt the stack of any program, and longer names are prime candidates. They might not even come from the user intentionally. Perhaps the game's root directory on the hard disc is different, and the longer pathname has just tipped you over the `MAX_PATH` limit of 260 characters.

Hardware Problems

First, check the obvious: make sure your hardware is debugging the right file, that it is truly a debug build, and that the previous memory contents are not having any adverse effects.

When using a debug build, we often write dummy data into any newly allocated memory to prevent this. This dummy data might be just potent enough to keep it working. It is, after all, the "other" random number generator.

If we can't find the bug without trace messages and we can't add trace message without losing the bug, how do we break this catch 22 scenario? We do so by spreading the same trace information across other output methods.

Screen

Rendering trace messages to the frame buffer is an easy, if obstructive, way of covering what's going on inside the machine. The screen is refreshed 60 times per second, so we need to store each string in a buffer and render the last, say, 10 messages every frame. Keeping a history actually works in our favor, as any bugs that occur (or disappear) *solely* as a consequence of writing out new trace messages will no longer happen because the message is not written out in the traditional fashion. It also eliminates the possibility of disc or network caches being flushed. Naturally, however, render time increases significantly (usually because nobody ever optimizes the graphics engine for 2D text rendering) and prevents the tracing of the low-level graphics driver.

Second Sight

As an alternative to displaying messages on the primary frame buffer, you can also render them to a second monitor. This requires a dual head display (which is fairly common on PCs today) and a compatible graphics engine that can cope with two contexts.

This also allows you to spot transient errors as you step through code on one monitor, while the frame buffer lies undisturbed on the other.

File

Writing everything to a file is the antithesis of writing it all to the screen. This one can completely obliterate the disc and I/O caches, but allows you to study what would be happening onscreen in those moments when the graphics driver has broken.

In a practical scenario, the trace message should *not* be written to the file when it is received, but it should be stored in a cache and written to disc at a more convenient time, perhaps when the other disc caches are flushed, to avoid any extracurricular activity. This is more beneficial when tracing a graphics driver because its comparative speed means the engine will spend most of its time waiting for the disc.

In situations in which the bug is liable to instantiate a crash and no messages will escape, you should write the trace message to disc at every instant. For this to work, make sure that every file write is followed by a flush and a file close. Closing the file should flush the buffer automatically, but it doesn't hurt. Also, if your API supports a means to flush the hardware caches (closing the file only affects the OS and/or API caches), you should do so. This will guarantee (as close as is computerly possible) that the file exists on the disc before the crash occurs.

In both cases, the filesystem we lovingly created in Chapter 5 should not be used because the retrieval of data is vitally important, and we might need more low-level control than its level of abstraction provides. However, be warned that the number of available file handles will decrease by one if you create your own using the platform equivalent of `fopen`.

Serial Port

Although most transmissions from the console to the host PC take place across some type of a serial connection, you can create a small driver to transmit the data via an alternative route. This could include creating a TCP/IP stack and employing Ethernet connectivity.

Unless this functionality is provided out-of-the-box, such a task may be outside the abilities of many programmers. Instead, alternative protocols might include flashing lights on the console or keyboard, rumbling the joypad, or issuing beeps through the speaker.

In all cases, having a number of alternative methods of extracting information from a game can only help because if one method disturbs the program, one of the others might not. Sometimes the best method of debugging a cross-platform game is to use tricks available on another, single platform.

MAKING DATA READABLE

Messages are only any good if we can read them. We've already decreed that the format for trace messages should appear as

```
Filename(linenum) : Message
```

to be compatible with the .NET debug window. But with so many messages, we might need to perform some postprocessing.

Like most windows in .NET, the contents of the debug window can be selected, copied, and pasted elsewhere. If we save this information into a file, we can load it into Microsoft Excel™ and extract information from it.

To do this effectively, we need to format the data in a way that it can be separated easily by the Excel Text Import Wizard. This supports both delimited and fixed-width data, although we'll use delimited because that more closely reflects the data we'll be generating. As Figure 6.1 shows, we can then split our columns according to a specific set of characters. We're using the colon as a suitable delimiter because it doesn't occur naturally in any of our data, with the exception of the Windows drive letter. That always comes first, however, so it's easy to isolate.

Writing out a comment with colons will allow us to parse our messages into columns, and therefore sort them according to certain criteria. Typical examples include file, module, processor time, and memory allocated.

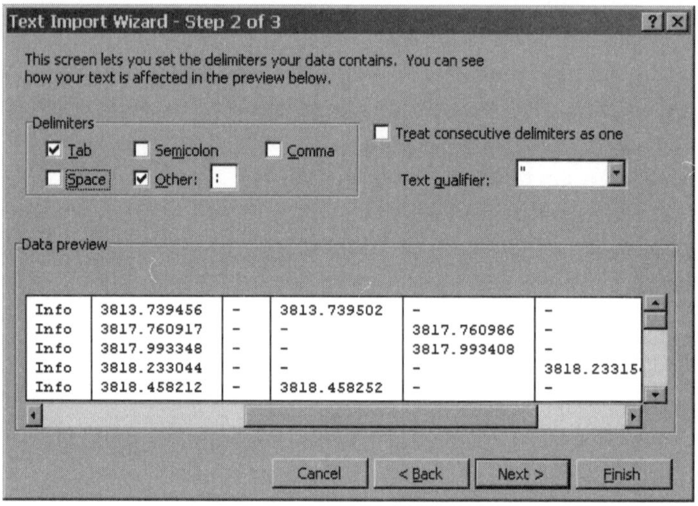

FIGURE 6.1 Text Import Wizard from Excel. (Screen shot reprinted by permission from Microsoft Corporation.)

Multithreaded Output

When working in a threaded environment, trace messages become very difficult to interpret because the time of the message might not correspond to the time of the event that caused it. Because the interesting part of thread development is how they interact, the order of these messages might not reflect the order of execution. Threaded development therefore requires the adoption of a timestamp on each message, and an indication of the thread.

The time can be picked up easily using the `CHardwareClock` class we abstracted in Chapter 4, and written to the trace message string with our colon separator. Each thread will then prepend its own specific string to the message so it can be distinguished in Excel. This can be accomplished in a number of ways, but the perpetual problems of variable argument macros means that one clever method shines above the rest. This involves creating a new `SID_xxx` macro and the token-pasting operator (`##`) to join our string to the message string given.

```
#define SID_THREAD1(Msg)  SGX_ERR_INFO,__FILE__,__LINE__,"T1:"##Msg
```

We can add as many of these as we need for the various threads. They work like any other trace call:

```
sgxTrace(SID_THREAD1("Thread Started"));
```

If we're loading this data into Excel, we can improve this macro by illustrating the relationship between the threads from a temporal perspective. This is a three-step process that can be seen with the basic macro:

```
#define SID_THREAD(Msg,Thread) SGX_ERR_INFO,__FILE__,__LINE__, \
"%s: %s",sgxThreadSafeGetInfo(Thread),##Msg
```

We've combined the token-pasting operator from our `SID_THREAD1` macro, with a new global function to build an information string. This string includes the time and current thread.

```
char *sgxThreadSafeGetInfo(tUINT32 thread)
{
    static char buff[256];
    const int MaxThreads = 6;
    tREAL32 time = g_Timer.GetTime();

    sprintf(buff, "%f ", time);
    for(int i=0;i<MaxThreads;i++) {
        if (i == thread) {
            sprintf(strchr(buff,'\0'), ": %f ", time);
        } else {
            strcat(buff, ": - ");
        }
    }
    return buff;
}
```

CAUTION

The preceding code is not threadsafe. It is an uncluttered version included to demonstrate the code required to implement the tracing feature. A real-world version would likely include multiple buffers and a mutex.

Provided colons are used to separate the data, the rest of the format is unimportant. Note that we are outputting the timestamp twice, once in the first column and once again in a separate column that belongs to a specific thread. This gives us one column to sort on, making sure the events are listed chronologically in Excel, and a group of columns that contain gaps, demonstrating how the individual threads interact with each other during runtime. Figure 6.2 demonstrates a sample output.

Note that `SID_THREAD` encloses all the trace parameters within itself, so we cannot pass extra arguments into the macro, or use the `%d` specifiers.

	A	B	C	D	E	F	G	H	I	J	K	L
1	c	\xp	Info	3813.739	-	3813.74	-	-	-	-	Thread Started	
2	c	\xp	Info	3817.761	-	-	3817.761	-	-	-	Thread Started	
3	c	\xp	Info	3817.993	-	-	3817.993	-	-	-	Play sound	
4	c	\xp	Info	3818.233	-	-	-	3818.233	-	-	Thread Started	
5	c	\xp	Info	3818.458	-	3818.458	-	-	-	-	Handle player	
6	c	\xp	Info	3818.687	-	-	-	3818.687	-	-	FX	explosions
7	c	\xp	Info	3818.932	-	-	-	3818.932	-	-	FX	smoke
8	c	\xp	Info	3819.163	-	-	3819.163	-	-	-	AI movement	
9	c	\xp	Info	3819.393	-	3819.393	-	-	-	-	Physics	

FIGURE 6.2 Timing events shown across threads. (Screen shot reprinted by permission from Microsoft Corporation.)

> TIP
>
> *Although the nature of multithreaded code makes it very difficult to determine where we are in a program, we can change the overscan color using platform-specific calls to the graphics driver.*

MAINTAINING CONSISTENCY

One of our key points in Chapter 2 was to ensure that every version of our game behaved identically on all platforms, all the time. As you saw then, there are many facets to this consistency. Let's now revisit those ideas and bring flesh to the bones.

Isolating System Calls

Without exception, any standard library function we intend to use should be isolated from the game, as should any system calls to the platform-specific API. We don't need to employ any additional namespaces or abstractions here, we just need create a simple wrapper function, and place it in a suitable file. We have split the standard library into the following categories:

- Memory
- STL
- Strings
- Mathematics
- Utilities
- System

The memory module, for example, will contain the wrappers to all the simple memory-handling functions, such as `sgxMemcmp`.

```
int sgxMemcmp(const void *pSrc1, const void *pSrc2, tMEMSIZE iNum)
{
    return memcmp(pSrc1, pSrc2, iNum);
}
```

This covers a multitude of sins. First, it provides a simple way to track the library calls within the game that can be useful for profiling (using the scope profiler we built earlier), and provides an easy way to hook into the standard libraries to perform supplementary error checking.

Second, the overuse of wrappers provide a visual reminder of the cross-platform nature of our code, and that we should always be using the `sgx*` versions of any standard function. By providing this, it also eliminates the use of vendor extensions because they can be trapped by the wrapper and ignored. On the flip side, any extensions that include good ideas can get stolen and placed in the cross-platform library for use by everyone, on every platform.

Finally, these wrappers provide an easy method of changing the implementation of the standard library if we need to. This happens more often that you might think, because the standard library is not standard—at least, not for cross-platform purposes. The best example, which we mentioned in Chapter 2, is `qsort`. Knowing its problems, we can use a single `sgxQsort` as opposed to the standard implementation. Furthermore, by implementing this ourselves, we can guarantee that the output is compliant and identical. Although writing a decent quicksort algorithm is not hard, it does feel like you're reinventing a fifth wheel. We can always download one with a suitable license or wrapper `STL::sort`, and deploy that instead.

The Files

The division of labor for the new standard library can be split three ways: into wrappers, reimplementations (both of which are cross-platform), and platform-specific versions. Each should have its own separate implementation file to avoid the unsightly appearance of `SGX_PLATFORM_XBOX` throughout the code, although each source file usually uses the same prototype-laden header.

Each subsystem will have a different balance between the implementation methods used, and can be grouped as described in the following sections.

Memory

For the `sgxMemset` and `sgxMemcpy` functions, it's sufficient to use wrappers to the standard library because the versions within have usually been written in assembler to provide us with as much performance as we're likely to need. There are some notable exceptions to this rule, but your profiler will indicate those platforms to you.

STL

STL is becoming a more extensive part of many games, and is invaluable within the tool chain. STL occupies its own directory of files. For us, this is a reimplementation of the vendor-supplied library to ensure the minor complaints (such as the difference in `erase` and `clear`) do not affect our game.

Although implementing a clean room version of STL is a mammoth, but possibly interesting, task, we have no need to do so because *STLPort* is a drop-in replacement and can be downloaded free from *http://stlport.org*. We'll look at this further in Chapter 11, "The Bits We Forget About."

Strings

Although the standard library includes prototypes for `strcpy` and its friends in `string.h`, we'll create our own file of string wrappers. This is because the string-handling functions in our environment will include debugging support; we'll also include our own `sgxString` definition that uses STL.

The `sprintf` function and its counterparts will not be rewritten because doing so is a significant undertaking for very little gain, particularly because STL provides much safer functionality with its `Format` method. For consistencies sake, however, we'll create an `sgxSprintf` macro.

Mathematics

Mathematics requires the most diligent programming, and contains a healthy mixture of wrappers, reimplementations, and platform-specific code for several reasons. First, the standard math library, as dictated by ANSI, is of little use for games development. We need functions to manipulate matrices, vectors, and quaternions. All these encompass new code that we must write.

Second, a large portion of our processor time is likely to be spent in these functions; our physics and animation systems both depend on high-grade mathematics, so we'll need to write platform-specific versions of these functions when they show up on our profiler. Over time, the math library will migrate from a fairly generic, cross-platform file, to several individual platform-specific files containing specially optimized versions.

If the situation arises that requires both a common and a single platform-specific version of a particular function, you should avoid placing guards around the functions, for instance:

```
#if SGX_PLATFORM_XBOX
SGX_INLINE void
sgxMthApply_Vector(sgxMatrix43 &Matrix, sgxVector3 &Vector)
{
    // Clever assembler
```

```
}
#else
SGX_INLINE void
sgxMthApply_Vector(sgxMatrix43 &Matrix, sgxVector3 &Vector)
{
    // Generic C
}
#endif
```

Instead, move each variation of the function into a separate file, as not to pollute the cross-platform code.

The final reason for creating custom versions of well-written functions is to ensure predictability during runtime across platforms. This extends in many corners of the development globe with functions such as `rand` and `sin` and the numeric constants such as π.

General Utilities

For the most part, general utilities exist as reimplementations of functions such as `qsort`, `min`, and `max`. This category also serves as a grab bag for those functions that do not fit nicely into any other area. If we add extensions to the standard library, they should live here.

System

System consists of wrappers for the basic system operations, such as `sgxYieldWait` and `sgxSleep`. In most cases, this is just a means of hiding the fact that one platform needs a specific function the others do not have. Particularly when some functions, such as the aforementioned `sgxYieldWait`, only make sense in a multithreaded environment. However, it does keep all similar functions together, and so warrants a place in our cross-platform standard library.

The Old Files

Despite programmer education, many still write `min` automatically, instead of the new cross-platform version's `sgxMin`. It's just human nature. But ideally, we'd like to prevent this as much as possible. To do so, we'll supplement the workflow solution with a technical one. Although there's no way of preventing it from occurring in every file, we can enforce it in most of them.

Don't Use Windows

Although our platform-specific code will require the `windows.h` header file, none of our other code does. So you shouldn't start every file with this:

```
#include <windows.h>
```

And you shouldn't add it to your `core.h` file, either. Doing so provides many functions and macros that we don't need within the project (such as the erroneous `min` and `max`[3]). Anything important that the header file contains should already have a cross-platform version that we've written (or wrappered) ourselves, so you should use that instead.

Undefine Defines

The C language preprocessor has a very useful command to remove macro definitions:

```
#ifdef TRUE
#undef TRUE
#endif

#define TRUE    1
```

This ensures that any truth that exists is our own.

`#undef` is used in two situations. First, it enables us to create our own macros without the hindrance of those that have come before. Second, it allows us to remove those functions masquerading as macros, and prevents any code that mistakenly uses them from compiling.

```
#ifdef min
#undef min
#endif
```

This should drop the hint that such facilities have been deprecated in the cross-platform world.

Tabulating Trigonometry

Implementing our own trigonometry functions ensures a predictable game, and can be done in a couple of ways. The traditionally taught methods include calculating a cosine through an expansion series (which is very time consuming), and using the processor's own cosine instruction (which returns us to a platform dependency). Instead, it's usually sufficient to use a simple lookup table, which produces a value between 0 and 1.

```
tREAL32 sgxSineTable[] = {
0.000000f, 0.006136f, 0.012272f, 0.018407f, 0.024541f, 0.030675f,
0.036807f, 0.042938f, 0.049068f, 0.055195f, 0.061321f, 0.067444f,
```

```
0.073565f, 0.079682f, 0.085797f, 0.091909f, 0.098017f, 0.104122f,
... and so on...

tREAL32 sgxSine(tREAL32 theta)
{
tUINT32 TableIdx;

    TableIdx = (tUINT32) ((theta * 1024.0f) / sgx2PI);
    TableIdx &= 1023;

    return sgxSineTable[TableIdx];
}
```

Or, for the function-impaired:

```
#define sgxSine(_theta) sgxSineTable[((tUINT32)\
(theta * 162.9746617261f)) & 1023]
```

Cosine is merely a sine wave out of phase by $\pi/2$ radians, and we know our table of 1,024 entries covers 2π radians, so we can create similar code for cosine with a minimum of fuss.

```
SGX_INLINE tREAL32 sgxCos(tREAL32 theta)
{
    const tREAL32 mul = 162.9746617261f;
    return sgxSineTable[(((tUINT32)(theta * mul))+256) & 1023];
}
```

The free lunch ends here, however, as we need a separate table for functions such as `asin`.

> TIP
>
> *When the processor is distanced from memory by caches, retrieving data in this way can actually be slower. In these situations, special fast routines are more likely to exist for computing sine and cosine functions. As always, profile.*

The size of our trigonometry table can vary as much as we want, but 1,024 entries usually gives enough precision (replete with an easy boundary mask) for most tasks. This 4 KB table can then, depending on the profiling results and capabilities of the platform, be stored in a local cache.

Generating these tables is very straightforward and can be done with a few lines of C:

```
printf("tREAL32 sgxSineTable[] = {\n");
for(int i=0;i<1024;i++) {
    sgxSineTable[i] = sinf( ((float)i * sgx2PI) / 1024.0f);
    printf("%ff, ", sgxSineTable[i]);

    if ((i & 31) == 31)  {
        printf("\n");
    }
}
printf("};\n");
```

Throughout these examples, we've been taking the sine of a floating-point number. This differs from the standard library where `sin` works with `doubles`, and `sinf` works with `floats`. We use floating-point numbers to achieve better performance on platforms such as the PS2.

TIP

If you ever need to move your engine onto a fixed-point machine, don't try to hide the floating-point types behind classes and abstracted types. Such machines may emulate floating-point calculations accurately, but they will be many thousands of times slower in doing so, making the endeavor worthless. If you're writing for a fixed-point machine, you should know its underlying number system to prevent fatally slow code.

General Accuracy

A floating-point number is stored in 32 bits and has a range of between 3.4^{e37} and -3.4^{e37}. In contrast, an integer using the same number of bits can "only" reference a total of plus or minus 2 billion. As you probably know, the trade-off for having such a large floating-point range is by suffering in the accuracy department, as not every number between 3.4^{e37} and -3.4^{e37} can be stored explicitly. So while any numeric constants will be stored identically, that is

```
tREAL32 one_thousandth =  0.0001f;
tREAL32 another_thousandth =  0.0001f;
```

the results from an equivalent calculation might not.

```
tREAL32 one_thousand = 10000.0f;

sgxAssert(one_thousandth == another_thousandth);
sgxAssert(one_thousandth == 1.0f/one_thousand);
```

In this (slightly contrived) example, the first assertion allows the program counter to pass without incident. The second calculates an identical value, but because the result is quanitized to the nearest representable value, the answer will actually differ from the desired result. It is therefore impossible to test such numbers with

```
if (one_thousandth == another_thousandth) ...
```

and have it return `true`. Instead, we have to test that both numbers are within a very small amount of each other. This small amount is called *epsilon*, denoted with the Greek letter *e*. We'll assign our own value to it, and write a specific equality test.

```
#define SGX_EPSILON     0.000001f

tBOOL sgxEq(tREAL32 fValue1, tREAL32 fValue2)
{
    return sgxAbs(fValue1 - fValue2) < SGX_EPSILON;
}
```

An alternative method is to test whether the values fall within 1% of each other. However, this requires additional time-consuming mathematics, and is less easy for a human to determine in advance if the computer would consider them identical.

NOTE

When looking at these numbers in the debugger, you'll often notice they appear identical, despite the fact the assertion still fires. This is because most debuggers round the numbers up or down to make them more human-friendly. To determine a more accurate value for numbers in the debugger, modify the expression to `fValue+1.0f`.

Sine Accuracy

For most applications within the game, the level of accuracy provided by a lookup table is enough, and worth the speed gains it provides. This often includes the physics system and world scene graph handling. Of course, there's always an exception (or exceptions) that proves the rule. These cases need to forego the simple sine implementation we've created, and use the full-blooded versions provided by the processor, or rather, by the floating-point unit (FPU) of the processor.

```
#define sgxSinFPU(theta)    (tREAL32)sin((double)theta)
#define sgxCosFPU(theta)    (tREAL32)cos((double)theta)
```

If your compiler suite is compatible with the C99 standard, these can be replaced with the faster (noncasting) versions of `sinf` and `cosf`, which work with floating-point numbers throughout.

TIP

Although this isn't a book on optimization, we should mention the benefits of creating `sgxSinCos`*, which computes both named functions from a single theta. This is beneficial because many algorithms use both values anyway and some platforms provide a "buy one, get one free" offer, when it comes to providing sine or cosine values. In some cases, you might be able to calculate two sine and cosine values from one call. If so—do it.*

The problem with the inaccuracies in a lookup table approach is that they are not always obvious during implementation. But as a guide, the numbers often break down in the following areas.

Player Control

Anything the player has direct control over, particularly when using analogue sticks, should be a prime candidate for the FPU version because the player is astute enough to notice when the control system is not as responsive as it should be. Having a quanitized control mechanism highlights the lack of responsiveness.

Animations

Anything that requires smooth transitions, such as IK and limb animations, should use the full-precision version of sine and cosine. If compression is used on the animation data (which it invariably will be), you don't want to lose any further accuracy with an imprecise math library. If your animations start getting the shakes, experiment with a more compute-intensive sine calculation.

Large Moving Objects

Any big object needs the extra precision because the smallest amount of movement will be amplified by its bulk or become apparent over time. This includes stationary objects that rotate (such as sky boxes), as well as physical objects such as trains.

Large objects that appear in a group among smaller objects should *not* generally be upgraded to an FPU version. A good example is a road scene where the traffic consists of one truck and a selection of cars. Even if the physical inaccuracies are invisible to the player's eye, the gameplay changes soon will be, when the vehicles begin to move in different traffic streams as the number system breaks down. If a positional variation is required to provide a human element to the cars, then provide it across all platforms as part of the AI, and not as a side effect of the mathematics.

Because of the processor hit involved in FPU calculations, it's no surprise that all consoles have specialized instructions for handling floating-point numbers. These instructions should invariably be used. Where one module makes excessive use of such functions, the entire module should be isolated and marked for possible optimization. One such task is animation, which can be parallelized very easily and consists of largely FPU-accurate calculations. It's no coincidence that such modules are often given their own processor or thread on which to work.

Random Numbers

Although no game is completely predictable, it's impossible for a computer to act in an unforeseen manner because it's completely logical. This is not a problem because any suitably advanced system can show signs that are indistinguishable from randomness. Part of the standard library provides a function, `rand`, to achieve this *pseudo*-randomness. This generates a number between `0` and `MAX_INT`, and can be scaled to any range we need. The process of scaling this number is difficult because a simple modulus limits the effectiveness of the random numbers produced.

```
// This returns a number between 0 and 1, but the results
// are not suitably random
num = rand() % 2;
```

However, this function, and its implementation, will vary according to the library. The trick in cross-platform development is to control this random appearance in such a way that we can reproduce the "random" effects of any platform.

Tabulated Rand

To maintain a good scope for our random number generator (that is, it's capable of producing numbers between 1 and 5, as well as 1 and 1,000), we'll build a table of numbers between 0 and 1 (inclusive), which can then be multiplied by our requested range to get a reasonably random number.

```
tREAL32 sgxRandomTable[] = {
0.840188f, 0.394383f, 0.783099f, 0.798440f, 0.911647f, 0.197551f,
0.335223f, 0.768230f, 0.277775f, 0.553970f, 0.477397f, 0.628871f,
0.364784f, 0.513401f, 0.952230f, 0.916195f, 0.635712f, 0.717297f,
0.141603f, 0.606969f, 0.016301f, 0.242887f, 0.137232f, 0.804177f,
0.156679f, 0.400944f, 0.129790f, 0.108809f, 0.998925f, 0.218257f,
0.512932f, ... and so on ...
```

We can have as many, or as few numbers in our table as we want. We've chosen to use 1,024 again because it lies on a power-of-two boundary, enabling a time-efficient bit mask when the table entries wrap around.

When a random number is requested, we simple pick the next number in the array, and increment the pointer. This has the same effect as the standard pseudo-random number generator insomuch as any specific seed (that is, the starting index of the array) generates the same sequence of "random" numbers every time. This is popularly seen in games like *FreeCell* to recreate completely different games.

```
void sgxSRand(tINT32 seed)
{
    sgxRndPtr = seed & 1023;
}

tREAL32 sgxRand()
{
    sgxRndPtr = (sgxRndPtr+1) & 1023;
    return sgxRandomTable[sgxRndPtr];
)
```

This should not be compressed into a macro because it can produce unpredictable results in expressions such as:

```
v = sgxRand() + sgxRand();  // get a value between 0 and 2
```

In this example, `sgxRndPtr` may get incremented twice, once, or not at all. Although the side effects will always be consistent and the actual result of `sgxRndPtr` is unimportant to us, the seed would change randomly within a macro-ized version. This is because the consistency is controlled by the manner in which the compiler treats the expression, and therefore the set of numbers that appear will vary across platforms. This is a very bad thing—even for a random number generator.

Calculated Rand

Several formulas can be used to calculate random numbers, and George Marsaglia's post at *http://www.ciphersbyritter.com/NEWS4/RANDC.HTM* (among others) contains 8 of them within just 17 lines of C code. Despite the quirkiness of the code, it's still a fast implementation, and certainly benefits from being processor-based as this gives it the opportunity of running in tight spaces that won't cause cache misses for other code.

The implementation has the standard components you would expect from any random number generator: an initialization routine to set the seed, a call to get a number, and a lot of impenetrable magic numbers—as you can see from the seed-creation routine.

```
void settable(UL i1,UL i2,UL i3,UL i4,UL i5, UL i6)
{
int i; z=i1;w=i2,jsr=i3;

    jcong=i4;
    a=i5;
    b=i6;

    for(i=0;i<256;i=i+1) {
       t[i]=KISS;
    }
}
```

The rest of the implementation is less clear to the layperson, but we're assured the numbers are indeed random by the comments provided at the end of the source. Access to the floating-point numbers, in the range of 0 to 1, can be retrieved with the `UNI macro`, which we'll hide behind our `sgxRand` function.

```
tREAL32 sgxRand()
{
    return UNI;
}
```

The floating-point implementation, as given, returns doubles, but can be adapted with a one character change:

```
#define UNI   (KISS*2.328306e-10f)
```

Note that if you're only including the UNI algorithm in your game and using a stripped down version of this code, many of the macros (and the 256-byte table) are unnecessary.

There are other implementations, including those at Numerical Recipes (*http://www.nr.com*), but the author has stated there is no copyright in the preceding code, and you're free to use it in any way you want.

Hardware Rand

This is not recommended lightly, but raised as a discussion point and possible inspiration. If your hardware supports low-level access to the sound card, you can always sample a few bytes from the current audio signal and use that as a seed.

Because the sound card will always have a certain amount of noise on the bus (generated by electrical interference), you can employ this as either data or a random seed to start one of the other more traditional random number generators.

Seeding Rand

The base seed can start anywhere in the table, with each seed creating a different gameplay experience. Depending on your game design, you might need to modify the game slightly every time by using a seed determined at random. But generating this random number requires a seed, which requires a random number, which requires a seed, and so on. You can retrieve such a value in several ways: the number of seconds since switch on, the time taken for the user to bypass the title screen, the number of games on the memory card/hard disk, or even the noise level on the sound card.

TIP

When using random numbers that must follow a pattern, don't forget to save the seed to disc with the game.

Using Rand Wisely

Normally, you shouldn't need to document how random numbers are used, but in this case, because we need predictability, there's an extra stipulation: If you're using a time-scaled algorithm, make sure the random element is compensated for. Returning to our simple physics code:

```
vPosition += vDirection * time_elapsed;
```

You can see that this scales very well for all time-related cases of `time_elapsed`. However, if we decide to add a small random variation to this position, the code will break very badly in some cases.

```
vPosition += vDirection * time_elapsed * (sgxRand() * fRandScale);
```

The error occurs because the random number generator call is not scaled according to time. If one instance calls the update function with an elapsed time of 0.2, and a second instance calls it twice with 0.1 and 0.1, then the position will have more randomness in it during the second version, and the number generator will be out of sync causing different results to be returned to the next function, and so on. This will be impossible to correct.

We must, therefore, always consider the number of times we *call* such functions (and not just the result), and write our algorithms to compensate. This example should be written by quanitizing the function into 1/10th of a second slots.

```
time_accumulate += time_elapsed;
while(time_accumulate >= 0.1f)
{
    vPosition += vDirection * 0.1f * (sgxRand() * fRandScale);
    time_accumulate -= 0.1f;
}
```

The Problems

A random number table does produce one bad side effect, however, it's sometimes possible to spot the pattern of numbers when they're used for special effects, such as rendering snow on a TV monitor. Because the monitor texture will probably contain fewer than 1,024 pixels, a very obvious pattern will appear if you use these random numbers directly in the renderer. Instead, you have to resort to a computed form of `rand`, either using the example `UNI` code shown earlier, or resorting to the standard library version of `rand`. You can also get a better snow pattern by reseeding the number generator on every line.

Beating Piracy with Random Numbers

Random numbers can change the gameplay in undetectable ways. Sometimes, this is a good thing. If you are sending a lot of copies of your game out to journalists or other third parties, you can secretly seed each game with a different random number. Then, if any copies get leaked out to the Internet, you can look at the seed value to determine the mole.

Also on the piracy issue, if you have a fast mechanism for determining an illegal copy of the game, you can use it to vary the random seed. So while a legal copy will apply `sgxRand` as normal, a pirated game will change the generator after the first or second level to always return a constant value (like 0 or 1) to produce a broken game experience. Check your code to determine which random number would kill the player more quickly, or cause the AIs to act more aggressively.

Pirates that crack games rarely play them. After they get rid of the "Illegal Game" message you generally put at the start, and they see the first part of the first level start up, they'll ship it out. Only later will someone realize it only works as a glorified demo mode and they have to buy the real thing. In the current climate, most games have a shelf life of one month, with the first week of that being critical. If you can hold the pirates up for that week, you have more chance of making money from the game, as they'll quit playing the hacked PC version, and go out to buy a genuine GameCube version.

Code Checking

Being a cross-platform product brings about one unexpected advantage—a much greater wealth of development tools. When working on a single platform, you are locked into a particular set of tools, libraries, and debuggers. If the game works cross-platform, a vista of opportunity presents itself. Furthermore, you don't have to develop for other platforms to gain the benefits. If the source is clean enough, avoiding the limits of language, compiler, and libraries, you can test the code on many other platforms. This will mostly benefit console programmers as the PC environment has a significantly more mature set of tools.

The following tools are not an exhaustive list, but serve as a guide for where to start looking.

Lint

Lint is probably the granddaddy of all code correctness tools, and checks the source for semantics as opposed to syntax. It highlights typical errors of programming style and usage and has a variety of settings. Usually thought of as an overzealous compiler, building any nontrivial program on a strict level build is next to impossible, especially if the project is started before Lint testing is applied. However, it's possible to use the Lint configuration file to treat different files with a different set of criteria. So, like most tools introduced mid-schedule, this should be adopted with a low-key roll out, treating new files harshly and old ones with more leniency.

No tool is ever the final word, and so *ALOA* was born. ALOA (A Lint Output Analyzer) provides a quality metric for the code under test. It works as a post-process for Lint, and takes the entire code base as an input to deduce the standard of code across various modules. This enables a game plan to be drawn up, and specific modules targeted for Lint-ing. ALOA can be found on the *C/C++ Users Journal* Web site at *http://www.cuj.com/code* or from the author's page at *http://pera-software.com/aloa.htm*.

Traditionally, Lint is configured by means of a simple text file. This is still the case with both the PC-Lint™ program (from Gimpel Software at *http://gimpel.com/*) and free variants such as Splint. However, this is no longer the case, as users of Microsoft Developer Studio can adopt a tool called *dsplinter* (available from the ALOA suite) to Lint-specific modules. This creates the configuration required automatically from Developer Studio project files, and applies a project policy that indicates the severity of warnings.

These configuration files hold the key to an untapped resource in development, where non-PC builds can be Lint-checked with the PC-only tools. From a simplistic point of view, Lint only ever looks for self-consistent code, matching whatever source you've written with the associated header files. This enables you to check the source of other platforms by simply adding their paths to the configuration.

Code Coverage

The code coverage tool often exists as part of other software, usually a profiler. During a sample run of your game, every line of code that was executed gets marked by the coverage tool for later perusal. You can then confirm that the code you've just claimed "didn't break anything" did in fact run.

Using a coverage tool is easy—it's a simple matter of point and click. A good workplan metaphor is needed, however, and this will vary depending on your studio. However, a number of small, well-formed tests will provide more detailed information than a single behemoth checklist, and it will certainly be easier to interpret the data.

Generating tests can be split into two halves, good and bad. A good test will call the functions, process the code, and run the game under normal conditions. A bad test will attempt to break it by generating out of range parameters, really slow frames (by force-feeding large time elapsed values), and other such conditions. Each test should cover a different section of code.

BoundsChecker™

This Windows tool from Compuware Corporation (*http://www.compuware.com/products/devpartner/bounds.htm*) validates access to and from memory by checking, among other things, the array bounds and resource allocation. BoundsChecker also performs deadlock analysis for those who have already taken the plunge into threaded code. When interfacing with the Win32 API, it will also check function parameters, and spot when invalid handles have been returned and used.

BoundsChecker requires a recompile of your source code to work, but in return provides more runtime information than you thought existed. Using it within a game requires an event loop giving constant time messages, because the extra checking can slow the game down significantly. This can also necessitate a means to capture and play back the joypad movements early on in development. You'll see how to implement this in Chapter 7, "System I/O."

ENDNOTES

1. The Heisenberg Uncertainty Principle states that if we have a particle with both velocity and position, we can only accurately determine one of them. This is akin to looking at a single frame of a film; if the image is blurred, we can work out the velocity from the shutter speed, but cannot accurately

determine its position within the blurred mass. If the image is sharp, we can ascertain its position, but its velocity is undetermined. Many systems, including debugging, exhibit a similar property, and change after we start to observe them. (The HUP can be stated in many ways, but this is the most commonly understood version.)

2. This term originates from Schroedinger's cat, which is a gedanken experiment whereby a radioactive particle is sealed in a box (with the aforementioned cat), and attached to a poison-release mechanism. After its half-life, the particle will either have decayed or not. The chance is a truly random 50-50. If the particle decays, the poison is released and the cat is dead. Otherwise, the cat remains alive. The interesting part of this experiment is that after this time we have no way of knowing if the cat is alive or dead. Until we open the box, the cat is both alive and dead, and our observance of the system causes the duality of state to collapse into one.
3. It's possible to exclude these macros by defining NOMINMAX before using windows.h, but that still doesn't justify including the Win32 header file.

7 System I/O

In This Chapter

- Abstracting Basics
- The Null Driver
- Input Devices

ABSTRACTING BASICS

We now move from keeping the internals of the software identical, to abstracting the various hardware and OS components to make them appear identical to anyone using them. This task is split into three areas.

First, the common architecture describes the naming convention and how the interface will appear to the game programmer. Second, the platform-specific code communicates directly with the hardware or middleware application. Third, the *null driver*, a fully functioning implementation of the architecture, is used as a reference for other platforms to derive from.

THE NULL DRIVER

The null driver is perfect. It does everything you need, never breaks, and doesn't rely on any hardware, compiler, or OS. On the negative side, however, the null driver doesn't do anything. By "do" we mean visibly, or audibly, "do." It still maintains the state of the engine, returns valid information when asked, and accepts data with the grace of any other function. However, the null driver never applies this data to the hardware, which is why it's possible to ensure that it works all the time, on every platform.

Although presumably useless, this driver has several uses in testing and debugging because you can execute an entire game using nothing but null drivers, which allows you to watch the output through trace messages and debug information. If a bug is suspected in any component of the game, you can replace that platform-specific module with a null driver and retest.

The functionality of this driver can be implemented through two design patterns: the *prepared singleton* and *double chance functions*. You'll see these stalwart functions of cross-platform development many times in this chapter.

Prepared Singleton

The prepared form of a singleton is useful for handling derived classes through its base class without ever having to `switch` between them. We saw a similar version when creating our `CHardwarePlatform`. In this case, however, each derived class has its own `Get` function that behaves identically by creating an instance of itself, but stores its instance pointer in a common variable shared among all derivations of the class.

```
class CGfxEngine {
protected:
    static  CGfxEngine *ms_pSingleton;
};
```

Unfortunately, for C++ purists, this requires the use of the `protected` keyword,[1] but the scope of its usefulness is limited so there shouldn't be any problem.

```
// Generic (aka null) driver
CGfxEngine *CGfxEngine::Get()
{
    if (ms_pSingleton == NULL) {
        ms_pSingleton = new CGfxEngine;
    }
    return ms_pSingleton;
```

```
}

// Platform-specific
CPS2GfxEngine *CPS2GfxEngine::Get()
{
    if (ms_pSingleton == NULL) {
        ms_pSingleton = new CPS2GfxEngine;
    }
    return ms_pSingleton;
}
```

This creates a suitable singleton for the entire game, provided the first call to `Get` uses the appropriate platform-specific class. Consequently, this initial call is placed as part of the `main` function to ensure that a suitable object is created and that the destruction order is correct. This *prepares* the singleton for the rest of the game.

```
CPS2GfxEngine::Get();
```

From here, we can retrieve the applicable pointer from our common `CGfxEngine::Get` function, while the virtual methods ensure the resultant call is made to the correct platform-specific code.

TIP

Never make the base class abstract as implementing 50+ different functions is a frustrating time sink when you start porting to a new platform, or new methods are added to the base class during development. Instead, make sure the null driver includes suitable functionality, even if it's just statistics gathering.

Some people may prefer to create the singleton with its own explicit function. For example:

```
CPS2GfxEngine::Create();
```

At this point, the `Get` is resigned to nothing more than the basic retrieval of the static pointer. This allows us to inline the `Get` function, eliminates the function call overhead, and prevents a singleton from being re-created accidentally due to unforeseen interdependencies between objects.

Double Chance Functions

This pattern relies on the use of virtual functions to give a derived method two chances at controlling a particular routine.

The first chance comes from the platform-specific virtual function. When this function is called, the derived class can either process it manually, or pass control back to its parent class (which is usually the base because few hierarchies are more than two layers deep). The base class, running a null driver, can then process this call using data or code from the derived class by calling another virtual function, giving the platform-specific code a second chance to handle it (see Figure 7.1).

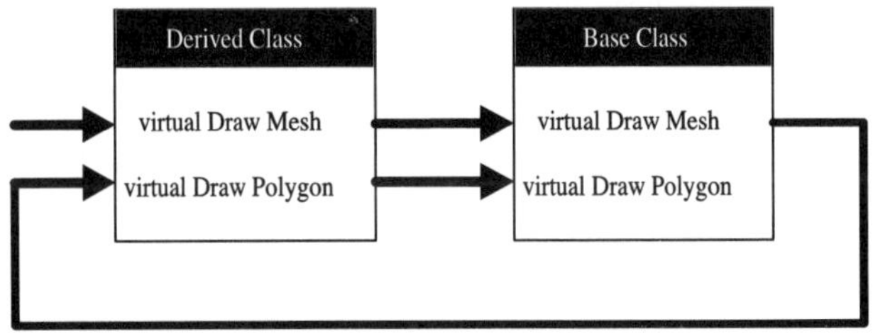

FIGURE 7.1 An example of a double chance function.

This allows the data to be held in either a platform-specific, or generic, format according to the needs of the machine without any code-oriented exceptions or changes to the design. It also allows the base class to use lower-level functionality held in the derived class, as this example shows:

```
// Generic
CGfxEngine::DrawPolygon(const sgxTexture &txt,
    const sgxVertex &vtx)
{
    // Null driver does nothing except keep statistics
    // It never renders anything.
}

CGfxEngine::DrawMesh(const sgxMesh &mesh)
{
    // Use the cross-platform structure
    for(int i=0;i<mesh.iNumPolys;i++) {
        DrawPolygon(mesh.poly[i].texture, mesh.poly[i].vertex);
    }
}

// The platform-specific version
CPS2GfxEngine::DrawMesh(const sgxMesh &mesh)
{
    // An optimal driver will handle the whole mesh here, and
    // not call the DrawPolygon routine.
```

```
        // Otherwise we call the base class, and let it call our
        // platform-specific DrawPolygon routine.
    }

    CPS2GfxEngine::DrawPolygon(const sgxTexture &txt,
        const sgxVertex &vtx)
    {
        // Platform-specific routine to draw a single polygon. Will
        // certainly be suboptimal from a performance standpoint.
    }
```

A simple trade-off happens here. The quickest route to a finished product is to use the null driver code from `CGfxEngine::DrawMesh` and the platform-specific version of `DrawPolygon`. In contrast, the route to the quickest product is to write specific code for the `CPS2GfxEngine::DrawMesh` routine, and ignore its `DrawPolygon`.

TIP

The interaction between platform-independent and platform-specific components is distinct; the platform-specific component indicates the limits of the device, whereas the platform-independent code enumerates and works within those limits to process the game.

This is just one example of where a double chance function can be used, and there are many others. In all cases, you are likely to waste a few bytes whenever the data is duplicated in both the null driver and the platform-specific version. However, the amount of memory is likely to be very small because there's only one graphics driver per game, which is very easy to spot if you want to remove it.

INPUT DEVICES

What makes the input module difficult is not the technical side (as we'll explain that later), but its role in tuning gameplay. The controller is the method by which the player interacts with your game. It has a language of its own, in which both speaker and listener must be fluent for effective communication to occur. This means the controller must be responsive, accurate, and intuitive for every platform. The input system stands alone in the cross-platform world as the only component to have more abstractions for gameplay than for hardware.

The low-level driver usually provides the basic information about the controller indicating no more than which buttons are down, and the position of each shoulder button and joystick. This requires a very simple abstraction, and data can be presented to the game programmer within a day of coding. However, determining the differences between buttons involves more than just renaming them. The physical position of the buttons on different joypads might make certain combinations more difficult for a player to press, causing functionality to get moved onto other keys, or even the joystick. There is then a further layer of complexity when supporting different joypad configurations, as the strafe control may move between buttons and joystick, for example. Instantly, the code will have to change from a Boolean button test to an analog range check; which is certainly not the most obvious abstraction, especially when compared to the other system components we'll be looking at later.

General Implementation

The input data follows a simple route from the hardware, through its abstractions, to the game code. We'll now consider each section in turn.

Hardware Abstraction

Of all the layers, hardware abstraction is probably the easiest to implement. This involves a basic input manager class to configure the basic hardware and handle the controller. Each platform has its own specific manager derived from a cross-platform base class.

The purpose of the manager is to hold information about the controllers in general (like how many there are, and which are plugged in), as well as the current state for each individual joypad.

```
class CInputManager {
public:
    // ...
    virtual void         Initialize();
    virtual tUINT32      GetNumControllers();
    virtual void         Update();
    virtual void         Release();

private:
    // ...
    CInputController    *m_pController;
};

CInputManager::Initialize()
{
    m_pController = new CInputController[GetNumControllers()];
}
```

All the common data is held in the input manager, inside `m_pController`. From a development perspective, this allows 99% of the input processing code to be written in the cross-platform `CInputManager` class. As the input functionality evolves, this will minimize our workload because any new features only have to be written once—in the base class.

A much more important reason for letting `CInputManager` handle everything is that it removes the platform-specific components from the equation. From here, we can determine when the current input state gets updated, and how. This becomes important when handling asynchronous input messages from an event system or interrupt as changing the controller status mid-way through a frame would be disastrous. Instead, all data received is stored in the platform-specific code, and copied into the common controller variables at the start of every frame when the member function `Update` is called.

```
void CPS2InputManager::Update()
{
    sgxMemcpy(m_pController, m_pInternal,
        sizeof(CInputController) * GetNumControllers());
}
```

A typical controller includes the following information:

```
class CInputController {
public:
    CControlButton    Buttons[eMaxButtons];
    CControlStick     Sticks[eMaxSticks];
};

class CControlStick {
    tREAL32           m_fPosX, m_fPosY;
    tREAL32           m_fRawPoxX, m_fRawPosY;
};

class CControlButton {
    tBOOL             m_bPressed, m_bReleased;
    tBOOL             m_bIsDown, m_bIsUp;
};
```

Input Controllers

Let's now consider the different types of controllers that are available.

The Keyboard

Although keyboard versions exist for several of the current consoles, the keyboard is only considered a necessary peripheral within the sphere of PC gaming. What's more, it's the only peripheral we're concerned with in an abstract sense; if we want to retrieve input from the keyboard, there's no reason to abstract its interface into that of a joypad by pretending it has 104 buttons and no joystick. Keyboards serve a different purpose when it comes to the input phase of a game, and so can reasonably have different abstractions. The abstractions to open the inventory screen, for example, will consequently exist in the gameplay arena, not the input driver.

Access to the keyboard and mouse will be hidden behind `CInputManager` functions, so that our common code can check for the keyboard state without having to clarify the platform with an `#ifdef SGX_TARGET_WINTEL32`.

Creating the keyboard module simply entails creating a unique set of IDs for each key on the keyboard (usually identical to the key's ASCII value), and a function to test for it.

```
tBOOL
CInputManager::IsKeyboardKeyDown(tKey key)
{
    return m_Keyboard[key].m_bIsDown;
}
```

Because of the asynchronous nature of keyboard events, the driver registers all stage changes in the platform-specific code before copying it into the cross-platform manager at the start of the next update cycle for retrieval by functions as shown in the previous code.

Additional features, such as auto-repeat, can be added later if required. Naturally, with all the necessary information (such as the time of keypress) in the common code, it can be applied to other platforms without any extra coding.

Mice

What's true for keyboards is also true of mice; that is, we don't have to lever its interface into that of a generic joypad. All we have to do is add a couple of extra support functions. Within a Windows environment, these might include designating the game's window handle to determine the mouse cursor position inside the client area. Because such information is platform-specific, we should use `void *` throughout, which you can `typedef` into `CPlatformWindow` or similar, to prevent it causing offense to the other platforms. If this information is available at game start, you might prefer to create the platform-specific input singleton and pass this information to the constructor.

Mice usually require additional information over and above the traditional `x,y` position. For example, a delta position indicating how far the mouse has moved along each axis is often a more useful piece of data. This has the additional benefit of being identical to the data returned by the trackball or mouse wheel, both of which have unbounded axes, meaning deltas are the only way to measure them.

Joypads

In its previous incarnation as a joy*stick*, this device had minimal control. It had one stick with two axes, and an assortment of up to three buttons. Since then, we have become accustomed to using and programming joypads with two sticks, shoulder buttons, analog buttons, directional pads, and 10 or more digital buttons. So how do we start to unify them?

In the first instance, we're not concerned with cosmetics, so we create a large list of anonymous enumerations for each type of control:

```
typedef enum {
    eButton0,
    eButton1,
    eButton2,
    // ... and so on, up to around 16 ...
    eStick0x,
    eStick0y,
    eStick1x,
    eStick2y,
    // ... and potentially more ...
} tControl;
```

This may appear rather frugal compared to the different types of control we have to manage, but they can cover the entire range of gadgets that appear on the standard suite of consoles. Notice we're using "buttons" as a catchall for both the digital and analog varieties. This is because, conceptually, they perform the same task in the same way, and they hold the same data. The only difference is that the amount of travel on a digital button is limited to 0 or 1, as opposed to the variable scale available with analog controls. The means our button state structure would appear like this:

```
struct {
    tBOOL    bState;
    tREAL32  fState;
    tBOOL    bPressed;
    tBOOL    bReleased;
} ButtonState;
```

When handling analog buttons, we need to scale the API result from the platform-dependent code into something uniform. The range can be anything, but a floating-point number between 0 and 1 provides a lot of scope with little or no quantization problems, so we need nothing more than the most basic scaling functions to handle it:

```
const tUINT32 iMaxRange = 64;  // arbitrary number, dictated by API

    State.fState = iStickValue / (tREAL32)iMaxRange;
```

We can then convert this state into binary by an equally simple piece of code:

```
if (State.fState < 0.5f) {
    State.bState = FALSE;
} else {
    State.bState = TRUE;
}
```

This is one of many different variations. Another might be the following:

```
if (State.fState < 0.1f) {
    State.bState = FALSE;
} else if (State.fState > 0.8f) {
    State.bState = TRUE;
} else {
    // Keep state unchanged
}
```

In both cases, the choice of numbers to indicate how far the button needs to be pushed or released to change state is completely arbitrary. You should replace these with your own variables, which can be controlled externally. Better still, have them controlled by the game component so it can determine which particular buttons have a hair trigger and which don't.

TIP

We can use this same structure to report the GameCube's shoulder buttons. These have an extra click state when pressed fully in, as first used in Luigi's Mansion. For this to work, we can limit the analog travel of `fState` *to the range of* `0` *to* `0.9`*, and set* `bState` *to* `TRUE` *when the button is clicked. Employing this technique is not a general solution, however, and depends on how your game is using the shoulder buttons.*

We then have to apply this unification technique to the joysticks. This process consists of three steps:

1. Rescale each axis, and clamp if necessary.
2. Apply a deadband around the center of the joystick.
3. Rescale the position to reflect the shape of the stick.

The scaling code is as simple as it was previously, only now we have a larger range (-1 to +1) to deal with. We could also employ extra clamping because the range of joysticks diminishes with age, so you would scale to –1.2 and +1.2 instead.

```
fStickX *= 1.2f;
fStickX  = sgxRange(fStickX, -1.0f, 1.0f);
```

TIP

Your game should never require the joystick to be in the outer 5% of its range because old sticks will never be able to move there.

No movement should be reported in the deadband area, even if movement is detected. This is necessary when dealing with some external devices, as a certain amount of electronic noise exists which causes a very small movement to show, despite the fact that the stick remains motionless.

Like the magic numbers given previously, the position of the deadband can be made to vary according to platform or controller. Generally, however, deadband is only used to eliminate noise around the center of the stick, so the platform-specific code supplies the bounds and the common `CInputManager` processes them.

```
if (stick.fPositionX > -fDeadband && stick.fPositionX < fDeadband) {
    stick.fPositionX = 0;
}
if (stick.fPositionY > -fDeadband && stick.fPositionY < fDeadband) {
    stick.fPositionY = 0;
}
```

TIP

When calculating the user-presentable values for the joystick, never throw the original numbers away. Keep them available as "raw" data because some parts of your game might require the data that the deadband removes. Targeting systems also can benefit from this precision.

The final part of our process involves another scale to correct the physical mounting of the joysticks. If you look closely at the surround of any joystick, you'll notice a plastic surround, or guard, to prevent the stick from moving beyond a certain region. The shape of this plastic is not uniform among consoles. The Game-

Cube has two sticks, both of which sit in an octagonal surround. The PlayStation 2 and Xbox both let the stick run around in circles (see Figure 7.2).

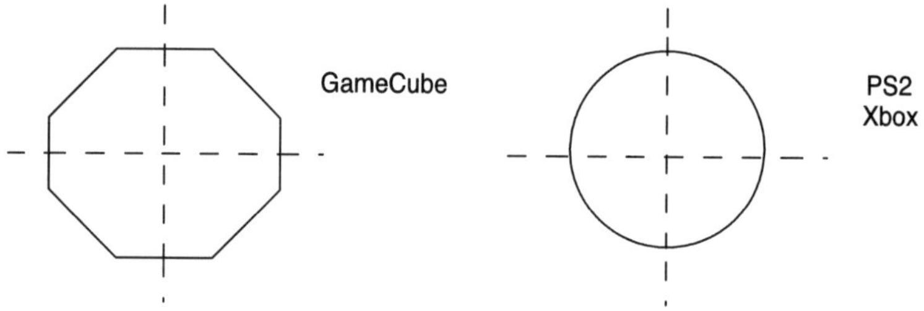

FIGURE 7.2 The range of various joysticks.

This poses two questions. Do we worry about the GameCube because an octagon is very nearly a circle? And do we need to remap the circles to cover the whole range of –1 and +1 in both axes?

The answer to both questions depends on how you plan to use the controller data. Whatever is returned to the game must be identical in all cases, so you might opt for the easiest route and use the low-level driver to return values between –1 and +1 as given, and let the gameplay code square the circle if necessary.

To reduce the GameCube's octagon to a circle, the easiest solution (other than to ignore it) is to measure the magnitude of the stick's position and clamp it to the largest circle that fits inside the octagon, as shown in Figure 7.3.

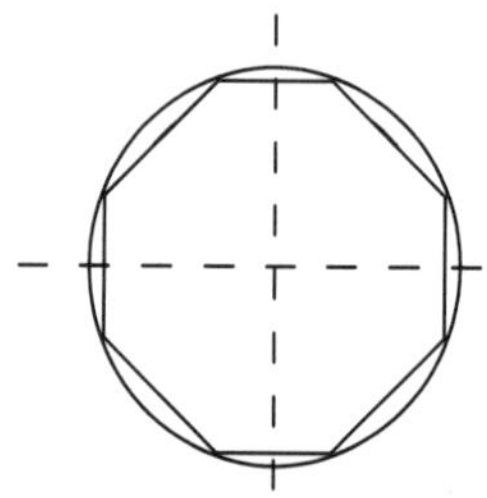

FIGURE 7.3 Converting the GameCube octagon.

We can then scale this circle up to cover a larger area than the octagon, covering the tiny bits we missed previously, and then clamp to unity as normal.

```
fMagnitude = sgxSqrt(x*x + y*y);
fMagnitude *= 1.1f;
fMagnitude = sgxMax(fMagnitude, 1.0f);
```

Other formulas and solutions are possible, but we'll leave that as an exercise for you.

Rumble Feature

All current consoles support a rumble, or vibration, feature of some kind that provides shocks and jolts to the player to reflect the experience onscreen. For the most part, this is an add-on feature when the player gets shot or the car runs over a bump in the road. The only gameplay consideration is that the player can turn off the rumble feature at will, so it cannot be relied on to exist.

NOTE

Some controllers, such as the Nintendo GameCube WaveBird™, do not have a rumble feature at all.

From a programming perspective, we have to abstract the rumble code according to purpose and then by process. So in the first instance, we would a trigger cross-platform rumble using an abstraction such as:

```
CRumbleManager::Get()->StartRumble(eExplosion, fStrength, fDuration);
```

Our common manager code then tracks each rumble being processed by modifying the strength across its duration. After all, an explosion will have a more gradual fall-off pattern than a gunshot. The manager code then sorts these rumbles into order, strongest first, and passes them on to the platform-specific handler.

TIP

The fall-off pattern for each type of effect should be as elaborate as possible because this data provides a very high degree of control to the vibration intensity, enabling more complex rumble effects to be produced in common code without resort to (or relying on) the platform-specific joypad.

The platform-specific code then processes these vibrations according to the limits of the console. This generally requires one of two generic solutions.

Single Rumble

Some platforms support a single magnitude vector for their rumble feature. This requires an accumulation of existing rumbles by simply adding the relative strengths together. You could use more complex calculations (based on the median of relative strengths), but with a single control variable, the results wouldn't be noticeably different. A customized fall-off pattern, as previously mentioned, will therefore give you the best results possible.

If the rumble feature supports different waveforms (such as square, sine, or sawtooth), then you need to choose a heuristic to combine them. Such a heuristic could be the most common waveform in the strongest five rumbles, or you could grade them according to abruptness and pick the most prominent waveform. The grading technique follows the ideas of Fourier, insomuch as every sawtooth wave can be composited from a selection of sine wave harmonics, and *every* possible harmonic of a sine wave produces a square wave. This means the most abrupt wave is square, followed by sawtooth, followed by sine.

Multiple Rumbles

When the platform-specific API supports multiple rumble "channels," the work is much simpler because you only need to apply the most prominent N vibrations (where N is the maximum number of channels).

CAUTION

Some technical requirements indicate how long the rumble can run uninterrupted. This requires some additional, simple code that exists at the cross-platform level, although it uses a timeout value given by the platform-specific code.

Some platforms have dual rumble units. These units can be used by way of a manager routine that divides the list of prominent vibrations into two, according to the suitability of each unit.

Platform Nomenclature

Every platform has its own special names for `eButton0` and `eStick0` and so on, and in many cases, we would prefer to use them because they make the code self-commenting and less impenetrable. We'll see the convenient places in which to do so when we look at the gameplay abstractions later. For now, we can create a duplicate enumeration in the manner shown. This explicitly shows the mapping between common name and platform name, and ensures that any new buttons added don't cause our platform names to go out of sync.

```
typedef enum {
    eCircle     = eButton0,
    eSquare     = eButton1,
    eTriangle   = eButton2,
    eCross      = eButton3,
    // ... and so on ...
} tPS2Control;
```

Logical and Physical Input

The input manager also needs to maintain a mapping table to convert logical input devices to physical ones. This technique allows a controller to be called "controller

1," but actually read the input data from port 3, for example. This means that whatever controller is initially picked up and used by the player can be termed the first, regardless of where it's plugged in. Sometimes this is a desired game design feature, whereas other times, it's a technical requirement from the console manufacturer. This is simple to implement, so there's no reason every game shouldn't support it.

```
CInputManager::CreateMapping()
{
    for(int i=0; i<GetNumControllers(); i++) {
        m_Mapping[i] = i;
    }
}
```

Note that there is always a 1:1 mapping between logical and physical devices. We can then write our `IsButtonDown` function like this:

```
tBOOL
CInputManager::IsButtonDown(tController controller, tButton button)
{
    if (controller >= eFirst && controller <= eFourth) {
        // Map logical button to physical one and recall ourselves
        return IsButtonDown(m_Mapping[controller-eFirst], button);
    }

    if (controller >= ePhysical0 && controller <= ePhysical3) {
        return m_Controller[controller].IsButtonDown(button);
    }

    return FALSE;
}
```

Our `tController` enumeration supports access to both logical and physical controllers because both are needed:

```
typedef enum {
   ePhysical0 = 0,
   ePhysical1,
   ePhysical2,
   ePhysical3,

   eFirst,
   eSecond,
   eThird,
   eFourth,
```

```
        eLastController = SGX_ENUM_PADDING

    } tController;
```

This enumeration can be extended by including support for an `eAllLogical` facility, which enables a twenty-first century version of the "Press Any Key" routine. The same idea can be applied to the `tButton` enumeration we used in the `IsButtonDown` example by adding logical keys for "select," "go backwards," and "next."

These are much more than cosmetic changes, however, as this allows a uniformed way of handling many of the UI (user interface) screens. All UIs have navigation keys dictated by the console manufacturer, so they can be placed here in the platform-dependent driver.

TIP

Always have a bypass function so you can query a second physical joystick, as this is very useful for controlling debugging features within your game.

Data Inference

We also need code to produce data that was not generated by the hardware or its messages. This occurs through *inference*, where we look at the state information we *do* have and the history behind it to determine the latest state information that we *don't* have. The best example in this category involves keypresses.

At a minimum, most platforms issue a message when a key is pressed or released. This allows you to infer when a key is down or up by looking at the current message and its previous state.

The inference layer is occasionally necessary because some platforms will provide *only* this functionality. Conversely, they may allow you to determine whether a key is up or down, but not when it was first pressed. It's easy to infer from this data, however, whether the key was pressed in the last frame or not.

One further point to raise is the language we use when specifying exactly what constitutes a pressed button. Is it one that's currently down, has been pressed since the last frame, or has been pressed recently? This last case needs to be clarified further. Many player control systems work on a state engine, and the "button pressed" event causes it to change state. However, the output from the following code will vary depending on the meaning of the word "recently."

```
bPress1 = CInputManager::Get()->IsButtonPressed(eFirst, eButton0);
bPress2 = CInputManager::Get()->IsButtonPressed(eFirst, eButton0);
```

Should `bPress1` and `bPress2` be equal? After all, the button was pressed since the last frame. Or, because `bPress1` has acknowledged the pressed button, does that flag now get cleared so that `bPress2` can return `FALSE`?

The answer to both questions is whatever the comments in the code say about it because they define how the function works for your game. For the sake of maintainability, however, we recommend that `bPress1` and `bPress2` both return the same value.

Input Logging

The input logging technique solves problems—lots of problems. By recording every input from the user, you can feed that data back to the game later. This input then reruns the entire game while you look on in disbelieve as it plays itself, like the player pianos from days gone by. This automated replay lets you track down bugs and validate optimizations in proven identical situations. However, you can also use it proactively as a test suite or game replay feature, either for letting the player relive past glories or as a demo mode.

For most programmers, input logging is difficult and tiresome. The cross-platform developer, however, sits quietly and contented because the input system he's already designed needs but a few tweaks to get it ready. The traditional cross-platform techniques you've learned throughout this book will ensure the level of predictability required for input logging.

The implementation pivots around the simple fact that the logger is just another input manager and no different from, say, `CGameCubeInputManager`. On every `Update`, another few bytes are taken from the log file and copied into the common data structure in the same way that every other input manager copies data from its controller.

TIP

Always make sure it's possible to retrieve the true physical state of the joypad because at some point, you'll want to hit the start button to exit the playback mode. If the only data received comes from a log file, this action won't be possible.

Log Format

The format of this data will vary according to the amount of time you have to develop your logger, and how small you want the end result to be. In the simple case, you can export the entire `CInputController` structure every frame. With 16 controls each occupying 16 bytes, you have a fairly chunky 256 bytes per frame to store. Table 7.1 shows how much memory this could occupy.

Using 256 bytes per frame might be acceptable for debugging purposes, but is prohibitively large for in-game features, such as action replays.

TABLE 7.1 Logging Capacity at 60 fps

Bytes per frame	*1 minute*	*5 minutes*	*10 minutes*	*1 hour*
256	900 KB	4.5 MB	9 MB	52 MB
64	225 KB	1.1 MB	2.25 MB	13.5 MB
16	56 KB	281 KB	562 KB	3.4 MB
12	43 KB	216 KB	432 KB	2.6 MB
8	28 KB	140 KB	281 KB	1.7 MB

To store the same information in a more optimal fashion, we need to compress it. One good way of doing this is to only store the data that changes, which is usually the joystick position (which can compress to 1 byte per axis), along with the appropriate button states. Because we only monitor changes, we can include each button change as a single reference without indicating whether the button is up or down (in another case of data inference). With 16 different buttons, we only need 4 bits of information, allowing us to store eight state changes in 4 bytes. This reduces the memory footprint to 8 bytes per frame. Analog buttons need an extra byte each.

However, we need to store one more piece of information: the time. In a perfect world, the game will take the same amount of time to process the frame if the inputs are identical in both cases. Unfortunately, because we're likely to be testing this data cross-platform, the timings are unlikely to be identical. Furthermore, the complexities of modern machines and threaded architectures mean that even on the same machine, the timings between successive runs could vary by a fraction of a second. As you've seen before, any fraction is too much, so each piece of data is prefixed with the time, taking our total to around 16 bytes.[2]

If we save the time out, however, we must apply it to the game loop on load. We already have our cross-platform game clock (Chapter 4, "The CPU") accepting a prespecified time elapsed value, so for our logging to work, we must extract this value from the log file and apply it to the clock. The consequential data flow is shown in Figure 7.4.

This log can also be used to replay the game at different speeds. This shouldn't introduce problems because we've compensated for time changes throughout the game, but it does let us replay parts of the game in slow motion or super fast "comedy mode." Slow motion enables you to look more closely at the interactions between objects without resorting to the stop-start handling of the debugger, whereas super fast motion lets you get to the problem area as quickly as possible

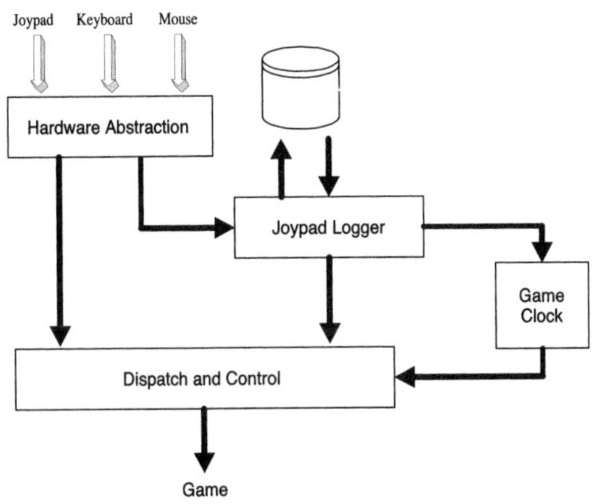

FIGURE 7.4 Input logging data flow.

Implementation

Adding an input logger to the source requires one additional mount point to indicate the destination folder for the log file. This could be in RAM, on a memory card, or on the hard disk.

```
// In the platform-specific main.cpp...
CSGXDeviceWin32Disc logfile("c:\\logfiles");

CSGXFileSystem::Get()->Mount(logfile, "/log");
```

We can then create our log file generically with

```
CSGXFile file("/log/input1.log", "w");
```

and then use a new `CLoggingInputManager` class which supports

```
void
CLoggingInputManager::StartPlaybackInput(CSGXFile &file)
{
    m_pFile = &file;
}

void
CLoggingInputManager::Update()
{
    if (m_pFile->IsSaving()) {
        *m_pFile << CGameClock::Get()->GetGameTime();
```

```
        // Calculate memory efficient deltas
    } else if (m_pFile->IsLoading()) {
        tREAL32 time_elapsed;
        *m_pFile >> time_elapsed;

        // Check for the terminator
        if (time_elapsed == 0) {
            StopPlaybackInput();
            return;
        }

        // Apply the game time
        CGameClock::Get()->SetModeConstant(time_elapsed);
    }

    *m_pFile | delta_stick0;
    *m_pFile | delta_stick1; // and so on...

    if (m_pFile->IsLoading()) {
        // Apply deltas to all sticks
        m_Controller[controller].Stick[0].x += delta_stick0.x;
        // and so on...
    }

}

void
CLoggingInputManager::StopPlaybackInput()
{
    if (m_pFile->IsSaving()) {
        *m_pFile | 0;   // a delta of zero to terminate
    }

    CGameClock::Get()->SetModeRealtime();
    m_pFile->Close();
}
```

NOTE

We're using the cross-platform filesystem because it shouldn't introduce any uncertainties because the timing is compensated for.

Potential Problems

Reproducing a complete game run from input data alone is a remarkable sight, as everything replays exactly as it did last time around. When it doesn't, there's an abundance of reasons why not, and it's never easy to deduce where the problem is. With this in mind, it's better to create your input logger earlier in the development process, and ask these typical questions.

- Are any random numbers being used that have not been seeded correctly? Some people prefer to have a random number generator for gameplay and engine code to prevent these problems. Ensure that the initial seed is constant between successive executions, at least for debugging. Or, if not constant, at least log its value so the game can be reproduced next time. Remember also that uninitialized variables constitute another random number generator.
- Have timing differences caused an `OnSoundComplete` message, or similar, to trigger an event at the wrong point in the game? Try running it with the null sound driver.
- Has the level or code changed in any way? Any subtleties, especially in AI will prevent log files from being reapplied identically. Create supplementary log files containing all the event messages sent between objects, and compare them.
- Does the current controller have fewer buttons than the machine that created the log file? Perhaps the game missed this input, and therefore processed a different code path.
- Did the game generate a log file? If the game crashes during execution, the data intended for the log file might not have been flushed to disc. Catch exceptions and write the log to disc in debug mode, and always run with logging on.
- Are you playing back in super fast or slow mode? If so, consider the rounding errors that can occur when `time_elapsed` is divided by 10, for instance, as the individual numbers might not accumulate to the same result as the original time.
- Is the floating point accurate, especially with the compression of joystick positions?
- Are random numbers being applied correctly in time-compensated code? See the "Using Rand Wisely" section in Chapter 6 for more information on this.

Gameplay Abstractions

When it comes to implementing gameplay, we have another set of abstractions to deal with. This comes from the need to provide different control configurations for the game and for the various consoles. Our first thought is to create a simple mapping:

```
if (CInputManager::Get()->IsButtonDown(eFirst, m_Mapping[eStepLeft]))
```

However, this is not enough as the step left can be carried out by a joystick movement instead of a button press. The idea of a mapping idea is correct; it's just not that simple.

The first task is to create a list of all the possible buttons that exist from a *game* perspective. Such a list might start with the following:

- Fire
- Jump
- Step left
- Step right
- Side step (a combination of step left and right)
- Move forward
- Move backward
- Movement (a combination of forward and backward)
- Turn left
- Turn right
- Open inventory

We can then map these to particular buttons on a dynamic basis by having a series of registration functions. These map the gameplay controls, like fire, to particular buttons that are specific to that platforms controller and in that particular configuration.

```
class CMappingControl {
public:
    CInputManager::tControl    ctrl;
};

void
InitializePS2ConfigOne()
{
    RegisterControl(eCtlFire, ePS2ShoulderR1);
    RegisterControl(eCtlFire2, ePS2ShoulderR2);
    RegisterControl(eCtlStepLeft, ePS2Square);
    RegisterControl(eCtlStepRight, ePS2Circle);
    // ... and so on ...
}
```

Because the PS2-specific buttons here actually map to the standard `eButtonO` definitions, we don't have to worry about any platform-dependencies. Nor do we have to worry about the large size of this function, as some buttons will be mapped to more than one feature in the list. With an eye to bug prevention, you might want to initialize each control with empty keymappings before calling the initialize functions. You can then test these keymappings afterward to make sure they have all changed and consequently contain a complete complement of controls.

Having specified what button, or joystick, maps to what feature, we now need to indicate *how* they all map. We put the onus on the game components to ask for the appropriate data. So, if the game asks "*is* the player trying to step left," we can interpret that in two ways.

If it's a button, we simply look at the controller and retrieve its state; if it's a joystick, we determine whether the stick is somewhere between –1 and 0 on its horizontal axis. From here we can return a simple true or false answer, just as an *is* type question would demand.

On the other hand, any code asking to "get the position of the side step" will expect an analog value between –1 and +1. This time around, controller configurations using the joystick for side step have the easy job, and the keypad variations have to convert `eStepLeft` and `eStepRight` into an appropriate number. You will recall the existence of both "side step" *and* "step left" and "step right" in the previous list; this takes care of these cases and allow us to handle the controller in any way the game sees fit.

The implementation of such a feature is not difficult, but can appear long-winded as each type of control needs its own mapping to tie the two separate "step" controls into one all-encompassing entity. This can be done with either a large switch statement or, more preferably, a callback function.

The suggestion of the callback might appear to bloat things further, but there's a lot of common code. Detecting the movement of a left side step can be achieved with a function like this:

```
tBOOL
StdGetButtonDownLeft(CMappingControl *pControl)
{
    if (CInputManager::Get()->IsControlButton(pControl->ctrl)) {
        return CInputManager::Get()->IsButtonDown(pControl->ctrl);
    }
    if (CInputManager::Get()->GetStickPosition(pControl->ctrl) < 0) {
        return TRUE;
    }
    return FALSE;
}
```

This is then tied to the button with an improved version of the `RegisterControl` function:

```
RegisterControl(eCtlStepLeft, ePS2Square, StdGetButtonDownLeft);
```

This gives us a great deal of scope. Not only are these functions standard and cross-platform, but also they can be used to enhance the control system. Let's consider the button-oriented version of the side step.

When retrieving the side step value as a floating-point number, there's a gradual change as the joystick moves to the left or right. If this were being returned from a button, it would represent an acceleration from 0 to 60. Although this is something the player could do (voluntarily) with the joystick, it isn't something the player would generally want from the keypad. So, we can extend the `CMappingControl` class with some generic data:

```
class CMappingControl {
public:
    CInputManager::tControl    ctrl;
    tBOOL       (*pFnForButtons)(CMappingControl *pControl);
    tBOOL       (*pFnForPosition)(CMappingControl *pControl);
    tMEMSIZE    iUserData;
    tREAL32     fUserData;
};
```

Because this structure belongs to the individual gameplay actions (like fire and jump), we have separate data for every type of joypad control. This makes it very easy to use `iUserData` to add auto-repeat to the side step so that, when used from a keypad, it increases in speed over a second or so. To achieve this, we need to add a special loop at the start of each frame to update each mapping control, resetting the auto-repeat to 0 if the button is not down, or clamping it to unity if the numbers get too large.

The Bottom Line

Despite all the techniques shown here, there will still be instances where the control system isn't quite the same on all platforms. That won't be due to any technical issues because we have them all covered, but due to some intangible feature of the controller. The watchword is *playability*. The game must be playable, and the control system is the most important part of that. So, if the game doesn't feel quite right because the GameCube controller is slightly different to the PS2, and multiplying the lookaround speed by 1.1 solves the problem...then do it.

```
#ifdef SGX_TARGET_GAMECUBE
    fLookSpeed *= 1.1f;
#endif
```

There's nothing wrong with this. Nor is there a problem with using the raw controller data you saw earlier. In fact, we added it in there for this very contingency.

CAUTION

Do not change any movement-based data with this approach, as that will cause the player to run faster, or jump farther, on different platforms, which can seriously affect gameplay.

Don't be afraid to hack the code if it will make a better game. Just make sure you check, double check, and triple check every gameplay feature connected to it, in case the change makes the game very easy or completely impossible.

ENDNOTES

1. Protected members are essentially public, but under another name. This is because there are no restrictions in being able to derive a class, and therefore no means to prevent a malicious programmer from deriving a class for the sole purpose of accessing protected members.
2. If we adopt a variable compression system, this can be reduced substantially. We can use the first byte to indicate how many axes (between 0 and 4) and button changes (from 0 to 16) are stored in the subsequent bytes, followed by the data itself. The time (stored invariably as a `tREAL32`, so consider the alignment problems carefully) should be stored at the head of this data.

8 The Audio System

In This Chapter

- High-Level Parameters
- Playing Music
- Playing Sounds
- Resourcing Data
- Mixer Control
- Video Playback Interaction

HIGH-LEVEL PARAMETERS

For many years, the audio engine has been playing a secondary role to the graphics engine. It has been afforded less time for development, fewer in-house resources, and usually had a minimal affect on the gameplay. This is not completely surprising, because the capability of sound cards was usually limited to squeaks and squawks on a single channel, being written by whichever junior coder had a week to spare to copy the sample code and wrapper it in a `PlaySound` function.

Over the past decade, this scenario has changed substantially, with a definite shift toward experienced audio coders, sound designers, and composers working in a professional recording studio producing CD quality soundtracks. This change has affected everyone it seems; except the cross-platform audio programmer. He is still doing what is perceived as a relatively simple job. On one level, this is true, but this generalization omits a very large part of the story.

Audio development consists of providing middleware between the game and hardware, and resourcing the data. In some cases, this hardware may be considered middleware itself (such as *MultiStream* on PS2), but regardless, the audio programmer always writes an abstraction between the way the game wants to call the hardware, and how the hardware will accept requests. This interface is considered simple because the requirements of the audio engine *are* very simple, and consist of basic commands to start, pause, and stop playing, along with a means to change parameters in real time. These should work across the various types of audio data we'll support and typically include the following:

- Background music
- One-shot music (or stings)
- Ambient effect samples (often looped)
- One-shot samples (gunshots, and the like)

These can be broken down or condensed into as many, or as few, groups as you like but essentially, every one has the same functionality.

And while we're busy making checklists, how about an example list of parameters, as follows:

- Volume
- Pitch
- Position in world
- Effect (for example, echo, reverb)

Because these requirements are uniform across platforms, a large gap exists between the function call layer and the hardware-processing layer. This gives us a lot of scope to handle the request in whatever way is suitable for the platform. It's almost as if after a cross-platform audio function has been called, we drop directly into platform-specific code, and continue as a native application. What differs is how the data assets are resourced by the different platforms, and how the various limitations of each platform are overcome.

PLAYING MUSIC

Of all the sound assets we'll cover in this section, music has the greatest scope. Every FPS is fully expected to have a variety of gunshot sounds, different ricochets for each surface, and an unhealthy selection of violent death screams. How the music should react is not so well understood. Should the music be continuous, vary according to location, or consist of occasional musical stings without an underlying score? Such decisions are usually in the hands of the audio designers. As programmers, we have to ensure that we can implement a music system to cope with the music on every platform.

As already discussed, the interface is straightforward; however, the data-resourcing component requires some thought. From the game programmer's perspective, the interface will use a simple function like this:

```
hMusicHandle = CAudioEngine::Get()->PlayMusic("main_theme");
```

This is a good level of abstraction because we might not know any more details about the theme at this point. Notice that we don't even specify a file extension. This helps us change the extension according to the platform, and stops the game programmer from making unwarranted assumptions about the data.

Storing music, on the other hand, involves more decisions; however, because music has a fairly low processor overhead, storage is usually governed by the disc and memory capacity available to us, instead of by platform capabilities. Provided the source material (in this case, the original music score) is recorded at the highest possible resolution, we can downsample to fit within the scope of our platform through a variety of methods. The medium we choose can (and probably will) vary between platforms, but we can base the format entirely around the machine because of the high level of abstraction.

CD Audio

Sometimes called red book audio by experienced people in the industry, this is the format used in commercial audio CDs. Some platforms, PC especially, make light work of handling CD audio because it's entirely processed by the sound card, leaving no marks on the processor at all. As you would expect from a normal CD, the quality is very good and gives people the option of listening to the game music on their car or home stereo systems.

The downsides are also what you would expect from a normal CD: CD audio takes up a lot of space, there are seek time issues, and you can only play one CD audio stream at a time.

MP3 and Ogg Vorbis

The term MP3 has been sullied and perverted since its first use. Originally used to describe a compression format, it has now become synonymous with piracy and file sharing. Despite this stigma, MP3 provides a good mechanism for introducing near CD-quality audio in a fraction of the space.

MP3 compression works by providing a target bandwidth for the data, say 128 kbps, into which the source material is then compressed by removing anything you're unlikely to hear. This means we can accurately determine the size and throughput of our streaming buffers, and how much disc space we need to store the file. On average, a 128 kbps-encoded MP3 uses about 1/12th of the uncompressed audio stream, requiring about 1 MB per minute of disc space for good quality audio. The MP3 standard also allows a variable compression rate across a single file, but this is not recommended because the decoder software is more problematic to write.

The legal issues with MP3 encoding and licensing has initiated the creation of other compression methods based on similar ideas. The most prevalent is Ogg Vorbis. Unlike MP3, Ogg Vorbis is a completely open solution that has no patent, copyright, or trademark issues to limit its growth or use. Indeed, Ogg Vorbis has been used by *Unreal Tournament 2003™* (and every other Epic™ game since), *EA™*, and *Crystal Dynamics™*, among many others.

There are two portions to the Ogg Vorbis format. Ogg is the container format, which contains generic information such as name and duration, and allows a standard Ogg decoder to access an arbitrary set of compression methods. This includes formats such as Vorbis, which has a similar style of lossy compression to MP3, but it measures the throughput as an abstract "quality" level, not in kilobits per second. The often-made comparison is that quality level 3 uses about 110 kbps, but gives better fidelity than MP3 files at 128 kbps.

Ogg Vorbis was intentionally designed by *Xiph.org* as a two-part standard that allows the Vorbis decompressor to be replaced at will. This has already happened, and a separate codec called Speex (*http://www.speex.org*) has been created that is specially tailored to handle compression for speech. The quality of its speech files currently outshines the Vorbis encoder, which is intended more for music.

MP3 and Vorbis data take a comparable processing hit during decompression, and is sent to the sound chip with all the other audio data. Unless compressed audio streams, such as these, are built-in to the start of the game, you're unlikely to be given the processing power required for their decompression later in the development cycle.

NOTE

Because of the way the decompression algorithms work, a slight latency exists between requesting an MP3 or Vorbis sound and hearing that sound.

MIDI

Musical Instrument Digital Interface (*MIDI*) has been featured in musical instruments since the wonderful *Sequential Prophet 600* in 1982. As a term, MIDI can mean either the interface to communicate MIDI data or the file format in which MIDI data is stored. We use MIDI here to describe the format, which is basically a list of notes to play and the time at which to play them. This data is then fed into a sound generator to play the notes themselves. Often this sound generator is a synthesizer, tone module, or a collection of sampled instruments in the computer's memory.

The use of MIDI-based audio in games no longer lives in the domain of Casio™ keyboards and 1980s synth-pop because the quality of the audio is governed by the sounds, not the music data. On a console, these sounds are generated by professional samples loaded into memory and played through the normal audio chip. With increases in memory budgets, these sounds can be very high quality, providing a compact solution for long pieces of music. In reality, MIDI files on consoles are more akin to the old-style trackers of the Commodore Amiga, but with a greater resolution in timing and sample rates.

The sound cards on most PCs come with a basic MIDI tone module, but these are usually so basic as to be useless. The more expensive sound cards allow custom samples to be loaded in place of the default tones, and generate listenable music. Because you cannot predict the user's sound card, any MIDI music often has to be processed in software, which is a very processor-intensive task. Fortunately, storage space is not normally a problem on PCs, enabling other solutions to be used.

To talk numbers, a complete MIDI score can be held in around 100 KB of data. The sounds, however, will occupy as much space as you give them. This could be between 2 and 4 MB, and total as much as an Ogg Vorbis file. Where MIDI scores highly, however, is that the same sample data can be reused for several pieces of music, so you only need to load a different 100 KB chunk to change the tune, giving you an hour or more of music for very little memory. Additionally, you can lower the quality of specific samples (usually those of low pitch, such as the bass drum) to claw back as much memory as necessary to fit within the budget. On the downside, however, all the MIDI sample data must be held in memory because determining which samples are currently playing and intelligently streaming them into, and out of, memory is very difficult and liable to leave embarrassing gaps in the soundtrack if the sample is missing.

Audio programmers trying to push the proverbial envelope will want to focus on MIDI playback as this is the only method in the current cross-platform crop that supports dynamic music to segue into other tunes, or to change individual notes and patterns to reflect the game's mood.

Customized Formats

Each platform SDK comes with a set of tools and sound samples. Invariably, this includes a tool to play music in a proprietary audio file format, which is usually just a specialized (and sometimes, optimized) version of the MIDI files we've just seen. Again, having such a clear distinction between the `PlayMusic` request, and the back-end process helps us here. Provided we ensure that our tool chain is able to create these custom formats from our common data, we can adopt this music format as transparently as the game code can play it. If the SDK examples do not provide enough access to these formats, then you are usually better off using your own format because an efficient tool chain is most important.

PLAYING SOUNDS

Unlike music, sound effects cannot be abstracted, so they must be reproduced as sampled data. The days where the sound chip was programmed directly with a white noise generator to produce an explosion are over. Fortunately, there are a couple of different ways to store sample data.

Raw Data

File formats such as WAV have a built-in mechanism for lossy compression that enables sounds to be stored in a smaller memory footprint without the overhead of expensive decompression code. This mechanism is called downsampling, where a sound is stored at 22,050 Hz, instead of 44,100 Hz. Sampling a sound at a lower rate omits the higher frequencies that are present[1], but reduces the memory footprint. This is often acceptable for short sounds, particularly as the sounds themselves, such as footsteps or bullet impacts, won't contain any high frequencies. Even those that do, such as ricochets, often survive a downsample like this.

Some platforms also support ADPCM (Adaptive Delta Pulse Code Modulation) compression on WAV data. This stores only the differences between successive samples, and can achieve around 4:1 compression. It's also very cheap to decompress.

Compressed Data

Taking a page from the music compression section, we can also apply the Vorbis or Speex decoders to normal sample data. Although compression can be applied to all the sounds, the processor overhead in doing so usually makes this prohibitive, especially given that they are likely to be played several times a second. If storage is the main problem, you can get better results by reducing the quality of the sample and saving it as raw data. It's better to limit the use of MP3 or Ogg sample compression to speech and ambient sounds when there is only one or two instances of it. This creates a double win, because the speech and ambient effects are likely to be the longest samples.

Compressed speech has another benefit in that its memory footprint is only usually apparent when the first playable version has been built. Compression of this kind can help you find an extra 200 MB of disc space. If your game has a lot of speech, one disc might need to hold duplicate copies of it for five different languages. Using compressed audio can save a significant amount of storage in this case.

> CAUTION
>
> *When auditioning and testing sounds, use the simplest audio player you can find. Windows Media Player™ supports plug-ins for a huge variety of audio decompressors that might not be available on the consoles or the asset building machine, causing broken audio.*

Metadata

Every sound in the game exists as more than just 44,100 samples per second. It also features a selection of metadata that describes the sound, and how it should be played *in situ*. This is typical of any file format and should come as no surprise. A texture, for example, includes its size and color depth alongside the pixel data.

The metadata in our sound file can be grouped into two categories. First, we have information about the sound data itself: size, compressor used, playback frequency, at what resolution it's stored, and so on. Second, we have the sound's properties. These are set up by the sound designer and include the traditional features such as an inner and outer range.

Looped Sounds

Although such a simple technique, the support for looped sounds varies between platforms because you can't guarantee an arbitrary start and end marker for your loop within each API. It's possible that some sounds will only start looping from the beginning of the sound, and some will only use the endpoint for its end loop marker.

Unfortunately, this functionality is commonly required because many game puzzles rely on the player starting or stopping some device to achieve their objectives. This involves a corresponding set of sounds (for start, looped middle, and end) that should be created by the tool chain from a single sound file, with automatically appended metadata indicating the next sound to load. This only needs to occur in specific cases because many sounds will naturally loop from beginning to end, which all platforms currently support natively.

The playback of these nonnative loops must use memory-streaming technology that we'll detail shortly.

RESOURCING DATA

The source data only tells us so much. Specifically, it only tells us about itself. When the game comes to resource this sound, we need some way of indicating how it's to be used, which generally breaks down into two categories: stored in memory and streamed from disc.

Sound data can include as much or as little information as we choose, as the rest can be inferred during the game. For example, the sound engine would notice when the ricochet gets played repeatedly, and would give it a high priority and not delete it from memory if space got tight. Conversely, we can add such a flag to the `Register` function so the game knows how the sound is going to be used and forces it to remain in memory.

```
CSoundEngine::Get()->Register("ricochet_brick_01", eInMemory);
```

If the sound is going to be streamed from disc, it's still vital to register the sound because this allows the audio engine to prepare resources for it and allocate anything it might need internally. Such tasks vary according to platform, so it's wise to preregister the sounds on all platforms. DirectX, for example, needs to set up the capabilities of any buffer you allocate, so knowing this sound is used for streaming an ambient effect would allow the engine to set up the `DSBCAPS_CTRLPAN` or `DSBCAPS_CTRL3D` flags correctly. The reason given to `Register` is, naturally, an abstraction of the actual flags required. Let's now look at three typical reasons.

In Memory

For most sounds, storage in memory is a good idea because it provides zero latency on playback, and can be handled by all the current platforms natively. Each sample can be played on one or more channels as required without any extra memory as the platform-specific API will process the data directly. The data can be held in whatever memory the platform sees fit to give it.

From a Stream

This covers a multitude of different variations. The one you choose depends on the inner workings of your sound engine, and the platform.

Disc Only

Disc only is an efficient way of processing very long pieces of audio with a minimum of space because it only touches a specific piece of memory; the playback buffer. Each sound that is being streamed has its own playback buffer and is allocated to a single channel (or two channels for stereo). When the initial data has been found, it's copied into the first half of the buffer and the playback begins as a looped sound. Then, while the first half is playing, a second block of data is loading into the second half of the buffer. After the play pointer has begun playing this second half, the first half of the buffer is cleared and the next portion of data is loaded into it. This see-saw effect continues until the sound has finished, at which point the buffer is cleared (to stop audio pops) and the playback is terminated. This is a fairly traditional technique for handling streams, and many consoles now support this automatically.

The buffer itself is usually between 1 and 3 seconds long depending on the platform, and based around the disc seek time and loading speed. If you are planning on two streams of data, then you can assume a data transfer time based on `load_time + seek_time * 2` (to seek to the other stream, and back). We have a cross-platform indication of this time through our `CHardwarePlatform` class from Chapter 3, "Memory."

This solution does have some latency, however, because a time delay occurs between requesting the sound and hearing it. This is governed by the load and seek time of the disc, but is a suitable method for playback of ambient effects and music streams. However, it can cause problems when trying to synchronize audio and video, such as animations and the gesticulations of a character. Our next solution solves that.

Partially Memory Streams

This behaves identically to the disc-only solution, with the exception that the sound can start immediately because the first 0.2 seconds, say, of the sound are already held in the playback buffer. When the sound is first registered, the initial data is copied into the stream buffer and looped playback begins. By the time the sound is ready to play the second half of this buffer, the data is located on the disc and loaded.

This solution is preferred for voice-overs and conversational speech. Individual shouts and screams are probably better placed in memory because they are very short and will be referenced a lot.

CAUTION

Loading data into any looped stream buffers can usually only occur when the buffer is locked. This can be a lengthy process, and locking data near the current play pointer can cause audio skips or worse. To circumvent this, all platforms can load their streamed data into a separate buffer first, if memory allows.

Memory Streams

The memory streams category is relatively new to games. It allows data to be streamed out of memory (as if it were a disc) and into, er, memory. The technicalities of such a system are very easy to implement because we can use our abstracted filesystem from Chapter 5, "Storage," to read from memory as if it were a disc. This gives us near-zero latency because the memory reads are several orders of magnitude quicker than disc access.

However, this system introduces more redundancy with yet another buffer, but it compensates by introducing a means to decompress MP3 or Vorbis files from memory with a minimum of extra code. It also provides a simple way of looping sounds on hardware that doesn't support arbitrary loop points (as you saw previously), and can then be evolved to a completely generic memory playback system where individual snippets of music can be pieced together and mixed into some form of dynamic music system.

Asynchronous Loading

When your game needs to load data in sections (such as the large cityscape example we've used previously), your audio footprint must follow the rules of everything else and only load itself when it's needed. This can be achieved by using the disc-based streaming solutions we've just discussed, as the amount of audio required usually precludes the use of anything that touches memory.

To combat this restriction, you need to drop further hints to the audio engine. When the level section is loaded, you should `Register` the sound as normal; when the object is within, say, 50 meters of the trigger, call a second function, `RegisterUpgradeToMemory`, to start the disc seeking process.

MIXER CONTROL

The mixer is the final stage of the audio pipeline. In truth, after the sound has been fully resourced and begins playing, it is actually the entirety of the audio pipeline because there's nothing else to do except adjust its volume according to the listener's position and orientation in the world.

TIP

The listener's position and orientation may not be taken from the same game object, so don't combine their implementation. A third-person game, for example, would take the position from the camera, but the orientation from the character. This ensures that an NPC talking to the character's left will be emitted from the left speaker, and that there are no odd side effects when a character turns on the spot.

The analogy between lighting models in graphics and mixing control in audio is not as prevalent as it should be. In the same way that a miscast shadow or overly bright light can ruin the ambience of a scene in graphics, so can a poor mix process in audio. Many musicians have claimed that what sounds bad in the studio can always be fixed "in the mix." Similarly, a bad mix can destroy a good album. The same is true in games. No matter how good the samples are, a bad mix can break the game.

UDE

In cross-platform audio, the best approach to take is one that seeks out the Utopian Development Environment (UDE). This is a completely opposite approach to the lowest common denominator we've mentioned before, as this assumes whatever audio resource or hardware feature we need is available. The game works by believing that it has everything it needs, while the platform-specific code can quietly scale back anything that is not available. And because so much of this code is buried in the platform-specifics, we do not have to amend our game, working practices, or architecture to implement it.

For many, the only two pieces of information they know about their sound card is the sample rate, resolution (usually 44,100 Hz, 16 bit), and the number of channels. This latter number can vary wildly between consoles, and equally so between PC sound cards. In our UDE, we need to consider the best we could hope for and work to that limit. As an example, let's say we'd like 256 audio channels available to the end user. This is an arbitrary number, for sure, but not completely unreasonable. These are our *logical* channels. By building our game to work within this limit, we cannot run out of channels on any single platform. It's an all or nothing solution. At present, no console has more than this many audio channels, so we're not limiting the capabilities of our game. However, in the future, this number might have to increase.

CAUTION

PC sound cards can make various claims about their capabilities that bend the truth a little further than most. For instance, many cheaper sound cards without on-board memory claim 256 channels. What is not stated is that they are all in software and therefore carry an immense processor hit. So, consider all data from the driver as tainted, and unless you can independently verify the capabilities, establish a safe cut-off point.

Each channel contains three main components:

```
class CLogicalChannel {
public:
    CSampleData       *pSampleData;
```

```
        CDeviceChannel    *pDeviceChannel;
        CMixChannel       *pMixChannel;
    };
```

The sample data is a reference to the static information concerning our sound; which includes the inner and outer ranges, the type, and its duration. This set of sample data is the only information within the logical channel that should not change throughout the game.

The device channel is an abstract class, from which each platform will derive to store its own data. This usually includes the previous channel allocated to the sound or the internal stream handles.

Finally, the mix channel contains the sound's parameters, such as position and volume, which the game can modify through the audio manager.

This data is then passed through the mixing pipeline to calculate the resultant volume and pan information for this channel. The pipeline stages are the gameplay mixer, the technology mixer, and the user mixer as shown in Figure 8.1. Every stage considers each sound and works out how loud it is and on which channel it should be played (if any). Throughout this pipeline, we maintain the complete `CLogicalChannel` structure, so that no information gets lost because some platforms will make decisions on data that the others won't.

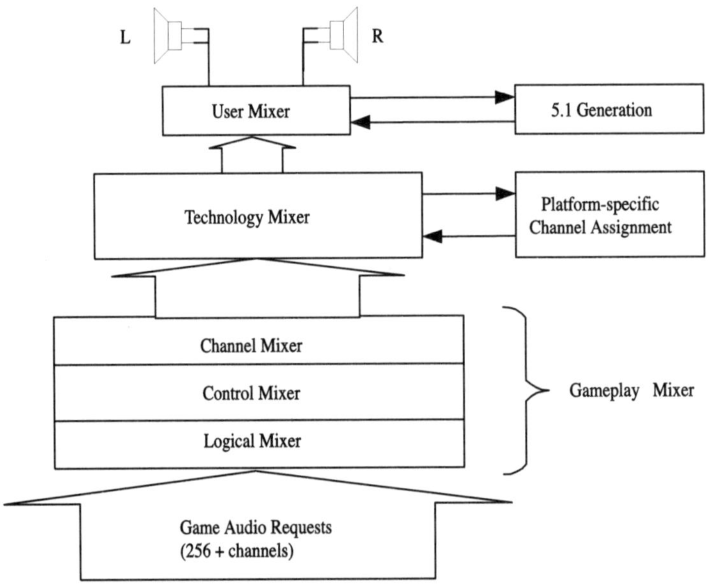

FIGURE 8.1 Cross-platform mixer control.

As each stage of the pipeline is executed, half of the data remains static (`CLogicalChannel`), acting as a reference point for all information about the current sound, while the second half is modified to reflect any changes. The scope of this data is usually very small. For example:

```
class CMixOutput {
    tREAL32    m_fVolume;
    tREAL32    m_fPan;
    tINT32     m_iChannel;
};
```

TIP

We use floating-point numbers for the volume because they reflect the fractional increase (and decrease) of our audio properties. This eliminates the need for range checking at every stage of the pipeline as a multiplication by any value between 0 and 1 will produce a valid result. Because floating-point registers are on the main processors, we're not losing any performance by using them.

Each instance of the `CMixOutput` class is initialized at the start of each frame, and then applied to the hardware channels at the end of processing:

```
void
CAudioManager::Update(tREAL32 time_elapsed)
{
    for(tUINT32 i=0;i<GetMaxChannels();i++) {
        m_MixOutput[i].m_fVolume  = 1;
        m_MixOutput[i].m_fPan     = 0;
        m_MixOutput[i].m_iChannel = -1;   // i.e. none

        ProcessGameplayMixer(m_MixOutput[i], m_Channels[i]);
        ProcessTechnologyMixer(m_MixOutput[i], m_Channels[i]);
        ProcessUserMixer(m_MixOutput[i], m_Channels[i]);
    }

    UpdateHardwareMixer(time_elapsed);
}

void
CPS2AudioManager::UpdateHardwareMixer(tREAL32 time_elapsed)
{
   // ... Process according to m_MixOutput ...
}
```

Following the idea that we should move as much code as possible into the cross-platform areas, `ProcessGameplayMixer` and its siblings will all get processed in the generic audio manager class. Derived versions are used only in special cases.

The Gameplay Mixer

The gameplay mixer is the front line of our defenses. Here we take the list of logical channels and narrow them down to the most prominent sounds. Any explicit control from the programmer to affect volumes is also considered here. To make the task easier, we've split the gameplay mixer into three separate submixers.

The Logical Mixer

The first stage of our mixing pipeline is to prepare the default settings for each logical channel. This data will be taken from the basic parameters set up by the user:

```
void
CAudioEngine::ProcessGameplayLogicalMixer(CMixChannel &channel,
        const CLogicalChannel &logical)
{
    channel.m_fVolume *= logical.pMixChannel->m_fBaseVolume;
    channel.m_fPan    += logical.pMixChannel->m_fBasePan;
}
```

This is always a very simple cross-platform component. Notice that the pan control uses an addition to accumulate the sound's position. The position can be represented on the very simple number line of Figure 8.2.

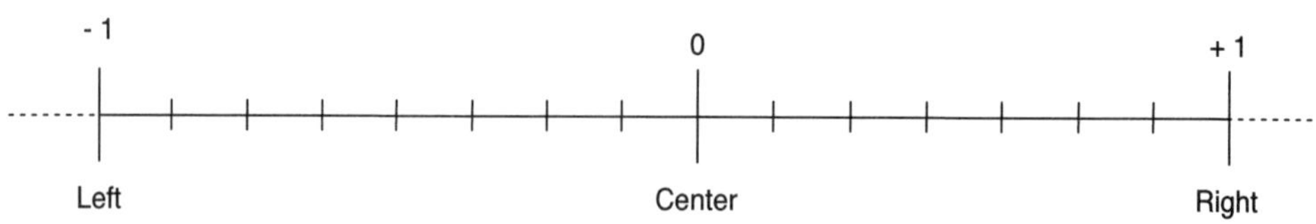

FIGURE 8.2 The panning control.

Whenever we want to move the sound right, we add the number 1, or some fraction thereof. To move left, we subtract 1. This allows each stage to readjust the positioning while still respecting previous changes. In reality, only one stage of the mixer is likely to change the pan position, but having a formal standard in place eliminates any arguments that might occur later. To be safe, however, we must remember to clamp the pan value before using it in `UpdateHardwareMixer`.

The Control Mixer

When fading sounds in and out, it's often tricky to know which volume parameter should be affected. There are often separate volume levels for the sample data, the channel, the current volume, and (usually) the hardware. By applying each fade to the `CMixOutput` result, we avoid this problem, because it's only ever applied to transient data.

```
void
CAudioEngine::ProcessGameplayControlMixer(CMixChannel &channel,
        CLogicalChannel &logical)
{
CMixChannel *pIn = logical.pMixChannel;

    if (pIn->bFadingIn) {
        pIn->m_fFadeTime += time_elapsed;
        pIn->m_fFadeMix = pIn->m_fFadeTime / pIn->m_fFadeDuration;

        if (pIn->m_fFadeMix > 1.0f) {
            pIn->m_fFadeMix = 1;
            pIn->bFadingIn = FALSE;
        }

        channel.m_fVolume *= pIn->m_fFadeMix;
    }
    // Repeat with other control parameters...
}
```

From here, we can control the volume and pan information of each sound according to its position in the world. This process is simple, and common across all platforms. When the platform supports Dolby Surround™ Sound, we can still prepare results for a simple left/right pan because it will still be useful if the user mixer at the end of the pipeline has the feature switched off.

```
channel.m_fPan += CalcAngleBetween(logical.m_vPosition,
                m_Listener.vPos, m_Listener.vOrientation);
```

NOTE

If you are developing this audio code as part of a larger general-purpose engine, be aware that `CalcAngleBetween` *should calculate this angle in three dimensions, not two. Although most sounds can ignore the Z-axis and be considered to originate from a plane, characters that crawl upside down will have their left and right hand sides reversed.*

The position is then used to determine the relative volume of the sound with the traditional inner and outer cones that are used throughout the audio field.

```
fDist = CalcDistanceBetween(logical.m_vPosition, m_Listener.vPos);
if (fDist < fInner) {
    channel.m_fVolume *= 1.0f;
} else if (fDist > fOuter) {
    channel.m_fVolume *= 0;
} else {
    channel.m_fVolume *= (fDist-fInner) / (fOuter–fInner);
}
```

This treats the volume as a linear scale, which unfortunately, it isn't. However, we need to maintain a consistent set of units throughout the pipeline, so these units are cross-platform and will stay until we're ready to pass the data to the platform-specific code. At that point, the data will be converted into the logarithmic scale of decibels. This decibel conversion should use our own attenuation scaling code to cope with the differences between fall-off in various platform audio drivers.

TIP

We can also use the control mixer to limit the sounds themselves. This could mean preventing any sound from playing more than three instances of itself, or to stop two identical samples from being played within 200 ms of each other. The latter causes phasing effects on most hardware and should be avoided.

The Channel Mixer

The channel mixer is the most important part of the gameplay mixdown because it assigns sounds to channels. Naturally, as seen in Figure 8.1, this combines generic channel assignment code along with platform-specific code to determine a suitable hardware channel.

Every frame, we reevaluate all the sounds being played to determine their status. Those that have gone out of earshot are removed and replaced with those that are currently audible. Also, some sounds will require access to specific channels inside the hardware so that they can, for example, trigger special effects. Streamed sounds can only be applied to one of the stream buffers that exist in the hardware, so this is catered to here. This all works on a basic priority system, which has the following default order:

- Music (background and stings)
- Looped sounds (ambient effects, such as air conditioning units or crowd noises)

- Voices (voice-overs and plot dialogue)
- POV sounds (coming from center speaker)
- Normal sounds (sorted by volume)

We can then order every playing sound into a list according to its priority (first) and then volume. We can then assign sounds from the top of the list into the pool of available channels, and apply them to the appropriate mix output.

The order of events is important because the channel assignment function, `GetFreeChannel`, can only exist in the platform-specific driver, as streamed sounds and special effects often have to be assigned to specific channels.

```
channel.m_iChannel = GetFreeChannel(logical);
```

As a result, we have a list of sounds and the channel to which they've been assigned. As a rule, each sound can only be added to, or removed from, a channel; it should never be *moved* between them because this can cause glitches. This occurs when the audio chip has started playing, as it might report that you're 1.2 seconds into the sound, whereas it might actually be 1.21 seconds. So when you start replaying the sound on a different channel, 1.2 seconds from the start, you'll repeat a fraction of it and sound like a stuck record.

TIP

The sound of three separate pairs of footsteps is indistinguishable from four pairs, at which point, only a single sample would be needed. In a more advanced audio system, you can reduce the number of channels in use and improve the mix quality by replacing groups of identical samples with single pregrouped sounds.

The Null Driver

Whenever a sound is playing, the hardware understands how much of it has been played so far. Its progress counters are accessible to us in this instance, but they are not under our control. So when a sound goes out of range or is removed from its physical channel because it's relatively unimportant, this information is no longer available, at which point we have to get the computer to start counting the seconds to emulate the progress counter. This is very simple code, and consists of:

```
m_fSoundDuration += time_elapsed;
if (m_fSoundDuration > m_fSoundLength) {
    // Remove sound from request list
    // Send any sound completion messages required
}
```

Instead of writing this explicitly for each platform, we should first write a null sound driver that plays all sounds this way. This not only makes sure we have the code ready, tested, and available for our platform drivers, but the null driver also allows us to work on the game without a sound engine present, and still have it *act* like there's sound. This helps us when the platform driver hasn't been written yet (new consoles and new engines always seem to leave audio until the end of the project), and when there's a difficult-to-solve bug that is being attributed to the audio code.

The Technology Mixer

A game can have a wide range of different sounds—from the delicate chimes of a spent cartridge hitting a wooden floor, to the explosion of an oil tanker at the end of the level. Although our gameplay mixer will cope with these dynamics admirably, our sample resolution will not.

Assuming we have 16-bit samples throughout the game, this gives 65,536 possible values for each audio sample. Although this is enough range to play any *single* sample with good clarity, it's not enough when these samples are mixed together. To ensure their relative volumes, an explosion would be using numbers ranging from 0 to 65,535, while the cartridge casing would be in the 6 to 7 range. Is this a problem if they'll never be audible at the same time? Yes. The same sample is used when the cartridge is heard on its own, giving the player the opportunity to listen to the casing more critically. In isolation, such a resolution (effectively 3 bits) will make it sound very poor indeed.

To fix this, we need to give each sample the fullest opportunity to express itself by letting it use all 16 bits of the resolution. That is, we normalize it. We can then reduce the volume in-game to a suitable level so that it matches the other sounds. Each sample needs the same treatment, which extends to many thousands of sounds. This is a lot of work, so we'll limit the work by splitting the sounds into categories, and normalize each sound to use the full 16 bits. The sound designer then builds an audio canvas to determine the ratio that each category of sounds should be mixed and *de*normalized in. Typical categories include:

- Bullet impacts
- Footsteps
- Music (main and incidental)
- General sound effects (doors, windows)
- Special effects (gunfire, ricochet)
- Ambient sound
- POV (such as an FPS weapon, or something always played center speaker)
- GUI sounds

- Explosions
- Speech

Your sound designer will determine the relative volume of each sound, although the list given here is approximately ordered from the quietest sounds to the loudest. Speech is more prominent as it's often crucially important to gameplay and the human ear is more attuned to its sound, so you need as much quality (read: memory) as you can spare.

Within the engine, this volume is simply another multiplier attached to the cross-platform mixdown code:

```
void
CAudioEngine::ProcessTechnologyMixer(CMixChannel &channel,
        const CLogicalChannel &logical)
{
    channel.m_fVolume *= m_fMixDown[logical.pSampleData->m_MixGroup];
}
```

The User Mixer

The user mixer is the final link in the chain, and usually the simplest. Here we allow the user, in our case a gamer, to vary the volume of various channels or mute them entirely. Typical categories include:

- Music
- Sound effects
- Voices
- Cut scenes

Voices and sound effects should be separated for the player because they fill different portions of the frequency spectrum, and people are sensitive to different frequencies in various ways. This simple split prevents the need for building complicated graphic equalizers that would be unusable on a console.

NOTE

If your cut scenes include a single premixed soundtrack, some of these settings will have no effect.

In all cases, you can provide a mute option, usually for music. However, the implementation for mute should not stop the sound from playing, rather it should just reduce the volume to 0. The channel assignment code in our gameplay mixer will prevent it from wasting any channel resources, and the fact that it's still (technically) playing means that we don't need to create any extra code to handle "sound complete" messages because the null driver will take over. Ideally, this sound should be consigned to the null driver so that the sound chip is doing no processing. This becomes a consideration when battery life is a factor, such as on the PlayStation Portable™ (PSP).

Our final mixdown comes courtesy of a master volume control. We then know how loud each sound is, on which channel it's playing, and how to affect it. At this point, we convert our linear (0 to 1) scale into a suitable logarithmic scale for the output. This conversion must be done because some platforms do not support logarithmic volume controls, and those that do might not be as good as ours. The perceived volume of a sound halves when it drops by 6 dB (decibels). It drops by one quarter at 12 dB, and so on. The conversion code is simply this:

```
iTableSize = sizeof(m_VolumeTable)/sizeof(m_VolumeTable);
fScale = 600.0f; // number of 'units' in a 6 dB drop

for (int i = 1; i <= iTableSize; i++)
{
    fLog = log10((tREAL32)i/iTableSize) / log10(2.0f);
    m_VolumeTable[i] = tUINT32(fScale * fLog);
}
```

Then one final pass applies all these changes to the audio hardware. This is always done at once, and by the platform-specific code. This is because there's usually a special mechanism to apply several audio changes at once, so that the volume changes are not staggered. DirectX, for example, uses `CommitDeferredSettings`, which need not occur every frame.

```
void
CDXAudioEngine::UpdateHardwareMixer(tREAL32 time_elapsed)
{
const tREAL32 fFreq = 1/20.0f;

    if (m_fHardwareUpdate > fFreq) {
        pDriver->CommitDeferredSettings();
        m_fHardwareUpdate -= fFreq;
    }
}
```

VIDEO PLAYBACK INTERACTION

Unless you're very lucky, at some point in the development cycle, you'll have to contend with video playback. For the most part, this involves copying the sample code from the platform SDK and modifying it to work with your engine framework. Additionally, this involves getting it to work alongside the graphics and audio engines. Because movie playback has such a vast throughput of data, these samples come with their own render and blit routines, making it easy to bypass the graphics engine. The audio engine is not simple, as a lot of movie code expects exclusive access to the sound chip, which requires you to shut down your audio engine and open it up again later...without losing any information.

In those cases, we simply jump into platform-specific land with a generic-looking call to `SuspendEngine`. The task is not particularly complicated because all the data, including sample durations and positions, are held in the base class or null driver.

ENDNOTE

1. The Nyquist limit requires you to sample at over twice the rate of the highest frequency present in the sound that you want to capture.

9 The Graphics Engine

In This Chapter

- History
- Techniques
- Resourcing the Data
- Engine Features
- Abstracting Special Effects
- Graphics on Television

HISTORY

For many people, graphics *is* the engine. When they talk about the *Quake*® engine or the *Unreal*® engine, they are generally referring to the graphics component of a much wider section of code. Although this isn't particularly fair to the nongraphics programmers, it's understandable because window dressing and eye candy really do sell more units than a scalable filesystem or an efficient memory manager.

Console and middleware vendors also engage in the same form of graphics-only promotion—60 million polygons per second must create a better game than 50 million, right? Every new machine pushes these statistics into the limelight to convince developers and the buying public alike that this is the most original machine on the market. The irony is that as the machines become more advanced, the cross-platform graphics component becomes simpler.

The 3D graphics cards in both PCs and consoles have followed—more than lead—the innovations made in software. True, pixel and vertex shaders were hideously expensive in software, but the concept had already existed, so the manufacturers picked up on the idea and re-created the routines in hardware. The approach of using polygon-based modeling, as opposed to voxels (volume pixels) in software, lead to its widespread adoption in hardware. And, the number of graphics cards optimized explicitly for *Quake* equated to a significant share of the market at one point.

So, although the internals of the hardware may change and require a different driver API to access it, the principle of 3D development is pretty much the same now as it has always been. That is, you have a bunch of polygons that you throw at the renderer. Many of the optimization techniques (such as state batching) that you've learned for other graphics cards still apply today, and across all platforms. So, before we start worrying about how to achieve some magical sparkle effect for our game, let's look at the basic commonalities between platforms.

Common Code

Graphics is one of the multilayered abstractions in our game. In fact, it's probably one of the most layered abstractions we have, as there is a very simple (and common) bottom line. That is, our graphics engine will render polygons to the screen. There will be several polygons with different textures, different sizes, and in different positions, but conceptually the entire rendering component of the engine can be written with a single function:

```
void
DrawPolygon(const sgxTexture &Tex, const sgxVertex &Verts);
```

Such an approach would be very slow, but it would work. Given this, let's first look at the common features of a graphics engine, and how they coexist in a cross-platform world.

NOTE

Throughout this section, we'll refer to a theoretical graphics engine. Because of the many ways we can represent scene graph data, some instances might not apply directly to the engine you are working with. However, the ideas should still be applicable, and make sense in similar environments. For example, we'll generally refer to a "texture," although this in reality might represent a full-blown material, including a texture map, normal map, specular map, diffuse maps, gloss maps, shaders, or other such enhancements.

General Handling

The first step is to create a graphics manager. Actually, the first step is to create two graphics managers. Always start by writing and testing under a single platform without worrying about the others. If you're starting the graphics component from scratch, by the time your first world drawing is onscreen, the code will have changed significantly from your first version. Functions will have been renamed or split into two, parameters and datatypes will have changed, and so on. You'll write everything twice, throwing the first away. So, don't waste time writing clever code to manage multiple platforms until you have a clean architecture for a single platform. That said, your finished version will invariably include two classes, involving a prepared singleton and a slew of virtual render functions.

```
class CGfxEngine {
public:
    virtual void DrawPolygon(const sgxTexture &, const sgxVertex &);
    virtual void DrawMesh(const sgxMesh &);
    // ... etc ...
};

class CPS2GfxEngine : public CGfxEngine {
public:
    virtual void DrawPolygon(const sgxTexture &, const sgxVertex &);
    virtual void DrawMesh(const sgxMesh &);
    // ... etc ...
};
```

This simple and over-familiar pattern ensures that we can reference any platform-specific engine without having to know its inner details, because a call such as

```
CGfxEngine::Get()->DrawPolygon(WallTex, WallVerts);
```

will automatically get dispatched to the correct platform.

TIP

The indirection involved here can harm performance because it increases the number of cache misses. Don't overdo them, and certainly don't call them from within tight loops.

Although the code gets processed immediately, it isn't necessary for the platform to draw the requested feature at the same time, because some implementations require (or recommend) that particular primitives are buffered and drawn later in the render cycle. For example, alpha faces (that is, those with translucent features) always have to be queued, sorted, and rendered at the end of the frame.

The code in the base class will be minimal, but should certainly exist. It will include the general-purpose tasks such as alpha face collection, state handling, general housekeeping, and message posting. You'll learn about all of these later. The base class should manage a self-contained, and more importantly self-consistent, null driver. The consistent aspect means that if a state is set up and later queried, new state information will be returned to the user. The null driver won't create any graphics output, but the game code will think it has, and react as if it were running on a genuine engine.

NOTE

Because each platform, PC excepted, will only ever use a single graphics engine, a class hierarchy is not strictly necessary and can be replaced with simple `Gfx_DrawPolygon` *and null driver functions such as* `GfxCmn_DrawPolygon`. *We'll demonstrate our engine using classes because it explains the methods more clearly.*

TECHNIQUES

We must always work toward the strengths of our engine. This might seem obvious, but it's often ignored in all forms of game development. If you're using a terrain engine that creates very large rolling hillside exteriors, it doesn't make sense to try and build the claustrophobic worlds of *Quake*. Similarly, any portal engine that works well with small rooms will not produce the particularly nice exterior environments of *Farcry*™.

The same advice applies to the techniques we use for cross-platform engines. Because we're making certain assumptions about the way in which our engine works to cope with the differences in platform, we should work *with* the code to make its job easier. This means giving the code the data it wants in the right format, and arranging objects in an order that makes it suitable for fast rendering. In each case, we'll present methods that will improve performance on one or more platforms. Such improvements will not be universally beneficial, but in the worst-case scenario, there will be no adverse effects by using them.

Static Texture Changes

Beneath the veneer of a cross-platform API, rendering a texture isn't a completely straightforward task. Nor is it particularly fast. Rendering a texture isn't a simple matter of pointing the graphics engine to a texture and saying "draw with that," despite the appearance of the code. What happens behind the scenes is more complex, for example:

- The texture might have to be copied into an appropriate area of memory so the graphics chip has direct access to it. This also implies that previous textures might have to be removed from this special graphics memory.
- The UV coordinates, indicating which portions of the texture to use, must be set up.
- Texture clamping might take place. This determines what happens when multiple copies of the texture are applied to a polygon.
- Mipmap selection might be automatic, depending on the driver.
- Various texture parameters, such as its size, must be stipulated.

Some or all of these steps might be required, taking a considerable amount of processor time to execute, so we must reduce the number of texture changes that occur to a bare minimum in all cases—which for us means on all platforms.

At the high level, we can ensure this by building our data correctly. The tool chain should export static meshes by grouping polygons into blocks that use identical textures. These can then be presented in a single block to the graphics processor to minimize texture state changes.

FIGURE 9.1 Texture tiling using four regions.

UV Coordinates

We can minimize texture changes further by including several images onto a single surface, as shown in Figure 9.1. You can then instruct your graphics engine to restrict rendering to a small portion of the texture by specifying its UV coordinates.

Although this processes the same amount of data as four individual textures, the approach is better suited to most graphics chips because it doesn't incur the extra overhead of re-transmitting texture data since you only have to indicate the new UV coordinates, and these are much smaller and therefore quicker.

These regions should be set up in the tool chain and exported with any texture your artists create. The regions themselves should be numbered or named, along with their coordinates within the texture. These coordinates can be integers describing pixel counts or floating-point numbers between 0 and 1. Either is acceptable, although with most platforms accepting floating-point UV coordinates, a range of 0 and 1 is certainly preferred. The question that usually hangs over floating-point usage is one of accuracy. For the range of fractions we'll be using, there's no issue with any size up to 1/512.[1] A major benefit of using floating-point numbers here is that the *fraction*al position of a region does not change if the texture size does. And when memory gets tight on one platform or another, the texture size is usually the first thing to go.

Always make sure that the regions are described as `minimum_x`, `minimum_y` to `maximum_x`, `maximum_y`, so you will always need to use

```
region_minimum_x = sgxMin(x1, x2);
region_minimum_y = sgxMin(y1, y2);
region_maximum_x = sgxMax(x1, x2);
region_maximum_y = sgxMax(y1, y2);
```

within the tool chain exporter. This is because some hardware considers the regions as the shortest distance between the two specified points. So referring to 0.8-0.2 will wrap around the 1.0 barrier and produce a texture that is 0.4 units wide, not 0.6 as would be correct if they had been specified in the reverse order.

Another point to note about the regions in the preceding texture is that they are all correctly orientated. We haven't squeezed on another character by rotating it sideways and including it along the edge because only some platforms can understand and render such UV regions. Because only some can, we should work on the principle that none can, and consequently avoid it. Tell your artists.

The maximum rotation limit is usually 45 degrees. Fortunately, many graphics (like the chain-link fence) have 45 diagonals across the entire texture. We can consequently rotate this image by 45 degrees so that all lines are now orthogonal to the texture edges, and therefore suffer less aliasing problems.

Materials

In addition to regions, textures also benefit from supplemental material information. This complements each texture with information about "what it is," "how it acts," and "how it looks." This material information encompasses many fields. For starters, it might include basic information as to the physical properties of the texture, indicating whether it's intended to represent stone, wood, or plastic. This can trigger the ricochet sound effect and determine the bullet hole graphic.

Additionally, we can indicate the visual properties: is any portion of the texture transparent, is it reflective, and what does the bump map look like. The transparency property is easy to add, but can vary between platforms. For some, it works by designating a single color of the image to be transparent which, for ease of resource creation, means that such textures are always palletized, and the color in question is invariably at index 0. In the DirectX world, this approach requires an RGB colorkey instead. Performance can be improved by using alpha tests instead; these tests require a complete alpha channel, which naturally increases the memory footprint. This is the usual development trade-off.

TIP

You cannot chromakey textures that will be mipmapped, because lower-resolution versions will not contain the same ratio of transparent to opaque pixels, and will ultimately lead to a monopoly of one or the other. Consequently, the texture becomes completely transparent (which is wrong) or completely opaque (which is also wrong).

We intentionally chose the "bump map" property to reemphasize the material aspects of the texture. In short, the material doesn't *need* a specific bump map. Nor does it even need to exist. Rather, we abstract the concept of the material into something suitable for the game, for example, a stone wall. We can then create slightly different materials for each platform, adopting suitable texture and bump map data for each. These materials can be as general or as specific as you like. Possible alternatives to bump mapping could involve a second texture, a custom pixel shader, or nothing at all.

TIP

Because of the expense in creating bump maps on a PS2, you should spend your texture budget on a larger texture instead of a bump map.

Dynamic Texture Changes

When dealing with dynamic game data, it might not be possible to group objects according to texture. We have to bring some order, however, to maintain a good cross-platform frame rate.

Wall Sprites

Wall sprites might include things like bullet holes, blood splats, and damage decals. These areas can conform very easily. If your game has a single loop that renders *only* the bullet holes, then you already have an engine-friendly method in place. A list that includes bullet holes and blood splats will not represent any kind of win because the texture will be changing at every possible instance. We can either scan the wall sprite list twice, picking out only those sprites featuring an identical texture map, or have two lists. The cost of loop iterators is very small when compared to texture upload time.

So far, we have assumed that your bullet hole is a single texture map; however, this is unlikely to ever be the case. For starters, each type of wall (such as brick, wood, or metal) will have a different bullet hole. And each material class of bullet hole will have several different variations. Switching between these variations of texture would be an extra drain on resources. Instead, we'll place all the bullet holes for a particular type of wall surface onto a single texture, and use UV coordinates to distinguish between them. This benefits all current platforms.

```
void
ProcessBulletHoles(tSurfaceType surface)
{
CBulletHole::iterator it = m_BulletHoles.begin();
tREAL32 u, v;

    UploadBulletTexture(surface);

    for(;it != m_BulletHoles.end(); ++it) {
        if ((*it).GetSurface() == surface) {
            // this assumes all textures have a 4x4 grid of
            // bullet hole images
            u = mthRand(3)/4.0f;
            v = mthRand(3)/4.0f;
            DrawBullet(*it, u, v);
        }
    }
}
```

Given the significant differences between game levels, you'll probably need a full quota of wooden hole decals for one level, but not another, so creating separate lists for each surface type, although easiest to handle, might lead to significant amounts of wasted space.

3D Objects

In addition to the 2D wall sprites, certain games, notably FPSs, will have a large variety of 3D objects that get rendered each frame, such as spent cartridge cases and pickups. These can be grouped in the same way as bullet holes, and rendered in a single loop. Because these objects are small, they should only have one texture on them, so no time is lost in the upload. However, if two or more textures exist, you won't get any performance increase by grouping these objects. Although you can modify the renderer to draw such objects in two halves (one for each texture), this is a lot of effort. Instead, it's better to persuade your artists to reduce the number of textures.

> TIP
>
> *The typical rule of thumb is that 1 texture state change takes the same amount of time as rendering 100 polygons. If necessary, you can bribe artists with 50 of these polygons if they remove the second texture for you.*

Simple FX

Effects such as smoke and muzzle flashes have the same optimization criteria as wall sprites. That is, group them according to texture. This is usually more difficult because smoke is likely to be emitted from different objects across the level, and not concentrated in one place. However, with some minor extra CPU processing, we can manage it.

```
CSomeGameObject::Draw()
{
// Draw nothing, but prepare any variables required
// to adjust this object's position/orientation in the
// world.

// We then indicate what textures we'll draw, given the
// chance.

    CGameWorld::Get()->RegisterOptimalTexture(this, “smoke1”);
}

CSomeGameObject::OptimalRenderByTexture(const sgxTexture &tex)
{
// Draw any component using the texture ‘tex’
// This function will get called once for each texture
// registered by the official Draw function
}
```

As you can see, each game object suspends its rendering process when requested to do so, and even then only draws those portions of the object that feature the texture map given. So our smoke example might get called twice; once for the "white puffy bit" (and yes, that is the technical description) of the smoke, and again for the graying soot particles. We then just need to set up a global controlling object to dispatch calls to `OptimalRenderByTexture` for each object that expressed a preference. This is best left to the game code as it can make more intelligent decisions concerning its needs.

Translucent Textures

As mentioned previously, all polygons with translucent textures (a.k.a. alpha faces) are kept in storage until the end of the frame, and sorted before being drawn. This is to make sure they have a consistent appearance as they move in front of, and behind, other alpha faces. The sorting needs to occur, but it doesn't need to be particularly exact, so we can use a bucket sort. Unfortunately, this hits us with a time penalty for the sorting, and a memory penalty for the duplicate copy of each alpha face. Although this is necessary and occurs across every platform, the amount of scope we have available to accept these penalties will vary.

Programming Solutions

If you have good direct control of your engine and main loop, the sorting and rendering can take place by the game using the `OptimalRenderByTexture` technique you've just seen. By employing this trick effectively, we can sort the alpha faces by object, not polygon, which requires a lot less memory and is quicker to sort. This means less granularity, however, so any large object—or one with multiple alpha faces—can demonstrate visual artifacts when physically close to another. For the majority of cases, such as simple polygonal effects and one-off alpha faces on an opaque mesh, this is an effective cross-platform solution inflicting very little overhead.

Memory Solutions

When the memory becomes the bottleneck, we have a couple of options. First, we can reduce the space taken by the bucket sort by storing fewer distinct depths of field, although this can cause more flicker when objects are close. Second, we can lower the total number of stored faces so the alpha face rendering would occur every time the buffer was filled. This would reduce the memory in an interesting manner; you get more control over the amount of storage used, but less control over when the buffer flushes and the scene's final appearance. Which faces were output would depend largely on the order of the objects in the game loop.

You might also care to extend control of the alpha sorter to support an explicit flush that could get executed before large groups of applicable polygons, such as smoke effects, were sent to the alpha sorter.

Resource Solutions

In some cases, the use of an alpha face is a nicety. As time progresses, more and more games include them for this very reason, without introducing any game-oriented reason for doing so. If your engine is struggling to keep up with the number of alpha faces in your game, you might try simply removing them.

Changing a security guard's tinted Perspex visor to a light gray opaque one might appear a little on the cheap side, but because this removes around 10 polygons from the alpha sorter, it might be worth considering. Especially if the guard in question is rarely seen close up, or there are several of them. Perhaps instead, a level of detail system could be introduced so the visor would become opaque when it's more than 20 meters away. This in turn would require smaller alpha sorting buffers.

With a suitable tool chain, these changes do not have to be made wholesale as any modifications to the security guard mesh could be tagged as "nicety alpha." This would translate to different things on different platforms, the default being "alpha face." But it could also mean "this material is opaque on PS2 after 20m." This is just another form of abstraction.

State Changes

State changes are present within all graphic pipelines and are the main cause of slowdown. The texture changes we've already seen are a large-grain state change, however, many others, such as the cull and shading modes, also come under this category. We must minimize these changes before we can be proud of our cross-platform code.

Abstraction

Every material in our game should have an abstraction indicating its type. This is not just to determine the ricochet sound, but also to generate suitable render states for the textures because the precise definition of each is platform-dependent. The more you abstract a concept, the more general it becomes, so the abstraction of "wall texture" would be at the very general end of this scale requiring many platform-specific state changes. Such changes would be made by the DirectX functions `SetRenderState` and `SetTextureStage`, for example. These two functions cover such a wide range of functionality (see the file `d3Dtypes.h` in your DirectX SDK) that abstracting them individually would be counter-productive. Instead, we abstract according to group, using one sgx-oriented state that is reflected by three or four DirectX equivalents, as you'll see with fogging.

Therefore, each material makes several changes to the underlying graphical state, which should be handled by a wrapper function, like this:

```
void
CDXGfxEngine::SetRenderState(D3DRENDERSTATETYPE type, tUINT32 state)
{
    if (GetRenderState(type) == state) {
        return;
    }

    pDXDevice->SetRenderState(type, state);
}
```

The gains made by first testing the existing state will vary and might not amount to great savings, but they should be done because the wrapper provides an easy place to check for each state change or texture stage. This can in turn be used to log the number of (attempted) state changes per frame, or perform other profiling tasks.

TIP

You might be able to get extra speed by varying the state order between each frame, so that on the first frame your state changes appear as `A->B->C->D`*, whereas on the second, they are* `D->B->C->A`*. Each consecutive frame then simply swaps the first and last state around, removing an extra state change between them. This is a micro-optimization and not easy to implement in this instance. When it comes to textures, however, reversing the entire scene order can mean that a large percentage of your textures will still exist in video memory at the start of the next frame.*

State Housekeeping

For the simpler cross-platform states, such as fill modes and Z-buffer control, you should adopt the same state change wrapper you saw previously. In these cases, however, the change of state should be delayed until we actually need it and so we must introduce the concept of a *dirty bit*. In the world of generic states, these changes do not occur immediately, and in some cases *cannot* occur immediately if the current frame is still rendering. One typical example involves disabling the fog before the HUD is rendered.

To manage these situations, we need two sets of data. One set holds the requested data, while the other (sometimes held by the graphics API itself) indicates the current state:

```
void
CGfxEngine::SetFoggingMode(const CSGXFogging &fog)
{
    m_Fogging = fog;
    m_FoggingDirty = TRUE;
}
```

This causes the state to lay dormant until it's needed. Then, before rendering anything that requires a fog, the dirty bit is checked, and the fogging is applied to the engine if necessary:

```
void
CDXGfxEngine::ApplyFogging()
{
    if (m_FoggingDirty) {
        tUINT32 mode = GetDXFogMode(m_fogging.iMode);
        tUINT32 color =  GetRGBA(m_Fogging.fRed, m_Fogging.fGreen,
                             m_Fogging.fBlue, m_Fogging.fAlpha));

        SetRenderState(D3DRENDERSTATE_FOGENABLE, TRUE);
        SetRenderState(D3DRENDERSTATE_FOGCOLOR, color);
        SetRenderState(D3DRENDERSTATE_FOGVERTEXMODE, mode);
        SetRenderState(D3DRENDERSTATE_FOGSTART,
                                  *(tUINT32 *)&m_Fogging.fStart);
        SetRenderState(D3DRENDERSTATE_FOGEND,
                                  *(tUINT32 *)&m_Fogging.fEnd);
        SetRenderState(D3DRENDERSTATE_FOGDENSITY,
                                  *(tUINT32 *)&m_Fogging.fDensity);

        m_FoggingDirty  = FALSE;
    }
}
```

Again, our platform-specific driver handles each of the `SetRenderState` functions before being passed on to the platform API. Because we intend to move the platform-specific information as far down into the driver as possible, it's not surprising that the generic `SetFoggingMode` function has unified parameters across all platforms. Parameters are only converted at the driver level, as you can see in the case of `color` (which we've elected to store as floating-point numbers, but could easily be held as bytes) and `mode`. The parameters must also remain unified when storing such numbers. So, if you later retrieve the fogging distance from the DirectX driver, you actually get the generic parameters returned and not the platform-dependent ones that were passed to `SetRenderState`, for example. This works automatically with our method as the null driver holds this information, so we can simply return the data from the cross-platform base class.

We can also apply this method of deferment to other areas inside each driver. A DirectX-based driver, for example, can save considerable time by clearing the Z and stencil buffer together.

State Blocks

In addition to postponing state changes to an appropriate time, you should also group changes together in blocks. They can then be written to the driver in a single step for greater efficiency. You'll probably be able to group the changes more efficiently than the low-level API, leading to the expression "never let the API do it for you." By using blocks, you can handle redundant changes as efficiently as the driver in the *worst*-case scenario can, but usually manual change groups will be much better.

TIP

Each state block can be assigned a particular bit pattern, making it trivial to match duplicate state changes for sorting and optimization purposes.

Mode Changes

The modes we're discussing here are, like textures, large-grain state changes. One of the big state change bottlenecks we can encounter is between the 3D render mode and 2D. Generally, this won't cause many people a problem because it's traditional to process them in two passes: 3D first and 2D second. However, not everything is clear-cut.

2D Graphics in 3D Mode

2D graphics in 3D mode is rare because most 2D decals appear in the form of screen overlays, displaying the score or health of the player, and occur post-3D rendering using a single mode change. However, this might not be true for muzzle flashes rendered at the end of the player's weapon, or special highlights on pickups indicating their worth. In these cases, some people consider switching to the 2D mode to render the textures, and then switching back to 3D for the rest of the scene. This isn't a good idea because the mode change takes up a lot of time.

Effects of this nature can all be achieved through 3D sprites that are rotated to face the camera, and then rendered in 3D space. These billboards, or forward-facing sprites, require some math processing, but this is invariably less than the time to change state.

TIP

You can increase the number of allowable billboard sprites under DirectX-based renderers because it supports accelerated point sprites.

3D Graphics in 2D Mode

3D graphics in 2D mode is perhaps more common, as it forms the staple of the heads up display in many games where 3D pickups, POVs, and other inventory items are placed alongside 2D overlays. In addition to the state change, an additional problem is caused by the 3D objects themselves: the Z-buffer. This needs to be cleared in-between the rendering of the main scene and the inventory meshes or otherwise they might not get rendered. This comes about because the Z-buffer already contains depth information from the scene we've just drawn, which may prevent these objects from appearing. We therefore need to clear the Z-buffer so that the objects can render themselves correctly.

Clearing the Z-buffer, however, is one of those tasks that despite being easy to write, has wildly differing response times according to platform; in fact, several unplanned Z-buffer clears can kill your frame rate. To circumvent this, we need help from the engine and we need to add an additional function, say, `RenewZBuffer`, which will clear a portion of the Z-buffer based on a set of screen coordinates. This function is our abstraction for the Z-buffer clear, which will react differently according to platform. Those platforms that are fast enough will just clear the whole buffer regardless of the parameters. Others will meticulously clear only that area to conserve processing time. Still others may renumber the range of the Z-buffer, so instead of rendering depths labeled as 0 to 99, the new Z-buffer will render them as 100 to 199. This way we can still respect the Z-buffer when writing our meshes, and consequently only need to *truly clear* the Z-buffer once every two frames.

This Z-buffer problem also manifests itself in FPS games where the POV is drawn as a 3D overlay, and not as part of the world. In these cases, an additional Z-buffer clear is required (or, at least, a `RenewZBuffer` or partial clear). With care, however, it's possible to position the POV in the world without spoiling the illusion. This is the preferable cross-platform solution because it avoids the problem altogether.

Pre- and Post Draw

With this information, we can now split the renderer into distinct passes that minimize the number of mode changes. Such an order might appear as the following:

3D game world
Worlds scene graph
Static objects

Dynamic and skinned objects
3D game features
Bullet holes (and so on), ordered by texture
Spent cartridge shells (and so on), ordered by mesh
3D alpha faces
Possible Z-buffer clear
3D inventory items
3D POV
2D inventory overlays

This ordering should ensure that the game can react with the fewest necessary state and texture changes.

Special Cases

Not surprisingly, a cross-platform game sometimes requires platform-specific solutions, especially when it comes to graphics optimizations. A quick look at the paper entitled "How Far Have We Got" found at *http://www.scee.sony.co.uk/sceesite/files/presentations/PSP/HowFarHaveWeGot.pdf* will show you several quirks that defy general belief. Many of these solutions will appear in your platform-specific driver. However, in some cases, it's possible for the game to help the driver out in much the same way that programmers have helped the compiler by specifying `inline` and `register` to certain sections of code. Typical hints include the following:

- This is a character, so don't use full clipping.
- This is a POV, so don't use clipping here either.
- This texture is to be reused, so don't dump it.

In all cases, there are two parts to the description: what it is and what to do with it. The first case is true for all platforms and becomes our generic abstraction, whereas the second describes how the particular platform should handle the abstraction. In no case are we describing platform specifics in place of general data. It's then up to the platform-specific driver to determine how it will interpret the hints. As with all hints of this nature, it can never harm the performance of any platform, only improve it, and so is always worthwhile.

RESOURCING THE DATA

The most vital part of the cross-platform engine does not take place within the engine, because it's actually part of the tool chain. The component in question covers many possible areas, usually centered around the meshes exported from 3ds max or Maya, and the data converters of your own engine.

In Chapter 5, "Storage," you learned about the mechanics of converting data. Here we'll look at the large-grain processes involved, as outlined in Chapter 1, "Introduction," and shown in Figure 1.1.

Textures

This is the biggest resource we'll generally deal with in terms of retail selling power and memory consumption. Textures also perform a multitude of different tasks:

- World scene graph
- Mesh characters
- World furniture
- Particle effects
- HUD displays
- GUI creation

Ultimately, however, textures add something dynamic to the level. In all cases, the texture data is connected to nontexture data, such as the mesh onto which they are drawn or the HUD description file. This leads to an interesting question: do we place them into separate data files or not? Both actions have their own advantages. By separating the data, we can:

- Unify common textures easily, cutting down on memory and texture uploads.
- Change textures in the tool chain with less data rebuilding.
- Maintain compact data formats for the nontexture component, leading to better source control methods.

Whereas keeping a single file ensures we can:

- Optimize the internal renderer of each component for greater efficiency.
- Limit dependency problems when one texture change affects three objects.
- Allow objects to cross between levels easily.

This question elicits a similar response to the question of how a game asset should be shared between levels; if a tree (for example, `level1_tree.msh`) is created for one level, it should be permissible to use it in a different level, or it should be copied to `level2_tree.msh`. The answer to *this* question varies according to the workflow patterns you have adopted, whereas our original question is a technical one for cross-platform development, so we must address it.

Essentially the question requires separate answers. This is significant because our one piece of texture data may require separate metadata for each instance. The first step in this process is to ensure that the asset hierarchy is identical for all our artists. The asset hierarchy includes the directory structure in which they're stored. So, we dictate a common directory name to consider the root (the `c:\work` directory, for example) and place all the textures beneath it so a replicated texture can be spotted easily.[2] We can then use the tool chain to build platform-specific assets using these common textures with asset-specific metadata.

TIP

When looking for filename duplicates, remember to do a case-insensitive comparison because our filesystem ignores case.

To remove all the problems discussed previously, the tool chain needs extra development and must be integrated into the workflow. For example, the tool chain now needs to keep track of the assets using duplicate textures, so that if this number increases, a warning can be flagged to remind the artist that there's a new dependency on this texture. Furthermore, if a texture gets changed (which can be determined by file checksums or datestamps), the tool chain (possibly the texture exporter) can remind the artist that it is used in three different places, and ask if they are sure such a change is warranted. Source control can then be drafted in to revert the changes, if necessary.

The case of objects crossing between levels generally occurs in one of three ways: as part of the generic gameplay (such as the player's inventory or user interface), as a repeated object in two consecutive levels (especially around the changeover point), or as a common object that appears throughout the game using a rolling, asynchronously loaded world.

Generic Objects

Generic objects fall into the "global versus game" argument discussed in Chapter 3, "Memory." When these objects are resourced, we specify the memory location from which they should be allocated. These generic features are global objects that exist throughout the life of the game, so a predetermined (and fixed) budget can be assigned to them at the start of the game. Because these objects are generally allocated in batches, we can specify the memory handler on a class-by-class basis with static functions.

```
CTextureManager::SetMemoryHandler(m_pGlobalMemory);
```

```
m_Handle = CTextureManager::Load("ui_main1");
// ... other global textures ...
CTextureManager::SetMemoryHandler(m_pGameMemory);
// ... load game-based textures here ...
```

Repeated Objects

To use a bland management platitude, this is a no-brainer. As the entire game memory will be destroyed when we switch levels, the only common data we need to keep is the data stored in the global memory. So, the idea of common data being held between levels is a misnomer. Although this means we're reloading data we just deleted, no time is lost because the level data is prestored in its own custom format for fast loading anyway.

Rolling Worlds

There are several arguments concerning how rolling worlds can best be achieved. The preferred method for cross-platform programming is to load each section into a fixed-memory size. This ensures that fragmentation does not occur, and makes it very easy to build the game world as everyone knows what is possible at any one time. Within this scheme, any texture would get copied into each level section whether or not it was a duplicate. As with the repeated objects, these sections are optimized for fast loading anyway, so very little processing time is lost.

One further improvement we can make, however, is to create a directory of common assets that appear throughout the game. These common assets can be used by any or all of the level sections in addition to those in the level-specific memory block. And because the filenames are placed in a common hierarchy for all our artists, it's easy to determine which assets will get reused.

Texture Format

Now that we've determined where and how to resource the textures, we finally can deal with the format itself. As you learned in Chapter 1, we should build everything as large as possible, because it's easier to reduce than increase. The target size is governed by artist-created parameters that may include an abstracted "detail" parameter (which indicates a different size for each platform) or a proposition for the minimum allowable texel size (indicating its scale onscreen).

Note that some swizzled[3] textures can't be converted to the correct format offline. The metadata should detail this, too.

Meshes

At its heart, a mesh is the ubiquitous "bunch of polygons" we always think about when developing a graphics engine. The data within meshes is presorted for maximum throughput by specially written code for each platform that usually resides in the tool chain. This means there will be a minimum number of state changes for the mesh's textures and the preformatting of vertex data.

On a deeper level, the tool chain can also vary the basic parameters of the target data, such as the size of the resultant textures or number of polygons used. By changing this data you can control the mesh's level of detail beyond endian conversion and without artist intervention. This is strongly recommended. The difference in data format is something you'll have to contend with no matter of how many platforms you write for. In a cross-platform environment, however, you'll always need better control of the target data because of the greater number of variables.

An artist's time is precious, and the character meshes and game environment are crucial to a game's success. Reworking your art assets for each platform is not an option. As time goes by and games increase in complexity, there will be an increasing number of art assets across increasingly complex platforms. The need to take action is great, so we'll prepare a suitable mechanism.

The Textures

As you've seen, the biggest hit for the graphics processor is usually the texture upload path. This is something we can't change, so we simply have to minimize it by using as few textures as possible (most small-to-medium sized meshes need only one), and getting our tool to order the polygons correctly to minimize the number of texture changes, if there is more than one. We can also combine several meshes into one, and provide code that enables specific portions of the object mesh on demand. This is suitable for drawing large numbers of very simple objects—such as boxes, crates, or pipes—where the textures required are intentionally uniform or unvaried.

To adopt this method effectively, we need to ensure that disparate objects that share textures are handled sequentially. This can be done at the game level (which holds a list of all the boxes using texture "crate47"), or the engine (that makes a note of every object passed to the renderer, and then orders them accordingly). Either solution is equally effective, so any decision you make can be based solely on how easy it is to implement and how your textures are stored.

The Polygons

After the textures are optimized, we can work on the polygon limit. For any console, one of the biggest selling points is how many polygons it can draw every second. This number is pointless, because the numbers quoted are for flat shaded polygons, and don't acknowledge the nonexistent game driving them. After our engine is written, however, we'll have a polygon limit, and that's something worth working within.

Keeping the polygon count down on a traditional game involves the artist modifying the model until he is within the limits prescribed by the lead programmer. A cross-platform game will have limits that differ between platforms. Building resources that fit within variable limits can be achieved in three primary ways.

First, we can ask the artist to create platform-specific versions of each mesh in the game. This is not practical, and rarely done. Second, we can modify the distances at which the level of detail (LOD) meshes change over. This doesn't reduce the number of polygons present in the model, but it does ensure the total number onscreen, which is the important limit, can be adhered to much more simply. Such LOD changes can happen through metadata and data-driven code and so are the easiest to achieve.

The third possibility is rather novel and involves progressive meshes. Although most advocates claim it benefits a runtime environment, we propose its use in the tool chain. What happens here is that the artist builds a large character (say 20,000-polygon) and gives it to the tool chain; the tool chain then duly reduces it to an appropriate level for each platform. The artist only builds one mesh, each platform gets a single mesh optimized for its platform (handling progressive meshes at runtime often incurs a time penalty as its buffers can't be prebuilt), and the data size can be scaled up or down according to the platform demands without any extra work.

ENGINE FEATURES

All platforms have surfaces[4] and Z-buffers.[5] The image that gets rendered onto a surface is determined by the geometry, and the position and orientation of the camera, which is common too. In fact, many of these basic tasks employ the same code demonstrated in Foley/Van Dam all those years ago. Let's now look at how to apply those techniques by implementing a selection of typical engine features.

Camera

Given a camera position and orientation (often specified by a look "at" value), we'll always need to transplant them into a common view matrix, which is used later to determine object visibility. The mathematics is identical, so the only platform-specific component is an API call to apply this matrix to the graphics pipeline:

```
void
CPS2GfxEngine::SetCamera(const sgxVertex &from, const sgxVertex &to)
{
    CGfxEngine::SetCamera(from, to);  // do common mathematics

    // platform-specific setup, if required
    OS_SetCamera(m_ViewMatrix);
}
```

TIP

Given the opportunity, create two cameras for your game: one from which the rendering will take place, and another from which you cull invisible areas of the world. During a game, these cameras will be at the same location. During development, however, it can help to have a flying camera that will let you see which areas have been culled out of existence, without destroying that information by moving the camera itself.

Viewports

Like the camera, the viewport is a well-understood concept in computer graphics, and so every platform will be performing the same calculations to specify the same visible portion of the world. Again, this code consists of a common set of mathematics, followed by the platform-specific `SetViewport` call.

To validate the parameters against the screen coordinates, we can incorporate this code into the generic driver too, because we can use other virtual functions to retrieve the platform-specific size information. This continues to limit the amount of platform-specific code we have to write, which is always a good thing.

```
tINT32
CPS2GfxEngine::GetWidth() // virtual fn
{
    return m_ScreenWidth;
}

void
CGfxEngine::SetViewport(tINT32 orgx, tINT32 orgy,
        tINT32 width, tINT32 height)
{
tINT32 sizex = width, sizey = height;

    if (sizex > GetWidth()) {
        sizex = GetWidth();
```

```
        }
        // ...
    }
```

Additionally, you have to set up other parameters, such as the clip planes, world transforms, and the screen clipping area in a similar fashion. These parameters are more likely to vary between platforms, but the common code can still handle them because the mathematics is identical in all cases. They can be set up from the platform-specific `main.cpp`.

TIP

When setting up a frame, move the near clip plane out as far as possible to increase the accuracy of the Z-buffer, and set the far plane to infinity as this reduces the amount of necessary clipping, which on some platforms is a very expensive operation.

Lights

Creating an effective lighting model can really highlight the beauty of a graphics engine. Careful use of lighting can make safe environments appear scary, and make scary environments appear terrifying. However, dynamic lights are used sparingly because of the processing cost.

To begin with, the world is usually prelit using light map textures overlaid onto the scene geometry to apply shadows into the world. Being offline, these textures are not our concern. Similarly, the dynamic lights are processed according to the capability of the platform. Some platforms have hardware lights that are willing to take the strain. On other platforms, the lights only affect small portions of the environment that have been set up explicitly to manage it. Or, the lights only affect dynamic objects, and even then only affect the overall brightness of the object in the scene, and not the individual polygons the object contains.

Managing this from the game side requires a simple set of abstracted functions that allows us to set and get the various lights in the world. This should be done by providing the entire light structure, so that any changes can only be applied through a similarly verbose function:

```
tBOOL GetLight(sgxLight &UserCopyOfLight);
tBOOL SetLight(const sgxLight &light);
```

TIP

By only returning a copy of the structure, it becomes impossible for the game to change a parameter without first calling a separate function to apply it. This makes sense in all development, but it's more vital with graphics drivers because we may be rendering a frame behind the update cycle and so we need to queue the updates for a specific time (such as the end of the frame).

The platform-specific code underneath is then able to determine how the lights are to affect the scene, and modify the engine accordingly. The platform-specific code is not alone in making this decision, however, as it will still have a close relationship with the generic engine, because determining the most prominent light affecting object X will always be determined from the base class.

The Scene

The scene presents the general work area for the graphics renderer over the course of a frame. It consists of a time before the current frame is drawn, the drawing of the frame, and the blitting and flipping of that frame to the TV set. Different names may be used, but the concepts always remain the same. Our first set of virtual functions is therefore very simple:

```
void CGfxEngine::BeginScene();
void CGfxEngine::DrawScene();
void CGfxEngine::EndScene();
```

The platform-specific versions will be able to call whichever functions are pertinent for their API, without having to know how much, or how little, work each platform has to do to manage the task.

The only addition to make to this set of functions is to adopt the *Rule of 3*.

TIP

The Rule of 3 says that there is always a beginning, a middle, and an end for everything. This includes our `BeginScene`, `DrawScene`, *and* `EndScene`, *meaning our* `BeginScene` *would actually split up into* `PreBeginScene`, `DoBeginScene`, *and* `PostBeginScene`. *This overblown rule ensures we have all our escape routes covered. When profiling, for example, we can start our timers running on the* `Pre` *function to capture the time involved in preparing a frame. In smaller grain tasks, such as animating a character, we can flush buffers and prepare render states both before and after the main task, giving greater opportunity to use common* `Do` *sections. The smallest grain Rule of 3 appears in our alignment macros from Chapter 3.*

One good approach here is to consider the `Do` portion as cross-platform, and both `Pre` and `Post` sections as platform-specific initialization. The scene draw is a good example of this working well as each platform will be rendering the same game, so a common chunk of code handling the sequence of

```
void CGfxEngine::DoBeginScene()
{
    DrawSky();
    DrawWorldSceneGraph();
    DrawObjectsInWorld();
    DrawPOV();
    DrawOverlays();
}
```

would fit very well here. Our `Pre` chunk can then clear all the buffers, such as those used to store the alpha faces, and the `Post` code flushes these buffers to the screen. Because the `Do` function is also virtual, it too can be overloaded by the platform-specific driver to cope with any minor ordering discrepancies that cannot be handled with the `Pre-Post` setup we have here, such as a reversed order for the POV and world object rendering. This is like a double chance function in disguise.

When adopting this rule in general game code, its use becomes more natural as many objects will have interdependencies. If both objects tried to query the data of their dependents during a `StartGame`, for example, at least one would fail because of the sequential nature of their processing. However, by adopting a `PreStartGame` (and possibly `PostStartGame`), you can split the process down into three chunks and avoid these problems.

Abstracted Features

Several features in a graphics engine exist solely as abstractions for a specific set of API functions. In these cases, it doesn't matter if the results are not pixel-for-pixel identical; we only have to know that the facility exists to some extent. The implementation, from a game perspective, is unimportant.

Fog

By fog, we mean the global game fogging that affects the whole level, and not the localized variety. Fog has a set of known parameters that do not change between platforms. It has a near and far plane (to determine the area in which the fog shall be applied), a color, and a flag to switch it on and off. You may additionally support a fog density, and an option to vary how the fog varies with distance. The latter is usually limited by hardware to either linear or logarithmic fall-off. That doesn't matter. In these cases, we only need to indicate that we want the fog to appear, and if logarithmic fog isn't possible, then we can either emulate it in software *at the driver level*, or ignore it and use linear fogging. The latter is preferable.

Each implementation of fogging simply takes the generic structure, rescales the values, and passes that data on to the platform-specific functions. Some will manage it through render states, such as DirectX:

```
SetRenderState(D3DRENDERSTATE_FOGENABLE, TRUE);
```

Others will have a fog-specific function. In either case, you can safely ignore any parameters your platform doesn't support within the comfort zone of the platform-specific driver.

The only important fog parameter that must be clarified is whether it is range-based or linear. In a range-based solution, the fog exists at the same distance from the player, regardless of his orientation. With a linear fog, the reverse is true, and objects disappear if the player turns around on the spot, which can cause issues with gameplay.

The Sky

The sky is often a box (or sometimes nested boxes to create a parallax effect) with a texture on it. This is no different from any other static mesh, other than the fact that the texture is usually much larger. The sky interface consists of little more than an orientation, and perhaps a brightness control, for each layer of the box.

Texture Handling

As far as the game code is concerned, resourcing textures is a very monosyllabic task. A simple call is made, and a resource pointer is returned. This pointer, or handle, is then used to initiate the rendering process for the rest of the engine. It's rarely more complex than this:

```
m_WoodenBulletHoles = CTextureManager::Get()->Load("wooden_hole");
```

Thanks to our common interface, we can reference all our textures in this cross-platform manner despite the wide variety of methods each platform can use to load or reference the texture internally. Furthermore, it doesn't matter if the handle type differs between platforms, or if the value that `Load` returns changes—provided the texture data it references doesn't change.

The loading mechanism for textures also requires the obligatory cross-platform abstraction parameter; that is, it needs a *reason*. For the texture to be loaded into an appropriate portion of memory, the data has to be loaded for the purpose it will be applied to. The terms involved are all abstractions of the basic concepts in graphics, and a superset of properties can be created for all textures across all platforms. In some cases, the hint will go unnoticed by the engine. In others, it will be the most critical piece of data. To this end, every texture should be registered with the engine before the request to load occurs. Generally, the two will exist together, but if the textures are being loaded asynchronously into the main game, this distinction will become more important.

We have four basic hints as described in the following sections.

Dynamic

Dynamic textures are updated in real time by various algorithms in the game, such as a procedural fire effect. Under some platforms (DX9 at least), the texture surface cannot be accessed directly. It must first be *locked*. This copies the texture data from wherever the engine decided to store it, into a buffer in system memory so that it's accessible to the main processor. This flag should ensure that the texture is always placed into system memory so that the surface data can be manipulated with minimal overhead.

Video

Video indicates that the texture will be in constant use, and should be stored in video memory or as close to the video memory as the platform supports. Because video RAM is limited on all platforms, overuse of this hint can have a negative effect.

Render Target

Whenever a scene is drawn, it is rendered to this type of texture. This includes the main frame buffer and render-to-texture effects, such as mirrors.

Default

Default lets the platform-specific engine decide on the appropriate memory location for the texture. This usually begins with video memory, but switches to system RAM when it runs out.

Meshes

Within a game, there are a number of different types of meshes. On one level, the meshes are simple collections of polygons with a variety of properties assigned to each face, such as texture or surface material. On another level, they are the lifeblood of our game—and there's a lot of blood in a computer game. We have static meshes, animating meshes, skinned meshes, and shadow volume meshes, at the least. This mesh data is then built into vertex buffers, ready for rendering by the graphics hardware.

Fortunately for the cross-platform programmer, most of this code only needs to be written once because it is common. Even the vertex buffer creation can be abstracted to a large degree.

Static Meshes

Static meshes are the simplest because the graphics driver handles the preformatted mesh data directly. Vertex buffers can even be prebuilt for the target platform. Of all the parameters usually associated with meshes, only its position and orientation in the world can be changed, which doesn't affect the organization of the polygons at all—unless it contains alpha faces, which need to get queued as normal. These parameters *can* include scaling, but this can cause extra overhead on some platforms so it's best to build each mesh to the precise size you need. The tool chain can create additional rescaled versions if necessary; remember that the mesh data is very small when compared to texture space—and our textures can be shared.

Dynamic Meshes

Here we'll consider animated and skinned meshes together because they use the same cross-platform techniques (although the production algorithm differs). To get the quickest possible game, we'll have to write the animation code entirely wired to the platform. So, a typical function call such as

```
CAnimationManager::Get()->ProcessAnimation(pAnim, time_elapsed);
```

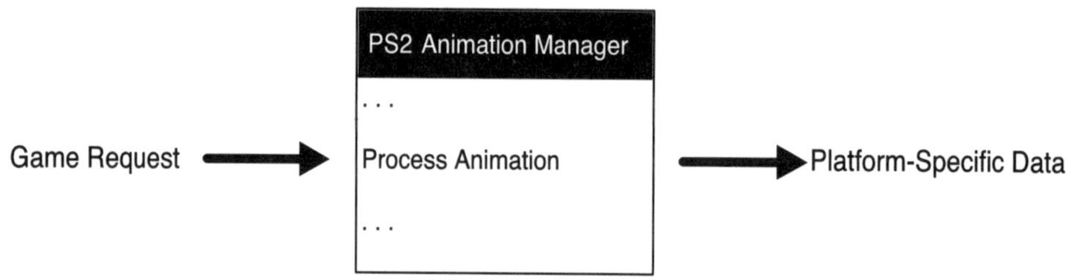

FIGURE 9.2 A fully customized (and therefore platform-specific) animation process.

will use the double chance function to find the platform-specific version of the code, and execute that. This does require a lot of custom code, but should be used to improve PS2 games by moving the processing onto custom chips, as seen in the program flow diagram of Figure 9.2.

We can exchange our speed of processing for speed of development by moving the basic animation code into the cross-platform component of the `CAnimationManager`, and generating the platform-specific mesh from this generic data. This requires opening the knowledge of the animation format to the graphics code, as shown in Figure 9.3.

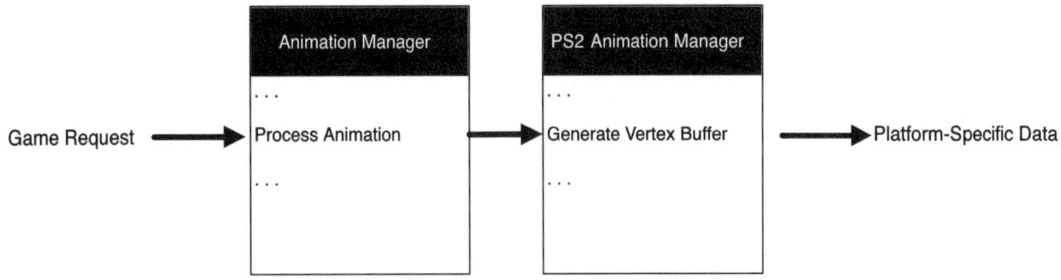

FIGURE 9.3 A half-customized animation process.

Vertex Buffers

To further expand our system within a cross-platform animation engine, we need to abstract the concept of vertex buffers. A vertex buffer holds preformatted vertex information in a platform-friendly fashion. This low-level data is then sent to the graphics chip. We can abstract this in a similar way to DirectX by implementing a set of primitive operations within the driver to build them, such as:

- Create
- Lock
- Reset
- Apply
- Unlock
- Destroy

If you are comparing this list with the functions available in DirectX, you'll notice our system has a specific function to `Apply` vertices into the buffer, rather than using `sgxMemcpy`. This is because we have a common format (say float-based vertices) for the cross-platform component, while the platform-specific vertex buffers may differ. This lets the platform-specific `Apply` function convert data into the correct format before copying it.

We can then use the common animation code to write generic vertex data into the platform-specific vertex buffer. This data path would appear as shown in Figure 9.4.

TIP

The vertex buffer code may appear as a spurious luxury, given that we'll often be wanting to produce customized animation code that runs faster than our generic version. However, almost every graphical component of the engine will require a vertex buffer, and this process will save a significant amount of wheel reinvention and provide the fastest road to market for a new game. Note that this is a useful low-level function in its own right, on par with our primitive `DrawPolygon`.

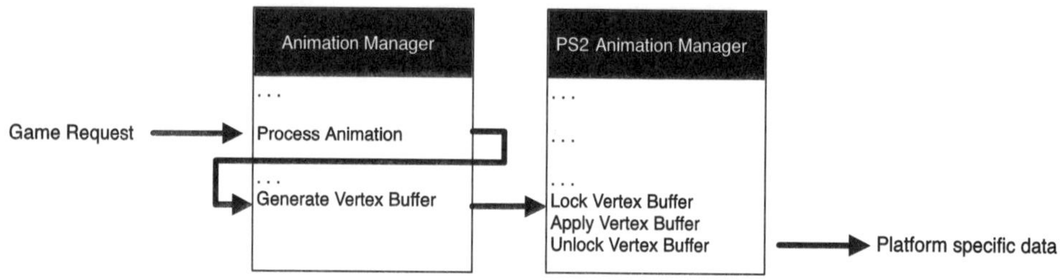

FIGURE 9.4 A cross-platform animation process.

Using platform-specific code to allocate and build the vertex buffers provides another important benefit. Some platforms require their vertex buffers to be allocated from contiguous memory. This restriction can exist in other places, and so it's preferable that the driver allocates its own memory as it deems appropriate.

Sprites

Sprites are possibly the simplest 3D objects to get rendered in a game because they consist of little more than a single face containing a texture. What makes them special is that they are likely to be a major cause of slowdown if not handled correctly. From the user's perspective, sprites are very simple: a set of points and a texture are specified, and the renderer takes care of the rest. However, as you've seen when discussing renderstates, this is incredibly inefficient, so we have to batch process them.

Batch processing involves storing each sprite request in a platform-specific buffer that is flushed in one operation at some later stage. This buffer will vary in size according to the platform.

```
void
CGfxEngine::DrawSprite(const CSGXTexture &tex,
        sgxVertex *pVert, tUINT32 num)
{
    if (tex.IsTranslucent()) {
        if (m_AlphaFaces.IsFull()) {
            m_AlphaFaces.Flush();
        }
        m_AlphaFaces.Add(tex, pVert, num);

    } else {
        if (m_SpriteBuffer.IsFull()) {
            m_SpriteBuffer.Flush();
        }
        m_SpriteBuffer.Add(tex, pVert, num);
```

```
        }
    }
```

When being flushed, this buffer should be sorted by texture to minimize texture uploads. Because of the amount of texture sorting that can occur during a frame, it's a good idea to set a maximum limit on the number of textures per level, and bucket sort the faces according to texture. On platforms where this compute-based process is too prohibitive, you can often forego the sorting, and just render the sprites with the Z-buffer tests enabled on read, but disabled on write. Particle systems work well using this method.

Fonts and 2D Overlays

Fonts and 2D overlays are among the first features to be included in an engine. They prove that the system's working, are very simple to write, and often feature as copy-and-paste code from one or more of the SDK samples. After the code is in place, it's rarely touched because there are more important matters to attend to. This often means the 2D code is—in general—nonoptimal, but will rarely show up in profiles because there's never a lot of 2D processing in a 3D game, although the changes between modes (as you saw earlier) does cause problems.

When implementing the font-handling code, remember to handle it in two halves. The first is the driver-level renderer that places each character on the screen. The second is the text handler that formats and justifies the text to fit in the appropriate areas of the screen. This is another multilayered abstraction because the text handler is generic.

TIP

Always reference strings using `tBYTE` *because this is unsigned and can cope with the whole range of accented ASCII characters. Even if your game is only intended for an English market, any foreign words in the script, or foreign names in the credits will need those accented characters. Add them to the font early so that you'll get a more accurate memory footprint. Those games intended for the CJK market (China, Japan, Korea) need to use Unicode and double-byte characters throughout.*

When drawing the text, further abstractions must be made. The style (its color, formatting, justification, font, and so on) must be considered separate from the text itself. This allows the selected menu items to change their appearance between platforms to include, say, a flashing entry where the requirements dictate.

We should also include code to handle line breaks, inline formatting changes, and special characters, such as those that are required to draw the console button symbols. Most in-game instructions need to refer to the buttons in a manufacturer-specific fashion, and so either the font needs to include the symbols or the font code needs to be able to escape them. We'll look at other issues with text when discussing the frontend system in Chapter 11, "The Bits We Forget About."

ABSTRACTING SPECIAL EFFECTS

A special effect is just that—special. However, in many cases, special effects are used to describe things that aren't remotely special, such as fog or smoke. Let's split them into three categories: engine effects, game effects, and special effects.[6]

Engine Effects

Engine effects are features of the engine that are standard across all platforms, such as fogging, and can be implemented without any extra effort within the confines of the published API. The abstraction exists as a thin layer that corrects the format of the data and scales the range of its parameters, according to the machine in question.

Game Effects

Game effects are the most common and work by using only the functionality of our abstract graphics engine. This generally covers transparent sprites (as used in smoke and fire effects), dynamic textures (for algorithmic effects like the noise on a TV monitor), and render-to-texture images (for TV screens showing an external view of the 3D world).

Such functionality is easily made common to all platforms with little overhead, so platform-specific work isn't necessary because all the new code exists in the cross-platform gameplay source. The biggest consideration is its affect on gameplay when one particular engine feature, say render to texture, is more significantly expensive on one platform than the others. In these cases, you have to look at the effect as a whole. For instance, does each TV screen need its own render-to-texture effect? Can you use different UV coordinates on the same texture? In some cases, you'll remove the effect from a room, move the room further away, or change it into a less processor-intensive routine.

The range of these effects can be astounding, as there's very little you cannot do with a batch of well-textured transparent sprites, and a couple of dynamic lights. Lens flares, explosions, and particle systems can all exist as game effects.

Special Effects

This final category covers the true "wow factor" of graphic engine programming. It also covers the least cross-platform programming we're likely to do within a game because the abstraction exists at a very high level as we indicate the effect we want, and let the driver handle it in whichever way is suitable for that platform.

These effects can be split into two categories: those that change the way in which other graphics are rendered (such as a full-screen blur) and those that create new graphics artifacts (such as shadows).

In both cases, the abstraction would exist as:

```
CGfxEngine::Get()->CreateEffect("shadow", (void *)&parameters);
```

With this example, the graphics engine uses a factory pattern that allows each platform to register a specific function to handle each named effect and its parameters. Any unregistered effect can then optionally be written and included as a game effect, using only cross-platform functions if so desired. However, after this function has been called, every other decision is in the domain of the platform-specific code.

This removes a great deal of the cross-platform decisions that would normally exist.

GRAPHICS ON TELEVISION

For the most part, an artist creates textures on a PC using a high-quality monitor. Most young gamers have the same portable television they bought six years ago. Even in the less extreme cases, the output from a television set is not comparable to that of a monitor. We must therefore consider these differences, and require that our artists do the same. This is one of the few cases where given two technologies, such as a PC monitor and a TV set, we must fully acknowledge the lowest common denominator.

Text

The alphabet conveys a lot of information and is the basis of language. And language is the invention that makes all others possible. Therefore, it's imperative that all text in the game conveys this information clearly, without fuzzy edges or hard-to-read artifacts.

Text may appear in either of our dimensional render modes (2D or 3D), but its role in each is significantly different. In the 3D environment, text is used on billboard signs and world furniture to signpost the player's route,[7] and enliven the game. The rules governing its creation are no different from any other texture. That is, it must be clear and reasonably visible.

In the 2D world, however, there are other considerations. For the text to be as crisp as possible, it should be rendered with a 1:1 mapping. This requires that you closely couple your interface design with its implementation. So, for text to appear 32 pixels high onscreen, the resource must also be 32-pixels high. Also, make sure you highlight the text by rendering it over a sensible background image, or use a drop shadow to make it stand out. You might also deem it appropriate to restrict yourself to uppercase letters.

When it comes to using the text itself, the key word is "minimal." Five to six lines of text is a reasonable maximum when it comes to listing items on the screen. Any more and the screen appears cluttered. This stems from the requirement that all text must be fairly large to be legible on a TV. Watch any television program and observe the text. Sports shows, such as the ESPN's Sportscenter™, are good examples because they have a lot of statistics to convey, but there are rarely more than a few lines on the screen.

Such guidelines are not the exclusive property of cross-platform games, but should be considered when writing your font-handling code because despite running on a monitor, the PC version of your game must still work within the rules (that is, don't overfill the screen), but you benefit from being able to work with a wider acceptable range of parameters.

TIP

Always create a complete font when you start writing your game. Belatedly adding the accented characters during translation will cause an unpleasant surprise with respect to the memory footprint.

Contrasting Colors

Real impact can be generated by sharp contrasting images. Unfortunately, a domestic television set cannot manage these any better than they can handle text, and so should be avoided as any high-contrast textures will cause artifacts when they appear onscreen. This is because bright colors cause a lot of particles from the TV's electron gun to be emitted toward the screen, and these electrons repel others in nearby pixels. This causes a blurred effect as the light colors appear darker, and the dark colors are lighter.

Image Sizes

As much as possible, make sure every 2D texture is drawn to the screen at the same resolution it was created in. This is the same argument we made with text rendering and normally involves inventory displays and frontend graphics. Although this can mean a slightly smaller or slightly larger graphic onscreen —relative to everything else—no platform will suffer odd stretching effects when a 2-pixel border has 2 pixels on one side, and 3 on the other because it has been stretched slightly.

Also, never draw a single pixel high horizontal line because when it's displayed on an interlaced TV set, it will appear to flicker. This is because interlace mode draws half the picture each frame, alternating between every other line. So, the first frame draws the line, and the second frame doesn't, which gives the appearance of flicker. By using a 2-pixel line, the flicker disappears, but only looks half as bright, comparatively speaking. There are similar considerations with high contrast images, as previously mentioned.

Balancing Colors

Unfortunately, changing the color balance is out of our hands as this is a function of the hardware. What we can do in some cases is tweak platform-specific hardware registers to adjust the basic look of the game. You can generate a testcard (or download a free one from *http://www.hippy.freeserve.co.uk/testcard.htm*) to match the images on each platform by tweaking these hardware parameters. To be effective, you should only do this on identical TV sets.

TIP

The individual textures should be effectively balanced too. Make sure the artists use the entire color range for their textures and then postapply gamma to darken them if necessary. This ensures that the maximum possible color resolution is available for special effects.

Some color balancing issues might exist between the PAL and NTSC versions of your game because highly saturated colors are not viable under NTSC. Again, you are limited to hardware parameter tweaking to fix this, as the effort required to create additional assets is prohibitive, and has a very low cause-to-effect ratio.

Physical Testing

Preparing a TV set to test your game is easy. Preparing it to verify your cross-platform artwork is more difficult. Ideally, you should use a set of identical TVs (preferably from the same batch) attached to each console and match their color balance, contrast, and brightness settings. A good artist can manage this manually, although for the rest of us automated light meters and so on can help. This ensures that we have a true WYSIWYG environment.

TIP

Don't use LCD televisions or monitors for this because they have relatively poor color-balancing capabilities.

You also should buy a cheap secondhand television for distortion testing. You'll be able to see how bad your game *can* look, determine whether all the textures are reasonably sized, and determine whether the text is legible.

TIP

Make sure you playtest the game on a TV in a bright sunlit room as not everyone will have the ideal gaming environment that involves a customized darkroom.

One more idea that may appeal to you is using dual-headed graphic cards that support a TV-out option to allow the artist to see his work on the monitor and TV at the same time. Although the output has been untainted by a console, it will highlight most of the issues we've covered here.

ENDNOTES

1. In fact, because all textures have a power-of-two width and height, floating-point numbers maintain their integrity for much larger images. A practical comparison of `fUV=iRegionX/(float)iWidth` and `iRegionX=(int)fUV*iWidth` will show that no precision is lost for textures up to 16,777,216 pixels wide.
2. You should be able to add code to the tools that prevent textures from being used outside this hierarchy, as it's not uncommon for artists to find a suitable texture and use it directly, without first copying it to the `work` directory.
3. Swizzling reorders the image data inside a texture so that renders faster by making sure the pixels—*as they appear onscreen*—are consecutive in memory. The swizzling format can vary between graphics cards, so it needs to be processed offline.
4. Although not everyone calls them surfaces, they have become a standard term for anyone coming into the industry because the first thing new programmers see is the DirectX documentation that uses this terminology.
5. With the exception of the original PlayStation.
6. For the purposes of this discussion, we do not consider vertex and pixel shaders to be special effects, as they are part of the generic properties attached to all textures. They merely exist in different forms, depending on the platform.
7. Any gameplay features that rely on being able to read worded signs are problematic when translations are necessary and should usually be avoided.

10 Network Programming

In This Chapter

- Packet Programming
- Networking Background
- The Physical Network
- The Null Network
- Cross-Network Programming

PACKET PROGRAMMING

Like every driver in the cross-platform world, three components reside within the network code: the common architecture, the null driver, and the platform-specific code. In general, our null driver is actually the most important because we'll be using it throughout the game for general-purpose message passing.

Our industry is moving in many different directions at the same time. One group is pushing us toward network play and an ever-engaging online experience. Another group is moving us into asynchronous worlds with entire cities accurately mapped out, but with never more than a few streets in memory at once. Others are showing us shiny new boxes with a lot of processors, each with its own separate cores. And yet another is increasing the load on our graphics engine with megabytes worth of assets that would take far too long to load at game start, resulting in just-in-time resourcing.

So who's on the right track?

They all are. At least from a technical perspective, because they all require the same *packet programming* metaphor. We hinted at this in Chapter 5, "Storage." This is where all requests for work (containing little bundles of code and data) are queued and subsequently dispatched by the main processor. These bundles are then dealt with by the processing pixies whenever (and wherever) there is time. After the job has been completed, the results are passed to predetermined callback functions, which then makes use of this data in the game environment. This is the architecture we want for asynchronous loading and for multiprocessor games. This is also the method we use when writing network games. So adopting this philosophy now gives us an easy route to implementing networking games, asynchronous worlds, multiprocessor environments, and just-in-time resourcing.

NETWORKING BACKGROUND

This section serves as a whirlwind tour that should give you a grounding on the basics of networking, so when we discuss the game architecture working under its principles, you'll be prepared. If the phrase TCP/IP doesn't scare you, feel free to skip this section.

A network operates through a series of layered protocols. At the high level, an *application layer* interfaces to the program, in our case, a game. This is usually accessed through an API with some variation on the name *sockets*, such as WinSock, which handles the high-level communication for us. As an antithesis to this, the *physical layer* describes how to build suitable cables for your network. Each layer can talk to the one "above" or "below" it, and according to the *Open Systems Interconnection* (OSI) *Reference Model* there are seven layers. However, in reality, some of these overlap one another, and others are squashed together, so generally we use a four-layer model. The advantage of using layers in this manner is that any layer can be replaced by another without affecting the overall network as shown in Figure 10.1. This is sometimes called the protocol, or TCP/IP, stack. It is also the epitome of abstraction.

There are a lot of acronyms here, many of which you've probably seen before in some context. *HTTP* (*Hypertext Transfer Protocol*) is used to request and send data on the Web, and *TCP (Transmission Control Protocol)* and *IP* (*Internet Protocol*) are usually used together to send most data (including HTTP request and response information) across the Internet as TCP/IP. We'll cover the other acronyms as needed.

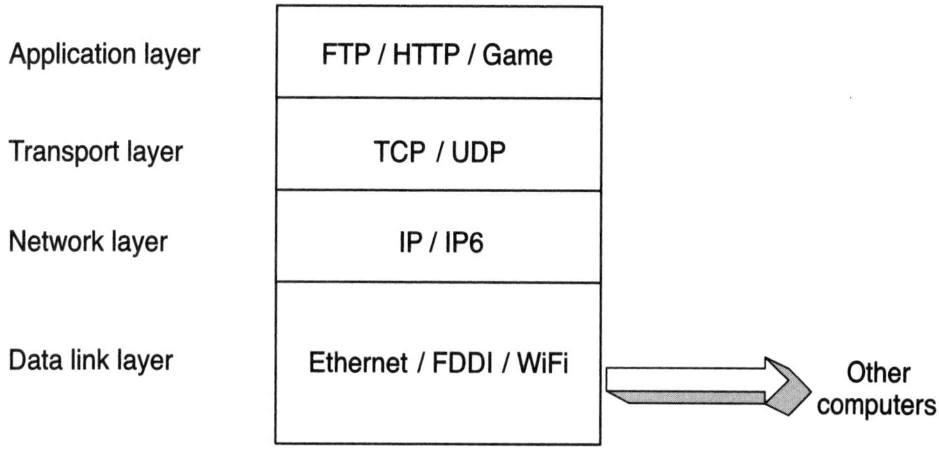

FIGURE 10.1 The networking model.

Every time a message is sent from one program to another, it must descend from the application layer to the data link layer of one computer, across the cables (which may include network switches and ISPs), and up from the data link layer to the application layer on the second computer. At each layer, additional protocol wrappers are added to the data, indicating how the other computer needs to interpret it. Each stage of this process is very fast, and not a direct concern. However, the final size of the data transmitted from the data link layer, known as a *packet*, will be different from what you sent from your game. So, if you want to profile the actual transmission data, you can't simply measure the data you sent because the resultant packets will be larger than you created, and consequently may be fragmented into separate packets for transmission. Profiling at this low level requires API calls that might not be available to you without a network sniffer.

Within the transport layer there are two protocols that interest us: TCP and *UDP* (*User Datagram Protocol*). Both package data for transmission between machines, but UDP does not guarantee it will arrive, or that the packets will be in the same order as they were sent. For this reason, UDP is sometimes termed *Unreliable* Datagram Protocol.

In contrast, TCP provides a guarantee of delivery through a system of acknowledgements. Every packet sent requires an acknowledgement from the receiving machine. If it doesn't get one, the packet is resent. This occurs with the exchange of every piece of data. If you send a lot of data across TCP, there will be a lot of acknowledgement packets, and therefore less throughput. This handshaking is not something we need to consider too closely, as TCP is available on all systems.

However, the ideas behind it will be useful later when we elect to send UDP packets and need to determine whether they have arrived out of sequence and should be dropped.

The trade-off between TCP and UDP is much the same as it is with image formats. PNG very accurately reproduces your picture, but is very large. This is analogous to TCP with its accurate data transmission but corresponding large packet-sending overhead. In contrast, a UDP packet is like a JPG image, which is much smaller but suffers quality loss in places. The loss in a JPG image is visual quality, whereas in UDP it's quality of connection and reliability.

We're now ready to go back to our game.

THE PHYSICAL NETWORK

The physical network is, in a word, slow—*very* slow. When you branch out from intranet to Internet, it becomes *incredibly* slow. A ping time on a good server is in single digits, but compared to the response of a processor, it's an eternity. Like the processor, the more data we transmit over it, the slower it gets.

Like disc speed, two major components govern the speed of the network: latency and throughput. *Latency* is the time a packet takes to traverse the network between sending and being received. This time is roughly identical for any packet of any size. *Throughput* is how many bytes per second the network can take after the connection has been made. Of these two numbers, latency is the killer. A typical FPS will probably send around 100 bytes of data on each update. Even for a user playing over a 28.8 kbps dial-up connection, that data will only take 3 ms to transmit. That's less than a fifth of the time our entire frame takes to process. Unfortunately, latency can add tens of milliseconds onto this total, instantly putting you a frame or more behind. As you might have guessed, this is another hard limit. We can't change latency. However, we can use some techniques to minimize the effect. Remember, however, no matter how much we minimize it, there will *always* be latency between sending and receiving so suitable safeguards and countermeasures have to be built-in to our game architecture.

The Conceptual Network Driver

The network component is little more than a glorified event system; the request goes in one end and comes out the other. However, those network-based differences require us to raise the bar.

Initial Handshake

With any online game service, there's always a method for signing up, introducing yourself, and searching for a game to play. This is one feature that is difficult-to-impossible to abstract. There will be many functions to handle the different stages of connection, but while they have some similarities, it's usually more trouble than it's worth to abstract them.

Instead, you can abstract the UI. In this scenario, a piece of platform-specific code queries the servers to find out about available games and generates a cross-platform menu structure. This information is then passed to the frontend engine to handle the menu, with the keypresses generating additional requests for the platform-specific GUI that controls the network code.

TIP

Think of this as abstracting the frontend for separate platforms, with the base class handling the GUI, and the derived classes processing the keypresses and controlling the network components. It's similar to the double chance function pattern you saw at the start of Chapter 7. We'll revisit this metaphor in Chapter 11, "The Bits We Forget About," when discussing memory cards.

As the online components mature, this will become easier to abstract, and there will be fewer special requirements for each platform.

Network Interface

This part of our network driver deals with sending and receiving messages. After we have a basic connection set up between our machines, we just send and receive the messages. So let those be our first two functions.

Sending Packets

When sending data, we need to consider the information itself, to whom it needs to be sent, and the manner of its delivery, for example, is this a guaranteed message?

```
void
SendPacket(const CDataPacket &packet, tUser who, tProtocol send);
```

At the moment, `tProtocol` only indicates whether it should be guaranteed or not, but in the future, it can be amended to reflect a broader range of abstractions, such as the capability to send only to fast machines, those that have a low ping time, or those that are physically close.

```
typedef enum {
    /* Individuals */
```

```
        ePlayer1 = 1,
        ePlayer2,
        ePlayer3,
        ePlayer4,
        /* Groups or teams */
        eClan1 = 1001,
        eClan2,
        /* Meta-users */
        eServer = 2001,
        eAll,
        /**/
        eLastUser = SGX_ENUM_PADDING
    } tUser;
```

Some APIs won't transmit the packet data immediately and instead place it in a queue. This means the game cannot safely free its data when `SendPacket` returns. There are three solutions for this problem.

First, we can copy all the data into a separate buffer (with our own headers) and ask the network API to send that information instead. By avoiding transmitting the user's data as-is, we can scale our network packet to cover any solution by adding as much header information as necessary. A separate buffer also handles the case of `SendPacket` transmitting local variables.

Second, we can adopt a callback approach where the network code triggers a function when the data has been sent, allowing it to be freed. This is cumbersome and increases the amount of code required, which will usually exceed any memory employed in buffers.

The third option is to do nothing, and spin in a loop until the network API indicates that it's safe to continue. This can cause a delay on each message and is not suitable unless the code sending messages and the network code reside on their own thread, away from the main engine. As this is unlikely, we opt for the initial hunch.

```
tBOOL
CNetManager::SendPacket(const CDataPacket &packet, tUser who,
    tProtocol send)
{
    DispatchMap::iterator it = m_Dispatch.find(packet.m_Type);

    if (it == m_Dispatch.end()) {
        return FALSE;
    }

    tBYTE *ptr = m_pCurrBuffer;
```

```
    CPacketHeader header;

    header.m_HeaderSize = sizeof(header);
    header.m_TotalSize = sizeof(header) + packet.m_DataSize +
        sizeof(tMEMSIZE);
    header.m_ID = it->second.m_iLastIDSent;
    header.m_Who = who;
    header.m_GameTime = CGameClock::Get()->GetTime();
    header.m_UsersHeader = packet;

    if (&m_pCurrBuffer[header.m_TotalSize] >
        &m_pTransmitBuffer[m_BufferSize]) {
        return FALSE;
    }

    sgxMemcpy(ptr, &header, sizeof(header));
    ptr += sizeof(header);

    sgxMemcpy(ptr, packet.m_pData, packet.m_DataSize);
    ptr += packet.m_DataSize;

    tBYTE *data_ptr = (tBYTE *)m_pCurrBuffer;
    *(tMEMSIZE *)ptr = (tMEMSIZE)m_pCurrBuffer;
    m_pCurrBuffer = ptr;

    // the TransmitPacket routine here is our own, and assumed
    // to be nonblocking
    if (!TransmitPacket(data_ptr, header.m_TotalSize)) {
          ReleaseLastPacket();
    }

    return TRUE;
}
```

NOTE

The thread-friendly mutex code has been omitted from this example for the sake of clarity.

Here we use `m_pCurrBuffer`, which points to a globally allocated block of data (so it doesn't impinge on the game memory of other platforms) that increments after each message. When this memory block runs out, we are forced to suspend all other messages until the backlog has been cleared. Sometimes we can increase the buffer size, but this is usually the root of a deeper problem—such as a game sending hundreds of redundant messages each frame—because network messages are usually dispatched quickly. The same situation can occur if the memory buffer gets fragmented, which is rare given its first in, first out (FIFO) approach.

Note that a header size parameter is used to version data because, during development at least, the format of the header can change. Whether version one of your game is allowed to talk to version two depends on the individual design of your game.

Receiving Packets

Each message arrives of its own accord in the platform-specific network driver. Depending on the platform, this either happens because of an interrupt or because we explicitly polled the network card. In either case, the time at which we dispatch messages is identical and handled by a specific function call in the main loop, which makes sure all messages are sent synchronously to the game engine, avoiding undue problems for the code. If you recall the problems that occurred when threads context switched from Chapter 4, "The CPU," you'll acknowledge the similar problems that occur with networking. For example, if an AI is in its update cycle, and halfway through it gets a message to die, then its state will be undetermined as it continues to process nondying animations. However, although network messages are very important, they generally don't take very long to process.

In both the sending and receiving, the packet is very simple and completely cross-platform:

```
class CDataPacket {
    CPacketType   m_Type;
    tBYTE        *m_pData;
    tUINT32       m_DataSize;
    tMEMSIZE      m_UserData1;
    tMEMSIZE      m_UserData2;
};
```

The `m_pData` is naturally specific to the event in question, and indicated by the `CPacketType`. This is an abstraction for the piece of code that we want to run on the other machine. However, because we can't pass function pointers (or any kind of pointer, for that matter) to another program and still have it make sense, we need to indirectly reference the code. We do so by using a `map` between a named `CPacketType` and its callback function.

Each component of the system that wants to receive messages must register itself with the network manager to provide the pairing between event name and callback. In this implementation, we'll adopt a text string for the `CPacketType`:

```
CNetManager::Get()->Register("getshot", cb_NetGetShot);
```

Every client involved in the game does this. The register code is straightforward and is similar to the object factories we built earlier when constructing arbitrary game objects determined by IDs stored on disc.

```
// Create our own name for ease of readability
typedef sgxMap<CPacketType, CPacketMapData> DispatchMap;

class CNetManager {
public:
    DispatchMap   m_Dispatch;
    // ...
};

tBOOL
CNetManager::Register(const CPacketType &name, cbNetDispatch dispatch)
{
    return m_Dispatch.insert(DispatchMap::value_type(name,
        CPacketMapData(dispatch))).second ? TRUE : FALSE;
}
```

With each message handled in this way, it's trivial to send and receive cross-platform messages, as any event that hasn't been registered is automatically ignored.

The network manager then invokes each callback function whenever a suitable packet has been received from the platform-specific driver. Again, this is simplicity itself.

```
tBOOL
CNetManager::DispatchPacket(const CPacketType &type,
    const tBYTE *ptr, tUINT32 size)
{
DispatchMap::iterator it = m_Dispatch.find(type);

   if (it != m_Dispatch.end()) {
       CPacketMapData &packet_data = it->second;

       (*packet_data.m_Callback)(ptr, size);
       return TRUE;
   }

   return FALSE;
}
```

Packet Metadata

The system described so far provides a reasonable communication mechanism for turn-based games and their kind. For action games, we also need to know the time of our message because this lets us deduce the speed of an object. Additionally, if we send data through the nonguaranteed UDP, we need some way of determining when a packet has been missed or arrives out of sequence.

So before we send any packet data to the network driver, we have to wrap it with our own transmission data. This is a catchall structure that can be used to detect dropped packets and determine the game time of the message:

```
class CGameWrapper {
    tREAL32    m_TimeSent;
    tUINT32    m_MessageNumber;
};
```

The message number is an incrementing counter that exists for each type of event packet, starting at one. We can then use this information to determine whether any packets have been dropped, and pass this information back to the game. This therefore requires an update to our map:

```
class CPacketMapData {
public:
    cbNetDispatch   m_Callback;
    tUINT32         m_iLastIDSent;
    tUINT32         m_iLastIDReceived;
};
```

If any packets arrive with a lower ID than the last one received, then the network driver can quietly discard them because we've already received more up-to-date news on the same topic. Conversely, any ID that is higher (by two or more) means that the network has dropped one or more packets in between. We still dispatch the packet in the usual way, but this time we'll append an additional flag to say that some information was lost. However, this is not strictly needed because the game should always interpolate between the previous, and current, data packet.

Packet Endian

When network packets traverse the Internet, they are all sent in network-order (or Big Endian) format. Fortunately, we don't need to convert to this format because the traffic is only going between machines of the same endian (either on a local machine within the null driver or to an identical machine across the network) and the console network API handles the low-level endian conversion of IP addresses and the like automatically.

Only on network games that bridge the Macintosh™ and PC communities do we need to consider this problem, and duplicate our filesystem endian swap code in the network layer. The more complex question of cross-network programming is handled later.

Game Topology

Although many computer science books show a number of network topologies (including star and bus), the only two we're concerned with are the client/server architecture and peer-to-peer, as each game's platform will support one of these.

In client/server architecture, all game data is sent to the server that holds the canonical game state. The server makes all the decisions, and then sends back new state information to the other machines, known as clients. The server can be either a console involved in the game itself, or a standalone program running in a faceless ISP somewhere. It can even run on nonconsole hardware.[1]

By contrast, a peer-to-peer (p2p) network allows the individual machines to communicate the game state among themselves. This has the benefit of supporting much faster network traffic (because it's sent directly to the machine in question via the server), but requires that each machine update its own copy of the game state, and be trusted to do so.

Although you can intimate the network topology yourself by controlling to whom you send messages, some consoles don't allow you to send packets directly between peers. So, although you can *request* that messages be sent to your peer, they might in fact pass through the server *en route* and not benefit from the reduced latency. As always, our cross-platform mantra of "say what you mean" should require us to send the messages to whomever requires them, and allow the networking code to handle it efficiently.

Half-way House

For those looking toward alternatives for the two topologies mentioned previously, you can always use decentralized servers. This is where several servers maintain a complete breakdown of the game state, each one interfacing with a certain number of game machines in a client/server architecture. The servers themselves then work in a p2p manner to establish the final game state. Writing such code is a large undertaking, and not recommended outside the field of massively multiplayer online games where there are hundreds of players, or the amount of processing per frame is substantial.

The Problem of Packet Hacking

Packet hacking exists and will always exist. You can't stop it; however, most of the time, you can survive by placing a simple encryption on the packets before sending them. In most cases, you don't need anything heavy because the data is only being sent between your machine and the server, which validates the information automatically.

Many PC games have chosen to adopt p2p networking, which needs each client to validate the data packets it receives. The encryption employed can be as simple as adding one to each data byte because it's only intended as a deterrent. If someone wants to divert your game's network traffic through a "sniffer" and modify certain packets on-the-fly, you don't have any in-game technology to help you. You simply employ the technique known as "not playing with the cheats anymore."

For a little more security, you can add a random number to each byte in the packet, and increment it periodically with special messages saying "increment random number now." These control messages, plus the initial random seed, can be sent using stronger encryption, because they happen infrequently. A public key system, such as PGP (Pretty Good Privacy), would stop all but the most determined hackers, but this should be used sparingly because the encryption and decryption routines are very processor intensive.

Protocols

Two forms of protocol are usually supported at the driver level: guaranteed and nonguaranteed. These roughly equate to TCP and UDP, respectively. For the most part, we'll be sending UDP-style messages. We're not saying games should *only* use UDP; in fact, many messages, such as major changes in player and AI state, *need* to arrive. Otherwise, the game state will drift out of sync and lose cohesion. However, such state changes are rare and should not be sent every frame. Otherwise, the bulk of messages will create contention, causing TCP to scale back its transmissions, leading to fewer messages actually being sent.

In contrast, each character's position needs to get sent more often (sometimes once a frame), but it isn't vital that it arrives because there's always another one along in a millisecond or two, at which point the game can calculate a new position for all the frames where a packet was not available.

NOTE

We can't affect the way TCP works, so this constitutes another hard limit. Consequently, the problems associated with TCP scale back are very serious and can stifle your game. We should therefore favor UDP packets over TCP after the connection has been established. Then we must replicate a method to guarantee arrival within our own code because this is a soft limit and available to change.

You can intentionally exclude even more network traffic because there's a genus of data that is below nonessential called *inferred data*. A lot of inferred data exists within every game, but we rarely think about it. Animation playback is a superb example as this is all inferred data. The game simply requests a "run" animation, and every part of the mesh animates accordingly. A network game never needs to send the position and orientation of every bone in the skeleton because it can be inferred from the basic event of "run *this* animation on *that* character, starting *now*." The same approach can be taken with most of the game data. After all, every state change we normally process in the game is inferred by keypresses from the joypad, so this is a reasonable extension of the same idea.

Because of the extra wrappers at each layer of the protocol stack, the amount of data available in a nonguaranteed packet might not be equivalent to what you'd expect. DirectX lets you retrieve this limit with `GetCaps`. If you exceed this size, the data is split in two, increasing the transmission time. Such situations should be tracked for profiling research. As a guide, a UDP packet with 982 data bytes is a reasonable size because the wire adds another 42 bytes of headers, bringing the total up to the magic 1,024. If your API documents the maximum size of a single UDP packet, then adopt a lowest common denominator approach and compress your data to fit. This can be done for all platforms because the processor overhead of compressing a couple of hundred bytes should not have an impact.

THE NULL NETWORK

Everything we've built to abstract the system I/O over the past four chapters has used the idea of a null driver. The networking component is no different, but more important. This stems from the fact that we'll use our null driver for nonnetwork games, too. Instead of calling the functions directly, we'll send a network message. Instead of sending packets through the TCP/IP stack, we'll simply copy them into another buffer and pass them on to the recipient.

By using the abstraction of a null network, we earn several benefits.

- Future-proofing for a hardware network.
- Network traffic monitoring for packet size and frequency.
- Provision of a network usage graph for any platform, even if the network hasn't been written yet.
- Debug-friendly code, enabling the game code to be tested without a network, which is useful if you get network timeout problems because you're working in the debugger for too long.
- The ability to emulate real network issues by dropping and delaying packets.

Implementing a null driver takes a little more work than most of the other cases we've seen so far. Essentially, we need to take a copy of every packet requested, store it for an arbitrary amount of time, and then send it back to the program, pretending to be a network.

Dropping and delaying packets to match fallen network traffic is no mean feat. However, we only have to *emulate* it, not *simulate* it, so the task becomes much simpler.

The basic approach is for every packet to be tagged and added to a list for later dispatch. How much later is determined by the virtual network traffic shaper we elect to throw at it. Each tag would contain the same information that any network protocol would:

- Source address
- Destination address
- Size and pointer to data
- Time before delivery

This last element is specifically for us. Before adding the packet to the dispatch list, we *pre*determine how slow the network is going to be. We also decide whether the packet will get through at all, before making the decision and adding it to the list. Knowing the final status of the packet ahead of time makes it easier to monitor various scenarios that reflect particular real-world situations, such as a lost subnet or a power outage at one particular machine.

Network Latency

After the initial connection between our two machines has been made, the speed at which the packets traverse the network is usually fairly constant. The real speed hit comes from the extra handshaking involved in guaranteed packets. We can model that handshaking like this:

```
fPingTime = fBasePing + m_DataSize * fNetworkSpeed;
if (packet.m_IsGuaranteed) {
    fPingTime *= 3.0f;
}
```

Balancing these times can be done by looking at the responses in the real world and adapting these *magic numbers* accordingly.

NOTE

Although we use the word "ping" to describe the network turn-around time, this isn't strictly true because a traditional ping only ever includes a few bytes in each packet, and is sent by ICMP (Internet Control Message Protocol), not TCP.

Because the connection between two machines goes through several others, it's possible that consecutive packets will take two different routes. This is one of the main causes of UDP packets arriving out of sequence. To re-create this we'll adopt a simple random element:

```
if (!packet.m_IsGuaranteed && sgxRand(100) == 0) {
    fPingTime *= 1.0f + sgxRand(100)/200.0f;
}
```

In this case, we increased the duration by up to 50% of the original time. Naturally, in a full implementation, such numbers would be stored in variables allowing you to change the behavior of the virtual network dynamically.

Dropped Packets

Networked packets tend to disappear for two main reasons. The first is that the target machine has run out of buffer space and is just ignoring them. The second is that there is a broken connection between the two machines.

Emulating a lack of buffer space is fairly easy to implement because we only need to count the number of packets destined for this machine and drop those over a certain limit. But balancing this is very difficult because we don't know the size of the buffer on the other machine, how many other machines are trying to communicate with it, or how fast it can dispatch the packets at the other end, making that limit very hard to determine. If you have achieved real-world data from your network code, then employ that. Otherwise, count the number of packets during a frenzied part of gameplay and drop a quarter of the packets above that level.

Physical outages occur for a number of reasons. We can simulate an outage like this:

```
if (sgxRand(100000) == 0) {
    // Drop this packet by not adding it to the list!
}
```

In some cases, network packets will look for (and often find) an alternative route to the target machine. This may increase latency to three or four times its original value immediately following the outage. But the network switches will then reroute traffic as they realize the new best route and the times will settle down again, usually to within 50% of the original duration. When the console causes the breakage, this will cause a sudden death for every packet because there's only one outbound connection.

Fortunately, this kind of hardware outage is rare, so it doesn't need to be modeled for normal game testing. Indeed, during the initial testing phase, you probably won't have *any* network problems installed. However, during the final stages of game testing, you should trigger this kind of event from a special keypress to see what happens. A similar keypress should also allow you to slow down the general packet speed to look at the game reactions under feasible, but low-quality, conditions. The case of a completely broken connection can be justifiably solved by kicking the player from the game.

The Two Modes

After you've written a complete null network driver, the next thing to write is a mode switch to disable it. This removes the complexities that occur when debugging the game's network code because network shapers can introduce uncertainties that make bugs much harder to find. These problems originate from the time delay between cause and effect of each message. Let's look at an example.

Consider a moving character that sends its new position across the network. The client's game code has computed a new position that it sends to the server, which in turn may get passed to the other clients. One or two frames later, this message arrives and the clients can then adjust their local state. This means the original client machine must maintain two sets of data: one that is internal to the moving character so it can accurately determine its next position, and one that the rest of the game sees to determine its visibility.

NOTE

This problem exists outside the realm of cross-platform development, although it may be less pronounced depending on the particular network servers in use.

The first task here is to produce a single opening through which we can retrieve information about the game characters (these can be any game-related objects, but for ease of description we'll only consider characters). This must sit across every character in the game to prevent information from leaking out, and maintain a consistent state. Furthermore, every *parameter* of every character must be equally well hidden to prevent an inconsistent state from being produced. As this covers a wide range of data, we'll place the functionality external to our character in a manager class. With this architecture in place, any external object can query the manager for the current state of a specific character, while the character's job is to refresh this state with new data when it's ready to divulge it. The manager can then use a simple mutex to prevent an inconsistent state from being generated in the same way as you saw in Chapter 4. The input and output state of this system are separated by the manager using a "Chinese wall" to prevent contamination, as shown in Figure 10.2.

By moving this data into the manager, we can prevent the issues of duality by distancing ourselves from the problem. During single-machine operation, we can collapse this wall to allow direct access to our state information. This can be used to help us with our enquiries if a difficult-to-find bug occurs that we believe is due to mismatched state information.

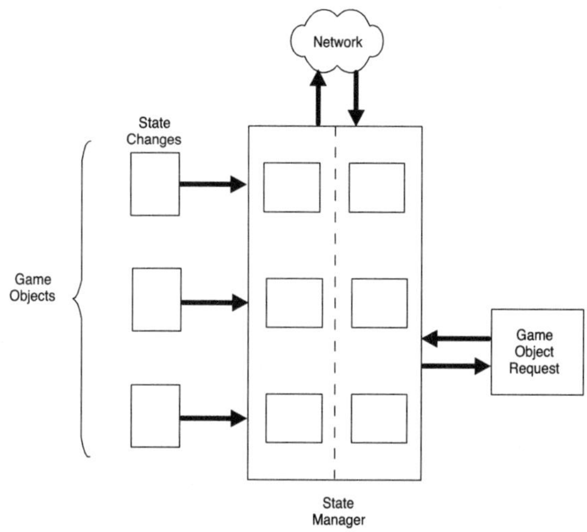

FIGURE 10.2 A sample networked game architecture.

CROSS-NETWORK PROGRAMMING

Because all the protocols in use are Open Standards, it seems appropriate to devote this section to writing a game that allows PS2 players to compete against Xbox players with the same game. Alas, this is not possible because the communication occurs through proprietary servers owned by the console manufacturers. Also, the protocol data that is given to the transport layer may involve vendor-specific wrappers, so you would have to pick out the data from the driver manually. From a technical standpoint, however, it *is* possible. And provided we apply all the guidelines presented here, not an insurmountable task. However, until the political winds have shifted, this will remain a very short paragraph.

ENDNOTE

1. The server machines that run such games are becoming increasingly Linux-oriented. Making sure your game runs cross-platform on other PC-based machines is therefore recommended if this becomes a desired target.

11 The Bits We Forget About

In This Chapter

- The Development Process
- Presentation Issues
- Operating System Considerations
- Handling Technical Requirements
- Artifacts of Code

THE DEVELOPMENT PROCESS

Cross-platform game programming isn't just about abstraction. The manner in which we write the code varies between platforms, too. These issues range from the high-level concepts of the *IDE* (*Integrated Development Environment*), to the real nitty-gritty of which type of end-of-line characters to use for the source.

The Environment

From the outset, it's best to have a good scalable build environment that is tested and working, even though it may change during its lifetime. But, to quote the mantra of the Perl community, "There's more than one way to do it."

Build Methods

For most people, development will begin on the PC under Microsoft .NET and progress on to Metrowerks CodeWarrior or the SN Systems compiler after the console hardware has been purchased. As each one of these tools provides a command-line interface, all the following approaches are available for a cross-platform development environment.

The Monolithic Workspace

In this scenario, one IDE (usually .NET) is used to control the entire build process. The prebuild and postbuild options are used to trigger the appropriate compilers and tools, and the project file contains build targets for all platforms. This keeps everything together, and means you only ever leave the IDE to use the console-specific debugger. On the downside, it can be difficult to integrate third-party compilers into the IDE, and you must ensure that each file is marked to only build on one platform in both debug and release, which is usually forgotten.

Separatist Projects

In this instance, every platform has its own project file. This is very easy to implement and get working, and fits nicely into the IDE with which it was supplied. On the downside, however, every new cross-platform file added to one project must also be added to all of the other project files, which can often be forgotten, leading to a broken build. Because most of the abstraction work involves pushing more code into the cross-platform arena, this happens more frequently than you might think. Additionally, project files are invariably binary, which makes it nearly impossible to merge them if two people change them at the same time. However, this is a good solution if you need a simple build process that can be understood by anyone, or you need tight integration to the ancillary IDE tools, other than the compiler. This solution is especially suited to small teams, and projects that don't extend over many platforms.

Using Makefiles

This fully command line-driven approach has the strains of a monolithic environment, but with the cross-platform benefit that, with no obvious exceptions, `Makefiles` are understood by every environment. By using a good make program, such as `gmake`, you can invoke a platform-specific compiler according to various build options without having to worry about dependencies, out of sync project files, or vendor lock-in. You can also get some IDEs to trigger the `Makefile` process through its prebuild step, although this can only usually happen from within a wrapper project of its own. If that project doesn't contain links to the external `Makefile`, then this approach can lead to the same problems as a separatist build, whereby IDE-specific project files get out of sync with each other if only some of them are changed.

This solution scales well and is recommended if you have a large number of platforms across which to work, or you need to automate builds in a large number of different configurations.

> NOTE
>
> *You can automate most IDEs, but this usually requires OLE (Object Linking and Embedding) controls and specific code for each platform. A simpler method of automation is to generate the necessary workspace files programmatically. This is easier under some environments than others, naturally, and also provides a means for keeping multiple configurations and libraries in sync.*

Jamfiles

Jamfiles is a relatively unknown technology that provides a modern-day cross-platform equivalent to `Makefiles`. They have the usual accoutrements associated with building large projects (such as dependencies and customizable options), but provide many enhancements over the traditional `Makefile` process. First, a clear distinction exists between the tools used to build the source (compilers, link, and so on) and dependencies themselves (inherent and epidemic in a large code base). This stems from the fact that Jamfiles are rule-based and can be specified with user-definable relationships, as opposed to `Makefiles`, which are limited to dependency information. This leads to an uncluttered view of the build process because all the cross-platform variants are built in.

Also, because the Jam build process involves a single executable, there are no multiple copies to spawn when a recursive project is built, as there is with make. This increases the speed of the build, and reduces the complexity of the Jamfiles themselves (which are already very simple). You can also parallelize the build process with comparatively little effort.

On the downside, Jamfiles, despite being available for more than 10 years, have failed to make a significant impression on the market. This means it's difficult, in the short term at least, to introduce Jamfiles into an environment that can't evaluate them effectively, as the majority of the staff will need to learn their structure and syntax. For the uninitiated, editing a Jamfile is easier than changing a `Makefile`, however, it can still be problematic at times. Additionally, every filename in the build tree must be unique, which can cause migration problems. To solve these migration problems, you can use Jam *grist* to make them unique, which is little more than a symbolic decoration or C++-style name mangling.

But after all the build elements are in place, the resultant process is much more resilient and better for shipping to junior programmers or customers.

Changing Between Builds

Because the same source will compile identically on all platforms, there needs to be an external influence to switch between them. This usually comes from the project file, whether it's a general purpose `Makefile` or IDE-specific project, to reference files that are specific to each platform. The `SGX_TARGET_PS2` define you've seen throughout this book is a typical example of the method by which you can switch compilation at the lower level. However, this must be held externally to the source to prevent excessive rewriting and recompilation of the header files. To this end, most compilers support the `-D` flag (or something similar) to define preprocessor macros from the command line or `Makefile`. This can be used to then include a platform-specific file containing all the appropriate settings or headers.

Compile Targets

Most people are familiar with the two main compiler targets: *debug* and *release*. We should also consider adding a third to this list called *final*.

One of the facets of cross-platform development that we have seen time and again is the prevalence of conditional logic that should occur at runtime, and not compile time. This means we prefer to write

```
if (sgxGetSettings("Profile")) {
    // do profiling code
}
```

instead of the more traditional

```
#ifdef SGX_PROFILE
    // do profiling code
#endif
```

This gives a faster turn-around between builds, a greater flexibility in-game (as either debug or release targets can be profiled), and allows us to enable additional functionality without changing the code footprint. This approach also limits the total number of build targets necessary within a project, which can spiral out of control very easily because there could be debug and release variations in each of the profile, editor, game, and testing versions.

The biggest problem with using runtime conditions is the amount of redundant code it leaves behind in release builds. The concept of the final build is to remove this dead wood and produce a polished product without the holes or trapdoors where debugging code could still be switched on by accidental keystrokes or button presses. After all, the debugging console, or second joypad, may still be useful in release builds.

You can remove this code by preparing a final build target that replaces the preceding function—and others like it—with

```
#define sgxGetSettings(option)    0
```

which relies on the compiler to spot the `if (0)` constant expression and remove it automatically. Naturally, in the rare cases where this doesn't happen, you'll need to surround the code with a new macro:

```
#ifndef SGX_FINAL_BUILD
    // original code
#endif
```

These instances are very, very, rare.

Source Code

Before we can begin writing our cross-platform game, we must first stipulate the methods by which the source code will be created. For the most part, our game code is written on the PC, and cross-compiled to the console. That is, the PC generates assembler for a target platform that is not its own. However, this is not always true, because it's possible (and becoming increasingly likely) that you'll compile it on a completely different machine, such as a Linux box or build farm. Due to the differences in compilers and platforms, you should take extra care with the source itself.

Filenames

Assuming we're not likely to be back-porting our game onto MS-DOS or CP/M®, we can safely use names with enough letters to make them readable—so we're not concerned with 8.3 filenames. We are, however, concerned with the other hidden properties of filenames.

First, we should adopt a convention in which every filename is written to disc and subsequently referenced using lowercase. This is common sense from a programming point of view as the C language favors it, so our `#include` lines will look more natural. It also avoids arguments with programmers about which letters should be capitalized[1] and helps when compiling code under a foreign platform where the filesystem supports case-sensitive naming, meaning `Aicharacter.h` and `AICharacter.h` would intimate different files and a likely failure on the `#include` line. We should also stipulate which extra nonalphanumeric characters should be used. Ideally none. Realistically, just the underscore, as too many other characters are illegal on one platform or another. This lowercase-only convention should also be applied to the naming of subdirectories for the same reasons.

Second, each filename should be unique within the entire source tree. Even if we have two files that we want to call `memorycard.cpp` and place in different directories, we shouldn't. This is because some platforms, and even some development environments, will mistakenly use the wrong file or disallow the file altogether. However, this is still beneficial in other situations; not just those that use Jamfiles. We therefore adopt a simple naming convention by prefixing the filename with a platform identifier, such as `ps2graphics.cpp` or `ps2main.cpp`.

Finally, we need to adopt a sensible convention for the directory slash used on the `include` lines. This fairly trivial point ensures that a single forward slash (`/`) is used in all cases because the current generation of compilers will all handle it correctly. This might appear counter-intuitive because the Windows platform, under which most code is compiled, uses the *backslash* (/) to separate directory names, but this has been a supported extension in Windows compilers for many years (probably due to the backslash character needing to be escaped) and is likely to continue for many more. Mixing the forward slash and backslash is also a bad idea because `directory/filename` and `directory\filename` might be considered different files, or the same file, depending on the compiler, platform, or phase of the moon.

Header Files

As we mentioned in Chapter 2, "Top Ten Tips," header files with relative paths can't be reliably included from other header files. This causes an increase in the number of header files present in the source files, which can be unwieldy and an unrealistic reflection of the development structure. Instead we have two main options.

First, we can use absolute paths, such as `core/engine/graphics`, which always descend from a specific root directory. We can then add this root as an *additional include* directory in the project file so that it finds our header files as easily as `stdio.h` or `string.h`.

Alternatively, we can prebuild all our headers into one, or more, overarching `include` files that cover each distinct area of the engine, such as graphics, audio, and core. This approach requires a rebuild of these files whenever changes are made, however, and should only be considered when the core engine is fairly stable.

The Windows Header File

Within the driver code, you must include a platform-specific header file, such as `windows.h` for the various API functions to be correctly prototyped. This file should also be abstracted to ensure that any special customizations could be carried out equally across the project. The typical contents of this file, such as `wincore.h`, are:

```
#define WIN32_LEAN_AND_MEAN
#define NOMINMAX
```

```
#include <windows.h>
```

Standard ASCII

No matter what anyone tries to tell you, standard ASCII is rarely standard. Although the character codes may be identical between platforms, the interpretation of these characters is not. Anyone who has copied text files between Windows and Unix machines to an abundance of `^M` characters can testify to that.

The safest approach is to adopt a simple line feed ('`\n`') to terminate each line, and ignore any carriage return ('`\r`') characters by preparing your text editor accordingly. This may be labeled as using LF line endings or Unix format. If this becomes a problem on your tool set (although most editors now support all variations of line end characters), you can instead configure your source control tool to fix the line endings upon check-in or check-out. Even if this option is not directly available, it can be implemented as a post-check-in script using `sed` or `Perl`. For example:

```
sed 's/.$//' <text_with_crlf >text_with_lf
sed 's/$'"/`echo \\\r`/" <text_with_lf >text_with_crlf
```

TIP

End each source file with a blank line, too. Some compilers won't parse correctly if the last line contains code, but no line feed.

PRESENTATION ISSUES

As far as the game player is concerned, the problems with abstracted filesystems and cross-platform memory managers are unimportant. The player wants a game, and it doesn't matter whether the GUI is running on PAL or NTSC or in English or French. For the game programmer, however, these are problems that—surprisingly—need cross-platform solutions.

PAL and NTSC

The switch between PAL and NTSC is more pronounced than just the quality of the image. There's a whole different ball game to be played out. Of the two important parameters, resolution and refresh rate (as shown in Table 11.1) are both vitally important.

TABLE 11.1 Resolution and Refresh

TV Standard	Typical Size	Buffer Memory (16 bit)	Refresh Rate
NTSC	640 x 480	600 KB	60 Hz
PAL	640 x 528	660 KB	50 Hz

Memory

Probably the first thing that most people notice is the amount of extra memory PAL requires. Because of the dominance of the American market, most development kits initially shipped are configured for NTSC, so it becomes the first completed version of the game. Unfortunately, this means the initial memory footprint is underestimated by 60 KB per buffer, so you should factor this in from the start. In addition, you must also consider the extra memory required for the Z-buffer, blur buffer, triple buffer, and any other screen-based effect buffers your engine may be using. This can total 300 KB or more (depending on the buffer size for each particular platform), which is not an insignificant amount of memory. You should allocate enough memory for the PAL frame buffer on the NTSC build at the beginning of the project to prevent yourself from being lulled into a false sense of security. If memory is tight, a PAL build can survive with a full-resolution front buffer, and reduced NTSC-sized back- and Z-buffers. Unfortunately, this generates lower quality visuals as it involves scaling the image every frame.

NOTE

The GameCube has 3 MB of internal SRAM to ease this burden. This memory is split into equal thirds and holds the Z-buffer, the back buffer, and a texture cache.

Refresh Rate

For most people, the issue of the refresh rate is a hidden gotcha. Switching from your first NTSC build to PAL will suddenly make everything appear faster because PAL gives you 20 ms to process each frame, instead of the usual 16.6 ms. Despite having a frame rate-compensated game loop, there are still some issues to consider.

You'll first notice that any constant rate effects (that is, those that process one *step* per frame) behave differently between PAL and NTSC. Rate effects could include sky rotations, any camera-based effects (such as lens flare), and movie playback code. The latter opens a can of worms because forcing a 50 fps movie to play back at 60 fps can cause horrendous problems with synchronization and timing. If you don't have the disc space to store both versions (naturally the preferred choice), you should opt to scale down instead of up, and store a 60 fps movie that can be played back at 50 fps. But with many games moving toward in-game cut scenes, this is becoming less of an issue.

Be sure to abstract the TV format away from the screen size and refresh rate because it's sometimes necessary to develop for 60 Hz PAL modes. This may further impact the storage medium if you can't add 50 and 60 Hz versions of the movies on the disc.

You may also notice issues with animations, events, or effects that exist for very short durations; essentially those lasting between 16.6 ms and 20 ms. Under NTSC, such effects will never be seen because they last for less than one frame, giving the engine no opportunity to render them. When the duration is more than 20 ms, both versions will display it normally. For anything in between, the NTSC version will display it for one frame, while the PAL version will ignore it altogether. Because your code will be time-compensated, this shouldn't cause a problem with the game logic, but may require some additional man management with eagle-eyed testers. Solving this problem outright is a case of making sure the minimum time for any such event is 20ms, which is high grain enough.

NTSC Limits

The physical limits of an NTSC signal are much lower than on PAL. So, instead of the brightest NTSC red being stored as 255,0,0, it's more likely to be 245,0,0. This is true for all the primary colors and all the secondary colors. These numbers must therefore be clamped (according to platform-specific limits) to prevent the additional harmonics from affecting the output signal.

After the technical considerations of differing screen sizes have been met, we can move on to the problems associated with the design of our frontend.

Frontend Screens

The user interface (UI) has traditionally been a simple affair. Your artist draws a screen, gives you a set of coordinates, and you create a composite in-game from a number of movie clips and textures. However, when the screen size changes, this approach doesn't work. Even the simple background movie fails to work correctly when switching between PAL and NTSC versions, as we've already seen. Furthermore, the TV signal includes a border around its edge that is invisible on many TV sets. The size of this border varies between TVs, so the console manufacturers have decreed a safe zone in which no important graphics may be placed. That safe zone differs according to platform.

So, instead of creating hard-coded designs, we need to describe the screen layout using a metalanguage. This could be as complicated as a micro-Web browser displaying XHTML, or as simple as an offset calculation function such as:

```
x = CGraphics::GetSafeX();
y = CGraphics::GetSafeY();
h = CGraphics::GetFontHeight();

for(i=0;i<3;i++) {
    CGraphics::DrawText(szMenu[i], x, y + i*h);
}
```

The in-game UI, usually displaying game statistics, should adopt the safe zone by rendering all objects using a specific number of pixels offset *from* the zone. Because these areas don't vary a great deal, you can simply anchor each graphic to a specific corner, and render toward the center of the screen knowing they'll never clash. The size of the graphic onscreen must reflect the texture size at all times because of the aliasing artifacts that can occur as you saw in Chapter 9, "The Graphics Engine."

TIP *Always abstract away the text properties by referring to the text "style." This allows you to change the color scheme or font size very quickly and makes it easier to flash selected menu items if featured in the technical requirements.*

Foreign Language Versions

In addition to the possibility that different PAL and NTSC versions may be shipped, you also have to contend with the existence of foreign languages. The problems here are generally no different from that of a single-platform game so we'll cover them briefly.

Graphic Resources

We've already seen the larger footprint required to handle a complete font with accented characters, but we must also remember to recreate any word-oriented gameplay textures for each language. German words are, in general, longer than English words, and so may require more texture memory to store if held as a single asset.

The Directory Hierarchy

Any assets that are language-specific will need to replace the common (or English) version dynamically at runtime. If you're using a good abstracted filesystem (as discussed in Chapter 5, "Storage"), you can mount two files for each game level, and create an abstraction across both. Here, a simple "file open" request is preceded by a "find file" request, which first looks in the language-specific folder, followed by the common folder to find the most suitable file for this language. This search order can be prepared after the language selection screen like this:

```
CFileSystem::Get()->SetSearchPath(szLanguageSpecificDirectory);
CFileSystem::Get()->SetSearchPath("game/english");
```

Because the directory hierarchy is in memory, no disc seek time is lost, and the appropriate file can be found with the minimum of effort. Naturally, there's an additional memory overhead to store both filesystem tables, which you should consider when testing your game.

Text Strings

Even the simplest data of all has issues with cross-platform development work. Fortunately, the data itself is very small so we can adopt the simplest solutions.

Text Resource Tables

The first stage is to develop a system in which text strings can be replaced *en masse* according to the language. One typical approach is to use string resource tables, similar to that of the Win32 API, but implemented from scratch to work cross-platform. Each line of text can be retrieved through any unique key you like, but the most efficient method is to use the string itself and access the translation with a function such as:

```
GetString(szTranslation, "Welcome to my game!");
```

This doesn't require changes to massive header files containing lists of `ID_TEXT_WELCOME`, nor does it require any extra work to complete a "translation-friendly" first version of the game because the implementation of `GetString` can render the ID (a.k.a. the English word) when no translation is found, making it easy to spot missing translations and identify them. To save time on tools development, the GNU `gettext` package provides a means to extract text strings from source files.

These resource tables must cover all the game text, as well as all the memory card strings with their officially sanctioned translations from the console manufacturers. The text data itself is therefore held in two separate tables: one for the generic game text and one for the platform-specific text, which includes all the memory card errors. These two tables can be chained together using a simple linked list, and searched (like the filesystem previously) so that if the string can't be found in the platform-specific table, the code attempts to find it in the common one.

TIP

When data can exist in two or more possible places, start searching within the most restrictive subset, and drop back to the common data if necessary.

This will result in several text files (English-pc, English-ps2, French-xbox, and so on), but the duplicate text strings will be kept to a minimum and separate from the game executable, following our data-driven principles once more.

TIP

Always add your credits in a separate platform-specific and language-specific file. There will always be more translators, testers, and hangers-on to add in later foreign versions that you hadn't planned for.

Word Order

Let's now look at the innocuous phrase "Sgt Pepper kills the meanies," which has been generated with this code:

```
sprintf(result, "%s kills the %s", szPlayer, szEnemy);
```

Any string requiring two or more replacements (of either a `%s` or `%d` persuasion) will break in foreign language versions if the word order changes. This is because the text could be translated as the equivalent of "The meanies are killed by Sgt Pepper." If you're creating a shooting game, you could avoid this problem entirely by asking your writer to avoid any such constructs. Anything with more complex literature will need a reimplementation of `sprintf` to support arguments such as `%1s` and `%2s`, which indicate the position of each subsequent word. The translator can then write the string as "`%2s are killed by %1s`" if necessary to ensure the correct grammatics.

If you're going to this amount of trouble for text, then be advised also that the concept of plurality differs between languages, requiring another set of text strings. Retrieving a suitable sentence would then require code in the form:

```
GetStringPlural(szTranslation, iNum, "%d bullet", "%d bullets");
sprintf(szResult, szTranslation, iNum);
```

Furthermore, consider the equally innocuous phrase, "You have the ammo." Depending on the language, the word "ammo" could be masculine, feminine, neuter, or plural. In English we always use "the." In other languages, this could vary between several different words, but for the most part, the rest of the sentence will be translated, providing context. However in some cases, you'll want to use the same word in two different contexts, with "Ammo" appearing on its own for inventory lists and menu selection routines, and a second instance within phrases such as "You have %s." Instead of coding grammatical rules into the game for each word, it's better to duplicate the text in two separate tables. The maintenance is simple, and the translator's time is cheap. Yours is not.

OPERATING SYSTEM CONSIDERATIONS

For the most part, the underlying OS has no part to play in our game. In fact, we've spent several hundred pages abstracting, isolating, and generally ignoring the OS altogether. In Windows games, we would rather rewrite an entire windowing GUI than suffer the 20 pixels of a menu bar at the top of the screen, because games are an immersing environment for the player, and any evidence of an OS beneath spoils that. With cross-platform game programming, any hint of an OS beneath spoils the programmer's illusion that this is really a cross-platform game. As this is something of a "grab bag" topic, we'll include those features that cover the OS, compiler, development environment, and anything else not generally covered elsewhere.

The Size of `size_t`

We've already established that `size_t` is the size of `sizeof`. It's the smallest type that can reference the whole of memory and has been abstracted in our engine with the type `tMEMSIZE`. For the current generation of machines, this is 4 bytes long and used in all code, such as `sgxMemcpy`, that references memory. We have also created a separate type, `tDISCSIZE`, to reflect the total accessible space on disc. In the future, this care will pay off when the disc sizes increase beyond their current range, and we need 8 bytes to represent it. The limit will be reached sooner than most people think, because the *memory* limit is already beginning to show signs of 64-bit incompatibility. This will become very important with the next cycle of development as the size and complexity of art assets increase to the point where 64-bit asset processing farms are a necessity, rather than a dream.

Code Overlays

As games grow, the amount of specific code required to control each level also grows. Within a typical game, the engine on its own is capable of performing very little gameplay. Indeed, without any specialization, each level is likely to be indistinguishable from the last. However, having the code for 20 different levels in memory throughout the entire game is a waste of resources. Instead we need to load the code for each level separately. This is certainly possible, and most consoles support some method of code overlays to manage this. The Windows OS uses DLLs to achieve this effect, for example. Abstracting overlays effectively is very difficult because of the interaction between game code and overlay code, as you have to determine entry points for a lot of functions, and provide a means to bind the code modules together as a whole.

Instead, it's preferable to use a scripting language and interpret this at runtime. The usual criticism leveled at this approach is that interpreted languages run slowly. This, like the old arguments of C++ being a slow and bulky language and unsuitable for games, is not necessarily true, as it's all a matter of how the language is used.

TIP

If your scripting language is completely C compatible, then you have the cross-platform option of interpreting it (on platforms with low memory), or compiling it within the hardcode (on high memory, slow processor machines).

For example, the *Lua*[2] scripting language has a highly optimized language structure that runs very fast when interpreted. A Lua compiler (called `luac`) is used to convert the language into a form of byte code that runs even quicker. Other cross-platform languages (most notably Java and those using Parrot) follow the same idea. While the code is certainly not as quick as a natively compiled binary, it's usually more than fast enough, given that the level-specific code will rarely be on the critical path, and certainly not the slowest part of your game. And you get the added bonus that the turn-around time is much quicker, as you don't need to recompile your overlays or main code base.

Initializing the OS

We've seen many cases throughout the book where parts of the OS are initialized. This could be for audio, graphics, or the file system. When creating and testing individual components, there's no required order to the initialization. But when two or more features are created, their order becomes important. All platforms have a mandatory hardware initialization order, and this will be dictated within the manufacturer's sample code and documentation. We must therefore make sure that it's impossible for our code to initialize the components out of sequence. Although we're unlikely to initialize them out of order intentionally, we must take some precautions to prevent out-of-order *implicit* initialization.

Singletons

Despite their problems when writing threadsafe code, singletons are still a very good design pattern for many components within our game. They are also very good at initializing themselves when we least expect it, and therefore, out of order. A simple trace call, for example, could create a `CGlobalTrace` class, which in turn might open a communications port to the host PC, which in turn could prepare the hardware registers in some undetermined way. Each step of this process will be handled by either global functions, or other singletons because there's no `this` pointer in their initialization. We can therefore ensure the correct initialization order by calling these functions explicitly at the start of our game:

```
int main(void)
{
    CXboxGraphicsEngine::Get();
    CXboxCommunications::Get();
    CGlobalTrace::Get();

    // Rest of code...
```

The `Get` function forces creation of the object if one hasn't been created before so we can explicitly order the singleton calls to ensure that the correct sequence of initialization is maintained. This is a feature of the prepared singleton pattern we saw at the beginning of Chapter 7, "System I/O," and it re-emerges here as a necessity.

By forcing the initialization order, we can also control the destruction order at the end of the game. Although this is not so important for consoles (because they have no quit option), a PC game is likely to have many dependencies that must be destroyed in the correct order. This is often dictated by the dependency of one singleton on another, or of one singleton holding access on an external resource that needs to be released at the appropriate time.

TIP

If you're primarily focused on console development, pay close attention to the debug window when you close down the PC version of the game. This may detail a lot of memory leaks or problems that would otherwise remain hidden on a console.

When singletons are used within the code "as and when they're required," the order of initialization cannot be guaranteed. In these situations, extra logic is required to store the order of allocation, and release accordingly. Andrei Alexandrescu provides some very good grounding on this topic in his book, *Modern C++ Design*, including the Phoenix Singleton, which can be recreated after it has been destroyed. During a game, all platform-appropriate singletons will be created at some point, and are therefore used as a pattern of convenience. Therefore, it's perfectly acceptable to explicitly create and destroy our singletons at game start and termination, respectively.

You also can adjust your function parameters to prevent singletons from being created implicitly. So, for example, instead of writing the input key logger as:

```
void
CInputKeyLogger::Start(const sgxString &filename)
{
CSGXSerializeFile file(filename, "rw");

   // rest of code goes here!
}
```

You could pass in the file handle directly:

```
void
CInputKeyLogger::Start(CSGXFile &file)
{
    // this code is no different!
```

This ensures that the logger won't create any singletons itself, giving the calling class complete control over the initialization order.

Global Variables

Don't use global variables because doing so can invoke the constructor of a class that causes other code to be run implicitly behind the scenes. For example:

```
tINT32 g_DefaultTraceLevel = CGlobalTrace::Get()->GetTraceLevel();
```

When multiple source files are involved, the order in which these global objects are constructed is undefined by the C++ standard, meaning they won't be created with any determinable progression. This code could be potentially damaging, as the hardware may be initialized out of sequence, as it was previously with singletons. What's worse with global variables is that the constructors are invoked before the `main` function is called, which gives us no opportunity to initialize anything else first, or understand the order in which they will be destroyed.

Where global variables are part of a larger, single module, consider using a special initialization function. This way, you can govern the order of their creation. When a global variable affects several modules, it's probably a good idea to move it into a singleton.

TIP

Some mobile phones prohibit the use of global variables altogether, which is another reason global variables should be avoided.

HANDLING TECHNICAL REQUIREMENTS

The business model for console development is interesting. Every console developer has complete control over the console and the software released for it. This is maintained by making the development tools (development kits, compilers, debuggers, and so forth) available exclusively from the manufacturer. All third-party products (such as middleware, additional tools, and your game) can only be released in conjuncture with the manufacturer. Every manufacturer can ensure that certain features in each game behave identically to every other by enforcing a set of technical requirements that ensure a high level of quality on each release.[3]

The technical requirements list might be called many things, depending on the manufacturer, but in all cases it lists the *technical* requirements for the platform. They include details such as the maximum load time for a game, the appropriate terminology and graphics for the controller and memory card, and how to handle the disc cover opening or the reset button. The list doesn't cover what content is impermissible on the grounds of taste or where it conflicts with the company's image, but there are supplementary rules that cover this.

Every console manufacturer has a different set of guidelines that must be adhered to or the game will not get released. This makes an interesting job for the cross-platform programmer because the differences between sets of guidelines can be profound. It makes a more interesting job for the cross-platform author because it would break NDAs to mention any of the guidelines. However, we can detail the typical requirements you would be expected to fulfill.

NOTE

These requirements can, and will, change throughout the lifetime of the console. Your code should be rechecked with each new update to ensure that it still conforms.

Title Screens

Preceding every game is a series of licensing, title, and copyright screens that are easy to implement, but vary on each platform. There might be additional rules as to how long each must stay onscreen, and whether or not the screen can be interrupted with a button press. And if so, which button should be used.

Because such code is trivial, the time taken to implement a generic license screen engine is generally wasted, so it's better to write a set of platform-specific frontend screens and begin the game on a different screen, as triggered by `main.cpp`. After these requirements have been fulfilled, you can use the cross-platform menu code to handle your own title screens, such as introduction movies and studio idents, as these don't fall under the technical requirements—although the publisher may dictate their own set of rules for them.

Attract Mode

Also called *demo mode*, attract mode occurs after a period of inactivity in one or more of the menu screens, at which point the game plays itself. This can be through either a movie of the game, or a genuine game level played through an input logger as discussed in Chapter 7. The purpose of this is to exhibit the game on shop floors and conferences to persuade the consumer to buy. This means it must be ultra-stable, as the game could potentially run for a day or more without interaction.

Achieving this should be simple because it's always among the last tasks on the schedule, when the game is fully debugged. For the paranoid, however, stability can be ensured by using only the bare bones of a gameplay system. This might mean that the AI used in the demonstration level consists solely of preprogrammed characters, or the physics system is limited to only a handful of objects. Better still, you could play a movie.

This latter option is normally more effective as it can provide a much better punch to the end consumer. Implementing this is no different from any other movie playback code, and follows the same warnings stated previously— remembering, of course, that a PS2 playthrough will look visually different from an Xbox one, and so replacement movies will be required.

The testing phase of this code needs only to periodically check the resources to ensure nothing is leaking. This is always necessary as the (rarely used) movie playback code may not clean up after itself as well as you might expect, or a texture in the frontend might not release its region, or tiling, data correctly and leak a few bytes on every transition between menu and movie. Neither of these leakage examples are noticeable in a real game because it never lasts that long; the level is either restarted or replaced with a complete fresh memory footprint before too long. But in attract mode that may not be true because it has to run for hours, even days. The testing is easy; just make sure you do it.

Reset Buttons

One of the biggest surprises with console development is that the reset button is rarely automatic. This is to fit in with the idea that, as a programmer, you're in complete control of the console. From a practical viewpoint, it gives you time to close any of the open files present on writable media to avoid corruption, and close down cleanly.

The only commonality here is the response time; the reset button must respond quickly or the user will believe it to be a fault with the console, which is obviously not good for the manufacturer's image—so they make a stipulation about it.

Achieving a quick response (how quick is up to the individual manufacturer) can be done in one of two main ways. First, the usual method is to poll the button every frame and handle it immediately. Second, you can run a second thread to handle the polling. Although this avoids many problems, it creates a need for threadsafe code, as we saw in Chapter 4, "The CPU." Unless your engine is already threadsafe, the overhead of this route makes it impractical. Note that if you adopt the polling method, all blocking functions (such as file I/O) must be replaced with nonblocking versions and the polling code must be included in the spinlock. Chapter 5 provides a practical example of this in the "A Blocking Wrapper" section.

You may also need to trigger the reset button manually with a special joypad combination. This usually involves some nonstandard button presses to prevent an accidental reset. Because this is very platform-specific and requires an intimate knowledge of the joypad, this code in placed inside the game loop in `main`. At this point, it can detect the keypress and trigger the traditional reset handling code outlined previously.

Memory Cards

The implementation of the memory card system is vital because more games fail their requirement checks because of memory cards than everything else combined. The memory card system is fraught with danger and NDAs. So although we can't show you how to avoid the submission failure, we can demonstrate how to build the cross-platform architecture for such a system in preparation.

The Interface

The basic premise is that a generic interface manages control of the entire memory card menu system, using low-level driver functions to perform the actual operations (to determine how many card slots to draw, for example), whereas the platform-specific frontend generates and handles the screens with error codes from information passed back from the driver. This effectively causes a high level of abstraction as the interface determines the primary differences of the platform, not the driver code (which acts as a black box).

The abstraction of the interface continues at all levels of the process. Rendering a list of possible save game files would exist as a generic menu using the data generated by the platform-specific driver functions such as `CMemoryCard::GetTableOfContents` and `CMemoryCard::IsCardPresent`. The interface can then be abstracted further (using double chance member functions) by allowing each platform to control the flow of each button press because the error handling might need to occur in different places. For example, some platforms may require that the player is not allowed to enter the Load Game menu if the memory card is empty, while for others this is acceptable. The same is true if the memory card is removed from the machine during a menu, because some platforms require you revert to the previous screen. Notably:

```
CPlatformSpecificFrontEnd::UpdateTableOfContents()
{
    if (!CMemoryCard::Get()->IsCardPresent(m_Card)) {
        PreviousScreen();
        return;
    }

    CFrontEnd::UpdateTableOfContents();
}
```

TIP

The frontend should be as dynamic as possible, because there will be menu differences between each of the platforms, as well as between different SKUs and languages.

A typical "save" operation might appear like this:

```
CFrontEnd::SaveGameScreen(tResponse selection)
{
    if (selection == eCancel) {
        GotoPreviousScreen();
        return;
    }

    CEngine::BuildSaveGameFile(&memory_block);
    CMCError err = CMemoryCard::Get()->Save(m_Slot, &memory_block);

    if (err.m_Code == 0) {
        SaveGameScreenEnd();
    } else {
        SaveGameScreenError(err);
    }
}
```

This produces two possible endings—success or failure—that can vary according to platform, so we use a `virtual` function for this and every other completion screen:

```
CFrontEnd::SaveGameScreenEnd()
{
    // No confirmation generated by default
    GotoPreviousScreen();
}

CPlatformSpecificFrontEnd::SaveGameScreenEnd()
{
    CreateGenericConfirmationScreen("Game has saved successfully!");
}
```

Similarly, the error-handling screen would be handled like this:

```
CFrontEnd::SaveGameScreenError(const CMCError &err)
{
    CreateGenericErrorScreen(err.m_String);
}
```

Notice the use of a specific memory card error class (`CMCError`) in this example. This is preferred over a simple integer or Boolean because of the vast number of different errors that can occur between the platforms. To save mapping error IDs to strings for each platform (some of which won't exist), we can get the `CMemoryCard` class to determine the correct string that we then duly apply to the generic error screen.

Most memory card operations (such as load, save, or format) require this level of consideration. The worst offender (if it can be called that) is the confirmation for overwrite. This confirmation can be required, optional, or denied, according to the specification of the target platform. The abstraction presented previously makes such code easy to write, and avoids nested `#ifdef SGX_TARGET_xxx` throughout the interface source. But, granted, it does introduce a large number of very small functions.

Blocks and Slots

One important consideration with a cross-platform save game is its size, or more specifically, its number of blocks. Each save game must fit into a save game slot, with each slot occupying one or more blocks on the memory card. Like network packets and disc clusters, any block that is partially used is unavailable to anything else, so it's worthwhile to bear this in mind. As for the total size of the data, the only advice is to "keep it as small as possible" as there are few other guidelines about usage. Game files are typically well under 100 KB, so they should not be a drain on resources; no game should ever fill an entire card or even a significant portion of one.

From a nontechnical perspective, however, larger save files means that fewer files can be stored on a single card. So if your game relies on the save-die-retry metaphor, this could prevent players from having more than a couple of saved waypoints, leading to frustration and a poor gameplay experience.

Low-Level Functionality

Low-level functionality shifts the focus from flexible generic components to tight specific platform code. When the game is ready, there's nowhere else to go except the platform-specific driver to save your game data. The following typical functional abstractions need to exist on all platforms:

- Load
- Save
- Delete
- IsCardPresent
- Format

Additionally, consoles such as the PS2 support a Multitap, requiring additional support when it comes to the interface and naming, as these will need special functions such as `GetCardName`.

Some of these functions, such as `Format`, exist only if the platform in question requires you to support the in-game formatting of memory cards. The interface consequently never calls them, so the driver can remain an empty stub.

The process of saving the data to the memory card is far from simple because of the technical requirements, but each console manufacturer documents the process because it's in their interest to have your game released. The best method to adopt was alluded to earlier, where we generate the save file offline (using `BuildSaveGameFile`) and write its data out as a single file. This minimizes a lot of the error handling that would need to occur if we allowed the game to control the memory card filesystem manually by writing individual bytes. Unfortunately, it doesn't eradicate all the problems, as we still need to make some checks.

Checking for the Reset Button

The memory card is the only read-write filesystem we need to worry about,[4] and an open file handle can cause corruption of your game file, other people's game files, or the card in general, which is definitely a Bad Thing. So throughout the save process—which we've now limited to a single `write` by creating the file in memory first—we must poll for it, and close the file safely should a reset occur. This requires an open interaction between the hardware requirements code and the memory card handler.

Handle Spinlocks

In many places throughout the code, we'll have to wait for the memory card to finish its operation. This often results in platform-specific tight loops such as:

```
while(sgxGetMemCardInfo() == SGX_MEMCARD_ISBUSY)
{
}
```

This prevents any interrupts from being serviced and, contrary to popular belief, may be correct for your platform. Check the requirements documentation carefully about this.

Corruption

Any writable media can suffer corruption. When that media is a memory card in the excited and impatient hands of a gamer, that corruption could happen more often than normal. Often platform-specific functions are used to test for memory card corruption, but these check the *card* and not the data on it. To this end, you should verify the game data during load and save. A simple Cyclic Redundancy Check (CRC) check will suffice in most cases. However, be sure to validate all incoming data during load as, like network traffic, it could be tainted and open a back door as we saw in Chapter 10, "Network Programming."

TIP

You might find it easier to save the game to a temporary location on the memory card, verify the integrity of the data, and then copy it into the correct slot.

Memory Card Icons

To show the icons in-game, a simple numeric identifier can be stored inside the file to indicate which graphic to display. This is considered metadata for the file, and exists alongside our corruption-testing CRC data.

The icons shown on the console's own menu are handled specifically on each console when the game data is written out through one of our abstracted driver functions. This information is under NDA and therefore beyond the scope of this book.

Disc Covers

Handling an open disc cover is an interesting problem. It's also a fairly rare requirement, because the user has already requested it to open, so reporting an error might seem importunate. In fact, some consoles (such as the Xbox) reboot themselves if the drawer is opened, thus removing the necessity. However, like all technical requirements, they are *requirements* that must be obeyed at all times.

The basic premise here is to suspend all engine components when the cover is open and resume them when closed. You must ensure that the error reporting is immediate, which means the use of any synchronous file operations will preclude the execution of the disc cover check. This requires using a separate worker thread or replacing all synchronous calls with asynchronous ones. Although the former appears a more general solution for detecting the error, responding to it requires more work as each engine component must be threadsafe and able to suspend its operation at any time. In contrast, the only potent blocking functions are in the filesystem—and these will be asynchronous anyway to cope with the problems outlined as "The Blocking Wrapper" in Chapter 5.

ARTIFACTS OF CODE

Programmers coming from a PC environment may introduce algorithms to the console arena that are too heavy for it, either in terms of memory or processor usage. We'll now briefly look at some traditional development techniques that might not be appropriate for cross-platform game development.

The Consequence of STL

The Standard Template Library, although part of the C++ language, has taken on a life of its own, spawning books, magazines, and fervor like few other libraries. But although STL has not always been considered suitable for game development, it's beginning to filter into the mainstream of many developers. For those using STL in a cross-platform environment, the following considerations must be made because despite its name, the STL is not completely standard. This must be dealt with because the implementation between vendors can vary a bit, and even a minor discrepancy is enough to destroy the predictability we have worked so hard to achieve.

The Problems

Let's being by taking the simple case of a vector growing in size, courtesy of `push_back` calls. When a vector increases in size it will, at various intervals, need to allocate more memory for itself. How much memory, and how often, is determined by the STL implementation. This will vary the amount of memory any particular `vector` occupies on each platform. When this occurs in the game memory, it can cause problems with our memory footprint.

You can always employ the "swap trick" to reduce this footprint to the minimum amount possible like this:

```
vector<sgxVector3>(m_Vertices).swap(m_Vertices);
```

But, like Scott Meyers says in his book, *Effective STL*, this is only the minimum amount possible *using that implementation* and therefore will still vary between platforms.

There are more problems when the memory comes to be freed as the call

```
m_Vertices.clear();
```

may not release the memory it was using to hold the vectors. The size is now 0, certainly, but the STL implementation is not obliged to release the memory. An obvious solution is to avoid `clear` by writing

```
m_Vertices.resize(0);
```

which not only avoids the implementation ambiguity, but releases the memory and makes life easier for the memory manager.

Even the algorithms are not identical, as the STL equivalent of our friend `qsort` returns here for one final time as `std::sort`, which can exhibit the same problems.

A Common Base

By using the same code on all platforms, we can eradicate all the problems mentioned in the preceding section. However, STL is a very big library, and would take a significant amount of time to develop fully. Fortunately, the hard work of rewriting a common STL has been done for us in the form of STLport, which is available from *htttp://www.stlport.org*. This is a cross-platform version of STL that can be employed under any of the current suite of consoles, and we believe it will still perform admirably under the next generation, too.

Usage Hints

Once the code is identical, we must then ensure that we use it well, because for many people the STL means slow and bulky. However, *any* language or tool can be slow and bulky if it's not handled correctly. These are probably the same people that five years ago said that C++ was bulky and would never be suitable for games.

Excessive `push_back` calls will slow down *any* vector implementation, so it's better to reserve the required memory with:

```
m_Vertices.reserve(m_Count);
```

This is possible because most (if not all) scenarios of this kind will work with a fixed data set, and so can prepare the vector ahead of time. This has the added bonus of preventing wasteful allocations we'll never use.

Now that the `std::sort` algorithm is common across all platforms, we can use it in preference to `qsort`, enjoying the better type safety that STL provides as we go.

Many other STL optimization hints are available on the Internet and in books, so it's unnecessary to repeat their advice here. By way of a finale, however, we'll note Boost, which is a set of templated libraries (akin to STL++, to use the geek parlance) that performs many other useful tasks and comes under a suitably flexible license for games developers. Boost can be found on the companion CD-ROM in the software/libraries/directory.

Exceptions

An *exception* is a category of runtime error that gets *thrown* when something problematic occurs and can be *caught* by an exception handler in the calling function. It was introduced into C++ as a standard means of handling errors. Any uncaught exception causes the program to halt. Exceptions can be thrown by the user's code, library code, or by the system in situations like a divide by zero or an illegal memory access. A simple try-catch block can prevent such errors from appearing:

```
try {
   UpdateGameLoop(time_elapsed);
} catch (...) {
    // Something would have crashed in the game. We caught it,
    // so life goes on as normal for the code...
}
```

Exceptions can be caught at any level in the program, with uncaught exceptions being rethrown to the calling function above it in an attempt to find a handler for the error.

This is very useful for the unpredictable world of games, but only in debug. In release builds, exceptions add a usually unacceptable overhead to the executable. To remove exceptions between builds requires an abstraction macro, as we've already used for assertions and trace messages.

```
#define SGX_TRY         try
#define SGX_CATCH       catch
#define SGX_THROW(thro) throw  thro
```

These will get replaced in nonexception builds, usually release and final, with:

```
#define SGX_TRY          if (1)
#define SGX_CATCH        if (0)
#define SGX_THROW(thro)
```

In addition, we might also need to modify the project settings, and switch the processor-based exceptions off with a simple (but platform-specific) assembly instruction.

Problems in Release

By far, the biggest problem for game developers is the speed hit that exceptions cause, followed closely by the 10% increase in code that is automatically added to unwind the stack. If exceptions stopped all known problems, it might be worth it, but in a game environment an exception is only likely to come from the processor, STL, or third-party library, as many game programmers[5] don't use exceptions. Therefore, any thrown exception will cause the game to be left in an unstable state, so although you could try processing another frame, it's highly likely another exception will get thrown and cause a cascade of further problems. Despite claiming the world of games is unpredictable, we do have the added bonus that, in fact, most games are *very* predictable as they only have to work within their own enclosed environments. Every input and process can be predicated within very tight bounds, so these exceptional circumstances should never occur, thus negating the need for exceptions in release builds.

NOTE

Exceptions can only be removed from the build as a whole if all the libraries and third-party code are free of them.

Check out some other well-made points about exceptions in the presentation given at *http://www.gdconf.com/archives/2004/isensee_pete.ppt.*

Uses in Debug

Exceptions are wonderful in debug, once you remember to switch them on (with either a compiler switch or the little platform-specific magic we mentioned previously). Throughout the development of your game, you should treat exceptions as seriously as you treat assertions. When an exception is thrown, it means there's something wrong. Find the problem and fix it. Don't simply check for the error case and return `FALSE` from the function.

The biggest use of exceptions is in the math field where a divide by zero or a manipulation of a signaling NaN will throw one. The first case is very important in cross-platform development because not all platforms will throw exceptions on divide by zero. The same is true with signaling NaNs, as illustrated in Chapter 6, "Debugging."

Exceptions also are useful when logging the input device, as a crash will usually eradicate your logfile. Instead, we can use `catch` to trap the exception and output the logfile, which now contains the exact steps required to reproduce the problem.

Game Configuration

Throughout this book, we've impressed the need for cross-platform game programming to favor runtime parameters over compile time parameters, such as the maximum number of alpha faces to buffer or the frame rate limiter. What we have yet to do is give any clues as to where this data comes from.

Your first instinct might be to create a set of hard-wired parameters into the platform-specific `main.cpp` file. This, admittedly valid, solution omits our desire for a data-driven approach, so this configuration data must come from outside the game. A basic configuration file stored in the root directory can provide all the parameters necessary to initialize the game at a minimal cost. By parsing this file with low-level code, we can retrieve our configuration parameters for the entire game, including the filesystem if necessary, before initializing any other module.

This information should be stored in a global configuration structure to prevent access to the disc during the game, and should be written to the trace output after it has been loaded, as part of the debug messages. This also allows the defaults to be registered and written back into the executable code if so desired to fully recreate the scenario.

The layout of this data is immaterial to our discussion, but each platform should use the same format, so it can be inspected and edited at will, and copied between platforms to experiment with different settings and to help isolate configuration-specific bugs. Plain ASCII, using only line feeds, is naturally preferred.

Hacking It

We're all friends here. If you've taken the effort to read this far, it's very likely you're not a code correctness spy, and will appreciate the honesty of this section. Because sometimes, you just have to hack it. There might be one specific issue with a compiler, platform, or piece of data that can only be fixed with a quick piece of hard code. Perhaps a formal solution *is* possible, but impractical, as you would need to reexport all your data just to fix the single binary digit that's changed on one specific level on a single platform. In these cases, there's nothing wrong with:

```
#if SGX_PLATFORM_GAMECUBE
if (g_Game.iLevel == 10 && pObject->id == 9345) {
   iNodeMask |= 1;
}
#endif
```

It would, however, be preferable to minimize the instances of this hack. We can therefore control these situations by creating a new global variable, called `g_MegaHack`, and treating it as a set of flags, enabling us to keep all the problems referenced in one place. Each bit of this variable controls a different problem case as it arises. We can then create a separate header file with numeric IDs representing each problem, and include it in *only* those files that need to be hacked. There's no point in making this a general header file because we want to keep the compile times down, and it's still a hack (and we don't want to promote the fact too widely).

Each instance of the hack would now appear as:

```
if (g_MegaHack & HACK_WRONG_BIT_SET_FOR_GRUNT_AI) {
    iNodeMask |= 1;
}
```

This buys us a couple of benefits. First, it ensures that if this hack has to be applied in more than one place, the numbers will still match and object 9345 isn't accidentally mistyped as 9354. Second, it means that when our `g_MegaHack` variable has no bits available, you'll have 32 hacks in the code. This enforces a reverse form of natural selection, as no game needs 32 hacks. So at this point, you should have enough cause to rebuild the data set, fix the mesh exporter, change the datatype, or do whatever is necessary to eradicate all these hacks from the game.

ENDNOTES

1. The other favorites capitalize the `InitialLetterOfEachWord` and `everythingExceptTheFirstWord` (called studly caps or camel case).
2. Lua means "moon" in Portuguese.
3. The PC has no such restrictions. However to achieve a "Designed for Windows XP" logo, or similar, does require a good level of cooperation with specific Microsoft technologies. Computer games have no need for such certification.
4. Excluding the Xbox hard disc (which the OS should help protect) and the memory (which is lost when the power goes anyway).
5. In fact, many programmers are unaware of how exceptions work, nor their intricacies.

Appendix

A About the CDROM

The CD-ROM supplied with this book is comprised mostly of source code. This includes both the code from the book, plus additional APIs and libraries that can be used as part of your own cross-platform development project.

BOOK CODE

The source code from the book demonstrates a memory manager, filesystem, and null network driver using the principles shown within the various chapters. It also contains example code that uses these libraries, and all the basic header files that form the basis of a cross-platform project.

To use this source, you should copy the project and all its associated files into a folder on your hard drive, and open the workspace in Microsoft Visual C++ (.NET will convert the project automatically on load). You then need to set up an additional include directory to include this path so that the header files can be found. You can then build all the code, and use the debugger to step through each line to re-emphasize the points made. This code does not include a graphics or sound engine, so the requirements are fairly minimal, but you should still ensure that your machine fits the specification given.

SOFTWARE

All the other source code on the CD-ROM provides an implementation of one or more of the major areas of cross-platform development, including graphics engines, audio systems, and utility libraries. All necessitate the system requirements given later in this appendix, although naturally, if you're using them to process a large number of data assets, the requirements will increase beyond these. Installation in all cases involves extracting the zip file to your hard drive and following the instructions included within. Some (such as the Microsoft DirectX SDK and OpenGL) perform this step automatically through their own install executable files. Each file also details the specific license requirements of each piece of source (that you should adhere to). Along with the full installation or compilation instructions, you'll usually find Web addresses and online forums where you can find more information and discuss the product.

The code is split into separate directories as follows.

Audio

The Audio directory includes both LibOgg and LibVorbis (*http://www.xiph.org*), the patent-free audio codec system that is outlined in Chapter 8 to handle high-quality compressed audio streams. The packages contain their own documentation and demo tutorials. A sound card is required in addition to those specifications given.

BuildTools

The source code to build Jam can be found here (or at its Web site at *http://public.perforce.com/public/index.html*). This is the cross-platform build tool covered in Chapter 11 as an alternative to `Makefiles`. For a practical example of a Jamfile, review the *Boost* library (also included on the CD-ROM). Version 2.5 of Jam is supplied here. You'll need to uncomment lines in the `Makefile` to reflect your current system. Users of Developer Studio will probably use the `nmake` tool to build it.

Graphics

Three of the most often-used 3D graphic libraries are located in this directory: OpenGL *(http://www.opengl.org)*, GLUT (the OpenGL utility toolkit from *http://www.xmission.com/~nate/glut.html*), and the Microsoft DirectX SDK *(http://www.microsoft.com)*. All three are mentioned throughout the book, and occupy a significant portion of the Web-surfing public's time. Installation involves running the executable, and following the instructions included.

Libraries

We've supplied four utility libraries here. Both STLport and Boost exist as numerous header files of high-quality, general-purpose templates that can be `#included` as part of your project and used as normal. STLport (*http://www.stlport.com*) is listed throughout the book as an essential replacement for cross-platform STL work, whereas Boost (http://www.boost.org) is a valuable supplement that perfectly complements STLport. Further installation information can be found in the archive.

To further the influx of Linux tools into the Windows arena, we offer an implementation of POSIX threads for Windows (*http://sources.redhat.com/pthreads win32/*). This opens up a vista of opportunities for those working on threaded code, as they can now use many existing books and references on the subject of pthreads.

Finally, we present PLib, the Portability libraries from *http://plib.sourceforge.net*. This requires OpenGL for its graphics component, but contains a wealth of game-specific routines such as a scripting language (PSL), GUI and font handling code, and joystick routines. Although PLib is cross-platform focused on Windows and Linux (among others), the amount of support for each can vary between modules.

Scripting

The self-contained scripting language Lua is included here (*http://www.lua.org*). This requires you to add the files given to your project and recompile. Source is included for both the Lua interpreter and Lua compiler, along with the basic Lua core that is required by both.

SYSTEM REQUIREMENTS

This CD-ROM requires an IBM PC or 100% compatible, 128 MB RAM (256 MB recommended), 100 MB of available hard-disk space (500 MB additional space is required for the full DirectX SDK), and a copy of Microsoft Visual C++, version 6 or above. An Intel Pentium 90 Processor is required, although Pentium II or higher is recommended for the majority of the code. A Pentium III, 1 GHz is recommended for the DirectX SDK. Windows 98 SE or later is required with a VGA or higher-resolution monitor (Super VGA recommended). The DirectX SDK requires a DX9-compatible graphics card with suitable drivers.

Appendix

B PlayStation 2 Glossary

TABLE B.1 Processing

Main CPU	295 MHz (Sony, "Emotion Engine")
Graphics	150 MHz (Sony GS)
FPU	6.2 GFLOPS
Other features	Instruction cache: 16 KB (2 way)
	Data cache: 8 KB (2 way)
	SPRAM: 16 KB
	Scratch: 16 KB
	VU0 (4 KB instruction and 4 KB data)
	VU1 (16 KB instruction and 16 KB data)

TABLE B.2 Memory

	Size	*Type*	*Latency*	*Bandwidth*	*Ext. Bus Speed*
Main memory	32 MB	RDRAM	–	3.2 GB/sec	202.5 MHz
VRAM	4 MB	DRAM	–	48 GB/sec	150 MHz
SPU RAM	2 MB				

TABLE B.3 Disc Storage Medium

Type	24x CD-ROM/4x DVD-ROM
Access speed	150 ms[a]
Read speed	5.5 mbps[a]
Capacity	650 MB (CD-ROM), 4.7 GB (DVD-ROM)

[a] Based on a typical PC CD/DVD drive.

TABLE B.4 System I/O

Performance	66 million polygons/second (75 peak)
Fill rate	800-1200 million pixels/second (in game)
Texture layers	1
Texture compression	1:1
Audio channels	2x24
Sampling rate	44.1 KHz / 48 KHz (selectable)
Memory card	8 MB

TABLE B.5 Machine Properties

Byte Order	***Little Endian***
`char`	1
`short`	2
`int`	4
`long`	8
`size_t`	4

TABLE B.6 Compilers Available

SN Systems ProDG/GNU C	
Web site	*http://www.snsystems.com*
Web site	*http://www.gnu.org*
Preprocessor macro	`__GNUC__`
Alignment	`object__attribute__ ((__aligned__(align)))`
PreAlign	
PostAlign	`__attribute__ ((__aligned__(align)))`
Inline	`__inline__`
MetroWerks CodeWarrior	
Web site	*http://www.metrowerks.com*
Preprocessor macro	`__MWERKS__`
Alignment	`object __attribute__((aligned(align)))`
PreAlign	
PostAlign	`__attribute__ ((aligned(align)))`
Inline	`__inline`

TABLE B.7 Web References

Official site	*http://www.playstation2.com*
Developer site	*http://www.ps2pro.com*
Homebrew	*http://www.aceshardware.com/read.jsp?id=60000286*
	http://www.gamecrazy.com/ps2/faq.aspx
	http://www.ps2ownz.com/

Appendix

C Xbox Glossary

TABLE C.1 Processing

Main CPU	733 MHz (Intel CISC with SSE)
Graphics	300 MHz (X-Chip, Microsoft/nVidia®)
FPU	2.93 GFLOPS

TABLE C.2 Memory

	Size	***Type***	***Latency***	***Bandwidth***	***Ext. Bus Speed***
Main memory	64 MB	DDR	–	ππ6.4 GB/sec	200 MHz[a]

[a] Effective 400 MHz.

TABLE C.3 Disc Storage Medium

Type	4x DVD-ROM, 8GB hard disk
Access speed[a]	150 ms (DVD), 9ms (HD)
Read speed[a]	5.5 mbps (DVD), 30 mbps (HD)
Capacity	650 MB (CD-ROM), 4.7 GB (DVD-ROM)

[a] Based on a typical PC drive.

TABLE C.4 System I/O

Performance	100 million polygons/second
Fill rate	4000 million pixels/second (in game)
Texture layers	4
Texture compression	6:1
Audio channels	256
Sampling rate	48 KHz
Memory card	8 MB

TABLE C.5 Machine Properties

Byte Order	***Little Endian***
`char`	1
`short`	2
`int`	4
`long`	4
`size_t`	4

TABLE C.6 Compilers Available

Microsoft .NET	
Web site	*http://www.microsoft.com*
Preprocessor macro	`_MSC_VER`
Alignment	`__declspec(align(align)) object`
PreAlign	`__declspec(align(align))`
PostAlign	
Inline	`__inline`

TABLE C.7 Web References

Official site	*http://www.microsoft.com*
Developer site	*http://www.xbox.com*
Homebrew	*http://www.activexbox.com/xbox/inside_the_xbox.shtml*
	http://www.xbox-linux.org/index.php

Appendix

D GameCube Glossary

TABLE D.1 Processing

Main CPU	485 MHz (IBM RISC, "Gekko")
Graphics	162 MHz (ATI, "Flipper")
FPU	10.5 GFLOPS
CPU capacity	1125 Dmips (Dhrystone 22.1)
Other features	L1 instruction cache: 32 KB (8 way)
	L1 data cache: 32 KB (8 way)
	L2: 256 KB (2 way)

TABLE D.2 Memory

	Size	*Type*	*Latency*	*Bandwidth*	*Bus Speed*
Main memory	24 MB	1T-SRAM	10 ns	1.3 GB/sec	202.5 MHz
ARAM	16 MB	DRAM	–	81 MB/sec	100 MHz
Embedded Frame buffer	2 MB	1T-SRAM	5 ns	2.6 GB/sec	162 MHz
Embedded Texture cache	1 MB	1T-SRAM	5 ns	0.5 GB/sec	

TABLE D.3 Disc Storage Medium

Type	Proprietary CAV (Constant Angular Velocity) disc
Access speed	125 ms (average)
Read speed	16-25 mbps
Capacity	1.5 GB

TABLE D.4 System I/O

Performance	6-12 million polygons/second
Fill rate	~800 million pixels/second (in game)
Texture layers	8
Texture compression	6:1
Audio channels	64
Sampling rate	48 KHz
Memory card	0.5 MB

TABLE D.5 Machine Properties

Byte Order	***Big Endian***
`char`	1
`short`	2
`int`	4
`long`	4
`size_t`	4

TABLE D.6 Compilers Available

SN Systems ProDG/GNU C	
Web site	*http://www.snsystems.com*
Web site	*http://www.gnu.org*
Preprocessor macro	`__GNUC__`
Alignment	`object __attribute__ ((__aligned__(align)))`
PreAlign	
PostAlign	`__attribute__ ((__aligned__(align)))`
Inline	`__inline__`
MetroWerks CodeWarrior	
Web site	*http://www.metrowerks.com*
Preprocessor macro	`__MWERKS__`
Alignment	`object __attribute__ ((aligned(align))`
PreAlign	
PostAlign	`__attribute__ ((aligned(align)))`
Inline	`__inline`

TABLE D.7 Web References

Official site	*http://www.nintendo.com*
Developer site	*http://www.warioworld.com*
Homebrew	*http://www.planetgamecube.com/specials.cfm?action=profile&id=60*
	http://www.extremetech.com/article2/0,1558,1152644,00.asp
	http://www.gc-linux.org

Appendix

E Code Guidelines

Most companies have a set of coding standards that you are expected to follow. The standards include things like naming conventions, tab stops, line lengths, and the use of classes. This appendix, presents a selection of rules to make your code more cross-platform compatible.

Use namespaces: Namespaces prevent name clashes with other libraries. As the number of libraries increases with each extra platform, so do the chances of a conflict. However, don't place `using namespace` in header files.

Order expressions explicitly: Add brackets judiciously; don't rely on your memory of the precedence table.

Don't modify the same variable twice in an expression: `a=a++;` is a no-no.

Set local variables: Explicitly set local variables to `0` or another pertinent value. Repeat with the default constructors.

Use enumerations instead of defines: The debuggers handle enumerations better. Also make sure the last element is `0x7fffffff` to ensure integers are used.

Don't use macros to save time: Use an inline or template function, unless a macro is strictly necessary.

Build macros with `do-while`: Place the construct `do { /* other code */ } while(0)` as part of your macro because it allows temporary variables to be created.

Enclose all variables in macros with brackets: This prevents erroneous ordering through precedence.

Don't allow macros to use the same variable twice: If the variable carries a modifier (for example, `macro(a++)`), undeterminable side effects will occur.

Place `{}` around all blocks of code: Do this even for one-line blocks. Apply on `if`, `while`, `do`, and `for`. This gives the debugger something to place a breakpoint on, and prevents new code from being added in the wrong scope.

Place code blocks on separate lines: This allows the debugger to hit the blocks.

Don't use `doubles`: The PS2 has to emulate `doubles` and is consequently sub-optimal. Use `floats` instead, and make sure every constant ends in `f`, for example, `1.0f, 0.5f`.

Always use the predefined types: Use `tMEMSIZE` for indexing memory, for example. Use signed and unsigned types (such as `tUINT32` and `tINT32`) consistently, too.

Don't end structures with `tUINT32 variable[1]`: It isn't portable, although it seems to work fine for all current platforms.

Use a temporary variable to swap values: You may have read it, but `a ^= b ^= a ^= b;` is not portable and it's slower.

Don't reuse variable names: Whether at different levels of scope or in different situations reusing variable names confuses humans and debuggers alike.

Be wary with variable arguments: Passing a set of variable arguments from one function to another (also with variable arguments) is not portable. Use platform-specific functions where necessary.

Create inline functions in a separate file: This allows the inline file to be included in headers for platforms where inline is supported, and in source code where it is not. This prevents two function bodies from conflicting in the linker.

Don't allow empty statements: Replace the semicolon with `continue;`.

Employ meta-comments: Add easy-to-spot comments that indicate potential problems, such as `TODO`, `FIXME`, `BUGWARN`, and `LIMIT`.

Index

M